DATE DUE

NOV 1 2002

www.wadsworth.com

wadsworth.com is the World Wide Web site for
Wadsworth and is your direct source to dozens
of online resources.

At *wadsworth.com* you can find out about
supplements, demonstration software, and
student resources. You can also send e-mail to
many of our authors and preview new publications
and exciting new technologies.

wadsworth.com
Changing the way the world learns®

Career Counseling Models for Diverse Populations

Hands-On Applications by Practitioners

Edited by

NADENE PETERSON, ED.D.
Our Lady of the Lake University

ROBERTO CORTÉZ GONZÁLEZ, PH.D.
University of Texas at El Paso

Wadsworth/Brooks Cole
Thomson Learning

Australia • Canada • Denmark • Japan • Mexico • New Zealand • Philippines • Puerto Rico
Singapore • South Africa • Spain • United Kingdom • United States

Counseling Editor: Eileen Murphy
Assistant Editor: Julie Martinez
Editorial Assistant: Annie Berterretche
Marketing Manager: Jennie Berger
Project Editor: Matt Stevens
Print Buyer: April Reynolds
Permissions Editor: Joohee Lee
Production Service: Matrix Productions, Inc.
Copyeditor: Joan D. Saunders

Frontis piece: "Work in the Lives of Diverse Peoples," framed in the Moorish-style motif influenced by the famous, hand-carved Rose Window at the San José Mission, San Antonio, Texas. Artwork by Richard Arredondo.
Cover Designer: Bill Stanton
Compositor: R&S Book Composition
Printer/Binder: Webcom Limited

Printed in Canada

2 3 4 5 6 03 02 01 00 99

For permission to use material from this text, contact us by
    web: www.thomsonrights.com
    fax: 1-800-730-2215
    phone: 1-800-730-2214

**Library of Congress
Cataloging-in-Publication Data**
Career counseling models for diverse populations: hands-on applications by practitioners/edited by Nadene Peterson, Roberto Cortéz González
    p. cm.
    Companion to editors' textbook: The role of work in people's lives: applied career counseling and vocational psychology.
    Includes bibliographical references and index.
    ISBN 0-534-34972-2
    1. Vocational guidance. I. Peterson, Nadene.
II. González, Roberto Cortéz. III. Peterson, Nadene. The role of work in people's lives.
HF5381.C265235 1999
159.3—dc21 99-28324

For more information, contact:

Wadsworth/Thomson Learning
10 Davis Drive
Belmont, CA 94002-3098
USA
www.wadsworth.com

International Headquarters
Thomson Learning
290 Harbor Drive, 2nd Floor
Stamford, CT 06902-7477
USA

UK/Europe/Middle East
Thomson Learning
Berkshire House
168-173 High Holborn
London WC1V 7AA
United Kingdom

Asia
Thomson Learning
60 Albert Street #15-01
Albert Complex
Singapore 189969

Canada
Nelson/ Thomson Learning
1120 Birchmount Road
Scarborough, Ontario M1K 5G4
Canada

Dedicated to the memory of Jane Becker-Haven   —RCG

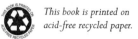

This book is printed on acid-free recycled paper.

Contents

Preface

This book is the result of our work as both professors and practitioners. As we and our graduate students worked with clients, we realized there were few resources for adapting vocational counseling skills to various populations. While we are aware of various emphases within theories and approaches, there has been little actual application of these theories to individual cases in which a particular client's background, needs, and options were basic to the success of our intervention. This book is offered to fill that void in the field. The intent of the book is to describe a variety of career and vocational counseling models that can be used for many types of individuals and groups across the life span, from age four to age eighty-four. By presenting this broad range of options for exploring career and occupational possibilities, we hope to help individuals define more clearly the role of work in their lives.

The authors of the various chapters were selected by either the age group or the specific population with which each has worked. Most of the authors are vocational practitioners who have worked for several years with the population about which they write. They have found that their interventions promote positive outcomes. The order of chapters is by age or developmental stage, beginning with preschool-age children and ending with adults in the last stage of life. In the chapters regarding adults, the considerations of several unique populations and topics are addressed. It is our hope that the models described will have sufficient information to be used or adapted easily to individual clients.

Contained within the twenty-two chapters is specific information as well as practical aids and techniques to help vocational and career practitioners work with each client. These tools can be used for building an effective means of securing the best type of work for individuals as well as for helping them toward a richer understanding of their values and lifestyle considerations. It is important to incorporate specific vocational concepts, assessments, and decision-making and goal-setting skills for each person, from children through older adults.

The ranges of populations included and the approaches illustrated will assist practitioners and clients in making the transition into the world of work in the next century. The first six chapters describe programs that can be implemented in schools through high school. The next five chapters focus on community college and university students, including the integration of technology and group counseling in career decision making. (The information in Chapters 9 and 11 is appropriate for adults as well.) There are models for two of the fastest-growing populations, older adults and prison inmates (both juveniles and adults). Several chapters deal with changing governmental rules regarding welfare and disabilities and how these laws affect our work as vocational practitioners. Three of the chapters can be used in residential settings: women's shelters, children's homes with at-risk youth, and the chronically mentally ill. These can be adapted to provide a conceptual framework for assisting day programs at hospitals, alternative schools, and social service agencies as well. A successful model for young single mothers is included as well as one for single-parent families. Practitioners working with employee assistance, work-force development, and career development programs will find useful models that will help their business organization stay current with governmental employment demands. These models will also help such practitioners better aid employees in their career development, in reaching aspirations, and in finding outplacement services. The chapter for military personnel can easily be adapted to many adults in career transition.

Finally, there are chapters that consider spirituality and genograms with ideas that can be incorporated into career counseling across the life span.

Each chapter includes an introduction that describes current research, the chapter's model(s), and strategies for implementing the techniques presented. A brief biography of the author is also included.

No book can be complete or meet every practitioner's needs. What is intended is that the material presented provide a specific model to be used or adapted by a practitioner in a manner that will be helpful to clients as they cope with the changing world of work.

While this book was written to fill a current need for practitioners in a variety of settings, it is also a companion book to our textbook *The Role of Work in People's Lives: Applied Career Counseling and Vocational Psychology* published by Brooks Cole/Wadsworth.

We are grateful to the reviewers for their valuable comments and suggestions: Paul Blisard, Southwest Missouri State University; Alan Davis, Montana State University, Billings; Cass Dykeman, Oregon State University; LeeAnn Eschbach, University of Scranton; Stephen S. Feit, Idaho State University; Marie E. Nowakowski (private practice); Lewis Patterson, Cleveland State University; Ann D. Puryear, Southeast Missouri State University; and Zark Van Zandt, University of Southern Maine, Gorham.

We want to thank each of the individual authors for their time, expertise, and commitment to this project. We are grateful to Eileen Murphy for her encouragement and understanding. We also want to thank Robert Peterson, Lyla Haggard, and Rachel Nichols for editorial and technical assistance and Amy Smith Doar and Marjorie Kyle for research assistance.

Nadene Peterson, Ed.D.,
and Roberto Cortéz González, Ph.D.

Experiential Model
for Career Guidance
in Early Childhood Education

MARJORIE T. KYLE, M.ED., M.S.

MELANIE HENNIS, M.S.

INTRODUCTION

Early childhood is a complex and exciting time in an individual's life. Jean Piaget (1977) stresses that children are not simply ignorant adults but are individuals who process information differently than adults. Early childhood, which usually ranges from three years of age to eight years of age, is a developmental period described as egocentric and concrete by Piaget. Young children in this age range are able to perceive order, understand that inherent properties do not change, and classify information. However, they are not yet able to comprehend possibilities and they only attend to the immediate environment.

This is a time when children believe the whole world revolves around them, and it is difficult for them to tell the difference between reality and fantasy. When asked, "What would you like to be when you are a grownup?" some children may reply with answers that correspond to the last unit taught to the child in which they took a special interest. For instance, if the above question was posed after the whole school participated in a beach/ocean field trip, some may reply "I want to be a fish when I grow up." When asked the same question after a zoo trip, the answer might be "I want to be an elephant when I grow up." It might be assumed that the students were not receiving the career information; actually, however, because of their developmental level, it does not make sense to young children when you ask them what they would like to be when they grow up.

Marjorie T. Kyle is a student in the doctor of psychology program at Our Lady of the Lake University and is employed as a consultant for the San Antonio Head Start Program. Melanie Hennis was a school counselor at a pre-K and kindergarten school in Seguin Independent School District, Seguin, Texas.

The questions young children are asked about career/job-related issues must be framed in the present moment. Young children are experts at *being* in the present moment. They do not understand tomorrow or yesterday—they are firmly planted in today. In the present moment they really might want to be a fish, an elephant, a flower, a book, Winnie the Pooh, or even Barney. This makes perfect sense to them at the time the question is asked. The answer they give reflects where they are *at that moment.* It is not unreasonable, therefore, to consider career awareness and vocational education of young children as different from that of older students and adults.

CAREER DEVELOPMENT
IN EARLY CHILDHOOD

Ginzberg, Ginsburg, Axelrad, and Herma (1951) proposed that fantasy in early childhood is the first stage of career development. Ginzberg et al. suggest that a lack of reality orientation and arbitrary choice of occupational preference characterize this fantasy period. In their study of second- and fifth-grade children's career aspirations and occupational role schemata, Wright, Huston, Truglio, Fitch, Smith, and Piemyat (1995) report that fifth-grade children were able to differentiate between real-life jobs and jobs depicted on television better than second-grade children. The authors also reported that children who "perceive television as socially realistic are apt to incorporate TV messages in their schemata and their aspirations" (Wright et al., 1995, 1706).

Yet studies of the career aspirations and vocational preferences of kindergarten children suggest that by kindergarten most children have developed stable career aspirations and vocational role preferences. In a study of 211 kindergarten children interviewed about their career aspirations, Trice (1991) reported that most of the kindergarten children had realistic and stable career aspirations. Stroeher (1994) described two qualitative research studies that examined the career aspirations and attitudes concerning gender-appropriate roles of sixteen kindergarten children. She found that even at that young age girls appear to have developed traditional ideas about gender roles. These established gender attitudes and career aspirations appear to be stable and difficult to influence. In their study of kindergarten children exposed to nontraditional vocational role models and curricular material, Weeks and Porter (1983) report that no statistically significant difference in traditional vocational role preference was found when compared to kindergarten children who were not exposed to nontraditional vocational role models and curricular materials.

In a web model of the structure of the growth stage of occupational development, Super (1990) proposes that during the early childhood years curiosity drives exploration, which in turn drives information gathering. Curiosity is a drive for something new or unusual, and exploration is the behavior that satisfies that drive. It is through this process of gathering information from their environment that children gain information about the world of work. The environments providing the information include television viewing, school, and home. Seligman, Weinstock, and Owings's (1988) report on a study of five-year-old children suggests that a relationship exists between the children's positive family orientation and the ability to express professional, occupational, and educational goals. David Elkind (1994) proposes that "historically, education has progressively assumed more and more family functions. In the modern era, to illustrate, schools took over the function of vocational training. . . . In the postmodern era this trend continued, but with added features. Post-modern schools have taken on what might be called a 'therapeutic function'" (Elkind, 1994, 453). These therapeutic functions include such educational initiatives as sex and drug education programs and before- and after-school programs.

The Early Childhood Curriculum

In recent years, there has been an active debate on the type of curriculum implemented in early childhood programs. On the one hand there are those who advocate formal academic skills, recommending teacher-directed execution of narrowly defined basic skills, usually in the areas of reading and computation. On the other hand there are those who advocate a child-centered curriculum, which emphasizes the development of the child's thinking processes and draws upon the child's cognitive, social, emotional, and psychomotor responses through play (Fraser, 1993; Williams, 1992). Over the past decade, research findings have supported the implementation of child-centered integrated curriculum in early childhood education (Seefeldt, 1992). The debate became so dynamic that the National Association for the Education of Young Children (NAEYC), the largest professional association of early childhood educators in the United States, produced a position paper and guidelines for the implementation of a child-centered curriculum with emphasis on a developmental perspective (Bredekamp, 1987).

The NAEYC position comprises the following guidelines:

1. Developmentally appropriate curriculum should provide for all areas of a child's development—physical, emotional, social, and cognitive—through an integrated approach.

2. Appropriate curriculum planning should be based on teachers' observations and recordings of each child's special interests and developmental progress.

3. Curriculum planning should emphasize learning as an interactive process. Teachers should prepare an environment that enables children to learn through active exploration and interaction with adults, other children, and materials.

4. Learning activities and materials should be concrete and relevant to the lives of young children.

5. Programs should provide for a wider range of developmental interests and abilities than the chronological age range of the group would suggest. Adults should be prepared to meet the needs of children who exhibit unusual interests and skills outside the normal developmental range.

6. Teachers should provide a variety of activities and materials, then increase the difficulty, complexity, and challenge of an activity as children are involved with it and as children develop understanding and skills.

7. Adults should provide opportunities for children to choose from a variety of activities, materials, and equipment and time to explore through active involvement. Adults should facilitate children's engagement with materials and activities and extend children's learning by asking questions or making suggestions to stimulate the children's thinking.

8. Multicultural and nonsexist experiences, materials, and equipment should be provided for children of all ages.

9. Adults should provide a balance of rest and movement for children throughout the program day (Bredekamp, 1986).

Different approaches are used to integrate the curriculum and meet the guidelines for developmentally appropriate early childhood programs. The most common are the theme approach, the unit approach, and the project approach (Bredekamp & Rosegrant, 1995). Through these approaches, the curriculum is conceptually organized to expand and build on the children's interests, enabling them to apply their new knowledge to problem-solving tasks.

The Early Childhood Classroom

The physical arrangement of the early childhood classroom reflects the integrated curriculum. The classroom contains learning centers where children interact with materials and each other as they acquire information, order information, judge, reason, and solve problems. Opportunities to discover and experience knowledge and skills in science, math, music, art, social studies (including career awareness), and language arts are integrated throughout the learning experiences in which the children are engaged (Bredekamp & Rosegrant, 1995). The activities, materials, and lessons are organized around a prominent theme, unit, or project.

A unit on Our Home and Family illustrates an integrated curriculum in an early childhood classroom. In the dramatic play area, children are acting out family roles and occupations. In the science area, children are exploring different types of houses for people and animals (the children are describing and discussing a hermit crab shell and comparing it to people's homes). In the block play area, children are constructing homes out of blocks and moving construction trucks around their buildings. In the art area, children are making collages out of pictures of families cut from magazines. There is a lively discussion about the number of people in one family. The library area, which contains many books about families, today is a role-playing area, and children are checking out books from a child who is playing the librarian. The "librarian" is writing the children's names and the book titles. Thus the children are engaged in activities that are associated with subject-matter disciplines within the context of their endeavors. Their learning becomes more meaningful through "learning opportunities that are contextually based, with ample opportunities for intellectual conflict, problem solving, and reflection" (New, 1992).

The Role of the Teacher

The role of the teacher in the early childhood classroom is dynamic and flexible. The teacher may be directive or nondirective. The teacher may use a number of strategies to engage in systematic and ongoing assessment of children's learning and development and construct an effective learning environment. These strategies may include: acknowledging, modeling, facilitating, supporting, scaffolding, co-constructing, demonstrating, and directing children's play, exploration, and learning (Bredekamp & Rosegrant, 1995). The teacher must have an understanding of how children learn and the importance of the sociocultural context in which that learning takes place. The teacher continually observes and interacts with the children, expanding their understanding by functioning as an information source, by asking questions, and by clarifying concepts.

Thus the children are able to engage in learning activities that draw from the goals of one or more subject-matter disciplines. The organizing topic or concept is "within the children's range of experience that allows children to explore, interpret, and engage in learning activities" that are meaningful to them (Brede-kamp & Rosegrant, 1995).

The Role of the School Counselor

The school counselor works closely with the teacher to provide materials appropriate to the age group, to bring special experiences into the classroom, and to set up projects that involve activities outside the classroom. There are many publishers and other sources of information that can provide books geared to various age groups. The use of these materials can be facilitated by the school counselor working with teachers. The following model for career guidance, which utilizes an integrated, learner-centered, experiential hands-on approach, is an example of an activity that teaches several important concepts to students. It can be organized by the school counselor to be implemented inside or outside the classroom.

EXPERIENTIAL MODEL FOR CAREER GUIDANCE

The goal of the Experiential Career Guidance Model is to create learner-centered, experiential hands-on activities that facilitate career awareness. The schools create career awareness activities through which children experience the rewards of work. These experiential activities are integrated into the daily activities of the children. The first activity involves the use of money. Some children do not understand the concept that one can earn money and, furthermore, that one can earn money by doing what one loves to do. Reasons for this lack of understanding vary, but may include the following:

■ The child's cognitive skills are not at the appropriate developmental level.

■ The child comes from multigenerational poverty.

■ The child's parents have jobs, but dislike what they are doing.

■ The child lacks the knowledge that work can be fun, exciting, and monetarily rewarding.

The schools participating in this Experiential Career Guidance Model have school stores. The children earn play money by coming to school, by earning good grades, and by performing activities and behaving in an outstanding manner. Once a month, the children are allowed to buy things from the store with money they have earned. The stores have penny items, books, toys, and games that may relate to the theme or unit they are exploring in the classroom. There also may be career-centered dramatic play kits, books, videos, tapes, records, games, and toys.

Children have a very concrete experience when they earn money at school and can spend it as they wish. Some school stores have a payment plan that allows them to purchase an item using layaway. Children become experts at how much they can earn in a month, the cost of different items, and at knowing that their job—school attendance—enables them to purchase these items. Through this activity children are exposed to learner-centered, experiential hands-on activities that create in them an awareness of the world of work and also allow them to experience and use computational and reasoning skills. Thus they internalize this process and take the information with them as they embark on careers and the life-long discovery of self.

Another activity in this Experiential Career Guidance Model is a field trip to a children's museum as part of a unit or theme. Many children's museums have interactive activities that are career centered. Field trips might also include visiting a press room, where children explore the role of news in their lives and the careers involved in producing a newspaper; an airport, where children experience worldwide travel and the variety of jobs involved in this vocation; a global communication station, where children are introduced to worldwide communication and careers in the communications industry; or the road works department of a highway system, where children discover how roads are built and see how heavy equipment operates. After a visit to a children's museum or a place of business, it is hoped that the children, when asked what they like to do, will reply with an answer that indicates an appreciation and growing understanding of jobs and careers.

Effective materials and programs for young children should incorporate a child's perspective and needs. Learning experiences should stimulate and involve a child's senses, mind, hands, and heart. Children learn through a coordinated, meaning-centered approach integrated across the curriculum. The Experiential Model for Career Guidance provides this type of approach to teaching very young children about the world of work.

CONCLUSION

By recognizing children as curious, self-motivated learners, and "accepting children's unique models of understanding instead of requiring the adult version, children learn to accept, modify, or reject their own hypothesis about the way the world works" (Bredekamp & Rosegrant, 1995, 175). Through this knowledge children may develop the self-knowledge and educational foundation needed to prepare for satisfying and productive careers.

REFERENCES

Bredekamp, S. (ed.). (1987). *Developmentally appropriate practice in early childhood programs serving children from birth through age 8* (expanded ed.). Washington, D.C.: National Association for the Education of Young Children.

Bredekamp, S., and Rosegrant, T. (1995). Transforming Curriculum Organization. S. Bredekamp and T. Rosegrant (eds.). *Reaching potential: Transforming early childhood curriculum and assessment* (vol. 2). Washington D.C.: National Association for the Education of Young Children.

Elkind, D. (1981). *The hurried child: Growing up too fast too soon.* Reading, Mass.: Addison-Wesley Publishing Co.

———. (1994). Young children in the postmodern world. H. Nuba, M. Searson, D. L. Sheiman (eds.), *Resources for early childhood: A handbook.* New York: Garland Publishing, Inc.

Fraser, D. L. (1993). Curriculum process and design: Pre-K through grade three. *Early childhood curriculum resource handbook: A practical guide for teaching early childhood (Pre-K–3).* Millwood, N.Y.: Kraus International Publications.

Ginzberg, E., Ginsburg, S.W., Axelrad, S., and Herma, J. (1951). *Occupational choice: An approach to a general theory.* New York: Columbia University Press.

New, R. S. (1992). The integrated early childhood curriculum: New interpretations based on research and practice. C. Seefeldt (ed.), *The early childhood curriculum: A review of current research* (2d ed.). New York: Teachers College Press.

Piaget, J. (1977). *The development of thought: Equilibration of cognitive structures.* New York: Viking.

Savickas, M. L., & Super, D. E. (1993). Can life stages be identified in students? Man and work. *Journal of Labor Studies,* 4, 71–98.

Seefeldt, C. (ed.). (1992). *The early childhood curriculum: A review of current research* (2d ed.). New York: Teachers College Press.

Seligman, L., Weinstock, L., Owings, N. (1988). The role of family dynamics in career development of 5-year-olds. *Elementary School Guidance & Counseling, 22*(3), 222–230.

Stoeher, S. K. (1994). Sixteen kindergartners' gender-related views of careers. The Elementary School Journal, 95(1), 95-103.

Super, D. E. (1990). A life-span, life-space approach to career development. D. Brown, L. Brooks, & Assoc. (eds.), *Career choice and development: Applying contemporary theories to practice* (2d ed.), 197–261. San Francisco: Jossey-Bass.

Trice, A. D. (1991). Stability of children's career aspirations. *Journal of Genetic Psychology,* 152, 137–139.

Weeks, M.O. (1983). A second look at the impact of nontraditional vocational role models and curriculum on the vocational role preferences of kindergarten children. *Journal of Vocational Behavior,* 23(1), 64–71.

William, L. R. (1992). Determining the curriculum. C. Seefeldt (ed.), *The early childhood curriculum: A review of current research* (2d ed.). New York: Teachers College Press.

Wright, J. C., Huston, A. C., Truglio, R., Fitch, M., Smith, E., and Piemyat, S. (1995). Occupational portrayals on television: Children's role schemata, career aspirations, and perceptions of reality. *Child Development,* 66, 1706–1718.

2

FOCUS

Finding Out the Child's Underlying Self:
A Career Awareness Model for Children

DEVELOPED BY TAMMY L. SMITH, M.A.

WITH CATHY JACOBS, JENNIFER LEVINE, LYN

MASON, AND BARBARA TERRACINA

INTRODUCTION

The intent of this chapter is to provide those who work with children ages eight through eleven with an age-appropriate perspective from which to view vocational exploration through the use of assessments. The goal of this type of counseling with children of any age group is to assist them in discovering their interests, skills, personality traits, and values. Such discoveries and exploration pave the way for children to seek work situations as they grow and mature with which they will be satisfied and compatible.

Career counseling as it is done with adolescents and adults appears to be inappropriate for children because school-age children span a wide range of developmental tasks unique to their age group (Sharf, 1992). Eric Erikson (1963) hypothesized that children aged six to eleven are in the "industry versus inferiority stage," which implies they must at this time develop a sense of industriousness in their creative efforts or they will instead possess feelings of inferiority in life pursuits. Briggs (1970) likewise offers that "The middle years of childhood are directed toward extending mastery and autonomy . . ." through a process of refining separateness and coming to believe they have something to offer (139, 140). The *FOCUS* model provides a way to assist in the negotiation of tasks through exploration of personality and interest preferences that are already present.

The encouragement of exploratory behavior can have eventual positive consequences in terms of career development and is a foundation upon which this model rests. Most children at this age are able to state strong and weak inter-

Tammy L. Smith is a licensed professional counselor in private practice in San Antonio, Texas, and is a doctoral student at the Saybrook Institute.

ests and discard some occupations because they are not interested in them, according to studies by Miller (1977) and Nelson (1963). These studies indicate that the development of interests is an outgrowth of exploration. Therefore, since the children of our society already face such a wide variety of influences, the *FOCUS* authors proffer the encouragement of exploring interests. Children's fantasies of occupations are affected by information about the world through exploration, then their fantasies evolve into interests. Such an approach fulfills what Clements (1977) sees as the major task for career education of elementary school children: the development of an awareness of self, occupational roles, the role of work in society, social behavior, and responsible actions.

THEORETICAL UNDERPINNINGS

Underlying Self

Rosenberg (1981), who is noted for extensive work on self-esteem, states:

> Although the answer to the question "What should I become?" has important consequences for the occupational system, it always emerges from the ulterior question "What am I like and what do I think of myself as?" (615).

The initial assumption upon which the *FOCUS* model is built is that each individual has an underlying self, an internal core consisting of innate interests, personality traits, and desires. Sylwester (1994) agrees that

> we have a basic personality developed early in life which is quite resistant to change. A number of others base their work on the idea of a fundamental self.

Rosenberg (1981) refers to one's "enduring disposition" while Coopersmith (1981) indicates that one maintains a fairly constant image of one's capability and distinctness as an individual, which remains consistent over a period of several years. Kohlberg's (1969) work on socialization and cognitive development is based on the assumption that there is a fundamental unity of personality, and Piers (1984) states that ". . . . individuals hold a relatively consistent view of themselves which develops and stabilizes during childhood" (43).

The most basic concept of the study and development of this "underlying self" is the belief that the mandate to "know thyself" is crucial to living a full, happy, and productive life. This allows a person to capitalize upon strengths and minimize weaknesses, permitting the development of a healthy self-concept. Stanley R. Coopersmith (1967) found from an extensive study that self-esteem in children is significantly associated with personal satisfaction and effective functioning (Coopersmith, 1981, 2).

A strong self-concept, because it includes confidence, identity, and purpose, is then crucial to the process of vocational exploration. Tarrant and Konza (1994) summarize this point well: "The development of a positive self-concept and self-esteem can affect thinking, feeling, attitudes, and behavior and determine what children are and their successes in later life" (abstract). Similarly, Wallace and colleagues (1994) found that self-esteem and identity achievement were positively related to career planning and exploration. Therefore, the development of self-concept is essential to the later process of career selection because those who possess high self-esteem "are goal oriented and motivated by dreams of what they want to be-come or what they want to accomplish, and they effectively utilize the resources available to them to accomplish their goals" (Reasoner, 1981, 2). It follows that children who possess a healthy self-concept will likely be more adept at focusing on interests and personal desires as they grow and mature. One can then conclude that a cyclical relationship exists between self-esteem and vocational and personal exploration.

Vocational practitioners today widely recog-nize that self-concept plays a major role in oc-cupational decisions. This idea has been most directly expressed in Donald Super's self-concept implementation theory of occupational choice. The selection of an occupation, accord-ing to Super (1963), depends on one's develop-ment of a self-concept (Rosenberg, 1981). Super asserts that the child's self-concept derives from the basic drive in early years of curiosity. Curiosity is satisfied through exploratory be-havior, which in turn leads to developing inter-ests and acquiring career information (Sharf, 1992,129).

Holland (1966) suggests that career choice and adjustment represent an extension of one's personality. Two of Holland's concepts that are directly addressed by the *FOCUS* model are the ideas of congruence and differentiation. Con-gruence is sought by assessing one's personality and attempting to match it with the appropri-ate occupational environment.

FOCUS could be considered a modified type of the trait and factor approach, which re-lies heavily on the use of tests and inventories to measure aptitudes, achievements, interests, values, and personality. *FOCUS* differs in that it incorporates gaining self-understanding by assessing interests and personality, obtaining knowledge about the world of work, then inte-grating these two areas of information.

THE *FOCUS* MODEL

Basic Model

The *FOCUS* model, "finding out the child's underlying self," is to be used as a discovery tool for vocational counseling with children. It is a four-tiered approach that can be adapted by the user according to his or her purposes. The basic four-step assessment of the child includes the following components: (1) self-report of the child about his or her interests, (2) assessment of the child's indicated interests in tasks and work situations accomplished through a mea-sure, (3) assessment of the child's basic person-ality through another measure, and (4) observa-tion of the child in a natural setting. This basic *FOCUS* model can be applied in a variety of ways. Figure 2.1 depicts the basic and applied models.

Recommendations for applying *FOCUS* are as follows: The first step, obtaining the child's self-report about interests, is usually best accomplished in some type of personal inter-view or conversation with the child or between children. (See Box 2.4 for a sample interview.) The goal here is to focus on what the child ac-tually *says* about his or her interests, desires, and dreams. The second step assists in the discovery of more specific interests and can be accom-plished through any measure designed to assess interests in children. Some examples of mea-sures suitable for this step are listed in Box 2.1. The third step, assessment of basic personality traits, may also be accomplished through any measure designed for this purpose and appro-priate for children. Box 2.2 lists examples of personality assessments appropriate for this step. Finally, the fourth step, discovering the child's observable behaviors and actions, is a qualitative measure and can be accomplished through par-ental report, teacher report, unobtrusive obser-

Basic Model

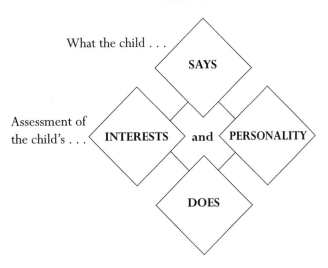

Applied Model

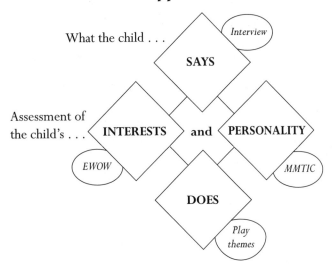

FIGURE 2.1   The *Focus* Model

vation in a natural setting, and even unique venues such as sand play. The point here is to actually observe what the child does and glean any useful understandings of unprompted interests, personality traits, and favorite settings from

naturalistic observation. Box 2.3 includes suggestions for this step. Steps 1 and 4 are most effective and informative if they contain multiple interviews and observations. The intent of such in-depth exploration of a child's self-report,

---

BOX 2.1 Resources Appropriate for Step 2 of the *FOCUS* Model

E-WOW: Exploring the World of Work (Grades 3–6)
Designed as a career awareness and exploration learning activity that has a game-like format. It helps students be aware of job activities, the job cluster concept, job titles, and the process of exploring, researching, and comparing jobs.

Career Trek (Grades 4–6)
Will help children become more aware of themselves, the people around them, and the occupations within their community and beyond. It will not teach children how to prepare for a career nor will it encourage them to decide what to be when they grow up.

JOB–O E (Grades 4–7)
Exposes students to the vocabulary of careers and information associated with occupational planning. If all objectives are accomplished, students will learn a great deal about occupational groups, career interests, specific jobs, and, most important, they will become more aware of themselves and the relationship of their interests and values to the world of work.

Dream Catchers (Grades 5–7)
Designed for developing career and educational awareness. Three topical clusters are Capturing

Your Dreams, The Stuff Dreams Are Made Of, and Make Dreams Come True; all three emphasize skill discovery, choices, and ability.

Elementary Careers (Grades 3–6)
Fun and interactive. It introduces the concept of occupational clustering and career choices to young students.

Children's Dictionary of Occupations (Grades 3–8)
A book introducing children to the world of work and the variety of occupations available. It includes nearly 300 occupations consistent with the latest information from the Department of Labor's *Occupational Outlook Handbook*. This is not a measure designed to assess level of interest.

All of the above resources can be obtained from: CFKR Career Materials, Inc, Attn: Elementary Dept, 11860 Kemper Road, Unit 7, Auburn, CA 95603, (800) 525-5626.

---

interests, personality, and actions is to assess a broad picture of who the child intrinsically is, that is, his or her "underlying self."

The importance of keeping the process as free from adult contamination as possible must be underscored. For example, during step 1, if children have a deep desire to please the adult who is conducting the interview, they will give answers not truly reflective of their thoughts.

Children need to understand that there are no right or wrong answers and that whatever they say is an acceptable answer. Likewise, during the observation in Step 4, what a child does must be observed unobtrusively within a natural setting. A contrived setting will affect who the child truly is when at play. It is also strongly recommended that the measures utilized for Steps 2 and 3 be standardized instruments, de-

---

BOX 2.2 Resources Appropriate for Step 3 of the *FOCUS* Model

Murphy-Meisgeier Type Indicator for Children (MMTIC)

    Ages: 7–13

    Publisher: Consulting Psychologists Press

Early School Personality Questionnaire (ESPQ)

    Ages: 6–8

    Publisher: Institute for Personality and Ability Testing (IPAT)

Children's Personality Questionnaire (CPQ)

    Ages: 8–12

    Publisher: Institute for Personality and Ability Testing (IPAT)

Comrey Personality Scales

    Publisher: Educational and Industrial Testing Service (EDITS)

Personality Inventory for Children (PIC)

    Publisher: Western Psychological Services

BOX 2.3 Suggestions for Step 4 of the *FOCUS* Model

- Any naturalistic setting where unobtrusive observation of the child at play may occur (school playground, backyard, and so forth)
- Parental report of child's most frequently used toys, activities often engaged in, and so forth
- Teacher report of child's playing preferences (alone, with others, conventional/unconventional usage of toys, play themes)
- Therapeutic observation (especially sand play)
- Play group observation

---

veloped and normed on this specific age population by test manufacturers.

Analysis and Synthesis of Data

After gathering all of the pertinent data from the four steps, the next task is to determine patterns and themes. This crucial step involves searching diligently for parallels between play, interests, personality, and self-report, looking for consistencies and inconsistencies. Themes that appear in all four areas and that are dominant are most important. Pointing out which personality patterns go with which interests should be done in general language, never as the final word, to expand possibilities and understanding. Consistent preferences, prevalent imagery and obvious personality characteristics are the type of useful information *FOCUS* is designed to elicit. After patterns are gleaned from careful observation of all information, the next step is communication of the patterns to those who will benefit from knowing them.

Communication of Discoveries

The guiding principle in communicating the information from *FOCUS* must always be that *words have power.* School-age children clarify and differentiate themselves through conversation. Teachers, parents, and people in positions of authority are all mirrors through which children come to perceive themselves. "Other people constitute a frame of reference, a backdrop, a perspective from which the self is seen" (Rosenberg, 1981, 613). Those who communicate with children are exceedingly important to the child's life by their very position. Any interaction with a child (especially as it relates to self-concept) must be positive and encouraging, filled with excitement about the child's potential and present personality. Communication of *FOCUS* discoveries must also be within this framework lest they be counterproductive to the entire purpose of the model.

Communicating Results

Because most occupational information for school-age children is provided in the classroom, this next section is primarily designed for teachers (Sharf, 1992). However, the principles apply to any situation in which *FOCUS* might be appropriately applied.

Communication of findings is first given to the children themselves. Providing children with feedback has been shown to encourage feedback, which in turn encourages autonomy and initiative (Coopersmith, 1981). The child should

be informed in language appropriate for the age group that he or she seems to possess certain personality characteristics and is demonstrating certain likes, dislikes, and interests. The child should be encouraged to think about these things in the future and challenged to continuously explore new activities and situations.

Such information should never be communicated in absolutes, but rather as possibilities, exciting avenues for exploration. By taking adequate time to explain and assist, teachers help children to believe in themselves. "By helping children recognize skills they already possess . . . teachers can help students develop self-confidence and determination" (Reasoner, 1982, 35). The teacher's excitement level will communicate volumes to the child because teachers make heavy contributions to a child's self-perception (Briggs, 1970).

Next the information can be communicated to parents to be used for guidance. The effect of parental encouragement is crucial to the entire process of identity development as well as to the understanding of vocational interests (Riley, 1995). The effect of parents showing encouragement and empowerment in a loving context of acceptance cannot be understated. Therefore, it is crucial that parents be educated concerning the critical nature of their position and influence. The *FOCUS* information in the hands of parents could be used to introduce after-school and summer activities based upon the interest/personality trait pairings discovered.

The themes and patterns should also be given to counselors, additional teachers, and any others who might be involved in the process of assisting career development. Simply knowing this information allows these significant others to encourage children in career fairs, field trips, and special seminars that seem compatible with the children's personality and interests. This model is designed to focus upon an intrinsic self, which, if nurtured, could find full expression through certain vocational and avocational pursuits. The goal of *FOCUS* is to reinforce in children that who they are is exciting, unique, and filled with potential. In no way should the information be used to categorize, label, or delineate a specific or narrow direction. "Encouraging children's merging interests is helpful in the development of their career maturity. Talking about those aspects of their life that are exciting can eventually be helpful in career planning" (Sharf, 1992, 134).

APPLICATION OF THE FOCUS MODEL: A CASE STUDY

As mentioned, each applied model might look somewhat different, depending upon the data-gathering techniques selected. Each step of an applied model utilized with a student is described below in detail, including the various instruments that were used with the case study presented. The application of the *FOCUS* model with the child "Beth" included an interview for Step 1, the Exploring the World of Work (E-WOW) instrument for Step 2, the Murphy-Meisgeier Type Indicator for Children instrument for Step 3, and play theme discovery for Step 4. Beth's results are examined in order to demonstrate how significant patterns and themes are discovered. She was in fifth grade at the time of the assessments. (Refer to Appendix A "Beth's Interview" for the verbatim interview, the E-WOW, and the MMTIC results.) The behaviors observed during this process (which constitutes Step 4), the child's self-report, and the information gleaned from the measures permitted the identification of a significant number of themes indicative of Beth's underlying self. Permission was obtained from Beth's parents (via a letter) prior to testing

and interviewing, all of which was completed within one day.

Step 1: What the Child Says

For this first step, Beth was interviewed with a questionnaire developed by the authors specifically for the *FOCUS* model. The interview was designed to elicit spontaneous responses concerning play, interests, and personality characteristics. Refer to Appendix A for the verbatim questions.

In order to ensure as standardized a process as possible (Beth was part of an entire classroom being assessed), the following was read to her prior to the interview:

> There are no right or wrong answers. As a matter of fact, every answer is right because it's about you and you are great just the way you are. So, just say whatever comes to your mind as soon as you hear the question. Please don't say 'I don't know' because these are questions you can answer in any way you like. It's about you—and we want to find out what you know about you. I'll ask you a question and you answer whatever you feel like. I'm not going to explain the question, I'm just going to ask it, so you can interpret it yourself however you'd like.

Interviewers need to be reminded to ask each question in a similar manner, to smile pleasantly and not to add to the questions even if the child responds "I don't know" and seems to be struggling with the answer. Interviewers need to look at each child pleasantly and confidently, as though the child is going to have a great answer that the instructor looks forward to hearing. Beth's answers were recorded verbatim.

Beth's interview is found in Appendix A. From this Step 1 interview, the following themes

---

BOX 2.4   Sample Interview for Step 1 of the *FOCUS* Model

---

1. If you could do anything you wanted when you grow up, what would it be?
2. What's your favorite thing to do?
3. Who is your hero?
   a. Why?
   b. Describe what you like best about him/her and what he/she does.
4. a. Do you like the job your dad has?
   b. What does he do?
   c. If yes, would you like to do what he does when you get older?
5. a. Do you like the job your mom has?
   b. What does she do?
   c. If yes, would you like to do what she does when you get older?

6. Would you rather
   a. go for a hike
   b. play sports
   c. write a story
   d. hang out with friends?
7. What toys do you still play with that you've played with since you were little?
8. What's your favorite thing to do on a summer vacation?
9. What do you remember doing a lot before you were in school?
10. If you were daydreaming, what would you be thinking about?
11. Describe your perfect day from start to finish.

---

emerged: is interested in teaching, enjoys writing stories, needs support and approval from significant others, is not interested in sales/persuasiveness, has a high imagination level, enjoys reading, is thinking about the future. Her "perfect day" scenario reveals that she is very expressive verbally, detailed in her thinking, concerned about her outward appearance, highly social, and enjoys a great deal of variety.

Step 2: Assessment of the Child's Interests

For Step 2 of the *FOCUS* model in working with Beth, E-WOW was chosen as the instrument for assessment of interests.

Interpretation The E-WOW can be interpreted by a comparison with Holland's trait theory, because the categories are quite similar. (See Holland's theory.) To examine the E-WOW itself, see Beth's results in the next paragraph. For other career interest measures, refer to the list of measures in Box 2.1.

Beth's Results Reviewing Beth's E-WOW allows for greater understanding through the following information: She scored very high in the artistic category and demonstrated interest in being a dancer, writer, or musician. Her scores were markedly low in the outdoor (forestry, agriculture, natural resources) category—Holland's "realistic." She also showed somewhat of an interest in mathematics, science, solving problems, research, building, working with her hands, teaching, and working with people. On the E-WOW, Beth chose "teacher" from all the vocations listed as the one that she would like to explore further. This corresponds directly with interview question No. 1 of Step 1, which asked what she would like to be when she grows up. She responded by saying "teacher." In Step 3 of the E-WOW, we notice Beth's unique pattern by the responses that she didn't choose: She prefers to work with others, is noncompetitive, would not like to be anyone's boss, and dislikes physical labor.

Step 3: Assessment of the Child's Personality

General Information For this step of Beth's *FOCUS* process, the Murphy-Meisgeier Type Indicator for Children (MMTIC) was utilized. It was developed for children in grades two through eight. The purpose of this test is to determine children's Jungian types in order to identify individual learning styles. The learning styles found through the MMTIC correlate with the Myers-Briggs personality types of: extroversion, introversion, sensing, intuition, thinking, feeling, judging, and perceiving.

Beth's Results The results of Beth's MMTIC indicate that her personality style is ENFP. She scored high on these four measures. "E," or extroverted, describes one who is energized by the external world, interested in thoughts and feelings, needs relationships, is friendly and talkative, and likes to share. "N" represents intuition, which indicates the enjoyment of fantasy stories, a child who is good at make-believe, who has imagination, and who lives in the future (or daydreams). "F" represents feeling and describes a child who is embarrassed by disapproval, who is focused on people, who uses words to express ideas, and who likes to work with others. "P" indicates she likes to explore, is curious, will work on many projects at once, and needs a great deal of variety.

Step 4: What the Child Does

Play Themes Within the guidelines of Step 4 of the *FOCUS* model, observation of what a child actually does is an effective method for gleaning an understanding of the child's underlying self. Therefore, observation of play themes in a naturalistic setting is suggested as a primary way to gather such information. By watching a child at spontaneous play in a variety of settings, many characteristics of the child and of his or her interests can be gleaned. The specific toys chosen for play can be identified as well as how the child uses the toys. Is it a conventional or creative usage? Does the child spend a great deal of time on one toy or switch quickly from one to another? Observations about children's traits can be made as well: whether they are bored, distracted, anxious, calm, hyperactive, neat or sloppy; whether they choose to play alone most often or seem to prefer playing with others. These are just a few examples of the information that observation of play themes might provide. Another unique assessment tool for Step 4 with great potential is sand play, to the extent that the sand play evolves spontaneously. Karen Signell discusses the use of sand play as a prognostic tool. She found that it frequently foreshadows the path that lies ahead (Signell, 1981, 108). Box 2.3 contains suggestions for completing this step.

Overall Synthesis

From the first three steps of the *FOCUS* procedure, combined with spontaneous observation of Beth throughout the entire process, it was possible to observe common patterns and themes for Beth. First, she is highly verbal, as seen in the story writing she referred to in her interview and in the number of conversations with others that she wrote into her perfect day. The verbal theme was also evident in her choices from the E-WOW, and the extrovert of the MMTIC is described as someone who is talkative and needs to process information externally, or verbally, as opposed to internally. A second theme is Beth's need for relationships and desire for approval within those relationships. Her perfect day included having many friends over and talking with them. Her interview also pointed to the support that her mother gives her as very important. The E-WOW indicated that she preferred not to be in situations that could cause conflict with others—non-competitive, nonsupervisory, and nonindependent all point to her need to work in an environment with personal contact. Her MMTIC results of ENFP describe her as a feeling individual who focuses on people, is embarrassed by disapproval, and likes to work with others and an extroverted person who is energized by the external, enjoys sharing, and is friendly. A third pattern that emerged is Beth's active imagination. The story-writing references in her interview, her high score in the artistic areas of the E-WOW, and her high intuition score on the MMTIC (good at make-believe, has imagination, enjoys fantasy stories) all indicate that Beth would best develop her potential in an environment that allows for active use of imagination and creativity. Still other themes emerge—her high perception score on the MMTIC and her description of her perfect day indicate a need for variety. Her high intuition score indicates she spends a great deal of time thinking about the future. This latter theme was validated by the interview question that asked what she might daydream about—her answer was "What I would do later." Another interesting theme was Beth's consistent response of being interested in being a teacher. She indicated this interest in her interview and in her E-WOW responses. What is striking is that she is an ENFP, and of all sixteen types utilized by the MMTIC and the Myers-Briggs Type Indicator, an ENFP is the most consistent type of teacher at all educational levels. Table 2.1 provides a more visual representation of these findings about Beth.

Recommendations and Final Comments

The intention for this model is that it be helpful and effective in discovering children's interests and personality at their most basic level. The discovery of the child's underlying self followed by the proper use of that information helps the child to develop the self-esteem that results from identifying one's strengths and to subsequently make vocational choices and pursue interests based on these factors. It is recommended that a longitudinal study of the model's long-term effectiveness be undertaken by comparing job and life satisfaction with FOCUS results.

It seems the experience of adults who work in vocations that mirror the play themes of their youth is a type of validation in and of itself. However, the optimal study would be to utilize the FOCUS model on a large, diverse group of children (representative of the U.S. Census) and follow these children as they grow and mature into adulthood.

One consideration when using the FOCUS model concerns the various cultural messages that may have influenced students. For instance, one might ask about Beth, "What does her choice of 'teacher' have to do with what she has been exposed to?" In addition to being cognizant of cultural influences, the FOCUS user must also pay careful attention to possible adult contamination. Such influence could come through the interviewer, teacher, parent, or other significant adult who means well, but might be subtly pressuring the child into interests, behaviors, and activities that are not a natural outgrowth of the child's underlying self.

Along these same lines, the manner, or spirit, in which the information is presented to children is crucial. The goal of the FOCUS developers is that it be an exciting, uplifting process of self-discovery for all involved. Therefore, teacher (or FOCUS leader) enthusiasm while working in all steps of the process is an important aspect of the model's effectiveness. This model can also be adapted for group or class use if time is allowed with each student for an interview and a follow-up.

TABLE 2.1 Application of the FOCUS Model:
Thematic Identification of Patterns

INTERVIEW	E-WOW	MMTIC
Interest in teaching	High scores in artistic	*E = Extrovert*
Enjoys writing stories	Dancer	Energized by external world, interested in thoughts/feelings, needs relationships, is friendly and talkative, likes to share
Needs support and approval of significant others	Writer	
	Musician	
No interest in sales/persuasion		*N = Intuition*
High imagination level	Low scores in outdoor	Enjoys fantasy stories, good at make-believe, has an imagination, lives in future, daydreams
Enjoys reading	Forestry	
Enjoys thinking about future	Agriculture	
	Natural resources	*F = Feeling*
Very verbally expressive		Embarrassed by disapproval, focused on people, uses words to express self, likes working with others
Demonstrates detailed thinking	Somewhat interested in	
Concerned with appearance	Mathematics	
Highly social	Science	*P = Perception*
Enjoys variety	Solving problems	Likes to explore, is curious, will work on many projects at once, needs great variety
	Research	
Daydream question: "What I would do later"	Building, working with hands	
	Working with people	ENFP is most consistent type of teacher at all levels
Said support her mother gives is very important to her	Prefers to work with others	
Multiple conversations in perfect day	Noncompetitive	
	Wouldn't want to be a boss	
	Dislikes physical labor	

REFERENCES

Briggs, D. C. (1970). *Your child's self-esteem.* New York: Doubleday.

Cattell, R. B., Ebert, H. W., & Tatsoka, N. M. (1970). *Handbook for the Sixteen Personality Factor Questionnaire.* Champaign, Ill., Institute for Personality and Ability Testing.

Clements, I. (1977). *Career education and vocational education.* Washington, D.C.: National Education Association.

Coopersmith, S. (1967). *The antecedents of self-esteem.* Palo Alto, Calif.: Consulting Psychologists Press.

———. (1981). *Self-esteem inventories manual.* Palo Alto, Calif.: Consulting Psychologists Press.

Erikson, E. H. (1963). *Childhood and society* (2d ed.). New York: Norton.

Holland, J. (1966). The psychology of vocational choice. Waltham, Mass.: Baisdell.

Kalff, D. M. (1980). *Sandplay.* Boston: Sigo Press.

Kohlberg, L. (1969). Stage and sequence: The cognitive developmental approach to socialization. D. A. Goslin (ed.), *Handbook of socialization theory and research.* Chicago: Rand McNally.

McCaulley, M. H. (1977). *Applications of the Myers-Briggs Type Indicator to Medicine and Other Health Professions.* (Monograph I) Gainesville, Fla.: Center for Applications of Psychological Type.

Meisgeier, C., & Murphy, E. (1987). *The Murphy-Meisgeier Type Indicator for Children Manual.* Palo Alto, Calif.: Consulting Psychologists Press.

Miller, J. (1977). *Career development needs of nine-year-olds: How to improve career development programs.* Washington, D.C.: National Advisory Council for Career Education.

Murphy, E. (1992). *The Developing Child.* Palo Alto, Calif.: Consulting Psychologists Press.

Myers, I. B. (1985). *The Myers-Briggs Type Indicator Manual.* Palo Alto, Calif.: Consulting Psychologists Press.

Nelson, R. C. (1963). Knowledge and interest concerning 16 occupations among elementary and secondary students, *Educational and Psychological Measurement, 27,* 741–754.

Piaget, J. (1977). *The development of thought: Equilibration of cognitive structure.* New York: Viking.

Piers, E. V., & Harris, D. B. (1984). *Piers-Harris children's self-concept scale manual.* Los Angeles: Western Psychological Services.

Quimby, V. (1967). Differences in the self-ideal relationship of an achieved group and an underachieved group, *California Journal of Educational Research, 18,* 23–31.

Riley, G. M. (1995). *Increasing self-esteem in children, 8–12 years old from dysfunctional families: A twofold solution to a twofold problem.* Nova Southeastern University.

Reasoner, R. W. (1982). *Building self-esteem: Teacher's guide and classroom materials.* Palo Alto, Calif.: Consulting Psychologists Press.

Rosenberg, M. (1981). Self-concept: Social product and social force. M. Rosenberg & R. Turner (eds.), *Social psychology: Sociological perspectives.* New York: Basic Books.

Sharf, R. (1992). *Applying career development theory to counseling.* Pacific Grove, Calif.: Brooks/Cole.

Shaw, M. & Alves, G. (1963). The self-concept of bright academic underachievers: II. *Personnel and Guidance Journal, 42,* 401–403.

Signell, K. A. (1981). The Sandplay process in man's development. S. Sternback (ed.), *Sandplay Studies.* (157–195). Boston: Sigo Press.

Super, D. E., Starishevsky, R., Matlin, N., & Jordan, J. P. (1963). *Career development: Self-concept theory.* New York: College Entrance Examination Board.

Sylwester, R. (1994). How emotions affect learning. *Educational Leadership, 52* (2), 60–65.

Tarrant, S., & Konza, D. (1994). *Promoting self-esteem in integrated early childhood settings.* Australia: Australian Early Childhood Association.

Wallace, B., & Wallace, A. (1994). Adolescent career development: Relationships to self-concept and identity status. *Journal of Research on Adolescence, 4* (1), 127–149.

APPENDIX A

BETH'S INTERVIEW

1. If you could do anything you wanted when you grow up, what would it be?
   Be a teacher.

2. What's your favorite thing to do?
   Write stories and color.

3. Who is your hero/heroine?
   My mom.
   A. Why?
      Because she's always there for me.

   B. Describe what you like about him or her and what he or she does.
      She's always nice when I need help and she gives me lots of help.

4. A. Do you like what your dad does for a living?
      Kind of.

   B. If yes, what does he do?
      He sells cars.

   C. If yes, would you like to do what he does when you get older?
      No.

5. A. Do you like what your mom does for a living?

   Kind of.

 B. If yes, what does she do?

   Stays at home and watches my little sister Leslie.

 C. If yes, would you like to do what she does when you get older?

   No.

6. Would you rather: (a) go for a hike, (b) play sports, (c) write a story, or (d) hang out with friends?

  (c) *Write a story.*

7. What toys do you still play with that you've played with since you were little?

  My stuffed animals.

8. What's your favorite thing to do on a summer vacation?

  Play and write stories.

9. What do you remember doing a lot before you were in school?

  Play with my mom and with all my old toys and reading.

10. If you were daydreaming during class and looking out the window, what would you be thinking about?

  What I would do later.

11. Describe your perfect day from start to finish.

  It would be Friday. First I would wake up and make my bed. Then I would get dressed in my rustler jeans and my white button-down shirt. Kelley would let me use her brand-new black shirt. For breakfast I could have a stack of pancakes. I would ask my dad to use his hair spray and he would say, "Yes!" My hair would brush out easy and stay in place. Then I would brush my teeth. After that I would give my mom and dad a kiss and hug. Then my mom would take me to school and I would get there at 7:11. I would get to the fifth-grade hall with Stephanie [for patrols]. Then in math Ms. B wasn't there anymore. I made all hundreds. In science we got some new students. They would be Valerie R., Julie A., Elizabeth A., and Christa R. In social studies Mrs. M brought her baby, Blake, to let us see him. For lunch my mom brought me Taco Bell. We received extra recess. For the rest of the day we had a pizza party. When we packed up, I received a $150 check from Mrs. R. Renee, Lauren, Stephanie, Brenda, Amanda, Val, Elizabeth, Julie, and Christa all rode the bus home with me and spent the night. For dinner we had pizza and for dessert we had Neapolitan ice cream. After that it was 5:35 and we went to Fiesta Texas [amusement park] until 10:00. Then my dad came home and went to my room and watched TV on my new TV. Also played tapes, and games, and talked.

3

Multicultural Career Exploration with Adolescent Females

MARIE PASCOE CRAIG, M.ED.

MARY CONTRERAS, M.S.

NADENE PETERSON, ED.D.

INTRODUCTION

This chapter is based on a project that was created out of an interest in understanding the development of adolescent females and their career decision-making processes.[1] Unfortunately, the identity of the adolescent female is often based on her physical attributes, not her talents, abilities, or interests (Herr & Cramer, 1996). These young women are valued more for their appearance, manners, and respect for rules than for their academic achievements. In describing herself, the adolescent female uses self-descriptors that are unflattering, reflecting low self-esteem (Sears, 1995). Pipher (1994) reports that gifted adolescent females lose IQ points as they become feminized, and therefore they tend to lose potential by devaluing their abilities. This devaluing is observed in every aspect of the adolescent female. In school, they often choose to avoid advanced math and science courses because they do not feel competent. Even when the confidence level is intact, these young women often minimize their abilities. Our society teaches the adolescent female that young men do not like smart girls. It goes without saying that these social influences will shape their future decisions. Career possibilities are limited by the minor courses chosen by the adolescent female. Without advanced-level math and science courses, careers relying on a scientific, technological, or engineering basis are often eliminated.

Marie Pascoe Craig is a certified school counselor and a licensed professional counselor in Texas. She is enrolled in the doctor of psychology program at Our Lady of the Lake University. Mary Contreras is director of the Second Chance and Think Nontraditional programs at San Antonio College, programs that provide vocational and career counseling for single parents, displaced homemakers, and nontraditional students.

[1]Even though this project was designed for adolescent females, many of the ideas may be used for adolescent males.

Emotional insecurities may easily overshadow academic ability and become the basis of a fear of success for the adolescent female. Sears (1995) suggests that a fear of success is further developed in adolescent females because of a need to have friends and to be attractive to boys. When girls excel academically, they believe they become less attractive to boys. Choices made by these young women to gain and maintain favor have strong consequences: Namely, young women are losing their authentic selves.

Adolescent females are a unique population. They have numerous cultural and societal issues with which they must deal. These young women are coping with some of the same issues their mothers dealt with in the '60s and '70s that arise out of cultural values and practices, and as they are assimilated more fully into the larger culture, gender issues and racial concerns become more pronounced. Pipher (1994) observes that American girls are growing up in a "girl-poisoning culture."

The self-esteem of adolescent females is much lower than the self-esteem level of preadolescent girls. Preadolescent girls are assertive risk-takers who believe that they are as smart as boys (Orenstein, 1993). They are interested in a variety of topics, unlimited in thought, androgynous, adaptive, and assertive (Pipher, 1994). Adolescence brings not only biological and hormonal changes, but emotional changes as well. These changes are reflected in a loss of resilience, curiosity, and risk-taking. Adolescent girls are more critical of themselves and often believe that they are less capable than boys. These feelings can lead to low self-esteem and depression. Girls tend to lose sight of their abilities and consequently do not perform at their actual level of potential.

The late French feminist, Simone de Beauvoir (1952) believed that adolescence was when girls realized that men have the power and that a female's power comes from consenting to become a submissive, adored object (Pipher, 1994, 21). This outlook paralyzes the growth of the adolescent female. She becomes like Shakespeare's Ophelia. She loses herself and lives for the approval of Hamlet and her father. Adolescent females who are not true to themselves lose themselves as did Ophelia (Pipher, 1994). Girls who change to please others become resentful, while those who remain true to themselves maintain their assertiveness and high level of self-confidence. To develop a healthy life, adolescent females need love from family and friends, meaningful work, respect, challenges, and physical and psychological safety (Pipher, 1994).

CAREER AWARENESS IN MIDDLE SCHOOL

Careers, jobs, and occupations are terms used interchangeably in our discussion of the world of work. Work adds the necessary ingredient to balance our lives, and dissatisfaction with jobs can lead to mental and physical problems. Herr and Cramer (1996) believe that a variety of life difficulties and mental problems ensue when work life is unsatisfactory. It is imperative that our career choices be made very carefully. Career awareness, exploration, and decision making are needed in order to ensure that individuals enter their careers/occupations with the best information possible.

Middle school female students are like no other group of students. Developmentally, they are risk-takers, explorers, investigators, and identity seekers. This is when young female adolescents discover who they are. Their penchant for exploration helps with the development of both self-concept and career awareness. Making sure that the adolescent female continues to value and enhance her talents, interests, and abilities is very important at this stage of development. Career exploration is a vehicle that will support the adolescent female's self-discovery. Super (1990) suggests that middle school students fall within two developmental levels—growth and exploration. The growth level identifies attitudes, interests, and needs associated with self-concept. The exploration level identifies interests, skills, and personality characteristics (Sears, 1995). Career exploration is an important complement to the intellectual and social development of the middle school student (Yatvin, 1995).

Bartholomew and Schnorr (1994, 246) suggest that expanding career horizons for young women through career counseling programs needs to include:

1. counselor awareness of gender role stereotyping,

2. finding ways to dismantle gender-based stereotypes,

3. helping females to reframe math and science stereotypes,

4. enhancing self-concept,

5. improving self-esteem and self-confidence,

6. facing fear of success,

7. looking toward balancing family and career goals,

8. understanding peer influences, and

9. finding support systems and role models.

Career counselors must be well trained in the issues of work and career development in addition to developing an understanding of minority students, including gender and racial concerns. Since work interrelates with an individual's personal and emotional welfare, coun-selors need to address all these issues in a well-developed career education program.

CULTURAL DIFFERENCES AMONG ADOLESCENT FEMALES

Since cultural differences need to be understood by career counselors, the following discussion is included.

African American Adolescent Females and the World of Work

Orenstein (1994) describes the African American adolescent female as an assertive, self-confident individual. She is often judged to be aggressive because of her lack of fear of making her presence and desires known. She is said to be very similar to the Anglo male. Her strong sense of self often creates problems, since she is often perceived to be aggressive. It is this aggressive behavior that often makes the African American female student appear to be difficult to manage. She tends to speak loudly and will not be minimized by anyone. Her behavior parallels the Anglo male's classroom behavior of demanding attention. This behavior is supported in the adolescent male but not in the adolescent female. The reaction to the African American adolescent female's behavior is more of a gender issue than a racial issue. Girls are to be seen and not heard.

The African American young woman is very resilient. Although her level of self-confidence is reported by Orenstein (1994) to be the most intact of all of the female adolescents, these young women do suffer. The icon of strength can and does work against her. It does not allow the African American adolescent female to accept her weaknesses or limitations—she must always be stronger and endure more than anyone else, male or female.

Counselors need to keep in mind the uniqueness of the African American female's historical development. Providing an appropriate career education plan will aid not only in economic development but also in personal health. The multiple roles of the African American female should be addressed. She is a female who is bicultural and perhaps bilingual (standard English and black English). She must operate in both worlds—the Anglo and the African American worlds. She is the one female whose self-esteem does not lessen as she becomes feminized.

Hispanic Adolescent Females and the World of Work

Hispanic adolescent females have unique cultural differences, starting with the primacy of family concerns about achievement, rank, and wealth. These patterns have a very strong influence on their development of values, beliefs and self-concept. Family primacy can be strong enough to negate independence, with the expectation that the female is to stay within family boundaries. Female development incorporates interdependence and consideration of others, making the individuation and the separation process very different for Hispanic females (Kuvelsky, 1981).

In the Hispanic culture, most girls are taught that motherhood is the highest calling and the greatest source of fulfillment. The *quinceñera* (the presentation of a female to the community as an adult at age fifteen) is the popular ceremony that identifies and celebrates the transition from childhood to adulthood, leaving little time for adolescence as a stage.

School achievement records suggest that there is a low mastery in math, science, and lan-guage skills in most Hispanic adolescent females. They also have a low rate of school completion. Herr and Cramer (1992) cite a report by the Hispanic Policy Development Project that indicates that the middle school years are an important time to discuss motivation and aspirations. The study suggested that a possible source of lack of motivation on the part of Hispanic students is the anonymity many sense and the lack of respect for their cultural values.

The National Council of La Raza reports that since 1980 the Hispanic population has grown five times as fast as the non-Hispanic population (De La Rosa & Maw, 1990). The future of our nation may be secured by guiding these bicultural students through positive self-discovery and educational growth experiences and providing them with various career options and opportunities. As with other groups, however, there is very little research available on Hispanic females of any age, and the research that is available is often influenced by Anglo researchers' misconceptions of the cultural and family norms and value systems. Individuals interested in Hispanic women are faced with a mass of undifferentiated information that appears to assume that the educational process and the self-development process are the same for Hispanic males and females (McKenna & Ortiz, 1988).

Government reports on the socioeconomic conditions and school achievement of Hispanics reinforce negative attitudes about the Hispanic populations (Valencia & Richards, eds., 1991). Although Hispanics are the fastest-growing minority group in our nation, they are least likely to graduate from high school or to aspire to a professional career. The lowest retention rates in school are among Hispanic students, with less than 50 percent graduating, and Hispanic females drop out at a rate that is 2 percent to 5 percent higher than Hispanic males. Additionally, Hispanic youth leave school at an earlier age than other groups, with 40 percent to 60 percent leaving before reaching tenth grade. Females begin the process of leaving school much earlier (Melville, 1980). The dropout rate of Hispanics is attributed to (a) the students' lack of motivation to continue their education, (b) the anonymity many of them feel in middle school, and (c) lack of recognition or respect for their cultural values (National Foundation on Secondary Education for Hispanics, 1985).

By age thirteen, females are more likely than males to have interest in career options and are more interested in seeking information (Orenstein, 1994). Traditionally a Hispanic female's personal goals, educational goals, and career choices are dictated by the family. The family is the most valued institution in the Hispanic culture. The individual owes his or her primary loyalties to the family (Grossman, 1984). A thirteen-year-old female Hispanic suppresses her dreams and needs if they do not correspond with the familial expectations. What occurs at the same time as this loss of self-recognition is a significant loss of self-esteem. It is likely that this decrease in self-esteem among adolescent females is the result of a struggle between caring for self and caring for others (Staitzeyl, 1995).

Cultural assimilation, level of acculturation, socioeconomic status, and value orientation are critical factors that must be considered by school counselors, teachers, and administrators when guiding Hispanic students. An understanding of these students may be established by developing rapport with the students, encouraging parental involvement, being aware of family values, listening to their communication patterns, and examining family status, achievement, and attainment.

The process of making career choices begins with educational planning during the middle and high school years. Designing curricula that are culturally sensitive and developmentally appropriate will foster growth, increase self-esteem, and allow students to formulate career goals.

Anglo Adolescent Females and the World of Work

Even though many adolescent girls' mothers have been in the work force and no longer follow the traditional roles, many of today's Anglo adolescent girls still exhibit patterns of low self-esteem, self-doubt, and self-criticism of their creative and intellectual potential.

In the American Association of University Women's (AAUW) research study (cited by Orenstein, 1994), the most dramatic gender gap in self-esteem is centered in the area of competence. When asked, girls indicate some aspect of their physical appearance as something in which they felt competent. And although boys state they are pretty good at a lot of things, girls are more likely to say they are "not smart enough" or "not good enough" to achieve their dreams.

The AAUW study (1994) also showed that adolescent girls' interest in math and science drops as they advance through high school. By age fifteen even girls who like math and science are only half as likely as boys to feel competent in these subjects. A confidence gap rather than an ability gap may help explain why the number of women in physical and computer sciences actually decreased during the 1980s. The authors found that the responses of thirteen- and fourteen-year-olds from three different cultures indicate that the majority want to pursue the occupations of medical services, doctor, lawyer, and other occupations that require an advanced degree. Even though the goals, aspirations, and confidence are present in middle school females, something happens by the time they reach high school that makes them avoid classes that would help them reach their goals.

Herr and Cramer (1997) suggest that girls tend to decide on careers earlier than boys, at ages thirteen to fourteen. Counseling for girls should be different than for boys since more emphasis needs to be placed on self-esteem, competence, and direct information about careers and their requirements. Girls have different problems of identity establishment than do boys; they need special assistance early in middle school to realize the educational and occupational opportunities available. Furthermore, they must learn the educational requirements needed to accomplish these goals.

THE DEVELOPMENT
OF THE MODEL

A Career Awareness Questionnaire was developed as an outgrowth of an idea to explore career development of middle school students. Although an academic curriculum is quite apparent in schools and readily available for analysis, a career education program is often not a part of the essential elements of a student's educational plan. Since the interrelatedness between academics and career education has not been recognized in many schools, students do not see the interconnectedness between education and the real world. Even though a career program plan is not integrated into a student's educational plan, career awareness, exploration,

and planning help to bridge the gap between the academic world and the world of work. Hogan (1995) believes the more that students know about careers and the world of work, the more likely they are to make better decisions about their future. The questionnaire was designed to measure a student's practical career awareness and experiences, with the goal of using the developmental level of the middle school student to its greatest potential.

Data collected from this questionnaire was used to create a new model. The middle school population was chosen as the focus of this project because of its inquisitive nature; furthermore, this age group represents a critical juncture in adolescent female development. At this time, the adolescent female may choose her authentic self as presented in Pipher's (1994) *Reviving Ophelia* or succumb to the Ophelia syndrome of becoming what others choose for her. Goal-setting and decision-making skills are put into action, since it is at this time that students, especially girls, begin to set their goals in motion. Our premise is that students who have no goals or career aspirations are more likely to fall prey to inappropriate choices such as gangs, drugs, pregnancy and other at-risk behaviors.

The focus of this project is both ethnocentric and gender related. As cited earlier, research indicates that the self-esteem and self-confidence level of the middle school female is very low. Orenstein (1994) found the passage to adolescence was not only a physiological challenge but also an emotional challenge. The low self-confidence level indicates what girls believe they can do. It is a period of great questioning of abilities. The ethnic groups represented in this project reflect the ethnic configuration of a city.

TECS
Teen Exploratory Career System

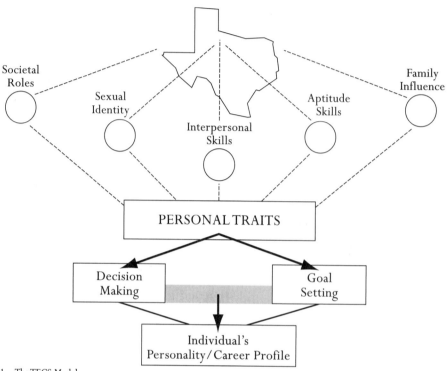

FIGURE 3.1   The TECS Model

THE TEEN EXPLORATORY CAREER SYSTEM/TECS MODEL

The Teen Exploratory Career System (TECS) (Figure 3.1) is the model that was designed to process adolescent female students through the growth and explorative developmental career level. Various areas were selected as integral to the process. The chosen areas are (a) societal roles, (b) sexual identity, (c) interpersonal skills, (d) aptitude skills, (e) family influences, (f) personal traits and strengths, (g) goal setting, and (h) decision making. Research cited above indi-

cates that these areas have an impact on an adolescent's personality and career profile. These areas influence the decision-making and goal-setting factors necessary for making career decisions. The TECS (pronounced TEX) model is general in nature so that every racial or ethnic group can be processed through the system without losing any of its integrity. TECS will work well for either gender group. It works especially well for adolescent females because this model deals with all of the issues that adolescent females face. It also encompasses those traits that need to be emphasized and supported in this age group.

STRATEGIES USED IN IMPLEMENTING THE MODEL

Decision Making and Social Issues (Sexuality and Taking Responsibility)

Rationale Learning decision-making strategies and applying them to daily life are important factors in the development of all teenagers. The consequences of their choices have a long-lasting impact on their lives. It is critical that they learn to extend the process of making good decisions into everyday life choices.

Objectives The student will:

- be able to think about choices carefully and thoroughly
- define priorities and values
- be able to list alternatives
- learn to weigh the alternatives in light of the consequences

Activity—Truth and Consequences

Sylvia and Benny's Story

Sylvia is a very smart and pretty girl. Her teachers respect her because she always acts responsibly and works hard to make good grades. She is very friendly and has many friends. Her parents have always encouraged her to have friends, but they don't condone boyfriend/girlfriend relationships at her age (thirteen). Both her mother and her father have decided to support that rule while she is in middle school. They are willing to discuss this again and change the rule once she's in high school. They have warned her that if she breaks this rule she will not be allowed to participate in any extracurricular activities during and after school. Additionally, her phone privileges would be limited to ten minutes per call.

Sylvia meets a new boy in school, Benny. She likes him, and Benny has demonstrated a considerable amount of interest in her. They eat lunch together and meet after school before band practice to talk and hold hands. Benny asks Sylvia to be his steady girlfriend and wants an answer by the next day. Sylvia tells him she is not allowed to have a boyfriend and that her parents will not let her date at this age. Benny says to her "That's all right; you don't have to tell them. We'll just keep it a secret from them. And when we want to see each other outside of school, you can tell them you're going to the mall with your girlfriend."

What does Sylvia decide to do?

Decision 1. Sylvia decides to keep the secret from her parents and lie to them when she goes out with Benny. What are the consequences?

Decision 2. Sylvia decides to tell her parents the truth and wants to know if they can either eliminate the rule or make it less restrictive. What are the consequences?

Oscar and Mindy's Story

Mindy is fourteen years old and is repeating the eighth grade. She is very attractive and dresses fashionably. She says, "My mom gives me a lot of money for clothes because she wants me to always look pretty." Mindy believes wearing nice clothes will get people to like her. Recently, Mindy has gained popularity with the boys at school, but not because of her clothes. She has been allowing boys to have sex with her. Sex is something she thinks she can use to get them to like her—just like the nice clothes. Nothing is more important to Mindy than to get people to like her.

She constantly brags to the other girls and boys, "I know what boys like, and I don't have to use anything for protection because I'm young and nothing will happen to me." Some of the girls at school think she's so cool because she acts real grown up, but most of the other girls are confused by her behavior and stay away from her.

The boys brag amongst each other and talk about how many times they have "done it" with her. They all laugh at her and say she wants to be their girlfriend. Oscar is one of the boys in the group that hasn't had sex with her. Oscar is shy and laughs with the other boys, but he really doesn't agree with what they are doing with Mindy.

Mindy likes Oscar and has made sexual advances toward him, but he responds reluctantly. He talks to Mindy and wants to be her friend, but she wants more than a friendship. Oscar knows he's not ready for more than a friendship and tells her, "Mindy, I like you as a friend and that's all I want right now." She insists and says to him, "I know your parents aren't there when you get home from school. I'll come over to your house right after school and we can talk more about our friendship."

What does Oscar do?

Decision 1. Oscar tells Mindy not to come over to his house because he is not allowed to have visitors while his parents aren't home. If she chooses to come over anyway, he will not answer the door to let her in. What are the consequences?

Decision 2. Oscar knows he isn't allowed to have visitors while his parents are not home, but he feels sorry for Mindy and he tells her to come over for a while. What are the consequences?

Identifying What You Feel Most Strongly About (Personal Traits and Goal Setting)

Rationale When students know what they like and what motivates them, they will want to explore their career options. If they understand what careers match the things they feel most passionate about, they will make smarter choices, and visualizing and planning their academic course work helps them to achieve their goals.

Objectives Students will learn what their passions are and why those passions are important in their lives. In preparing for a career they must discover who they are and what will make them happy.

Activity—Knowing What Your Passions Are

Sonia and Rudy's Story

Sonia and Rudy met at the mall while shopping for school clothes and they asked each other, "What's up?" Sonia asked Rudy what he had done while on summer vacation. He said he had read several books about faraway places and visited several museums. Rudy dreams of some day traveling to those faraway places and keeping his experiences and the scenery etched in his mind forever. He wants to learn to paint and draw so he can reproduce all the places he visits on a canvas.

Sonia likes Rudy and believes he will someday be a world traveler and famous painter. Rudy is always very active in the Spanish Club, and he likes to paint murals on the school walls.

"Someday when I graduate from high school and go on to law school and become a lawyer, I will buy one of your paintings and hang it in my law office," Sonia tells Rudy. She gives him a thumbs-up and says, "Good-bye, see ya in school."

Activities

1. Look up *passion* in the dictionary and write the definition on paper.

2. What does this definition mean to you?

3. Jot down three things that cause you to have "boundless enthusiasm."

4. Read Sonia and Rudy's story out loud.

5. Identify Rudy's passions. Did Sonia display any passions?

6. Complete the following statements. Don't be frustrated if you can't do it immediately. Take your time and be aware of your feelings.

My heart pounds with excitement when

_____

I feel especially good about myself when

_____

I lose track of time when _____

_____.

When I dream about the future I see

myself _____

_____.

If I could change one thing about the

world, it would be _____

_____.

Discussion This activity will cause quite a bit of discussion. The leader must promote the positive statements made by the students and encourage enthusiasm and feedback. The story may be lead by the facilitator or a student.

Needs and Values (Societal Roles, Family Influences, Personal Traits)[2]

Rationale In order for teenagers to explore and understand themselves, they must know the difference between needs and values. Needs and values are positive motivators in most people's lives.

Objectives Students will:

■ know the difference between needs and values

■ clarify their needs and values

■ utilize the results from their needs and values survey as filters for eliminating career and life alternatives that don't fit them

Values Activities Ask the following questions to begin a discussion on needs:

1. Do you know someone who is struggling through school and barely passing classes?

2. Do you know someone who has difficulty speaking to others and/or making friends?

[2]Adapted and modified from Boechaid, D., Kelly, J., and Weaver, N. P., Dubuque, Iowa: Kendall/Hunt (1992).

3. Do you know someone who makes good grades in class and plays well in a sport?

4. Do you know someone who is always bugging you to play a game or a sport?

5. Do you know someone who is always helping other students with something?

Give students enough time to think of someone for each question. After each question ask what needs this person might have and write the answers on the board. Continue by asking, "If a person behaves this way, what do you think they might value?"

Discussion The facilitator will define needs and values, and will give examples for further clarification. Needs are an urgent requirement for something that is essential.

Some needs are basic and shared by all.

Needs vary from person to person.

Unsatisfied needs provide energy that directs an action.

Needs develop from a perceived deficiency (physiological or social).

Values are learned and develop from life experiences.

Values guide us to current and future choices of action.

Values can be seen in our everyday actions as we make decisions.

Both needs and values change over time; however, values change far less than needs.

Needs Activity

1. Consider the things that are real needs at this stage of your life and write them down:

What I Need _____

_____

_____

_____

2. After completing your needs list, go back to the beginning of your list and after each answer put a P or an S (P for physiological need, S for social need).

3. Count all your P and S answers and write the numbers below.

Total P = _____

Total S = _____

4. Study this information carefully to help you understand your basic needs better.

Values Survey

1. From the list of possible values below choose those that are most important to you and place a checkmark on the line next to each value.

I value:

_____ wearing clothes that are in style

_____ having many friendships

_____ having challenges

_____ earning and having money

_____ working with a team or group

_____ having free time

_____ having a close family

_____ being able to travel to faraway places

_____ helping others

_____ getting good grades

_____ taking pride in my culture

_____ taking risks

_____ having good health

_____ being physically active

____ staying in school

____ being close to nature

____ my religion

____ gaining respect from others

____ controlling others

____ using my mind

2. Go back and review your list and narrow your list to your top ten. Place a second checkmark on those ten.

3. Look at your top ten choices and make sure they are things you must have in your life. Now write your answers down below. These are values that are absolutely important to you at this time in your life.

My Top Ten Life Values (Make a list from one through ten.)

Skills and Aptitudes
(Skills and Aptitudes)[3]

Rationale Teenagers fail to realize that the activities they engage in take skill and ability. Initiating a discussion to talk about what they love to do and what they think is cool will determine what skills they have.

Objectives Students will:

- build their confidence and self-worth
- identify special talents that they possess and label them as abilities
- understand that skills are developed through practice and study
- learn to speak about themselves more confidently

[3]Adapted and modified from Bingham, M., and Stryher, S. (1994) *Career Choices and Changes.* Santa Barbara, CA: Academic Innovations and from Gardner, B. (1993) *Work Wise,* Charlotte, N.C.: Kidsright.

Activities

1. Identify ten things you love to do.

   What's cool about these things?

   How do you feel after you do these things?

2. List all the things you do well at school.

   List all the things you do well at home.

   What gives you the energy to keep doing these things?

Discussion

1. The teacher or counselor always takes the facilitator role and participates as a member of the group.

2. As a facilitator the teacher or counselor can begin by sharing his or her reactions and experiences.

3. These experiences may be used as activities in developing group dynamics.

OBSERVATIONS
AND CONCLUSION

Our model was tested in a mixed-gender, mixed-social-skills classroom. Since all classes used in the study were coeducational, we chose not to select out the females. Perhaps the presence of the males inhibited the responses of the females. The students responded quite well to the design. The career activities were so varied that there was always some activity that appealed to most of the students. The boys were more interested initially than were the girls, whose participation was less enthusiastic. Boys talked easily about what they wanted to be when they grew up, while the girls were conservative in their discussion of the future. When the girls were pressed we found that they had careers in mind but were unwilling to disclose their dreams.

The issues of confidence and self-esteem were present. The boys tended to choose more fantasy careers, with professional basketball or football as top choices. The girls tended to choose careers that were more realistic, such as teachers and doctors. Adolescent females identified with the insightful activities and tended to perform exceptionally on the skills. The areas of the model in which the girls were most demonstrative were those of identity, personal traits, and roles. It appeared that these activities provided the most self-discovery for the girls, and they were more involved in them.

Goal setting, decision making, skills and aptitudes were either low-choice activities or activities that the girls did not respond warmly to in class. The confidence gap issue may have an impact here. As explained in the American Association of University Women's Report (1994), a confidence gap with adolescent females is more important than self-esteem. It is the confidence gap that restricts the growth of our adolescent females. Setting goals and making decisions is very difficult when one is unsure of capabilities or self-worth. The fear of success often leads to a sense of failure and to noncommitment, which in turn breeds a lack of confidence.

After completing the survey and listening to a presentation on skill areas, the students were allowed to visit two centers per week. Students visited the library to browse the Internet for career information. Questions about career preparation were sent via e-mail to school districts. Adding this technology phase better prepares the students for the 21st cen-

tury. The students preferred the interactive research style.

Each student completed a portfolio on their career awareness search. The portfolio contained samples of all activities, including the survey and printouts of computer research. Students also attended the Career Fair sponsored by the eighth-grade team. The students' evaluation of the program model indicated they wanted more speakers, mentors, and Internet time. Community service projects are an important part of public education at this point. When asked what community service projects could be developed from the Career Exploration Group, the students stated they wanted to present career information to fifth-graders in the elementary school.

The students appeared to learn much about themselves as well as about careers, goal setting and decision making. Middle school students are perfect candidates for a model of this type, since the exploration factor is exciting to this age group. More could have been done with the group process had there been fewer participants.

Boys and girls worked at the model differently, and most differences were addressed by gender variances. An observation of task-approach skills indicated that boys are bolder in their approach than girls. The girls were reticent. They tended to keep information about themselves private and were less willing to share their ideas concerning career choices. The mixed-gender class was nonnegotiable in this project, but an additional career exploration group for girls is recommended, since the girls participated more freely when in same-gender groups.

REFERENCES

Bartholomew, C. G., & Schnorr, D. L. (1994). Gender equity: Suggestions for broadening career options of female students. *The School Counselor,* 41, 245–255.

De La Rosa, D., & Maw, C. E. (1990). Hispanic education: A statistical portrait. Washington, D.C.: National Council of La Raza.

De Hoyos, A. (1971). *Occupational and educational levels of aspirations of Mexican-American youth.* San Francisco: Robert D. Reed, Publisher.

Gainor, K. A. & Forrest, L. (1990). African-American women's self-concept: Implications for career decisions and career counseling. *The Career Development Quarterly,* 39, 261–271.

Grossman, H. (1984). Educating Hispanic Students III. U.S.A. Charles C. Thomas Publisher.

Herr, E. L., & Cramer, S. H. (1997). *Career guidance across the lifespan* (5th ed.). New York: Harper Collins.

Hogan, C. C. (1995). Career awareness: Successful strategies that work. *NAASP Bulletin,* 79, 230–233.

Kuvelsky, W. P. (1981). *Gender differences among Mexican-American youth: A synthesis of results from Texas research 1967–1980.* Paper presented at the Southwest Sociological Association.

McKenna, T., & Ortiz, F. I. (eds.). (1988). *The broken web.* Encino, Calif.: The Tomas Rivera Center for Policy Studies.

Melville, M. (ed.). (1980). *Twice a minority: Mexican American women.* St. Louis, Mo.: Mosley Co.

Orenstein, P. (1994). School Girls: *Young women, self-esteem, and the confidence gap.* New York: Doubleday Dell Publishing Group, Inc.

Pipher, M. (1994). *Reviving Ophelia: Saving the selves of adolescent girls.* New York: Ballantine Books.

Sears, S. J. (1995). Career and educational planning in the middle school. *NAASP Bulletin.* 79, 570–573.

Staitzeyl, A. R. (1995). Maintaining the self in the relation among early adolescent girls. Doctoral dissertation. Ann Arbor, Mich.: UMI Company.

Super, D.E. (1990). A life-span, life-space approach to career development. D. Brown, L. Brooks, & Assoc. (eds.), *Career choice and development* (2d ed.), 197–261). San Francisco: Jossey-Bass.

Valencia, R. E. (ed.). (1991). *Chicano school failure and success.* New York: The Palmer Press.

Yatvin, J. (1995). Middle school experience the world of work. *Educational Leadership,* 52, 52–55.

4

At-Risk Students

Working to Raise *Students' Expectations and Motivation Using Career Goal Setting*

CHERYL BAKER, M.S.

INTRODUCTION

Exposure to career choices begins as soon as young children can identify their surroundings. Throughout children's schooling, individual values, interests, desired achievements, and needs are developed and goals are set that will ultimately carry over to career choices and quality of job performance. Children are continually taught that they can choose from thousands of jobs, which are modeled by parents, teachers, television, role models, and life experience. But what about children who have little choice as a result of academic failure, lack of occupational role models, or no foreseen goals? Unfortunately, many feel there is no choice but to drop out of school before they are even identified by professionals as being at risk. And what

does the future hold for a high school dropout? Survival isn't easy without a high school diploma. In fact, according to the National Center of Educational Statistics (1996), the unemployment rate for high school dropouts is twice that of graduates, and the median income of dropouts remains at a poverty level. Dropouts will also cost businesses nearly $25 billion a year in training costs and lost productivity (Center for Slow Learners, 1991). Yet, even with such statistics, a growing number of adolescents continue to drop out every year, and the dropout rates are again on an upswing (U.S. Department of Education, 1993). To combat this tragedy, at-risk students need a plan that utilizes academic, vocational, and career goals to give them the necessary tools to function successfully in a career-oriented world.

Who is the at-risk student? The term "at-risk" is used to identify those children and ado-

Cheryl Baker is a certified school counselor in the Northside Independent School District, San Antonio, Texas.

lescents who, for many and complex reasons, are at risk of educational failure. Failure in school drives at-risk students out before they graduate, which ultimately costs billions of government dollars in welfare, lost tax revenues, and incarceration (Center for Slow Learners, 1991). In order to address the issue, the U. S. Congress in 1988 adopted legislation that identifies those individuals who are either in danger of dropping out or show signs of possibly dropping out. The definition reads:

> The term "at risk" means students who, because of learning deficiencies, lack of school readiness, limited English proficiency, poverty, educational or economic disadvantage, or a physical or emotional handicapping condition, face greater risk of low educational achievement and have greater potential of becoming school dropouts (U.S. Department of Education, 1993, 8–9).

Congress continued its support of a solution to this problem the following year when President Bush pushed the second of the national educational goals. This goal stated that by 2000, 90 percent of all high schoolers will achieve graduation (U.S. Department of Education, 1993). This objective motivated schools to reform from traditional programs and work toward more individualized programs for students, emphasizing individual learning styles, skills, and training.

Thus the RAISE model was developed to give counselors a systematic foundation on which to build individualized plans for students identified as at risk in order to provide them with the tools they need to survive the world of work. The model focuses on methods that encourage goal setting in students who have little motivation. It further provides incentives such as the PASS, Edutrain, "I have a dream," and mentoring programs to increase a student's self-concept and engender a commitment to stay in school.

THE RAISE MODEL

Based on Super's Life-Span Theory (1990), the RAISE model focuses on the importance of helping children develop decision-making skills throughout each developmental stage of their life. According to Super, each stage is necessary in building skills that are needed for the world of work and for goal setting. Children and adolescents should be continually given chances to explore and work on their self-concept (values, interests, capacities), supported by exercises that will help them develop a time perspective, or sense of future. Thus, occupational information should be continually provided through classroom curriculum, small group settings, role modeling, and observation by means of field trips, videos, or special speakers.

Each RAISE step, therefore, continually works to help children and adolescents recognize their interests, abilities, and values and to expose them to a wide range of occupational information. This will ultimately help develop important values related to work. Following the progress of the child, then, is the ultimate key to successful career decision-making readiness. In the following sections, the RAISE steps are described, then followed by an overview of intervention strategies.

The RAISE model uses a number of effective, successful school at-risk programs as a foundation for addressing the ongoing concerns of the at-risk population and the attitudes that dropouts bring into the work force. Based on a five-step approach, RAISE is a systematic model useful for elementary, middle school, and high school counselors, administrators, and teachers that addresses the identification of potential dropouts and presents guidelines for intervention. The goal is to keep potential dropouts in school long enough to develop their own goals, which, in turn, helps them choose the appropriate tools to learn that they can carry over into the work force. The goal of RAISE is to identify as early as possible those students who may be at risk of academic failure, then to use continuous interventions at each stage of the at-risk child's educational track. If a student makes a dropout declaration despite the many interventions, contact should not be discontinued. The RAISE model should be used as a guide in developing a program that meets an individual's school and community needs. The steps of RAISE are as follows:

Step 1: **R**ecognize and identify early on who is at risk.

Step 2: **A**ssess student's academic needs and interests.

Step 3: **I**mprove student's interest by offering incentives.

Step 4: **S**tress parental, school, and community involvement.

Step 5: **E**valuate and follow up on student's progress.

Step 1: Recognize and Identify At-Risk Individuals

How do you recognize an at-risk student? Clothes? Low grades? Unemployed parents? Race? Identification of an at-risk student can be as easy as recognizing a kindergartner who shows signs of neglect or as hard as overlooking a gifted and talented student who becomes pregnant and feels an immediate need to drop out.

Unfortunately, many indicators of at-risk students are not visible, and educators can easily miss them. Dropouts do not leave all at once; they trickle out like water from a leaky faucet, and in the case of difficult students, their leaving is often to the relief of educators (Bottoms & Presson, 1992).

What are the motives dropouts cite for leaving school? Gerald Bracey (1994) worked to learn the answer to this question through interviews with actual dropouts. Disinterest in school, academic failure, academic pressure, the need to find a job, pregnancy, and drugs and alcohol were cited as the main reasons students left school (1994). Once the motive or motives are identified, a counselor may intervene by providing the student with the tools necessary for entering the work force when the student feels ready and sees the move as achieving a set goal.

In order to assist those students who may be in danger of dropping out, they need to be identified early in their schooling. There are some recurring characteristics that should alert counselors to the possibility of needed interventions. These characteristics can be grouped into three categories: familial, personal, and educational.

1. *Familial factors* include single-parent homes, guardians other than parents, stepparents, neglect, an abusive home, a transient lifestyle, low socioeconomic status, non-English speaking parents, uneducated parents, and being immigrants.

2. *Personal characteristics* include being sexually, physically, or psychologically abused; abuse of drug or alcohol; delinquent conduct and other behavior problems; limited English proficiency; delayed development; pregnancy; being an underachiever; being unmotivated; and handicap conditions.

3. *Educational performance problems* include poor performance on readiness tests or assessment instruments; being two or more years below grade level in reading or mathematics; failing in two or more courses; receiving compensatory or remedial instruction; being a slow learner; and having a poor attendance record (excessive absences, tardiness, late enrollment, many withdrawals, and truancy).

During this stage the counselor should have frequent contact with the student's teachers or adult supervisors in order to gather historical, biological, and sociological information about possible concerns. At all grade levels, the counselor should work on having students voice personal strengths, interests, and accomplishments through classroom guidance, small groups, or individualized counseling in order to identify students without personal knowledge of values or goals. Those students can be targeted as a result of this interaction with the counselor.

Interventions Some effective interventions at this level include the following:

1. interaction with the counselor;

2. exposure to occupational information;

3. student's verbal or written opinion of self (interests, values, accomplishments);

4. referral of possible at-risk students to an intervention program already in place;

5. information gathered about the student from which is created a portfolio showing grades, behaviors in different situations, family history, social and medical information, results of standardized tests, and any handicapping conditions;

6. a team meeting made up of counselor, teacher(s), specialists, administrator, and

anyone else who can help develop and carry out a relevant plan for the at-risk student.

Case Example David, a seventh-grader, was identified by one of his teachers as a possible at-risk candidate. He appeared lazy in class, often turning in incomplete assignments, never raised his hand to answer questions, and rarely initiated interactions with peers. The counselor began intervention as soon as David's name was given to her. She first traced David's history to develop a profile of David using his personal records, attendance records, past grades, and standardized testing information.

The counselor found through David's elementary records that his family was transient, having moved seven times since David was in the second grade. His mother was a single parent with three other children. All four children utilized the reduced-fee lunch program, an obvious indication of monetary need on the mother's part. David's grades showed him to be at grade level until the fifth grade. His standardized tests (Iowa Test of Basic Skills and the Cognitive Abilities Test) showed a bright boy with few learning gaps. His grades were As and Bs until the third grade. After this, his grades were poorer through the sixth grade, which he barely passed. A meeting with David's teachers showed him to be a disinterested student with few or no goals for a future. The counselor made suggestions to David's teachers, including modifications for work, continuous parent contact, and a daily assignment sheet. The assignment sheet included incentives within the classroom to motivate him. The counselor also instantly placed David in a small goal-setting group not only to develop rapport, but also to find out more about him and his specific needs.

Step 2: Assess Student's Academic Needs and Interests

According to Super's (1990) life span theory, the interests, values, and attitudes of an individual are all pieces of a puzzle that affect motivation, decision making, educational attainment, and, ultimately, occupational achievement. Assessment is one of the best tools for piecing together any missing information and for helping the individual fill in gaps that could be carried into the work force. In addition to pinpointing a possible learning disability or an attention problem, assessment can gather information about a child's needs, wants, goals, and motivating tools. Once a child becomes a concern or is identified as being at risk, assessment should help counselors and educators make decisions regarding (a) educational placement, (b) prediction of school success, (c) diagnosis of possible emotional disturbances, and (d) assessment of developmental delays (Garbarino & Stott, 1992). Counselors can use this valuable information to help an at-risk student set goals for continued education and career or occupational choices and to begin appropriate interventions to help bring about goal success. Since testing is often intimidating for children and adolescents, it is important that the adult carrying out the testing process do the following:

1. Create a comfortable, relaxed environment for testing.

2. Be familiar with the testing format, cultural implications, and testing scores, or bring in another qualified professional to perform testing and interpret results.

3. Be sensitive to responses that may be the result of variables in the child's life that are different from those of the individual doing the testing.

4. Give several different kinds of tests to get a complete picture of needs.

As stated in No. 4 above and depending on the concerns of the educators or the needs of the child, it usually is necessary for the counselor and/or psychologist to give the student different kinds of tests in order to determine the necessary remediations. The tests mentioned below do not represent an exhaustive list. For a more complete list, a school psychologist may be consulted.

Important areas to consider are:

1. *Language* Language tests such as the Test of Language Development (TOLD) or the Goldman-Fristoe Tests of Articulation and Auditory Discrimination should be given if a student speaks more than one language, has difficulty with language expression, has trouble with processing language, or may have a physical speech problem. Language assessments will help a counselor to determine whether the child needs speech services or special education help if a significant discrepancy appears in the scoring.

2. *Physical* It is important to obtain medical information about the student. By using doctors' reports, health histories (personal records or information given by parents), and results from medical testing, the assessor can evaluate the student's health and physical status, including vision, hearing, and motor tests. Some of the more formal physical tests include the Developmental Test of Visual Motor Integration (VMI) and the Motor Free Visual Perception Test (MVPT), which can be helpful in pinpointing and ruling out any physical conditions. For example, a child who appears at risk may actually just need glasses or medications for an existing health concern.

3. Emotional/Behavioral Tests such as Incomplete Sentence Blanks, the House-Tree-Person Projective, and the Rorschach can often help counselors evaluate a child's or adolescent's subjective experience of a problem or situation and may reveal underlying conflicts or feelings. Results can be determined through formal testing, observations, and personal evaluations.

4. Intellectual The intelligence, or IQ, test shows how the child's thinking compares with others in his/her age category. Tests like the Wechsler Intelligence Scale for Children III (WISC III) and the Stanford Binet Intelligence Scale demonstrate potential for problem solving and adaptation. Testing intelligence should not be regarded as a label upon which to base decisions, but rather as one descriptor among the many that help to understand the individual (Anastasi, 1988).

5. Educational Learning Competencies Educational achievement assessments focus on an individual's performance in academics. If appropriate, the assessments can include job-related skills.

6. Interests/Values/Career Assessments The Career Assessment Inventory (CAI), the Kuder Occupational Interest Survey (KOIS), the Work Values Inventory (WVI), and the Jackson Vocational Interests Survey (JVIS) are examples of personal evaluations that help determine goals, values, interests, and skills in relation to the work force. These assessments are especially helpful for students in the area of goal setting and range from an informal listing to a more formal evaluation. They can be used in classroom settings or small groups to help students focus on career choices in relation to their needs, successes, and limitations.

It is important to note that the majority of assessments should be administered by a school psychologist or an educational diagnostician. If neither a psychologist nor a diagnostician is available, it is imperative that the school counselor has the essential training and knowledge to determine which test is appropriate, to be able to interpret the results, and to make recommendations based on the information.

Interventions Some effective interventions at this level include the following:

1. creating a comfortable testing atmosphere;

2. testing the student in several different areas that will show needs;

3. using results and scores to remediate in the areas of (a) academics or instruction, (b) vocational, guidance and (c) support services. Some suggested interventions are shown in Table 4.1. These interventions may help a student in these three areas. They are not designed to operate simultaneously.

Case Example (continued) Once his counselor pinpointed David as an at-risk candidate, she saw some need for possible evaluations to take place. First, the counselor had his teachers and his single mother fill out an attention deficit scale to rule out any possibility of attention problems. Once ruled out, she had the school nurse check his hearing and eyesight for possible physical conditions that would keep David unmotivated in the classroom. His hearing and vision were not impaired. The counselor also had David's mother fill out a scale that looked at the possibility of depression, which was also ruled out. Next the counselor set up a team meeting that included the school psychologist, David's reading teacher and speech teacher, and

Table 4.1 Interventions

ACADEMICS/INSTRUCTION	VOCATIONAL GUIDANCE	SUPPORT SERVICES
Special education and/or related services	Cooperative work programs	Counseling programs (individual, group, family)
Cooperative learning programs	CVAE programs/cooperation education programs	Teen-parenting programs
Special reading programs	Life skills class	Life skills class
Bilingual education	Career inventories	Program/career guidance
Supplementary instruction	Occupational training	Mentor programs
Mentor programs	Mentor programs	Visiting teachers' program
Fine arts/technology classes (electives)		Drug abuse prevention
Statewide achievement test		Remediation programs
Summer school programs		
Tutorial programs		
Visiting teachers' program		

an administrator. They evaluated the results of David's sociological information and the results from the evaluations done so far. The entire group saw a need to test him further for the possibility of a learning disability. The school psychologist then gave him a battery of tests, looking at his language skills, his emotional/behavioral status, his intellectual capabilities, and his educational learning competencies. His competencies were equivalent to his intellectual ability and a special education referral could not be made. The counselor, in a small-group setting, gathered information on interests, values, and goal setting that would be used to create ongoing incentives to motivate David.

Step 3: Improve Student's Interest by Offering Incentives

When student's exhibit lack of interest they are usually quickly identified as possible at-risk candidates. Lack of motivation, which is often referred to as a behavior problem, is frequently the first clear sign of academic disinterest or failure.

Unfortunately, many times this disinterest carries over into performance at a paid job. The challenge, therefore, is to provide incentives for the student in order to stir an interest in education that will extend through the educational years and into occupational choices. According to Roe's Personality Development Theory (1956), interests, values, and needs all contribute to the process of selecting an occupation. The needs, founded on Maslow's (1954) hierarchy, work either for or against a child or adolescent—depending on whether or not the needs are met adequately—in terms of educational interest and, ultimately, occupational choice. Listed by importance, each need must be met before the next one can be satisfied. The following is a brief description of Maslow's hierarchy:

1. *Physiological needs*: basic needs required for survival.

2. *Safety needs*: the need for security and avoidance of danger.

3. *Needs for belongingness and love*: being cared for and caring for something or someone.

Table 4.2 Reasons for Dropping Out and Related Unmet Needs

REASONS FOR DROPPING OUT	POSSIBLE UNMET NEEDS
Uncaring teachers	Esteem needs
Attendance policy	Physiological needs, safety needs (trying to hold a job; illness; home problems)
Problems at home	Physiological, safety, belongness, esteem needs
School is boring and meaningless	Need for information; understanding, self-actualization
Personal problems (pregnancy, abuse, loss, legal, and so on)	Physiological, safety, belongingness, self-esteem and self-actualization

4. *Esteem needs*: liking and respecting oneself; receiving respect and like from others.

5. *Need for information*: obtaining knowledge about personal and cultural history as well as about the environment around them.

6. *The need for understanding*: having the knowledge to understand processes and information needed for school, work, and events taking place around them.

7. *The need for beauty*: finding appreciation in arts, such as artwork, writing, and music.

8. *The need for self-actualization*: to be the best that one can be.

Maslow's hierarchy of needs provides the foundation for Roe's theory and helps us to predict reasons for students' lack of motivation. When we are able to identify those unmet needs, we can then work to create incentives in order to satisfy them. An interview by Karol Gadwa Center for Slow Learners (1983) of students who have dropped out helps us understand how unmet needs provide reasons for dropping out. Table 4.2 shows some of these reasons.

Using the information in Table 4.2, incentives can be created to work on motivating students. This procedure can be a challenge, however, since each child and adolescent is different.

What works with one student may fail with another, so the process to find the right incentive may take some time. Some of the programs and incentives that have succeeded in spurring children and adolescents on to motivation and further goal setting are described below.

1. *Involving the child with community mentors.* A community volunteer comes in and spends an hour a week with a student, helping with homework or just playing a game of basketball.

2. *Choosing electives.* Electives often offer incentives that regular academia can't provide. Fine arts programs such as choir, band, orchestra, dance class, drama, art classes, and sports serve as powerful motivating tools because they are classes that tap into individual interests, that support a talent, and that surround the student with peers that have similar interests. Electives often provide recognition for students, which taps into their esteem needs, as well as a route toward a career that uses their individual talent.

3. *Developing vocational-education programs.* These programs are designed to prepare students for employment and to empower

them with skills needed to enter the work force. Vocational programs give hands-on experience that may motivate a child to stay in school.

4. *Receiving tangible rewards.* With the help of local businesses, goods and money are often contributed to help support school activities. Schools may receive supplies, sodas, T-shirts, coupons, candy, toys, gift certificates, or money to give as rewards for positive student actions (behavioral or academic).

5. *Receiving positive reinforcement.* Voices and actions that show praise and encouragement toward a desired behavior often succeed in renewing interest in school because the student sees that someone cares.

6. *Devising contracts.* Behaviors are identified and written down for the student to work on changing. Together with the counselor, the child or adolescent can specify how change will take place and when.

7. *Instilling self-management.* Children and adolescents are allowed to take control of their own program. They choose targeted behaviors and the type of reinforcements they want for making the change. Students monitor their own programs (Vernon, 1993).

8. *Using aversion therapy.* For destructive or aggressive behavior, a punishment that eliminates unwanted behavior by removing positive reinforcers or providing negative stimuli is given. This may take the form of in-school suspension (ISS), removal from peers, or time out (Vernon, 1993).

Some schools reported to be very successful in combating high dropout rates built motivational programs by first assessing the overall needs of their students. Once the needs were identified, the schools brought incentives into their programs to help create motivation and interest in kids who seemingly could not be reached. Three noted and successful programs are PASS, Edutrain, and "I Have a Dream."

PASS Memorial High School in San Antonio, Texas, focuses on utilizing positive reinforcements, community mentors, and tangible rewards to fight its dropout numbers. The PASS program (Professionals Assisting Student Success), coordinated by coach Terry Lowry (personal communication, April 18, 1993), recognizes students who have a passing average. Every six weeks, the students are given special tickets that release them from classes for two to three hours for a special school assembly. At the program, business leaders, local celebrity figures, city athletes, and musicians, who have volunteered their time, speak to the students with a motivational stay-in-school message. Following the assembly, the students are either entertained by a local act, served refreshments, or given tangible rewards donated by national and local food chains and sponsors. With the PASS program, all kids have a chance to be rewarded, not just the straight-A and A-B students. Memorial High School's dropout rates decreased remarkably.

Edutrain The Edutrain program was founded in Los Angeles. At-risk students are screened before they are accepted into the program. If a student was expelled from or dropped out of their former school, they may attend Edutrain. Students attend this charter school voluntarily and work in internships at local businesses that are provided through the school. Students design their own academic schedule, attend classes when able, and spend as much time as they want or need. The school is open from 7 A.M. to

7 P.M., and students can come and go as their schedule allows. Edutrain also has a day-care center, which not only serves a mother's educational needs, but also works to educate her with parenting skills. Each mother (or father) is required to take a turn supervising the children when not in class and is taught appropriate actions and reactions when taking care of the children. Classes at Edutrain are taught through interdisciplinary instruction and are presented in ways that are relevant to the students. For instance, math and economics are learned together, and the current events class examines homelessness as well as business trends to prepare the student for a world outside of school. This program has been highly successful in meeting the needs of students who may have had problems in their former school due to poor attendance. These classes bring meaning to many of the students that their former school could not provide. Overall, Edutrain is successful in helping adolescents who couldn't perform in the traditional system to create goals and a future (Pisano, 1994).

I Have a Dream The I Have a Dream program, initiated by Eugene Lang, may be one of the most well-known programs for at-risk students. Lang began adopting classes of disadvantaged students, promising them that he would cover certain college costs if they committed to graduating from high school. This reward for hard work and perseverance created a strong incentive for students to set goals and strive to better themselves (U.S. Department of Education, 1993).

Many other programs and sources for at-risk students exist. For example, many businesses are eager to offer services if only approached. Not only are they willing to offer incentives, but many have organized programs in place that provide students with valuable work experi-

ence, evaluations, help with goal setting, and guidance in the work world. School personnel who are responsible for at-risk students should seek help from these potential sponsors, which can be found locally as well as nationally, to minimize costs to the school.

Another method for motivating an at-risk student to stay in school is to involve the student in the system. For instance, the student can:

- read to a kindergarten "buddy" once a day or help a younger student with homework
- become a "helper" to the principal or vice principal, running errands and so forth
- become a "buddy" to a handicap student or to a child who is in the Pre-school Program for Children with Disabilities (PPCD)
- help the librarian
- help the physical education teacher and sports team coaches
- run errands for a teacher

The needs for belongingness and love as well as esteem may be met when at-risk students feel as if they are contributing or serving. They therefore may be inclined to work harder and stay in school. The school then has the opportunity to motivate the at-risk student and help the student realize personal successes that may result in goal setting, which, in turn, may carry over to achievement in the work force.

Interventions Some effective interventions at this level include the following:

1. assessing the student's needs, values, or interests;

2. setting up a plan for using incentives that tap into the student's needs in order to increase motivation (includes schoolwide programs and personal rewards).

Case Example (continued) Once David was assessed, the counselor worked closely with his teachers to identify a mentor and incentives that would increase his motivational level. Comments by David's computer teacher revealed that David was quite skillful on the computer and often lingered in her classroom after the dismissal bell rang. The counselor and the computer teacher then worked together on a contract for David that provided the reward, or incentive, of extra computer time in the computer lab when he finished and turned in assignments in each of his classes. The computer teacher became a mentor for David. She also scheduled a time for him to help a sixth-grade class with their computer learning. His other teachers also created incentives for success in finishing and turning in assignments (grades did not matter so much at this point). These incentives were in addition to the extra computer time in the contract. The teachers used personal motivators for his improvement, such as a can of Coca-Cola for showing a week's worth of improvement, inviting David and a few of his friends to eat lunch with them in their classroom, making David an errand runner for a short period of time, positive telephone calls to David's mother, and vocal or written affirmations of his accomplishments. Modifications on work were continued by the teachers, since their first goal was to encourage David to see that he was capable of success.

Step 4: Stress Parent, School, and Community Involvement

Children often follow their parents' footsteps in terms of education, career, and family habits. Parents who express negative messages about the education system and the work world are instilling the same negative attitudes in their children. It is important for the counselor to take advantage of the connection with the student in order to help the student perceive the education system and the work world in a more positive light. It is also important to involve key figures in supplying students with observations, role models, and information that provide the student with positive images. Lee Manning (1993) notes that the most effective at-risk programs are those in which a team made up of teachers, parents, and community all work together to set objectives and to determine methods and materials to use that will focus on improving the at-risk student's self-concept, which, in turn, will create positive feelings in the student about the future. When everyone works together, the student often feels support and even despite setbacks is hopeful that successes will continue.

Parent Involvement Even among the most effective at-risk programs, one of the biggest ongoing challenges that educators face is getting parents involved. There is a direct correlation between parents' attitudes and participation and their children's performance in school. In fact, Dorgu (1994) found that when parents participated in school activities—whether it was helping with a homework assignment or attending a PTA (Parent-Teachers Association) meeting or open house night—the child's achievement level improved. In two studies, Dorgu found the following to be true as well:

1. At-risk students in elementary and middle school had less school support and less involvement on the part of their parents than students who were not considered at risk. Further, teachers were likely to give less support to at-risk students in middle school than to those in elementary school.

2. Those students who had poor test scores showed negative perceptions of parent structure and teacher autonomy support. For a student who has been recognized as at risk, the bond between home and school is usually very weak (1994).

School personnel often encounter problems in getting parents involved in parent-teacher conferences, in following through with contracts, and in providing motivation for their child to do schoolwork. So how do educators get parents of at-risk students involved? Oftentimes, the parents want to get involved, but just do not know how. The major problems in achieving successful parental involvement are identified by educators as (adapted from the San Antonio, Texas, Northeast Independent School District At-Risk Plan, 1992):

1. non-English speaking parents, illiterate parents, and parents who lack a formal education;

2. cultural and value system differences that alienate parents from the schools;

3. single parents who, because of work, often have scheduling conflicts when setting up conferences or attending school meetings;

4. adolescent parents who are still immature when their children enter school;

5. the lack of a clear legal guardian

Since there is poor involvement on the part of many parents, educators need to replace their traditional ways of conferencing and create new and imaginative ways to encourage parents to support their children's educational efforts. Presson and Bottoms (1992) believe that one way to keep the parents involved starts with not allowing them to be apathetic. They note as an example that schools with effective programs have gone to such an extreme as having the teacher hold on to the child's report card until the parents come to pick it up. When first begun in one school, only 50 percent of the parents showed. By the second grading period, more than 90 percent came to the school.

Interventions with Parents Some effective interventions at this level include the following:

1. continuous teacher/parent contact via phone calls, conferences, home visits, and letters;

2. parent training sessions and parent consultation centers;

3. teacher/student/parent workshops;

4. GED preparation courses;

5. ESL (English as a Second Language) courses;

6. parent/child playgroups;

7. social events with motivational speakers (events such as a parent breakfast, "Sundae" Nights, potluck dinners, auctions, and flea markets in the school setting);

8. newsletter;

9. parenting library that provides informational books and videos;

10. parenting workshops taken to local businesses.

Teacher Involvement Teachers are another important part of an at-risk student's success. Part of motivating an at-risk student is the student's needing to know that the school has a place for each student and will care for each student. The student initially perceives this through the teacher. Also, the teacher is usually the one to first identify a student who may be displaying at-risk characteristics, so it is crucial to involve the teacher in a decision-making role about the student.

A teacher's behavior can actually improve a student's motivation. A teacher who shows caring, offers praise and encouragement, builds esteem, and displays interest, attention, and enthusiasm has an overall positive affect on student's attitudes toward school. Unfortunately, by middle school, teacher involvement with those children who are considered at risk usually lessens (Dorgu, 1994).

If a student is identified at risk, the teacher needs to take extra measures and make modifications. Modifications can include shortening assignments, reinforcing or paraphrasing directions of an assignment, setting up tutorials, teaching to the student's individual learning style, setting up a contract, providing incentives to motivate the student, and helping the student to set goals.

Interventions by Teachers Some effective interventions at this level include the following:

1. developing reading and literacy programs to target the child early;

2. developing teams in which teachers of at-risk students can collaborate, brainstorm, or plan;

3. staff development and further training in dropout prevention programs, learning styles, applied instructional techniques, how to improve students' basic skills, and classroom modifications;

4. providing special-help materials to assist at-risk students.

Community Involvement Why should the community get involved with the rising number of dropouts? Though the dropout problem is continually handed off to educators, it is a societal problem that should concern everyone. Rossi and Stringfield (1995) note that the average annual income of dropout students has fallen by 49 percent since 1973 as a result of the increase in sophisticated technology needing skilled workers and the decrease in low-skill jobs that offer adequate pay. Factories with low-skill jobs at adequate pay now have the option of hiring employees at a lower wage in developing nations.

Some businesses actually work counter to the educational programs when they allow students to work night shifts before school days or require them to work during school hours. Due to family poverty nearly 20 percent of dropouts cite an inability to attend classes, because of work commitments, as a reason for dropping out of school. Educators have the responsibility to seek the cooperation of businesses in making education the first priority for those students who need to work (Bottoms & Presson, 1993).

While drastic measures such as penalizing students and their families for truancy have been introduced, local community members can take more positive steps by involving themselves as mentors, tutors, and big brothers/big sisters or through general support of school programs. Community agencies need to offer services such as family counseling, health and dental services, employment training, substance abuse treatment and rehabilitation, and other social services. Community volunteers can also make a tremendous impact by offering their time as speakers or sponsors for parent-teacher meetings, student assemblies, and parenting consultation centers.

Interventions with Community Some effective interventions at this level include:

1. inviting local business members to be part of a committee to develop an at-risk program;

2. establishing mentor programs to involve community members;

3. using local community members and businesses in tutorial and job training programs;

4. speaking with individual businesses that employ students during school hours;

5. developing community reading and literacy programs and incentives for participation;

6. asking community members and businesses to provide incentives to schools for academic improvement/recognition

Case Example (continued) Though David is not at a legal working age, intervention and education are necessary in order for him to make good career choices and establish the tools he needs in order to be successful at whatever job he chooses. At this step, the counselor includes David's mother to help him set goals through contracts and frequent contact. An assignment sheet is sent home nightly for David's mother to monitor and sign once the work is completed. The teachers check this sheet daily for his mother's signature and reward David for keeping up with the sheet. Notes focusing on positive aspects about David are sent home daily with the assignment sheet. His mother responds to the notes quite frequently. The counselor brings different career role figures into David's small group to provide the students with positive role models and work experiences. The teachers, focusing on all their students, also bring in key figures from time to time to provide their students with images of different experiences and choices. David, at this point, has made significant improvement with his work habits and, after a visit with the whale trainer from Sea World in his science class, has even talked about being a marine biologist. The counselor continues to have him set weekly goals and checks his progress.

Step 5: Evaluate and Follow-Up on Student's Progress

Educators must be able to determine what is and is not effective in their dropout prevention programs. To do this, it is crucial that there be follow-up after each step of an intervention. Information on the student's progress must be gathered in order to determine what does and does not work for that specific student. Information about the student's progress can be obtained through counseling sessions, assessments, grades, work samples, personal records, the teachers and school specialists, the student's parents, and mentors that are working with the student.

With even the best interventions and programs in place, a student may still choose to drop out. Often counselors may find themselves frustrated after giving time and energy to an at-risk student who drops out, and they cut their contact with the student as soon as he or she drops out. While the student should be given full responsibility for the decision, follow-up is still a very crucial step. A follow-up plan can include:

1. Planning an interview (personal or by phone) with the student who makes a dropout declaration. Information from the interview should include the reasons for leaving school, academic history, future career and educational goals, and any special services the student may need.

2. Contacting either by letter, phone call, or personal home visit those students who have disappeared.

3. Providing options and contacts for dropouts, including:
   a. employment counseling
   b. parenting training
   c. night school
   d. information concerning the General Education Diploma (G.E.D.) Program and other continuing education programs
   e. career information/employment leads
   f. community job-training programs

Interventions Some effective interventions at this level include the following:

1. continuous follow-up throughout the educational years;

2. information gathered continually about the student's progress;

3. RAISE Steps 2 through 4 repeated as needed;

4. interview of the student if a dropout declaration occurs;

5. information given regarding dropout options.

CONCLUSION

The counselor serves as an overall role model to help at-risk students solve problems, develop a healthy self-concept, and recognize their individual contributions, successes, and limitations. However, the counselor should step back and give the child or adolescent full responsibility to make choices and experience the consequences of those decisions. The at-risk problem is not just the individual's problem. It is shared by educators, parents, and the community.

Rossi and Stringfield (1995) estimate that by 2020, the majority of students in America's public schools will be living in circumstances that would presently place them at risk of educational failure. Unless programs are developed and the number of potential student dropouts is addressed, we will see the dropout rate increase. The rising numbers can be reduced if schools, parents, and community see the dropout rate as a priority for the whole society. Parents, especially, play a large part in preparing their child for school and the work world by helping the child set goals and manage money and provide opportunities for the child to get involved in the community. Businesses need to provide opportunities for children and teenagers to view working role models, they need to provide mentors, and they need to provide educational and vocational opportunities. When action is taken by all, we can begin giving students the incentives they need in order to set goals and create a brighter future for themselves in school, at home, and at work.

REFERENCES

Anastasi, A. (1988). *Psychological testing* (6th ed.). New York: MacMillan Publishing Company.

Bottoms, G., & Presson, A. (1992). A reason to stay in school: What educators can do to reduce dropout rates. *Educational Digest,* 1–16.

Bracey, G. W. (May 1994). Dropping in on dropping out. *Phi Delta Kappan, 75,* 726–727.

Center for Slower Learners Institute. (1991). *Success strategies for at-risk students.* Seminar Report: Dallas, Texas.

Dewlen, B. (1997). P.S.D. Sharing library and testing information. Paper presented as Psychological Services Inventory Checklist: Northside Independent School District, San Antonio, Texas.

Dorgu, S. (1994). Determinants of parental involvement in a support program: A study of communication behavior and information sources (Doctoral dissertation, Syracuse University, 1993). *Dissertation Abstracts International,* 54 (8), 2796.

Garbarino, J., Stott, F. M., and Faculty of the Erikson Institute. (1992). *Using tests and other instruments: What children can tell us.* San Francisco: Jossey-Bass.

Manning, L. M. (1993). Seven essentials of effective at-risk programs. *The Clearing House,* 66 (3), 135–138.

Maslow, A. H. (1954). *Motivation and personality.* New York: Harper & Row.

National Center for Education Statistics. (1991). *Dropout Rates in the United States: 1991.* U.S. Department of Education. Office of Educational Research and Improvement.

———. (1996). *Dropout Rates in the United States: 1996.* U.S. Department of Education. Office of Educational Research and Improvement.

Northeast Independent School District. (1992). Northeast At-Risk Plan, San Antonio, Texas: Author.

Pisano, L. (1994). Charter school for at-risk kids. *Educational Digest,* 59, 64–66.

Ramirez, D., & Robledo, M. del Refugio. (1989). *The economic impact of the dropout problem,* IDRA Newsletter. San Antonio, Texas: Intercultural Development Research Association.

Roe, A. (1956). *The Psychology of Occupations.* New York: Wiley.

Rossi, R. J., & Stringfield, S. C. (1995). What we must do for students placed at risk. *Phi Delta Kappan,* 77, 73–76.

Super, D. (1990). A life-span, life-space approach to career development. D. Brooks, L. Brown & Assoc. (eds.). *Career choice and development: Applying contemporary theories to practice.* (2d ed., 151–167). San Francisco: Jossey-Bass.

U.S. Department of Education. (1993). *Reaching the goals. Goal 2: High school completion.* Washington, D.C.: Office of Educational Research and Improvement, Programs for the Improvement of Practice, Government Printing Office.

Vernon, A. (1993). *Individual counseling process: Counseling children and adolescents.* Boulder, Colo.: Love Publishing Company.

5

High School Students in Transition

Meaningful Vocational Counseling
for the Twenty-First Century

BELINDA McCHAREN, ED.D.

INTRODUCTION

Developing an effective high school career guidance program is dependent on a clear vision of what the school and community seek for its students. In other words, a vision of the knowledge and skills students should possess when they leave high school is essential. In addition, the school should find a guidance model that is comprehensive and can be adapted to fit local needs and structure. No model can be successfully adopted without some modification. The school should initiate research to discover which career guidance programs have been effective with high school students within their area, across the state, and nationwide.

According to Gray and Herr (1995), almost all (94.7 percent) high school students express the intent to continue their education; most (83.9 percent) say they want a degree from a four-year institution. However, statistics indicate that, in 1994, on average, only 30 percent of high school graduates would complete a four-year degree within four years. Obviously, a mismatch in student goals and actual accomplishment persists. The case has been made by the Southern Region Education Board (SREB) that high school career guidance programs are ineffective at best (Bottoms, Presson & Johnson, 1992).

According to authors Gray and Herr (1995), it is a widely held misconception that students in U.S. high schools are tracked into a regimented set of courses that limit their options. In fact, the opposite is true. Today, students can take nearly any course they or their parents choose. The implication of this trend is that successful preparation of students depends first and foremost on parents' and students' course

Belinda McCharen is the state coordinator for the School to Work program for the state of Oklahoma.

selection. This perhaps is a contributing factor to ineffective guidance and preparation for post-secondary education and work.

Many guidance programs in today's high schools still resemble those found in schools during the 1970s. Such a program is counseling-based with emphasis on academic achievement, is largely reactive, and does not systematically address the needs of all students as they gain experiences and maturity. As a result, many counselors are responding to the critical needs of the few and ignore or do not systematically plan for the needs of the majority of students. Career guidance must exit the counselor's office and enter the classroom and community (Paris, 1995).

To respond to the current realities, schools must explore developing career guidance programs that incorporate school counselors, teachers, and business/community liaisons in an ongoing interactive process. These programs should embody: (a) the concept that all students are prepared for both work and post-secondary education; (b) an established career guidance process with clear goals; and (c) curricula that integrate career development in every major content area. The guidance program should provide all students with the skills to manage their own career development, enabling them to fully prepare for their own future. Such skills should include the abilities to plan the future, to access and use career information, to identify tentative career goals, and to apply decision-making skills to career selection.

MODELS OF HIGH SCHOOL CAREER GUIDANCE PROGRAMS

In the past few years, several initiatives have shown promise in revitalizing high school guid-ance programs by incorporating career development and by widening the focus to serve all students. The Southern Region Education Board's High Schools That Work initiative has levied sound criticism toward current guidance programs. The SREB initiative is providing a "real life" model for schools in developing a guidance program and instructional processes that serve all students, rather than focusing on the college bound. The students who enroll in vocational education and those who plan to work after high school or after receiving an associate's degree need as much quality career planning and the same rigorous courses as their university-bound friends. The High Schools That Work initiative places a strong emphasis on a systematic career planning and advisement process that is not restricted to the services only a counselor can provide. SREB also advocates the early identification of a "career major" for students so courses taken in high school have a focus. This helps to ensure that students are taking the courses they need in order to move into the next stage of their education and career pathway, rather than leaving it up to chance. The School-to-Work Opportunities Act of 1994 [(see following paragraph) requires that a "career major be identified no later than the eleventh grade." A trend that career focus be identified as early in the high school career as possible is emerging both in practice and in legislation. While no definitive grade level has been unequivocally determined, there is a growing consensus that the senior year is too late. The ninth or tenth grade seems to be a time when a tentative career major could realistically be identified by students.

A major national initiative that is having an impact on high school guidance programs is the School-to-Work Opportunities Act of 1994. School-to-Work has provided the venture capital to stimulate the creation of new systems of education in order to make truly substantive changes in the way high school students are advised, including advice about the classes they choose to enroll in. In fact, the School-to-Work legislation, which addresses guidance program processes for all students, is the only piece of legislation since the 1960s focused on changing guidance (Hamilton & Hamilton, 1995).

The School-to-Work act recognizes that without quality guidance processes in place students will not have the education, knowledge, and skills to access high-wage, high-skill jobs. According to the act, partnerships receiving funding must "provide career awareness and exploration for all students at the earliest possible grade, but not later than the seventh grade." The School-to-Work initiative recognizes that in order for high school students to be prepared to make good career decisions, a background of career awareness and exploration experiences is essential. This model builds on the work of Gysbers and Henderson (1988) and the SREB's initiative in identifying critical processes that must be in place to serve all students. The good news is that these processes work.

IMPLEMENTING AN EFFECTIVE HIGH SCHOOL MODEL

Many examples of successful strategies are evolving, most of which are based on career development patterns and theory, and are being utilized to restructure high school guidance programs. The traditional high school developmental guidance program is composed of three domains: (1) personal-social, (2) educational success, and (3) career development (Burgess & Dedmond, 1994). In the past, few programs matured to include the career development domain in more than a cursory manner. The most

effective of the emerging guidance programs focus heavily on the career guidance domain.

The state of Oklahoma developed a statewide School-to-Work model upon which the dual foundations of academic achievement and career development are based. The Oklahoma model advocates that career awareness be integrated with academic education each year from kindergarten through sixth grade. Career awareness establishes an understanding of the role of work in society. Children learn to distinguish among occupations by examining work roles of people close to them and in their community.

The model supports career exploration in seventh and eighth grade. Career exploration examines a variety of occupations and emphasizes the relationship of careers to life situations. Students learn how to access career information and how to link school subjects to careers. Career exploration should be integrated in academic courses as well as in elective subjects such as technology education. Career awareness and career exploration serve as the foundation for career planning and preparation. This portion of the model is parallel to academic education in elementary and middle grades, which forms the necessary foundation for advanced courses in high school.

A pivotal feature of the Oklahoma model is the six-year plan of study, which was based on early SREB recommendations and site experiences. The model advocates that an "individual plan of study" be developed jointly with the parents, the school, and the student at the end of the eighth grade. The plan of study identifies tentative career goals within a cluster of careers, rather than a discrete career choice. The choice of career is determined later in the high school career when a tentative career major is identified. Selection of high school courses should be based

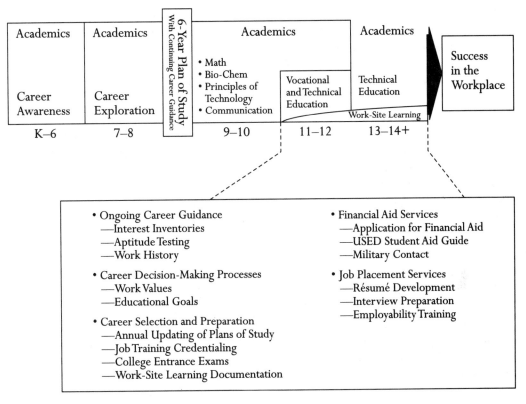

FIGURE 5.1   Guidance Model School-to-Work Transition

upon the cluster focus. The high school guidance emphasis is on career preparation with the individual plan of study serving as the blueprint. The plan of study is essential for determining the appropriate courses and post-secondary education options to prepare for the identified career major or cluster. The career major or cluster also helps to determine whether additional learning experiences from a work site would be appropriate to assist students to prepare for the next stage of education. (See Figure 5.1.)

Within the Oklahoma School-to-Work model, a variety of guidance processes are inherent. An important process that is one key to the success of the model is the identification of student career competencies for each grade level. The National Career Development Guidelines (NOICC, 1996) have been used to help schools structure career competencies into a clearly defined delivery system. (A copy of these competencies is available upon request from the NOICC.) The competencies have helped shape activities to be integrated into the curriculum and delivered by classroom teachers. Once a competency is identified, activities are attached to it. The grade level and course in which the activities will be delivered must then be determined. In this manner, students are receiving career information and building career development competency throughout high school. In the past, one career day for senior students was supposed to "inoculate" students with a one-time "shot" of career information, presumably giving them all the skills they would need for the future. Obviously, this is now viewed as a Band-Aid approach to the need for an organized system of career guidance.

The development of a six-year plan of study and the creation of career guidance curricular activities based on student goals or competencies are essential foundation pieces of a high school guidance program. More than ever before, career guidance is needed to prepare today's students for an increasingly complex future (Carnevale, Gainer and Meltzer, 1988). Further, the six-year plan of study must be updated as students experience more activities that help shape their career maturity.

In addition to career awareness and exploration, career assessment (interest and achievement measures) is an important element prior to career planning. In Oklahoma, the State Regents for Higher Education invested in the ACT Plan and Explore assessments, called the Educational Planning and Assessment System (EPAS). The State Regents provide the EPAS to all schools requesting it. By using the EPAS with all eighth- and tenth-grade students, the interest inventory and achievement tests provide an excellent foundation of career information and projected course-taking patterns for career planning purposes. An exceptional feature of the EPAS is that it generates the student's self-identification of both a tentative career goal and the number of years of English, science, mathematics, and social studies the student plans to take in high school.

Parental involvement is critical to changing the current career guidance process. School staff must learn how to communicate clearly with parents and must view them as partners in de-

livering career guidance information to students. The high school should offer frequent opportunities for parents to interact positively with the school so that they learn about current trends in the job market and expand their knowledge of career and educational requirements. Such collaborative interaction is useful when advising students and helping them plan for their career goal.

The EPAS, in conjunction with a six-year plan of study, provides parents with a wealth of information concerning their child's goals, course-taking plans, and assessed interests. This information provides the basis for examining the degree of reality and maturity with which the student is making decisions about future education and careers. When objective assessment information is provided to the parents, the school counselor or advisor is relieved of the burden of trying to tell parents that their child is not prepared to enter college or does not possess the skills to enter the work force after high school. Gray and Herr (1995) state that since the 1960s high school educators have grown leery of giving parents anything but good news concerning the student's post-secondary plans. This is understandable because increasingly parents either blame the school or ignore the message, if it is anything other than that their children should go to college. Thus, counselors have taken a passive role in guiding students into other post-secondary options (Gray & Herr, 1995).

This attitude must change. Tools such as the EPAS and the six-year plan will help counselors to clearly explain what is required of all students to prepare for career choices and post-secondary education and what is expected of them in the high school courses they need to take. Providing this objective information to parents and students for planning reinforces that it is the role of educators to provide the best education possible to achieve these career goals and academic success. This also requires that middle and high school counselors be trained to use the Explore and Plan assessments so as to best serve the students and parents.

High school guidance programs must be transformed from primarily focusing on the basic requirements for entering college to advising on courses needed for success in college or for any post-secondary training. The emphasis is different. By focusing only on minimum requirements for college entrance or other post-secondary options, the level of discussion with students never approaches selection of high school courses containing the rigor and relevance needed in order to prepare for completion of a college degree and/or completion of a specific credentialing program or on-the-job training.

CASE STUDY

The Oklahoma School-to-Work model has been implemented in reality with the CREATE School-to-Work Consortium in Oklahoma City, Oklahoma. The CREATE Consortium is composed of five school districts in a suburban area of northwestern Oklahoma City. The need to change the direction of school guidance programs toward more of a career development focus was apparent when the statistics showed that 85 percent of seniors indicated they would attend college, but only 30 percent were able to complete after six years (Oklahoma Educational Indicators Report, 1995). One community college in the area estimates that 70 percent of entering college freshmen have "undeclared" listed as their college major upon being accepted for college entrance. So this raises the question, should all these students be going to college and if not what other options are available to them? The district has an excellent vocational center with high-tech, high-wage career programs, but the number of secondary students enrolling was far below capacity and far below the demand of local employers. Putnam City High School was the first to embrace the new approach. The high school principal realized the instructional and guidance program was not effective with all students. He instinctively believed these programs could be strengthened by focusing more on student-centered activities in the school.

Putnam City began its transformation by implementing a planning process in the eighth grade, before students began their high school careers in the ninth grade. The plan was based on an interest inventory given to all students that revealed their interests. The school district spent a great deal of time determining how to complete a six-year plan of study for each student with only two counselors at the school. They had to develop a guidance program based on a different model (SREB, 1992), one that was based on the total school and delivered by more than just the counselors. Attention was given to the career-planning sessions that were structured according to cluster areas. It was soon discovered that the cluster-area planning was critical. Each day the cluster-planning process focused on a different career cluster or broad occupational area. Students who had an identified interest in that cluster met with their parents and an advisor to develop a plan of study based on that cluster area. As the model plan proceeded, the junior high school counselors became very concerned about the extra work involved with the parent meetings and about the pressure to implement a successful process. The pivotal, and innovative, decision made by Putnam City was to involve counselors from the high school, the area vocational center, the community college, and the four-year university in their area in the cluster parent meetings. They also invited instructors from the area vocational center and community college whose courses were related to each cluster to assist with the planning sessions.

An orientation meeting was held to acquaint these "new" advisors with the plan of study and to show them how to use the career resource materials provided and how to interpret the career assessment information to parents and students. When an advisor was presented with a difficult question about vocational enrollment or college entrance, that advisor would immediately call for the appropriate expert, who could be accessed in a very short period of time. These experts were available from the spectrum of educational professionals assembled in a particular cluster area. This program was exceptionally well received by the parents involved because of the high level of commitment from the school and the level of individual assistance offered. As one parent stated, it was comforting to know there were so many people at the school concerned with her child's future.

Since that first planning session, Putnam City has also committed to integrating career-competencies into academic courses through a career-academy approach. The school is developing six career academies that correspond with careers that families identify in the EPAS system. The district is truly developing an educational process that focuses the entire high school curriculum and guidance process on the career development of students. It has also invested a great amount of time identifying business and education partners who are willing to assist in revising curriculums.

The CREATE Consortium has maintained certain progress measures to determine the impact these changed guidance practices have had on students. They discovered that the 440 students enrolled in the health cluster showed a zero percent dropout rate in high school compared with a 12 percent dropout rate in the general student population of 1,400 students in grades nine through twelve. In addition, none of the health cluster students changed their class schedule, compared with the more than 1,400 schedule changes made by the student body as a whole in the first four months of school in 1996.

Teachers and professionals who worked with the students in the health cluster reinforced the relevancy of course work and how it leads to successful post-secondary experiences and careers upon graduation. The high school counselors stated that students in the health cluster pilot were much more aware of why they needed to take their high school courses.

In addition, a survey completed by Putnam City in 1997 revealed that at Putnam City High School, 46 percent of the parents participated in developing the six-year plan of study for their child/children. This is an encouraging statistic, since the previous parental involvement rate for in-school activities was barely 15 percent.

Further, an exciting trend emerged in the area vocational center. In 1991, when the career-planning process first began in Putnam City, 188 secondary students from the Putnam City School District were enrolled in courses at the area vocational center. This number was far below the number of secondary students that the school could serve (approximately 400 students). In 1992, the number of secondary students increased to 214 and held relatively steady through 1994. All the Putnam City junior high and high schools were participating in the eighth- and tenth-grade planning process by 1994 and the schools also began using the EPAS system. That year, the area vocational center enrolled 210 students. In 1995, the number increased to 270. In 1996, the number rose to 275, and in 1997 a record of 403 secondary students enrolled. The amazing fact is that the area vocational center began participating in the career-planning process and ceased traditional recruitment efforts (sophomore tours, radio commercials, and printed brochures). Vocational center counselors and instructors worked with the guidance staff and instructors from the public schools and post-secondary institutions as part of the career advisement team to accomplish the means by which students and parents could participate in a focused, effective guidance program. The philosophy of supporting a student-focused guidance program is paying off for the counselors, parents, students, and schools involved. The student, parental, and vocational enrollment data presented supports that the process is working, and working well.

Although the School-to-Work model has not been mandated in Oklahoma's state statutes, the model is being adopted by other states because it offers a blueprint to schools for and creates an awareness of the need for guidance of a different type. This awareness develops as schools implement tenets of School-to-Work (career awareness, career exploration, school-based learning, work-based learning, and connecting activities). In 1996, approximately 60 percent of the eighth-grade students in Oklahoma public schools had developed an individual plan of study (ODVTE, 1995). This is encouraging for high school guidance, since students are beginning to enter high school with planning and

decision-making experience and a focus for their academic and career studies.

CONCLUSION

We must learn to view a career guidance program not as a discrete activity, but as a way of doing business in schools: a way of thinking and behaving toward students. We must help others see that even though implementing a career guidance program does involve some change in thinking and behavior, it does not require counselors to give up anything that is important to them. In fact, it can enrich what they are already trying to do, such as eliminating a large number of schedule changes and tracking students.

Occasionally, some individual will insist that we do not need a career guidance program. After all, that person will say, we have gotten along very well for years without such programs. However, one must wonder what would happen if we had a school-to-work transition system with strong career guidance programs at earlier grade levels. Perhaps schools could eliminate the situation of students leaving high school commencement ceremonies, diplomas in hand, asking, "Now what do I do?" Or perhaps more of those going to college would have something besides "undeclared" to put as their major. We have a moral obligation to students to help them identify and prepare for their future. If we could envision high school students entering college, community college, or vocational/technical programs with an identified career major, having taken high school courses and having participated in work-based learning experiences that appropriately supported the career major they seek, perhaps parents and the community would view the effectiveness of high school differently. Perhaps more high school counselors would again feel they were helping students find a direction in life and value in their high school experience.

When one tries to come up with a process for addressing these questions, the answer is always the same—a career guidance program that has impact on all students and involves the entire school. What is required to develop a career guidance program? A school or community need merely have a vision of what it wants their students to be able to know and do. They also need the will and conviction that school must not only prepare students for college but also prepare those same students for future employment. They must believe that school exists for the benefit of all students and the community and to provide all students with access to the best post-secondary options.

This is a courageous and very rewarding process that will pay many dividends in the form of deepened support of the school on the part of the community, the parents, and the students. After all, today's students are tomorrow's parents and taxpayers, who, in turn, will be asked to support the schools.

Failure to ensure that every young person has considered career and educational options and has the knowledge, skills, and support system to pursue any of these options—or all of them—is to circumscribe the individual's choices for life (American Counseling Association, 1992).

REFERENCES

Bottoms, G., Presson, A., & Johnson, M. (1992). *Making high schools work: Through integration of academic and vocational education.* Atlanta, Ga.: Southern Regional Education Board.

Burgess, D., & Dedmond, R. (1994). *Quality leadership and the professional school counselor.* Alexandria, Va.: American School Counseling Association.

Carnevale, A., Gainer, L., & Meltzer, A. (1988). *Workplace basics: The Essential skills employers want.* Alexandria, Va.: American Society for Training and Development.

Gray, K. & Herr, E. (1995). *Other ways to win: Creating alternatives for high school graduates.* Thousand Oaks, Calif.: Corwin Press.

Gysbers, N.C., & Henderson, P. (1988). *Developing and managing your school guidance program.* Alexandria, Va.: American Association for Counseling and Development.

Hamilton, S., & Hamilton, M. (1994). *Opening career paths for youth: What can be done? Who can do it?* Washington, D.C.: American Youth Policy Forum.

National Occupational Information Coordinating Committee. (1996). *National career development guidelines.* Washington, D.C.: Author.

Oklahoma Department of Vocational and Technical Education. (1996). *Plan of study survey of schools.* Stillwater, Okla.: Guidance Division.

Paris, K. (1995). *The road to school-to-work: A manual for implementation.* Bloomington, Ind.: Agency for Instructional Technology.

6

Students with
Severe Disabilities

Functional Vocational Assessment

BARRY DEWLEN, PH. D.

HARRIETTE L. SPIRES, M.S.

INTRODUCTION

In the 1970s and '80s, vocational rehabilitation assessments could be requested for students prior to their graduation. Students in special education needing comprehensive vocational assessments generally were referred to local psychologists and/or the local vocational rehabilitation counselor. Results of these assessments would often indicate an "unfeasible for employment" outcome for students with severe cognitive deficits. This was of little use to the schools.

With the advent of transition-to-work systems, schools have had to adopt a rehabilitation approach to assessment. This became apparent with the onset of supported employment and the concepts of "place and train" and community-based instruction and work training. In vocational rehabilitation assessment, there are formal and informal testing components. As our experience found that there were limitations with a reliance on just one assessment component, we wanted to incorporate the best of both for the severely disabled student. The resultant battery led to the functional vocational assessment (FVA). This chapter focuses on the development of the FVA, which has assisted teachers in recognizing the unique strengths of students and to redefine specific goals and strategies. The format is generally for use by nonschool professionals working with individuals who have a variety of disabilities. Through task analysis, performance and behavioral observations, and work environment considerations, all common to vocational assessment, the professional can

Barry Dewlen is director of psychological services for the Northside Independent School District, San Antonio, Texas, and is currently vice-chairman of the Texas State Board of Examiners of Psychologists. Harriette L. Spires is the vocational assessment specialist in the psychological services department for the Northside Independent School District.

compile recommendations for training strategies and accommodations or modifications to the task. This brings us full circle. What started as vocational rehabilitation led to the development of the functional vocational assessment for schools. And now the FVA can be generalized into the rehabilitation setting.

DEVELOPMENT OF THE FUNCTIONAL VOCATIONAL ASSESSMENT

Since the inception of the Supported Employment model in the late 1980s for students with severe disabilities, the placement continuum has included work contracts in a school or sheltered setting and community-based training, then supported employment with job coach assistance. The focus has shifted from prevocational objectives to the concept of "place and train." Many students prior to this movement were assessed with standardized tests, such as the Apticom (Harry & Dansky, 1982), Career Survey (Ohio Department of Education, 1984), and the Prevocational Assessment Screen (Rosinek, 1985), in which most of the normative data disclosed levels of performance based on the norm of competitive employment standards and "normal" performance scores. Testing was conducted for the less severe student in special education, but for the autistic, for the moderate to profoundly mentally retarded, and for the physically involved student, vocational assessment was not even attempted.

Because the severely disabled were not tested, we felt a need to develop a vocational assessment system that would provide data. With this information we could assist in vocational training and placement. As a starting point we

used standardized tests that contained a sample of the mentally retarded population in the norm group. The tests we found most valuable had strengths not found in other vocational instruments; however, there were limitations that made application of the results difficult.

One of the first tests that we used with students having mental retardation, learning disabilities, and other disabilities was the McCarron Dial Work Evaluation System (MDWES) (McCarron & Dial, 1986). The MDWES utilizes a neuropsychological approach. The system is designed to (a) describe the individual's abilities and limitations in cognitive, emotional-coping, and sensorimotor functions; (b) provide predictive information regarding work potential; (c) suggest appropriate strategies for rehabilitation; and (d) provide information in predicting the individual's response potential to an education and rehabilitation program. The result is a comprehensive profile from which a prediction of performance can be made. However, for severely disabled students such as J.N., described in a case study later in this chapter, the predicted potential from the MDWES would look very dismal because the scores indicate no employment potential. The MDWES is not easily administered to individuals who have such extreme deficits in sensory/cognitive, motor, and language areas without the evaluator having exceptional clinical skills. Thus, if the student is unable to complete one of the sensory or motor subtests, the profile becomes skewed and the results are not completely valid.

A second instrument used in test trials was the General Aptitude Test Battery, (GATB) (United States Employment Services, 1982). The test components are: General Learning Ability, Verbal, Numerical, Spatial, Form Perception, Clerical Perception, Motor Coordination, and Finger and Manual Dexterity. Six of the nine subtests of the GATB require no reading: Spatial, Form Perception, Clerical Perception, Motor Coordination, and Finger and Manual Dexterity. While this test requires the completion of all the subtests to produce an occupational aptitude pattern, students with mental retardation were unable to complete the verbal and numerical portions that required reading. In addition, since each subtest had a timed component, the mentally retarded student appeared to be penalized. However, it was found that some of the students with IQs above sixty were able to perform on each of these six subtests. By piecing together information from the six subtests and by factoring out the speed factor we were able to determine vocational strengths and limitations.

Another instrument, The Perceptual Motor Assessment for Children (P-MAC), (Dial, J., McCarron, L., & Amann, G., 1988) was used successfully with students having an IQ above sixty. We found that students with mental retardation above the age of fourteen could be successfully evaluated by this test. Even though the ages of these students were older than the recommended age range (kindergarten to tenth grade), the application of the test procedures worked well and the interpretations of the results appeared valid. The vocational interpretation of the P-MAC focuses on areas such as sensory perception, sensory discrimination, fine motor skills, gross motor skills, and right/left sensorimotor functions. As part of the interpretation, performance is grouped and ordered by severity, that is, "probably limiting" and "possibly limiting."

Experimental trials with the P-MAC for students in the lower IQ ranges (below fifty) allowed the evaluator to examine what parts of the test could provide useful information. It was found that students had greatly splintered scores in perceptual memory, in sensory functions, and in motor performance with scores ranging from average to severely deficient. These trials revealed that the students had strengths that had not been previously identified.

The Assessment of Learning Style—The Perceptual Memory Task (McCarron, 1984) was also used in experimental trials to provide a test profile of the spatial/conceptual, visual, and auditory processing and discrimination recall factors. This test appeared to provide a reliable index for measuring one's ability to recall units of information. It was found that the use of the colored blocks from the Auditory-Visual Memory subtest provided a means to assess cognitive skills in naming or matching colors. In addition, the auditory and visual subtests tended to confirm the observed classroom difficulties that the student exhibited when processing information.

As the assessment procedures evolved, several attempts were made to modify interest inventories. Two such inventories were the Reading-Free Vocational Interest Inventory (RFVII) (Becker, 1981) and the Vocational Interest Exploration System (VIE) (McCarron & Spires, 1991). Both tests were selected because there was no reading requirement (the RFVII) or a low reading level was required (the VIE). Even though reading was minimized, both tests had to be modified to such an extent that the validity of the results was questioned. Thus, in order to evaluate interests, situational assessment was felt to be more appropriate.

What has been observed at Northside Independent School District in San Antonio, Texas, during the development of assessment procedures for students who are severely disabled is that they are not a homogeneous group. On the contrary, they are somewhat heterogeneous as a result of their splintered abilities. Many of the autistic students have strengths in fine motor skills, such as sorting small parts. But if these abilities are not discovered, then vocational activities may not be steered in the direction of the student's strengths. The concept that we work best at what we are most capable of doing (discovering our best aptitudes) and in those areas of most interest is inherent in the vocational assessment process for all individuals, regardless of sex, race, or disability. In turn, are we not most interested in an activity that we do well?

Establishing the Framework

In the development of testing procedures for this program, the decision was made to explore how to effectively examine this population. We wanted to utilize the fundamental elements of standardized aptitude tests, for example, gross motor skills, finger dexterity, spatial relationships, and the realism of a situational assessment. Three major areas, motor performance and perceptual/cognitive and task-oriented behaviors, define the framework for the functional vocational assessment. These major areas as well as their subcomponents were derived from the predominant assessment areas of the instruments discussed earlier. These subcomponents are to be observed when a student is being assessed. Included within these areas are representative questions to be asked when one observes a student in the assessment setting. (See Appendix B.)

Situational Assessment

Once it was determined what normative tests would be used with the severely disabled student we had a second problem to resolve. This problem was how to provide work experiences for students who had not worked. (This group of students was primarily eighth-graders.) The solution to this problem was to develop a set of activities that would simulate the training tasks they would be undertaking in the following years. The simulated activities became our situational assessment. In the situational assessment for the eighth-graders, the evaluator physically demonstrates the task, and as the task is being performed the evaluator provides an explanation of how to complete the task. If a student has difficulty understanding oral instructions, then only visual demonstration is provided. Additional help, such as cueing, prompting, and hand-over-hand assistance may be provided, but it is important to allow the student to initially work as much as possible without assistance. This allows the evaluator to make an assessment of the student's proficiency. The following tasks do not have to be administered in any given order; however, the order of presentation generally follows the order in which they are listed in the following paragraphs.

Collating and Packing Catalogs Twenty labeled catalogs, a container of small rubber bands, and the work sample container are provided. The evaluator demonstrates the task by laying out five stapled and folded catalogs approximately a half-inch thick. Each catalog has a colored label affixed on its side. The catalogs are then collated in a stack with the labels facing the same direction and a rubber band placed in the midsection to secure them. The catalogs are placed facedown in the larger container.

Packaging Picnic Packs Four sets of plastic knives, forks, and spoons, small plastic milk straws, napkins, and zip-lock bags are provided. The evaluator demonstrates the task by laying out one of each item in front of the student. Napkins are placed in a stack on the table while the other items are mixed together and placed on the lid of the work sample box. The sequence is shown by picking up the zip-lock bag and inserting a knife, a fork, a spoon, and a straw into the bag. A napkin is folded in half and inserted last. The zip-lock seal is then pinched to close the bag. The completed pack is placed in the work sample container.

Preparing Mail-Outs Four sheets of standard-sized paper, four envelopes, a small roll of colored labels, one ink stamper, one ink pad, and one small desk stapler are provided. The evaluator demonstrates the task by folding one piece of paper in thirds. The paper is slid under the desk stapler and stapled in the middle approximately one inch from the edge. Then the ink stamper is inked once on the ink pad and stamped in the center of the folded paper. The mail-out is then inserted into an envelope and the flap is tucked inward. The envelope is turned over and a label is pulled from the roll and placed on the upper right hand corner (simulating a stamp). The completed mail-out is placed in the work sample container.

Folding/Packing Washcloths Eight washcloths of the same color are provided. The evaluator demonstrates the task by picking up one washcloth and folding it in half with the label on the inside of the fold. The washcloth is then turned and rolled tightly with the fingers of both hands and packed tightly with the edges folded under in the work sample container.

Counting/Packing Pencils Twenty-four pencils of four different colors (red, yellow, green, and blue) are provided. The evaluator demonstrates sorting the colored pencils from the total group and placing six of each in a plastic bag. The bags are then placed in the work sample container.

We decided to utilize a situational assessment through a video approach because behav-iors could be captured and reviewed for analysis. Prior to this, when work behaviors were observed it was difficult to recall the specificities of the areas being assessed. Even with a behavioral checklist, not all of the behaviors being observed could be checked adequately.

After the student is videotaped, the evaluators review the tape and complete the forms addressing the functional aptitudes and task-oriented behaviors. The form contains (a) a task analysis with observations of each step, (b) work behaviors, (c) strengths, needs, and training recommendations, and (d) work environment (refer to Appendix A).

FUNCTIONAL VOCATIONAL ASSESSMENT

Combining the best portions of the standardized assessment with the videotaped situational assessment has resulted in our functional vocational assessment. The resultant functional vocational assessment report will address such referral questions as:

1. the student's occupational interests

2. the student's strengths and limitations

3. the type of work activities that match the student's interests and aptitudes

4. awareness and demonstration of work-related behaviors

5. the training activities needed for the student to acquire relevant work-related skills and behaviors

6. the types of accommodations needed on the job

7. the degree of generalization that has taken place from previous training experiences

CASE STUDY

J.N. is a thirteen-year-old student in the eighth grade at a public middle school. He is eligible for special education services under the categories of Autism and Mental Retardation. He has a Full Scale Intelligence Quotient of 46. His Verbal Score is 46 and his Performance Score is 50. His adaptive behavior indicates age equivalents from two to five years. Next year J.N. will be entering part-time vocational training in a work contract center. His Individual Transition Plan (ITP) indicates that as a long-range vocational goal the family would like to have J.N. in competitive employment. Transition services indicate the need for community agency support. J.N. will be able to receive special education services until the age of twenty-two.

An Admission, Review, and Dismissal (ARD) meeting has been planned to determine J.N.'s program for the next year. The individual education plan will be developed by the ARD members, usually a school administrator, a special education teacher, a regular teacher, the parent, and the student. Since assessment is to be discussed, an assessment specialist is present. J.N.'s mother has arrived for the meeting. His father could not attend. His special education teacher is present. Also present are a couple of staff members from the school J.N. will be attending next year. The school principal has made an effort to attend this ARD (although he doesn't always make each one). He is curious about this ARD meeting. He has heard there is a new assessment. It's a functional vocational assessment—whatever that means. He remembers seeing a dolly being wheeled in one day and a camcorder on top of the stacked boxes. So, what's new?

The scene at the ARD is different from the typical paper shuffling that takes place. Everyone is staring at the television and making comments. It's a videotape of J.N. working with his hands on different work samples. Following the brief video, the vocational assessment specialist presents a report. The report contains information regarding the task analysis, observations, work behaviors, strengths and needs, and training recommendations (see Appendix A). The vocational assessment specialist then asks J.N.'s mother about any health concerns she may have regarding the work environment. She relates an asthma condition that has not been disclosed to the school nurse. This information is attached to the report. The functional assessment presentation has taken fifteen to twenty minutes. Five recommendations have been presented. These will enable J.N. to progress more quickly toward his vocational goals. They are:

1. Accommodate for left-handedness in setting up work tasks.

2. Provide two- to three-part assemblies to increase dexterities.

3. Use color in manipulatives to attract attention to the task.

4. Provide matching and grouping tasks through sorting activities.

5. Utilize a jig for teaching how to fold into fractional parts and for counting.

The functional vocational assessment evolved out of the limited information provided by normative test data and the situational assessment. Over time, we were able to take the best of both types of assessment data to produce a report that more accurately addressed the student's strengths and limitations

CONCLUSION

The functional vocational assessment has resulted in a better understanding of the student's strengths and limitations. With this information, the ARD committee has become better informed, which has led to a truly individualized educational plan.

The factor that seems to have made the difference was the introduction of the videotape. In other words, "a picture is worth a thousand words." The opportunity to observe the student eliminated reliance on an assessment based on memory and notes. Parents and teachers alike have commented on areas they had overlooked in their own observation of the student.

The resultant information provided by the functional assessment has made a difference in the teachers' instructional methodology. Teachers are now providing more manipulative activities for students and they are relating basic skills (counting, sorting, naming) to real work tasks in the classroom. At this point in time, our data is indicating that teachers are becoming more cognizant of the importance of early vocational training experiences that recognize the individual's differences. For the severely disabled student, it is anticipated that these early training experiences will generalize to the community and lead to long-term supported or competitive employment.

REFERENCES

Becker, R. (1981). *Reading-free vocational interest inventory.* Columbus, Ohio: Elbern Publications.

Dial, J., McCarron, L., & Amann, G. (1988). *Perceptual-motor assessment for children.* Dallas, Texas: McCarron-Dial Systems.

Harris, J. A., & Dansky, H. (1982). *Apticom.* Philadelphia, Penn.: Vocational Research Institute.

McCarron, L. (1984). *Assessment of individual learning style: The perceptual memory task.* Dallas, Texas: McCarron-Dial Systems.

McCarron, L., & Dial, J. (1986). *MDS McCarron-Dial work evaluation system.* Dallas, Texas: McCarron-Dial Systems.

McCarron, L., & Spires, H. (1991). *MDS vocational interest exploration system.* Dallas, Texas: McCarron-Dial Systems.

Ohio Department of Education. (1984). *Career Survey [Interest].* Iowa City, Iowa: American College Testing.

Rosinek, M. (1985). *Prevocational Assessment Screen.* Cleveland, Georgia: Piney Mountain Press.

United States Employment Service. (1982). *USES General Aptitude Test Battery.* Salt Lake City, Utah: Western Assessment Research and Development Center.

APPENDIX A

Northside Independent School District
Psychological Services Department
Vocational Assessment Section
692-6133

FUNCTIONAL VOCATIONAL ASSESSMENT

Name _____ Soc. Sec. # _____ Campus _____

Date _____ M _____ F _____ Age _____ Grade _____ Eligibility Code(s) _____

Work Location _____ Teacher/IA _____

Materials/Equipment Used _____

	Task Analysis of Work Activity	Observations/Comments
1	Pick up one booklet	Uses left hand to pick up booklet; watches visual directions and performs task
2	Pick up four more booklets	Needed help in counting out five and placing in same direction
3	Collate the booklets	Uses both hands, needed encouragement to continue work at this step
4	Place a rubber band around the set	Uses pincer grasp to pick up bands; however, bands are placed haphazardly
5	Place collated sets in container	Places in container and stacks each set neatly
6	Pick up a plastic bag	Works very slowly in picking up a bag; states he is tired
7	Place a knife, fork, and spoon in bag	Picks all three as a group and places in bag; places these easily
8	Place a straw and napkin in bag	Uses left hand primarily; has difficulty positioning one of the napkins
9	Pinch the edges to seal the bag	Pinches the bags with both fingers; does not check work; some bags left unsealed
10	Fold the paper in thirds	Unable to fold in thirds; accommodations made for this step

_____   _____
Vocational Assessment Specialists   Date of Videotape

_____   _____
Licensed Specialists in School Psychology   Date of Interpretation

Name _____ Date of Birth _____

1	Use rubber stamp, stamp in middle	Uses good control of stamper, stamps as shown in demonstration
2	Staple edges with desk stapler	Initially has poor control of stapler; shows better progress with help
3	Place paper in envelope	Forgets this step; needs assistance in continuing task; working very slowly
4	Place a label in upper right corner	Peels off label with no difficulty; remembers to place label as shown
5	Fold the flap inward	Forgets this step; needs help in manipulating flap in envelope
6	Sort the twelve pencils by color	Sorts green, blue, yellow, and red pencils with no difficulty; can name the colors
7	Place the colored sets in a bag	Places each set in a bag
8	Place the sets in a container	Places each set as completed in the container
9	_____	_____
10	_____	_____
11	_____	_____
12	_____	_____
13	_____	_____
14	_____	_____
15	_____	_____

FUNCTIONAL VOCATIONAL ASSESSMENT—WORK BEHAVIORS

Name _____ Date _____ Observer _____

Please rate the behavioral characteristics listed below using the following rating scale:

NOT DEMONSTRATED 1	RARELY DEMONSTRATED 2	OCCASIONALLY DEMONSTRATED 3	OFTEN DEMONSTRATED 4	ALWAYS DEMONSTRATED 5

Focused Attending: Concentrates on task; easily directed to focus on task: Needs prompting and encouragement — 2

Cooperation: Willingly follows directions and procedures: Needs frequent assistance to elicit cooperation — 2

Verbal Direction-Following: Listens to verbal instructions and performs task: Appears to understand oral instructions combined with visual — 4

Visual Direction-Following: Watches instructor and copies visual directives: Copies physical demonstrations; needs additional practice — 3

Effort: Shows interest in performing task: Shows limited effort—appears fatigued; wipes over his face with his hands often — 2

Cognitive Flexibility: Readily understands the nature of the tasks: Not always sure he understands the nature of the task — 2

Organization: Works in a consistent sequence: When work is structured, can follow a sequence — 3

Self-Monitoring: Aware of mistakes and corrects errors: Picks up a part he drops; not aware of some mistakes — 3

Self-Assurance: Performs tasks with confidence: Performs tasks with limited display of assurance — 2

Frustration Tolerance: Remains patient/calm with stressful demands: Wrings hands frequently—orally is quiet — 3

Impulse Control: Controls impulse tendencies: Counted picnic packs impulsively—miscounted the last three — 3

Reality Contact: Aware of what is going on around him/her: On occasion is distracted by noise from another room — 2

Positive Attitude: Optimistic, positive outlook, pleasant disposition: Displays facial grimaces—flat affect majority of time — 2

Endurance: Stays on task until completed: Needed encouragement to complete task—anxious about class, lunch, and being finished — 2

Information Processing: Remembers and follows directions: Followed directions fairly well with assistance; needs structure and attention — 3

FUNCTIONAL VOCATIONAL ASSESSMENT—SUMMARY

Strengths	Needs
Follows oral directions when combined with visual	Needs frequent assistance in working steadily
Completes tasks with encouragement	Appears very lethargic
Uses both hands on occasion	Uses a lot of extraneous hand movements
Understands some simple spatial concepts	Needs structure to work continuously
Names primary colors	Demonstrates limited problem-solving skills
Groups six parts together (on picnic packs)	Needs a jig for folding paper and for counting

TRAINING RECOMMENDATIONS

1) Accommodate for left-handedness in setting up work tasks
2) Provide two- to three-part assemblies to increase dexterities
3) Use color in manipulatives to attract attention to the task
4) Provide matching and grouping tasks through the use of sorting exercises
5) Utilize a jig for teaching to fold into fractional parts

FUNCTIONAL VOCATIONAL ASSESSMENT-WORK ENVIRONMENT

Mark Areas of Concern:

Working Areas

_____ Indoor

_____ Outdoor/Sheltered

_____ Outdoor/Not Sheltered

_____ Both Indoor/Outdoor

Environment Conditions

_____ Central Heat and Air

_____ Extreme Cold

_____ Extreme Heat

_____ Wet and/or Humid

_____ Dust

_____ Fumes

_____ Odors

_____ High, Exposed Places

_____ Moving Mechanical Parts

_____ Explosives

_____ Toxic/Caustic Chemicals

_____ Electrical Hazards

_____ Noise Intensity Levels

Mobility

_____ One Floor Level

_____ Handrails for Stairways

_____ Slick Floors

_____ Carpeted Floors

_____ Steep Grades

_____ Protrusions

_____ Narrow Doorways (less than 32 inches)

_____ Curb Ramps and Walks

_____ Handrails for Ramps

_____ Other: _____

Accessible Accommodations

_____ Equipment Materials Placement

_____ Switch Locations

_____ Table Heights

_____ Chair Heights

_____ Water Fountains

_____ Accessible Toilets

_____ Toilet Room Compartments

_____ Grab Bars Provided

_____ Hand Washing Accessible

_____ Cafeteria Accessible

_____ Elevator Accessibility

_____ Parking Accessibility

_____ Entry Doorways

Equipment, Materials, and Tools

_____ Hand Tools (nonpowered)

_____ Power Tools

_____ Stabilizers (holding materials)

_____ Jigs

_____ Clamps

_____ Accommodations for Strength (i.e., lightweight materials)

_____ Accommodations for One Hand

_____ Accommodations for Organization (dominant left hand)

_____ Visual Coding (i.e., color-coded)

_____ Adaptive devices

_____ Specify: _____

Special Accommodations Needed:

Watch for asthmatic symptoms; has a heat intolerance _____

_____

Description of student's stated preferred environment: Prefers to work indoors; quiet environment _____

_____

_____

Information taken by:

APPENDIX B

Areas to be Assessed

Motor Performance

1. Gross Motor Performance

   Movements with Dominant Hand – Does the student use a dominant hand?

   Bimanual Movements – How well does the student use both hands together?

2. Fine Motor Performance

   Pincer Grasp – Can the student pick up small parts with thumb and index finger?

   Persistent Control – How well does the student maintain precise control with finger movements?

   Finger Dexterity – How smoothly can the student coordinate using fingers of both hands?

3. Motor Coordination

   Visual Motor Coordination – Can the student coordinate movements to manipulate materials?

   Body Coordination – How easily does the student use his/her whole body in walking, sitting, standing, and bending?

4. Muscle Power

   Speed Factor – Can the student increase speed when encouraged?

   Upper Body Strength – Can the student pick up and lift lightweight materials easily?

5. Mobility

   Walking – Is there a need for improvements in the area of mobility?

   Balancing – How well can the student balance entire body, such as when carrying materials and walking at the same time?

Perceptual/Cognitive

1. Learning Concepts

   Concrete – How easily are concrete operations learned, such as using a stapler, stamper, making a fold, and bundling papers?

   Conceptual – Can the student count, name colors, follow directions, name objects, and understand procedures?

2. Perceptual Organization

   Discrimination of Visual Details – Do accommodations appear needed regarding visual acuity and/or visual perceptual difficulties?

   Spatial Orientation – How well does the student apply spatial concepts, (up/down, under/over, right/left)?

3. Associative Relationships

   Differences – Can the student recognize differences in sorting, color, shapes, and sizes?

   Similarities – Can the student follow a model or sort similar items?

   Categorizing – Can the student group items, such as by color, shape, or size?

4. Memory

   Sequential Auditory Processing – How many steps of oral information can the student remember?

   Sequential Visual Processing – How many steps of visual information can the student follow?

5. Temporal Concepts

   Time on Task – Does the student show awareness of work time?

   Calendar Time – Are accommodations needed relative to work schedules?

Task-Oriented Behaviors

1. Personal Management

   Physical Presentation – Are any areas in need of remediation, such as grooming, hygiene, body image, and dress?

   Social/Emotional – Are there observable problem areas to prioritize?

2. Motivation

   Focused Attending – Can the student be directed to focus on the task?

   Cooperation – How well is the student cooperating with procedures?

   Effort – Does the student appear to be interested in the task?

3. Cognitive Flexibility

   Constructive Criticism – Can the student correct errors when told or shown?

   Self-Monitoring – To what degree is the student able to correct errors?

4. Interpersonal Relationships

   Self-Assurance – Does the student show confidence in performing?

   Response to Supervision – Can the student work with an unfamiliar person?

   Working with Peers – Is the student cooperative with peers?

5. Overall Task-Related Behaviors

   Strengths – What are the positive and desirable behaviors demonstrated?

   Needs – What are the undesirable behaviors/mannerisms demonstrated?

7

Low-Income Populations in Community College

Occupational Development

MARY CONTRERAS, M.S.

INTRODUCTION

A Welfare Fable

Since long ago times women have been socialized to believe that someone would always be around to take care of them and their children. So they waited for their knight in shining armor or for their mailman to deliver their welfare check. Each month after receiving their check, they sighed with relief and felt safe again. But their children grew in numbers and the money rapidly disappeared. The people of the village grew weary of the increasing taxes to help these poor women. The people

shouted in the streets to the lords of the castle, "Enough is enough. We have grown tired of supporting all these wenches and snotty-nosed kids. Let them toil and sweat to earn their keep." The king and the lords heard the village outcry and arranged a roundtable session to discuss this problem. One of the lords spoke and said, "It is true the numbers of needy mothers and their children have doubled in size and the taxation money is rapidly depleting. We must do something quickly to keep the people at peace." They discussed this problem for hours and finally voted on a plan. This plan would force the poor mothers to work the lands of their king and become fully responsible for the welfare of their young. This plan was called "Welfare Reform."

Mary Contreras was director of the Second Chance and Think Nontraditional programs at San Antonio College, programs that provide vocational and career counseling for single parents, displaced homemakers, and nontraditional students.

During the 1992 presidential election candidate Bill Clinton promised to "end welfare as we know it." Four years later President Clinton signed the Welfare Reform Law. The new welfare law is called the Personal Responsibility and Work Opportunity Reconciliation Act of 1996, PL104-193. This is a major revision of the nation's welfare system as we have known it. Legislation modified many programs, including Aid to Families with Dependent Children, child-care programs, and child support enforcement programs. One major change in the law is a dramatic increase in the state's responsibility for planning and conducting welfare programs. Additional changes include limiting eligibility, decreasing benefits and ending welfare programs altogether. The intended goal of the welfare reform laws is to decrease welfare dependency.

"Dependent nonworking mothers" is a pejorative label in today's society, a society that not so long ago taught that women should be dependent and subservient and that men should be independent and productive. Today's values include all of the middle-class ideals of hard work, two family incomes, and education to improve our earning potential. At one time industrialized America valued motherhood, family, and the home as part of the middle-class value system (Gordon, 1990). "Woman's place is Home, and she must not be forbidden to dwell there. For woman's work is race preservation, race improvement, and who opposes her, or interferes with her, simply fights nature, and nature never loses her battles" (Dorr, 1910, 330).

Another contributing factor to the so-called feminization of poverty has been the increase of single-family homes in this country. "Mothers account for the vast majority of single parents. In 1994, there were about 9.9 million single mothers versus 1.6 million single fathers. Thus,

single mothers represented 86 percent of all single parents . . ." (Rawlings, 1995, 23). Divorce and bearing children without being married are the primary causes for this increase. And the custodial parent must assume all social and economic responsibility for themselves and their children.

Laws, policies, and federally funded programs were formalized and secured to maintain women and their children. "The United States' first national welfare measure was the Sheppard-Towner Act, that tied health policy to motherhood and made social protection a gender benefit" (Gordon, 1990, 109). This has created *the belief of entitlement* among the economically disadvantaged female in our country.

For over forty years government assistance has financially supported mothers and their children by means of a federal program called Aid to Families with Dependent Children. There are over 4.5 million families in the United States on AFDC. The majority of these recipients are single mothers with an average of two children. Most of them receive no child support from their children's fathers. This aid encouraged women to stay home to care for the children and foster their domestic skills. Seemingly, these women often have low skills and so their income is below the poverty level. According to the official government definition of poverty, one out of every two single mothers is poor (Koon, 1997). In all fifty states the income for mothers receiving AFDC is below the officially established poverty level (Koon, 1997).

Economic and social conditions gradually changed the country's perception of welfare-dependent mothers, making dependency behavior no longer acceptable. In the 1970s the period of discontentment and protest against the welfare culture began. "For despite her political invisibility, woman was nevertheless assigned a weighty political significance as the guardian to male virtue and reproducer of the [white] Republican order" (Gordon, 1990, 63).

As we approach the twenty-first century, we are faced with a welfare culture that has had over forty years of development and entrapment. As educators, administrators, and counselors, we are faced with tremendous social challenges. How do we reverse a belief system in a populace that has embraced dependency for over three generations?

In order to define the welfare culture, we will first examine the profile of a welfare mother. The typical welfare mother is a single parent with one to two children; her average age is thirty with little or no work experience (TDHS, 1997). The different occupations and vocations they can explore as a means to become self-sufficient and independent are all new to them.

The majority of these mothers began having their children at a very young age, often without the benefits and rights of marriage. These individuals come to our community institutions with many personal needs. They know very little about academic and educational structures, therefore going through the process of applying for acceptance and admission to such institutions is intimidating at the least. Filling out forms, taking an exam, and asking for help is not easy, and they try to avoid these situations as much as possible. These women are usually filled with fear, anger, and unhappiness because of past or current experiences. The institutions they have come in contact with have not demonstrated any regard for their human suffering. Hence, their egos are fragile and easily damaged by rejection, ambivalence, and inconsideration. Lack of support from their families and friends is prevalent, which is often hard to accept. It is painful to realize that no one supports or listens to their

plans. All of this makes it easy to give up when things get tough. No one believes in them and when they experience failure, it only validates their unworthiness. Taking risks is not valued in this culture and deciding to change takes a tremendous amount of courage. Despite the lack of support, the negativism, and the rejection, some individuals forge on toward their plan to change their lifestyle. But they face many internal and external barriers that make their goals difficult to accomplish.

Getting off welfare and becoming self-sufficient and independent is no easy task. It is especially hard for women with intergenerational traits of dependency. Changing and becoming independent means a sudden shift of values and attitudes toward working, child care and time management for many of these welfare mothers. These are significant lifestyle changes that do not come easy.

Currently most states do not provide incentives that would assist with such transitions. The reform plan used to include incentives such as increased support for job training programs, increased maximum amount a working mother could earn and still receive AFDC, and increased benefits for families making the transition to work.

The goal now is to decrease the number of welfare-dependent mothers significantly in a short span of time. In the name of responsibility, this initiative has devised a system that (a) disqualifies many people for benefits, (b) decreases the entitlement of eligible people to assistance, and (c) empowers states to cut benefit levels and impose sanctions on individuals who do not comply with the new rules (Castro, 1997).

All physically and mentally able AFDC mothers are mandated to participate in short-term academic and skills training programs. If the AFDC mother has a G.E.D., a high school diploma, or a skill, she will be required to seek employment immediately. These welfare policy changes are implemented to produce a behavior change and reduce the incidence of poverty.

A MODEL FOR TRANSITIONING THE NONWORKING POOR INTO THE WORKING POOR

The following observations are based on the experience and knowledge the author has gained as project director and counselor for a program designed to assist single-parent nontraditional students, displaced from homemaking, to transition into a community college. The Second Chance/Think Non-Traditional program (TNT) is funded with Carl Perkins Funds/Discretionary Grants. Child care, textbook lending, tutoring, transportation tickets, and personal counseling are support services available to the Second Chance/TNT participant. The emphasis of this project is to support the student in meeting her educational and personal challenges while she is attending college. Maintaining a household; caring for children; attending mandatory food stamp, AFDC, or school meetings, and studying are all daily challenges for Second Chance/TNT participants. Coping with such demands is not easy, and the Second Chance/TNT project offers the support a student needs to help her through the many times when quitting seems easier than the struggle.

Many of these mothers enter an institution with a myriad of problems. These problems revolve around the following: (a) lack of confidence, (b) no sense of control, (c) feelings of isolation, (d) no motivation, and (e) little or no self-esteem. They may display behavioral defi-

ciencies such as being loud and aggressive or timid and withdrawn. What can we do as professionals to help re-create and shift their attitudes so that they become motivated, goal-oriented risk-takers? It is not an easy task, and one person cannot do it alone. If change is to occur, a comprehensive system of support services encompassing caseworkers, counselors, psychiatrists, facilitators, job placement coaches, employment readiness trainers, and mentors is the ideal program. Child care is an obvious necessity. The mother needs a safe and competent environment for her children while she is at work, school, and/or training.

Some welfare mothers will be mandated to work. These individuals are not familiar or comfortable with being part of the work force. Others will be placed into training and basic skills programs and will be expected to find employment once they complete their skills training and/or academic upgrading. All of these individuals will be experiencing a change in lifestyle and life situation. Therefore, counseling and intense case management are critical components of this intervention system. Because of the exceptional transitions, changes, and demands these welfare mothers will experience while learning and training, there may be severe adverse effects on their emotional state, which in turn will affect their children. The counselor who is dealing with these individuals must take on a culture-centered perspective when assisting them in coping with and resolving issues that surface. The goal of the counselor is to socially empower these women and to help them sustain and understand those feelings of empowerment.

When entering an institution of higher learning, these students are faced with issues and challenges that affect their self-esteem tremendously. There is a need in all community colleges to establish programs managed by a professional staff who have career and vocational development training and who can effectively assist these students with the discovery and the unfolding of their untapped potential.

The applications and objectives discussed below were formalized to create a nonthreatening system that can be utilized with the Second Chance/TNT participants. The applications help facilitate the counselor/staff/participant interaction and intervention process.

Project Objectives

1. Provide a nonintimidating system that will offer continuous support through an effective intervention plan.

2. Create a user-friendly environment that encourages participation and regular workshop/seminar attendance.

3. Promote learning and study skills by requiring a 2.0 grade point average each semester and providing tutoring.

4. Build self-confidence in all participants, which helps them to become more adaptive and innovative when faced with new demands and expectations.

5. Guide and develop the participants' personal insight by introducing personal growth issues and thought-provoking ideas in a workshop, seminar or counseling session.

Specific Interactions and Applications For the Counselor

I. Counseling Interviews and Sessions

1. Be cognizant of value judgments.

2. Lack of immediate eye contact from your participant does not indicate disinterest. Eye contact will happen with time.

3. Limit your note taking when interviewing and conducting sessions. Note taking can be intimidating.

4. Draw a genogram of the participant's family and ask questions that will give you an understanding of the family's style of coping and communicating as well as information about the occupations of family members.

5. Reconfirm periodically in your sessions that whatever your client says is confidential.

6. Encourage your participant to talk about current and future plans. Let her dream, and guide her dreams into reality.

7. Give her a gift of a notebook or a nice folder with notebook paper in it and ask her to keep a journal. Explain how journaling provides insight and assists in gaining confidence and a sense of control. Demonstrate a four-step method of keeping a journal and ask the client to write down this method on the first page of her journal.

Step 1. What are you feeling and thinking right this moment?

Step 2. Reflect on and examine those thoughts and feelings and why you feel and think this way.

Step 3. Write those things down in the journal.

Step 4. (optional) Share these thoughts and feelings with someone.

Caution: Some participants (students) may not feel comfortable carrying around a journal or having it in their home. Provide a space that can be locked and opened only by you and tell them they can store their journal in this space.

Also allow them time during their sessions to write in their journal if they wish.

The following is an actual journal entry taken from a participant's journal. Rosa F. is a second-year participant of the program. She is majoring in Child Care Administration and is graduating next semester. The entry is an example of the personal insight and processing she allows herself to experience through her journaling. It also illustrates the participant's fears and changes discussed throughout this chapter.

> *This past week I have been thinking maybe I should start working at daycare centers so I can gain work experience. I'm going to have the education for my chosen career, but no work experience. I know that no work experience will hurt me once I receive my degree and start looking for work. I feel I'm going to be way at the bottom of some employer's list. If I start now I'll have some experience along with my degree that could lead to a promotion or a raise. One thing I've discovered about myself is that I'm scared to work. All my life I've been living with my mom, then lived that horrible life with my ex-boyfriend, and presently I have the government to support me. I say support me because I'm receiving subsidized housing, a utility check that pays for part or all of my electricity, Medicaid, food stamps, daycare, Pell grants that pay for my school tuition, and a welfare check. I'm afraid that if I work any kind of hours I won't receive the same kind of benefits I just described, but I know I need to get started with building a career.*

II. Orientations Orient participants (students) to your program by providing enough time for interaction between staff, mentors, and other participants. A short formal orientation for staff,

mentors and program participants with a reception held afterward can provide time. A program album with pictures of past program events and past participants can be exhibited at the reception for all to view. Additionally, the counselor can schedule small tour groups guided by staff and faculty. This will help socialize the client into the new environment and culture.

Resources and ideas that can be utilized for the following activities are found later in this chapter.

III. Self-Development Seminars and Workshops

1. Develop a calendar of events with times, dates, and topics of workshops.

2. Post calendars on bulletin boards and make them available to your client.

3. When conducting workshops, incorporate participatory exercises.

4. Use activities that apply to your client's real-life situations.

5. Use analogies when trying to explain methods and or concepts.

IV. Support Groups

1. Utilize group-counseling strategies in all support groups.

2. Develop a calendar with times and dates of support group meetings.

3. Post calendars on bulletin boards and make them available to your clients.

4. The counselor must initiate topics and act as facilitator. Topics must be preselected before meetings. Select topics that will identify and clarify issues the clients are currently dealing with.

5. Utilize modern parables and stories to initiate a topic.

V. Mentors, Role Models, Peer Educators

1. Mentors can be recruited from faculty, staff, advisory boards, and working mothers who were once on welfare.

2. Mentors must meet with their protégées at least once a month.

3. Mentors and protégées may participate in activities that are provided by the counselor.

4. Role models may be members of the community who are asked to speak during a scheduled seminar/workshop.

5. Peer educators are clients/students who have been in the program and volunteer to tutor or to simply show new participants around their newenvironment.

VI. Supervised Study Hall

Welfare mothers who have been allowed to participate in training or a basic skills upgrading program or who volunteer to gain work experience must often demonstrate participation of twenty hours a week. If enrolled in school, twenty hours a week is unrealistic. Therefore, providing a supervised study hall with a personalized sign-in and sign-out sheet that is verified by a staff member will assist the student in demonstrating to her caseworker fulfillment of the twenty-hour requirement. The study hall is also a good place to utilize the peer educators. They can sign up to help a peer with homework.

RESOURCES AND IDEAS FOR ACTIVITIES DISCUSSED IN ITEMS III, IV, AND V

The following ideas for activities are examples of activities utilized for the Second Chance program. Some of these activities were created, others were taken from various resources and modified to meet the needs of the Second Chance participant. The reader is invited to adapt and modify the following examples or find other resources that will accomplish the task at hand.

1. | *Topics for Workshops* | *Topics for Support Groups* |
   |---|---|
   | Self-Esteem Building | Who am I and where am I? |
   | Assertiveness Training | Who do I want to be and where am I going? |
   | Decision Making | Identifying choices |
   | Relieving Math Anxiety | How am I going to get where I'm going? |
   | Feel the Fear and Do It Anyway | Where does fear come from? |
   | Overcoming Test Anxiety | Using relaxation techniques |
   | Parenting | Balancing act (school, studying, and kids) |
   | Learning Styles | What about me? |
   | Sex-Role Stereotyping | Work hard for the money! |

2. *Analogies Used When Introducing Topic*
   A. Goal Setting
      A runner participating in a marathon needs a specific finish line. Knowing the finish line is somewhere beyond those trees is not good enough. She'll get lost and then have a very low chance of winning the race. What does your finish line look like? Where are you headed in this race?

B. Knowing Your Learning Style
When shopping for a dress, you may try on a couple of styles. When you get up and move around in them you may not like how they feel. They don't feel comfortable, but you like the colors. Do you buy them anyway?

C. Self-Esteem Building, or What Is Self-Love?
When you go watch your favorite baseball team, do you stop cheering for them when they are not scoring or are losing? Don't you cheer them on to give them support and encouragement? When you take action and do something for yourself, do you cheer yourself on or do you criticize yourself?

3. *Parables*

The following parable can be used when discussing dreams. It illustrates the hard work that goes into realizing a dream and demonstrates how important it is to always envision your dream even if others do not.

Three men were laboring in the field of rocks. Each is asked what he is doing. The first man says, "Can't you see? I'm breaking rocks!" The second man replies, "Can't you see? I'm earning my salary!" The third man answers, his eyes gleaming with enthusiasm, "Can't you see? I'm building a cathedral!"

4. *Stories*

The following stories were adapted and modified from the *Career Choices and Changes* textbook (Bingham & Stryker, 1994). The story below may be read to the students to initiate discussion on the topic of fears and how to overcome them so they don't keep people from realizing their dreams.

At first Sonia was delighted to be offered a full scholarship at a well-known community college in the city. Then the anxiety set in: The college was way across town and she had always hung out in her barrio where she grew up. She had to take two buses to get there and two to get back to her side of town. She doesn't know anyone. What if the other students don't like her? After all, her family is not wealthy, and they don't belong to any of the social clubs that everyone else does. But she knew the education she could get there would help her prepare for her dream of becoming a dental assistant and eventually a dental hygienist.

The following story can be read when discussing the topics of Goals, Decision Making, and Identifying Choices.

Terésa decided she wanted to be a nurse the day she took her young daughter into the emergency room. Her daughter had fallen from a tree and was unconscious. Terésa was frightened and scared of losing her daughter. But the staff at the emergency room calmly took her daughter and tended to her while assuring Terésa that everything was going to turn out fine. She watched them work on her daughter and how they saved her life, as though they did this sort of thing every day. "Of course," she thought later, "they do!" She could not imagine a more wonderful job.

Terésa also wants a car because she's tired of relying on public transportation. She would have to find an evening job for additional income to help her pay for a car. But if she works at night her grades may drop, and she would not be able to get into a nursing program with a low grade point average. She also thinks that it might be a good idea to volunteer at a hospital in order to get some experience and increase her chances of getting accepted into nursing school.

The following story of Spider Grandmother comes from the Kiowa Nation, once the largest tribe of nomadic people on the North American plains (Edwards, 1995). Like the spider, the Kiowan women are given low status. Much like in our modern culture, they were unable to participate in government or in the hunt. When a woman can assert herself and seize an opportunity to demonstrate her talents and skills, she, too, like the warrior who is the hero for his people, can become the heroine.

Spider Grandmother Finds
Light for Her People
A very long time ago, the world was young. There was no light. It was night all the time, even in daytime. One dark day, the animals gathered together to complain. "We must have light!" they told one another. "We can't see anything—not even the ground we walk on."

Rabbit held up his foot. "Don't worry any longer," he said. "I will find light." So away Rabbit hopped to find light. But he came back with nothing.

Fox shoved his way to the center of the crowd. "Our people have nothing to fear," said Fox. "The Great Fox is here! I will find light." The Fox strode off to find light. But Fox came back with his head low. He, too, had not been able to find light.

Then Eagle drew himself up to his full height. When he spoke, all the other animals were quiet. "I will bring my people

light," said Eagle. And he soared away on his great wings.

But Eagle came back with his wings drooping in discouragement.

Eagle could not find light either. Woodpecker thought he would try his luck. "I-I-I ca-ca-ca-ca-can f-f-f-find lie-lie-lie-light," said Woodpecker. But Woodpecker returned as the others had, without light.

The animals continued to complain and brag among themselves.

Then suddenly, they heard a tiny voice that sounded very old. "I believe I can bring light to our people," said the voice.

"Who's that?" shouted Fox.

"Yesssss, who sssssaid that?" asked Snake.

"It's Spider Grandmother!" guffawed Fox, slapping his knee.

Eagle put up his wing to hide his beak. Then he threw back his head and laughed. "If even I can't find light, how does Spider Grandmother think she can?" he chortled.

Then the other animals snickered and chuckled. "Spider Grandmother? Ha! She's too little and she's too old."

Well, Spider Grandmother had lived a very long time and she was very wise. So it wasn't that she didn't hear the animals laughing at her. She did hear them. She just didn't pay them much attention. Instead, she set out on a journey to the Land of the Sun People. She crossed vast deserts. She climbed up high mountains and down their other sides. She walked around huge lakes. All the while she walked, she spun out her thread behind her so that she would be able to find her way back to her people. She traveled through the dark of many days and the dark of many nights. Once she stopped to make a bowl of some cool clay she had found. Then, carrying her bowl, she pushed on, spinning her thread behind her and moving closer and closer to the Land of the Sun People. Finally, Spider Grandmother saw an orange glow at the edge of the darkness. It began to turn pink, and Spider Grandmother knew that she had arrived in the Land of the Sun People. Closer and closer she crept to the huge fire that lit the Land of the Sun People. Then quickly and quietly, so quickly and quietly that none of the Sun People noticed her, Spider Grandmother broke off a piece of the fire, put it in her bowl, and began to follow her thread back to her people.

To her surprise, however, the fire in the bowl began to grow. It grew bigger and bigger, and hotter and hotter. It got so hot and so big that Spider Grandmother could stand it no longer. So, small as she was, she hurled the fire into the sky, so high that it stuck. And there it stays to this day, where it is the sun that lights our days.

But Spider Grandmother remembered to save a tiny piece of the fire in her bowl. That piece she took back to her people. That is how the people got fire to cook their food, to bake their bowls hard, and to light their campfires at night.

And that is why, to this very day, when people sit around their campfires at night, they tell stories, like this one, about Spider Grandmother. (Edwards, 1995, 26–28)

Tales such as these can be found in the book *Sun Stories*, which is referenced in the bibliography.

5. *Mentoring Activities*
   1. A potluck lunch coordinated by the protégées honoring their mentors.
   2. Job shadowing.
   3. Feedback paper turned in at the end of the semester or program year from both mentor and protégée addressing the following:
      a. What did I learn from my mentor/protégée?
      b. What was good about this match?
      c. What are some of the things my mentor/protégée does that I appreciated?
      d. What can I respect about my mentor/protégée?

CONCLUSION AND FOLLOW-UP

The author's participation in the program started in 1995. Students were encouraged to continue participation until their educational goals were met, and most of them are currently enrolled in college courses. Ninety to 100 percent of the students have been retained over the past two years.

The support services, which include child care, textbooks, bus tickets, and an array of personal/career counseling interventions, facilitate accessibility to educational opportunities that otherwise would not be attempted by these students. With the consistency of these services, the students stay in school until completion of their education goals.

REFERENCES

Bingham, M., & Stryker, S. (eds.). (1994). *Career choices and changes.* Santa Barbara, Calif.: Academic Innovations Publishing.

Castro, K. (1997). Welfare Reform: How the New Law Affects LHAs, *Housing Law Bulletin.*(January/February).

Dorr, R. C. (1910). *What eight million women want.* Boston: Small Maynard & Co.

Edwards, C. M. (1995). *Sun stories.* San Francisco: HarperCollins Publisher.

Gordon, L. (ed.). (1990). *Women, the state, and welfare.* Madison, Wis.: University of Wisconsin Press.

Josefowitz, N. (1980). *Paths to power.* Reading, Mass.: Addison-Wesley Publishing Company.

Koon, R. L. (1997). *Welfare reform.* New York: Garland Publishing.

Norris, D., & Thompson, L. (eds.). (1996). *The politics of welfare reform.* Thousand Oaks, Calif.: Sage Publications, Inc.

Rawlings, S. W. (1995). Households and families, *Population Profile of the United States: 1995, U.S. Bureau of the Census, Current Population Reports* (series P 23–189): 22–23. Washington, D.C.: U.S. Government Printing Office.

Rusk, T., & Read, R. (1986). *I want to change but I don't know how!* New York: Price Stern Sloan, Inc.

Texas Department of Human Services. (1997). Region 8 Home Page. *http://dhs.state.tx.us/ regops/reg08* (February).

8

The Student-Athlete
Life-Career Portfolio

The Personal Organization of Change

H. RAY WOOTEN JR., PH.D.

INTRODUCTION[1]

Issues and concerns plaguing the student-athlete have been well documented (Chartrand & Lent, 1987; Danish, Petitpas, & Hale, 1993; Frauen-knecht, 1996; Murphy, Petitpas, & Brewer, 1996; Parham, 1993). These problems involve a cadre of developmental issues (identity, personal competence, and career planning) that cover the life span of the student-athlete (Jordan & Denson, 1990; Pearson & Petitpas, 1990; Wooten, 1994). Coleman (1961) first identified potential developmental difficulties when he reported on the centrality of athletics in develop-ing adolescent peer groups. Since that time other researchers (Denson, 1994; Goldberg, 1991; Pearson & Petitpas, 1990) have described transitional, academic, and developmental threats that result from overidentification with sports. Potential threats of distress include iden-tity issues, perceptions of control, social support, and transitioning out of sports. The extent of these threats dictates the severity of difficulty athletes experience as a function of their termi-nation from sports.

Identity issues for athletes are influenced by the degree to which they define their self-worth as related to their participation and achievement in sports (Geendorfer & Blinde, 1985; Ogilvie & Howe, 1982; Svoboda & Vanek, 1982). Athletes who focus solely on sports activities to the exclusion of involvement in other activities develop a self-identity that can be characterized as unidimenisonal, or fore-

H. Ray Wooten Jr. is a counselor, educator, and sports counselor at Lenoir-Rhyne College in Hickory, N.C. Research interests include psychosocial and career development of student-athletes.

[1]Editors' Note: Although this model is applied to the student-athlete in particular, much of the chapter is applicable when building a portfolio for others.

closed. Pearson and Petitpas (1990) suggest that without input from their sport, these athletes have little to support their sense of self-worth. Furthermore, Gorbett (1985) suggests that social identity can be affected, as athletes have reported a loss of status and importance upon transitioning from sports. Ogilvie and Howe (1986) coined the phrase "role restricted" to characterize athletes whose socialization process occurs primarily in the sports environment. As a result, alternative role-taking due to termination from the sports context can be inhibited or limited (Greendorfer & Blinde, 1985).

Athletes who have foreclosed on an athletic identity are at risk of losing their primary social support system when athletic involvement ends. Social support for athletes revolves around the sports environment and may diminish substantially when they are no longer an integral part of the team. Jordan and Denson (1990) suggest that a support system based entirely in the sports setting constricts the athletes' ability to acquire alternative roles and assume a nonsport identity.

Kleiber and Brock (1992) suggest that a profound lack of control also exacerbates the distress experienced in transitioning from sports. The causes of termination from sports are found most frequently to be a function of aging out, getting "cut," and injury. These factors are clearly out of the control of the athlete and create a potentially negative and threatening situation in terms of self-identity, self-efficacy, and helplessness.

With the aforementioned information on the potential pitfalls, one would think that athletes would sensitize themselves to the stressors and proactively involve themselves in preventive activities. However, a common theme in the research literature about athletes is their denial of their inevitable termination from sports. Substantial research supports the notion that a significant number of athletes do not acknowledge the reality that their sports career will end (Blinde & Stratta, 1992; Haerle, 1975; Lerch, 1981; Svoboda & Vanek, 1982). As a result athletes are often plagued with issues concerning reconstructing an identity outside athletics, developing personal competencies, and developing career-life plans for when the "game is over" (Wooten & Hinkle, 1991).

Many career and transitional programs have been designed that address the career and life problems of the student-athlete (Chartrand & Lent, 1987; Coleman & Barker, 1991; Danish, D'Augelli, & Ginsburg, 1984; Jordan & Denson, 1990; Wooten, 1993). However, the typical approach is a "one-shot" career planning program. These programs cover a plethora of topics that include knowledge of self and of the world of work as well as decision-making skills. While occupationally focused crash courses are a good introduction, they fall short when student-athletes' problems are more developmental in scope. One method to expand the focus and duration of the career/life process is the student-athlete life-career portfolio.

THE STUDENT-ATHLETE LIFE-CAREER PORTFOLIO MODEL

Portfolios have been used historically in the fields of music, art, and drama, and more recently in the fields of teacher education, graduate education, and business. The portfolio concept allows an individual to demonstrate competencies and accomplishments through a selection of representative work. It also includes written self-reflection of these experiences. Portfolio development and construction emerges over time and captures the complexities of the individual. Thus the portfolio is a purposeful collection of work that provides a thick description of the student-athlete's range of abilities and growth as athlete and student.

The portfolio as a process develops reflective practice and allows for an in-depth portrayal of the personal organization of change. Reflective practice provides a formative or developmental evaluation, as opposed to the traditional summative evaluation process. The formative portfolio process produces evidence of issues relevant to the student-athlete. These issues may include the learning process and educational experiences and may highlight the student-athlete's multiple knowledges (cognitive, social, personality, and cultural). The content of the portfolio provides evidence that is far more illustrative of the individual's abilities, achievements, and skills than the traditional one-dimensional résumé.

The focus of a life-career portfolio for student-athletes can be facilitated to engage the process of self-definition inside and outside the athletic milieu. Researchers (Goldberg, 1991; Pearson & Petitpas, 1990; Petitpas, 1978) have outlined the deficits of individuals who overidentify with sports and as a result have foreclosed on age-appropriate exploratory activities. The portfolio process can set into motion developmental changes in identity, competence, relationships, and different conceptions of self. The process facilitates student-athletes in self-reflection and critical analysis by way of assignment sequencing, journal writing, group work, and reflection. By constructing a running commentary of work done over each semester and by meeting periodically with an academic athletic advisor, the student-athlete can investigate and study the parts (self-assessment and analysis, field of study, and decision making) to understand (1) what meaning these components have, (2) how they work in everyday life and the future, and (3) why they are important.

Reasons for constructing the student-athlete life-career portfolio vary according to the wants and needs of the student-athlete, the institution, academic and sports counselors, and the athletic department. In the case of student-athletes, a life-career development portfolio could provide a comprehensive and integrated view of growth and development over the entire collegiate (or high school) experience. This approach addresses the developmental issues (identity, competencies, and career planning) that are often deemed deficient in student-athletes. The life-career development perspective provides a framework to develop life and career consciousness. This awareness allows for the student-athlete to explore the possibilities of new identities, develop new competencies, plan short- and long-range goals, and make decisions based on new data. The portfolio process of life-career development is a holistic approach to development that recognizes the interactive nature of all aspects of a person's life.

Pertinent mental health issues may arise from the life-career focus process. Corbishley and Yost (1989) suggested that during the career development process certain issues and concerns (low self-esteem, cognitive dysfunction, ineffective coping styles, and unsatisfactory relationships) cannot be ignored because they may interfere with the life-career goals and process. These issues and concerns can be simultaneously integrated into the life-career development portfolio process.

Soodak (1997) suggests that the portfolio process can assist in reversing feelings of learned helplessness by providing an opportunity for students to showcase work representing their accomplishments, thus focusing on strengths rather than deficits. This can restore the student-athletes' sense of control over their own learning and may empower otherwise passive learners to become more engaged. Borkowski, Milstead, and Hale (1988) suggest that reflections on successful and unsuccessful outcomes by students can help identify faulty attributions and depersonalize the effects of failure. Many student-athletes have labeled themselves as poor performers in the classroom. Thus, many students lack the initiative and self-regulating strategies to compete in the classroom and become involved in college life. Via the portfolio process, academic athletic advisors and instructors can encourage a new self-reflection and help transfer competitive athletic strategies and goals to the classroom and alternative experiences. Because the portfolio is longitudinal, student-athletes can begin to change their limited attitudes about themselves and develop more accurate self-perceptions.

A life-career portfolio, developed over time, integrates an individual's life roles and explores various aspects of life to discover sources of satisfaction that heretofore may have been neglected. A multifaceted approach expands the possibility of personal choice to include occupational, social, personal, educational, and leisure interests.

For academic advisors and the institution, the life-career portfolio process can serve as an authentic assessment as opposed to solely focusing on grade point average and test results that are assumed to be conclusive. The life-career portfolio can (1) inform advisors and instructors as to the underlying processes of learning (learning strategies, self-monitoring skills); (2) illuminate individual changes over time; and (3) utilize the flexibility of multiple assessments (writing, divergent thinking). Positive attributes to life-career portfolio development include: empha-

sizing tasks that are open-ended and reflective of actual learning activities; encouraging a variety of different kinds of experiences; encouraging collaboration between student, teacher, and athletic advisor; and providing feedback. These attributes can be used with both individuals and larger groups. The portfolio process of using descriptive information can more realistically describe how a student-athlete performs in the classroom and in life.

Information Needed for the Student-Athlete Life-Career Portfolio

The student-athlete life-career portfolio should be initially designed to reflect the goals and purposes of the individual. The emphasis may change periodically (that is, per semester) but the overall goal of a comprehensive developmental picture of the student-athlete remains constant. A freshman may focus on more exploratory career issues (the world of work and choosing a major) while a junior may be in an action stage of investigating the subtleties of a chosen profession.

A wealth of information is generated during any given semester and needs to be organized into subdivisions. Subdivisions initially need to address fairly broad areas, including educational and academic experiences, athletic experiences, career development, and self-improvement. After sufficient time is spent on collection and reflection, the student-athlete may develop more specific areas of concentration within the broader areas of development. For example, the student-athlete may aspire to be in sports management. With guidance from the academic athletic counselor, the student can be directed toward exploring this area. If the area continues to be of interest, the student-athlete then focuses on its intricacies. This focus is documented in the portfolio with specific information and self-reflective writing. The concentration of self-reflection and writing, regardless of the emphasis, demonstrates to potential employers the strengths and commitment of the student-athlete.

The basic task is to gather the documentation needed and begin to collate the material that best represents the student. There are many sources for potential documentation and reflection that can be utilized. The most common are: (1) autobiography or lifeline, (2) career and personal inventories, (3) communication skills, (4) collaborative activities, (5) course content knowledge, (6) use of technology such as programming and spreadsheet and other software, (7) perceived abilities and skills, and (8) personal achievements. The documentation can be kept in a three-ring binder, an expandable file, or any other organizational system. Appropriate documents should be stored on computer disk for continuous updating and reflection.

The goals in the collection of documentation and reflection are to (a) integrate these sources of information to help gain insight into the past, present, and future; (b) help identify strengths and abilities; (c) help identify difficulties or deficits that may impede current or future functioning in the athletic, academic, or occupational world; (d) develop short- and long-range goals; and (e) make decisions based on these goals for next the semester, the next year, and the future.

The use of alternative sources of information—writing samples, self-evaluation, taped performances—can help develop a more accurate picture of the student-athlete. The portfolio provides a rich description of the individual's work and progress. A good portfolio has a balance of components with accompanying self-reflective writing that coheres these components. A compilation of data from different sources leads to a more credible portrayal of the student-athlete.

Practical Applications

A typical student-athlete life-career portfolio can include the following areas:

1. **Introduction**
   - Title page
   - Table of contents
   - Introductory comments

2. **Self**
   - Autobiography
   - Genogram (visual representation of occupations across extended family members)
   - Cultural and personal values
   - Life roles
   - Goals, motives, wants, values
   - Personality inventories (Holland codes, MBTI)
   - Abilities
   - Aptitude
   - Achievements (extracurricular)

3. **Education**
   - Schools attended
   - Favorite courses and teachers
   - Special abilities (writing, research, speaking)
   - Skills (computer skills)
   - Achievements (high grades, significant reports, projects)

4. **Athletics**
   - How athletics have benefited the individual
   - How athletics will be integrated into the world of work
   - Past athletic achievements as an individual and as part of a team
   - Individual goals for future athletic accomplishments
   - Goals for fitness and training

5. **Career**
   - Description of ideal job

- Volunteer/work achievements
- Interests inventory (Strong Interest Inventory)
- Work values clarification (DISCOVER)
- Investigation and reflection on occupational information (publications, audiovisual aids, programmed instructional materials)
- Direct observation, internship, externship, co-op
- Information interviews

6. **Summary**
   - Setting goals for next term (academic, personal, athletic)
   - Evaluation and reflection on content and process of past term (academic, personal, athletic)

EVALUATION OF THE
STUDENT-ATHLETE PORTFOLIO

Student-athletes can meet with academic athletic advisors, sports counselors, career counselors, or faculty advisors on a periodic basis to discuss and reflect on pertinent issues and concerns. These meetings can include discussion concerning self-appraisal, role clarification, performance expectations in the classroom and in sports activities, and setting parameters or processes for evaluation. The student-athlete and the career counselor can set the expectations of the portfolio and evaluation by developing questions to sensitize areas for periodic evaluations.

The following is a list of subdivisions and some possible questions.

Self:

What are some early experiences (or persons) that continue to influence you?

What are some principles that guide your actions?

What is your philosophy of life?

Education:

What experiences have had an impact on your learning?

How do you learn best?

What has influenced your educational focus?

Who has been your role model or mentor and what have you learned from him/her?

Athletics:

What does it mean to be a college student and athlete?

How does athletics influence you on and off the field?

Career:

What goals have you set and how did you achieve them?

What have you learned about yourself?

What have you learned about the world of work?

What is your decision-making process?

How did you choose your major and minor?

These focus questions are not rules but sensitizers that require creativity and judgment when used as an evaluative format.

Evaluation of the portfolio can begin with a self-evaluation by the student-athlete at the end of each semester as to how the expectations of the semester were met. The self-evaluation is a learning process for the student and gives the athletic counselor feedback on the individual's progress. The self-evaluation can be scored using a scaling score ("1" being the lowest, "10" the highest). The score serves as a concrete indicator for each component of the portfolio. Keep in mind that these self-evaluations are reported verbally, as long as the written reflective component has been completed. The purpose of the evaluation is individual development and is concerned with the student-athlete's actions as actually practiced and implemented. The evaluation is then scored by the counselor in order to determine areas that need additional attention, refinement, or polishing.

Overall scores can be of any configuration yet need to accurately represent the portfolio. For example, an outstanding score indicates that each section is complete, including reflections. Such a score describes a portfolio that illustrates professionalism, creativity, and reflection. On the other end of the continuum, an unsatisfactory score would indicate that sections and information are missing or incomplete and that the portfolio does not adequately communicate the expectations and respond to the questions generated at the beginning of the evaluative period. Such a score would lead to a plan being devised to correct inadequate areas.

Adjustments to the process can be made based on the evaluation of the portfolio and the student-athlete's stated goals. Student-athletes are accustomed to developing goals and strategies for effective performance in sports and can likely transfer those techniques toward the development of self. The life-career portfolio is also a good vehicle for group discussion with student-athletes. Pyle (1986) views groups as (1) helping individuals understand that their problems are not unique but are shared by others, (2) enhancing the opportunity for feedback, (3) providing assistance in understanding and personalizing information, (4) balancing affective and cognitive learning experiences, and (5) enhancing members' motivation for exploration. The group portfolio experience can provide a venue for student-athletes to experiment with new thoughts and behaviors, and it can provide training and modeling in problem solving and in re-evaluating and revising expectancies. It can also provide individuals with novel feedback on expanding self-image.

CONCLUSION

The portfolio process can lend insight into the student-athlete's philosophy, sense of self, motivation, resistance, expectations, and priorities. Feedback can be given to help facilitate readiness, to motivate, to elicit thoughts and feelings, and to offer support. Results of the life-career portfolio are unique and illustrate the complexities of the individual. As the individual constructs the portfolio with his/her reflections and specific evidence, a multifaceted portrayal of present and future self emerges. Neither the one-shot crash course on career planning nor the traditional résumé or transcript compares to the construction of the life-career portfolio.

REFERENCES

Blinde, E. M., & Stratta, T. M. (1992). The "sport career death" of college athletes: Involuntary and unanticipated sport exits, *Journal of Sport Behavior,* 15, 3–20.

Borkowski, J. G., Milstead, M., & Hale, C. (1988). Components of children's metamemory: Implications for strategy generalization. S. Ceci (ed.), *Handbook of cognitive, social, and neurological aspects of learning disabilities.* 2: 147–174. Hillside, N.J.: Erlbaum.

Chartrand, J., & Lent, R. (1987). Sport Counseling: Enhancing the development of the student-athlete, *Journal of Counseling and Development,* 66, 164–167.

Coleman, J. S. (1961). *The adolescent society: The social life of the teenager and its impact on education.* New York: Free Press.

Coleman, V. D., & Barker, S. A. (1991). A model of career development for student-athletes, *Academic Athletic Journal,* 33–40.

Corbishley, M. A., & Yost, E. B. (1989). Psychological aspects of career counseling, *Journal of Career Development,* 16, 43–51.

Danish, S. J., D'Augelli, A. R., & Ginsburg, M. R. (1984). Life development intervention: Promotion of mental health through the development of competence. S. D. Brown & R. W. Lent (eds.), *Handbook of counseling psychology,* 520–544). New York: Wiley.

Danish, S., Petitpas, A., & Hale, B. (1993). Life development intervention for athletes, *The Counseling Psychologist,* 21, 352–358.

Denson, E. L. (1994). Developing a freshman seminar for student-athletes, *Journal of College Student Development,* 35, 303–304.

Frauenknecht, M., & Brylinsky, J. (1996). The relationship between social problem-solving and high-risk health behaviors among collegiate athletes, *Journal of Health Education,* 27, 217–227.

Goldberg, A. D. (1991). Counseling the high school student-athlete, *The School Counselor,* 38, 332–340.

Gordett, F. J. (1985). Psychosocial adjustment of athletes to retirement. L. K. Bunker, R. J. Rotella, & A. Reilly (eds.), *Sport psychology: Psychological considerations in maximizing sport performance,* 288–294. Ithaca, N.Y.: Mouvement.

Greendorfer, S. L., & Blinde, E. M. (1985). Retirement from intercollegiate sport: Theoretical and empirical considerations, *Sociology of Sport Journal,* 2, 101–110.

Haerle, R. K., Jr. (1975). Career patterns and career contingencies of professional baseball players: An occupational analysis. D. Ball & J. Loy (eds.), *Sport and social order,* 461–519. Reading, Mass.: Addison-Wesley.

Jordan, J., & Denson, E. (1990). Student services for athletes: A model for enhancing the student-athlete experience, *Journal of Counseling and Development,* 69, 95–97.

Kleiber, D. A., & Brock, S. C. (1992). The effect of career-ending injuries on the subsequent well-being of elite college athletes, *Sociology of Sport Journal,* 9, 70–75.

Lerch, S. H. (1981). The adjustment of retirement of professional baseball players. S. L. Greendorfer & A. Yiannakis (eds.), *Sociology of sport: perspectives,* 138–148. West Point, N.Y.: Leisure Press.

McPherson, B. P. (1980). Retirement from professional sport: The process and problems of occupational and psychological adjustment, *Sociological Symposium,* 30, 126–143.

Murphy, G. M., Petitpas, A. J., & Brewer, B. W. (1996). Identity foreclosure, athletic identity, and career maturity in intercollegiate athletes, *Sport Psychologist,* 10, 239–246.

Ogilivie, B. C., & Howe, M. (1982). Career crisis in sport. T. Orlick, J. T. Partington, & J. H. Salmela (eds.), *Proceedings of the Fifth World Congress of Sport Psychology,* 176–183. Ottawa, Canada: Coaching Associate of Canada.

———. (1986). The trauma of termination of athletics. J. M. Williams (ed.), *Applied Sport Psychology: Personal growth to peak performance,* 365–382. Palo Alto, Calif.: Mayfield.

Parham, W. D. (1993). The intercollegiate athlete: A 1990s profile, *Counseling Psychologist,* 21, 411–429.

Pearson, R., & Petitpas, A. (1990). Transitions of athletes: Pitfalls and prevention, *Journal of Counseling and Development,* 69, 7–10.

Petitpas, A. (1978). Identity foreclosure: A unique challenge, *Personnel and Guidance Journal,* 29, 558–561.

Petitpas, A., & Champagne, D. (1988). Developmental programming for intercollegiate athletics, *Journal of Student Development,* 29, 454–460.

Pyle, K. R. (1986). *Group career counseling: Principles and practices.* Ann Arbor, Mich.: ERIC.

Soodak, L. C. (1997). Using portfolios with students who have learning and behavioral-emotional problems. R. Wiener & J. Cohen (eds.), *Literacy portfolios: Using assessment to guide instruction.* Upper Saddle River, N.J.: Prentice-Hall.

Svoboda, B., & Vanek, M. (1982). Retirement from high level competition. T. Orlick, J. T. Partington, & J. H. Salmela (eds.), *Proceedings of the Fifth*

World Congress of Sport Psychology, 166–175. Ottawa, Canada: Coaching Association of Canada.

Wooten, H. R. (1994). Cutting losses for student-athletes in transition: An integrative transition model, *Journal of Employment Counseling,* 31, 2–10.

———. (1993). The "indecisive disposition" and the college student-athlete, *TCA Journal,* 22, 54–59.

Wooten, H. R., & Hinkle, J. S. (1992). Career-life planning with college student-athletes, *TCA Journal,* 20, 41–46.

9

The Résumé as a Career
Development Resource

HOWARD MEYERS, PH.D

INTRODUCTION

Pliner (1990) discusses four characteristics of the most successful career planners. The successful career planner (a) has a high level of awareness of self and marketplace, (b) demonstrates flexibility in response to changing circumstances, (c) constantly seeks out information about self and trends in business, and (d) is not afraid to venture beyond existing boundaries. A good career manager carries a résumé in hand just in case an employment opportunity arises. A résumé does not guarantee employment, but it should ensure an interview, and with a foot in the door, the chance for being hired goes up

dramatically. To this end, résumé writing will be examined as a function of the qualities used by the most successful career managers.

To start this chapter, the foundations are laid for individuals at the front end of their career development. Next, the bases of career theory and the basics of résumé writing are examined. The second half of the chapter views career development through the lens of a chronological résumé in relationship to the major career theories. This section may have more salience for the more mature career manager.

Sound career management begins with having a good grasp of career direction. In examining the literature of career development of individuals, four aspects emerge repeatedly (Lent & Hackett, 1994). First, the process is developmental (Ginzberg, 1971; Gottfredson, 1984; Super, 1994). Second, a relationship exists between the

Howard Meyers is associate director of the Counseling and Career Development Office at the University of Texas at Arlington. He can be reached at the following e-mail address: meyers@.uta.edu. He is also a licensed professional counselor.

individual and the work environment (Dawis & Lofquist, 1994; Holland, 1992; Parsons, 1909). Third, types or traits predispose people to particular careers (Borgen, 1986; Holland, 1992; Rounds & Tracey, 1990). Fourth, learning experiences play an important role (Bandura, 1977; Krumboltz, 1994; Krumboltz & Mitchell, 1990). These four aspects will be used as focal points in examining career development through a résumé later in the chapter.

Career development can be dichotomized as either "Have-Do-Be" or "Be-Do-Have." Have-Do-Be career planners believe that you must *have* a degree (or diploma or certificate). Once you *have* a degree, you can *do* whatever it is your degree is in, and then you *be* whatever it is. For example, if someone has a philosophy degree, he or she can start philosophizing and become a philosopher. The problem for Have-Do-Be career planners is that when they graduate with their philosophy degree and find there are no want ads in the paper for philosophers, they must scramble to figure out what it is they will be doing with their degree. However, there are those who know who they *be,* and they *do* whatever that is, and, hence find they must *have* the right credentials. For example, a career planner knows in her heart of hearts that she *be* a psychologist, and she *do* psychology already (counseling others, listening to problems). Since she *do* it and she doesn't want to get in trouble with the law, she finds that she has to *have* the right degrees.

It is important to keep the characteristics of the most successful career planners in mind, along with the formal and informal theories of career development, while developing a résumé. The start of résumé development begins with characteristic No. 1: awareness of self and marketplace, along with reckoning of self in terms of Be-Do-Have.

THE MODEL

Step 1. Awareness of Self and Marketplace

The first step in writing a résumé begins with answering a question, "Who do I be?" More formally, the question reads, "What can I honestly see myself doing, enjoying, and being successful at?" Rather than quickly dismissing the question by saying, "I just don't know," career planners should take pen and paper and record any thoughts that come to mind. If nothing comes into consciousness, they should respond to the "fantasy" question, which is "If you could create the fantasy career for yourself (forget training, education, salary requirements, and employment outlook), what would you be doing?" Figure 9.1 contains three questions to begin the self-examination process.

Another helpful exercise for career planners requires that they take a sheet of paper and a pen and draw one line across the top of the page and two lines down, separating the page into three equal columns with three section headers: column 1 – Academic or Knowledge Skills; column 2 – Transferable or Work-Related Skills; and column 3 – Personal Knowledge Skills. Starting with column 1, career planners should review old course syllabi. What were their course objectives? What problems were they trained to solve? Inventory and list in column 1. Next, work history should be considered. Examine old job descriptions. What skills were used? Inventory and list in column 2. Finally, what characteristics make the individual unique? Perseverance, dedication, honesty? Inventory and list in column 3. If this exercise leaves the career planner feeling ill, it should. The career planner just developed the MUMPs: "My Unique Marketing Potentials." Figure 9.2 can be used to check for MUMPs. As will *be* seen, the career planner does *have* many skills to offer to an employer.

What can I honestly see myself doing, enjoying, and being successful at?

_____

_____

_____

_____

If a miracle happened one evening and you awoke the next morning with your
fantasy career waiting, what do you see yourself running to do?

_____

_____

_____

_____

The last time you were in a bookstore, what was the first section you went to?
the second? What career ideas are suggested by your book selection preferences?

_____

_____

_____

_____

FIGURE 9.1   Three Key Career Questions

Given a case of the MUMPs, where does the career planner stand relative to the marketplace? Leonardo Da Vinci knew he had the MUMPs. His résumé from 1482 fully demonstrates the depth of his understanding of self and marketplace. (See Figure 9.3.) Having just researched self, it remains for the career planner to research the world of work. Research can begin with such typical resources as the _Dictionary of Occupational Titles_ (1991), the _Occupational Outlook Handbook_ (1998), and the _Guide for Occupational Exploration_ (1979). A tremendous amount of career information, including these books, exists on the World Wide Web. For example, the _Occupational Outlook Handbook_ is online at _http://stats.bls.gov/ocohome.htm_. The _Dictionary of Occupational Titles_ is online at _http://www.doleta.gov/programs/onet_. _The Riley Guide_ at _http://www.jobtrak.dbm.com/jobguide/_ contains wonderful career information and links to many different career resources. Try the _Monster Board_ at _http://www.monster.com_ to post a résumé as well as search for career leads. A simple Net search should deliver numerous sites to explore in detail.

My Unique Marketing Potentials

Academic or Knowledge Skills	Transferable or Work-Related Skills	Personal Knowledge Skills

FIGURE 9.2   Check Your MUMPs

Leonardo Da Vinci to the Duke of Milan, 1482

1. I can construct bridges which are very light and strong and very portable, with which to pursue and defeat the enemy; and others more solid, which resist fire or assault yet are easily removed and placed in position; and I can also burn and destroy those of the enemy.

2. In case of a siege I can cut off water from the trenches and make pontoons and scaling ladders and other similar contrivances.

3. If by reason of the elevation or the strength of its position a place cannot be bombarded, I can demolish every fortress if its foundations have not been set on stone.

4. I can also make a kind of cannon which is light and easy of transport, with which to hurl small stones like hail, and of which the smoke causes great terror to the enemy, so that they suffer heavy loss and confusion.

5. I can noiselessly construct to any prescribed point subterranean passages either straight or winding, passing if necessary underneath trenches or a river.

6. I can make armoured wagons carrying artillery, which shall break through the most serried ranks of the enemy, and and so open a safe passage for the infantry.

7. If occasion should arise, I can construct cannons and mortars and light ordnance in shape both ornamental and useful and different from those in common use.

8. When it is impossible to use cannons I can supply in their stead catapults, mangonels, trabocchi, and other instruments of admirable efficiency not in general use. In short, as the occasion requires I can supply infinite means of attack and defense.

9. And if the fight should take place upon the sea I can constuct many engines most suitable either for attack or defense and ships which can resist the fire of the heaviest cannon, and powders or weapons.

10. In time of peace, I believe that I can give you as complete satisfaction as anyone else in the construction of buildings, both public and private, and in conducting water from one place to another.

(Note: Leonardo got the job and held on for 16 years when the French invaded the city and captured the Duke.)

Source: The ABCA Bulletin. *(1975). A classic letter of application. December, 19.*

FIGURE 9.3   Leonardo Da Vinci to the Duke of Milan, 1482

Step 2—Demonstrating Flexibility
to Accommodate Changing Circumstances

The second characteristic of a good career manager is flexibility to accommodate changing circumstances. Being flexible requires that a résumé always be in hand ready to submit. Good career managers update their résumés every six months. But just what is a résumé, and what needs to be updated? Résumé basics follow.

A résumé is a synopsis of an individual's educational and professional qualifications. Résumés are one to two pages in length. Experts disagree as to whether a résumé should be one or two pages in length. Enelow (1997) and Kennedy (1987) recommend two pages; Meyers (1984) recommends one. The curriculum vitae, an academic style of résumé, typically runs two pages, frequently many more. There are other kinds of résumés besides the chronological (or traditional) résumé and the curriculum vitae, including the skills résumé, the combination résumé, the synoptic/amplified résumé, and the creative résumé. The focus in this chapter is on the traditional/chronological résumé.

At the top of the résumé is the heading. The heading includes name, address, and telephone number and may include a fax number or an e-mail address. This information enables potential employers to contact the job seeker for an interview or confirmation of hire. Figure 9.4 is a worksheet for beginning the development of a résumé. Heading information can be placed at the top of the worksheet.

Although no one correct order exists for the sections of the résumé that follow the heading, research indicates that the most important information should be placed as close to the top of the page as possible (Meyers, 1984). Frequently, the section that follows the heading is the objective, in which applicants express the kinds of opportunities they desire.

The objective is optional. From a career planning perspective, however, it is a very important section and should be considered required. Having an objective forces individuals to think about where they are going and how they are going to get there. It also sets the tone for a résumé and, in a way, turns it into a term paper. The objective is the thesis, and the rest of the résumé is the proof (that the applicant can do what is claimed in the objective).

At its simplest, the objective describes the job title or occupation desired along with area of specialty. But for many, more than one title exists for the kind of work sought or professional interests held. The vocationally diverse, for whom the simple title or specialty area often falls short, can choose from four different styles of objective: short-term/long-term, skill, environment, and equal interest.

The *short-term/long-term* style has the greatest relevance for the entry career manager. It's a two-part objective that calls upon the career planner to state the immediate career goal followed by the long-term career goal: "Seeking an entry-level accounting position in industry. Desire to progress to comptroller function with responsibilities for a number of accounting systems and fiscal affairs of a corporation." *Skill* format objectives focus on skills that the individual wishes to use professionally: "Looking for a position requiring knowledge of decision-making models and the application of such models to marketing and production planning." A *work environment* objective describes the professional arena desired: "Seek a general sales representative position with a company producing soap, toiletry, or food products." When an individual is unsure of career direction or does not want to be limited to one area, *equal interest* formats can be applied: "Would like a position in sales of consumer products, or office administration, or marketing of new products. These are areas of equal interest. Would

Heading data:

Name
Address
City, State, Zip
Telephone
(Optional) Fax, E-mail

Career objective (choose one of the four format syles from page 98 and develop below)

_____

_____

_____

Education (reverse chronologically)

Institution last attended	Degree, diploma, certificate received	Date degree, diploma, certificate received
Institution attended	Degree, diploma, certificate received	Date degree, diploma, certificate received

Relevant course work, projects, honors, and/or extracurricular activities

Experience (reverse chronologically)

Company Name	Title	Dates of Employment (Mo./Yr.–Mo./Yr.)

Description using action verbs and showing successes (e.g., Developed marketing plan that led to a 50 percent increase in sales.)

Company Name	Title	Dates of Employment (Mo./Yr.–Mo./Yr.)

Description using action verbs and showing successes

Optional Section:

Honors and Activities
Professional Memberships or Professional Organizations
Personal

FIGURE 9.4   Résumé Worksheet

function well in any one." The "equal interest" statement allays employer fears that the applicant, if selected in one area, won't leave for another. Campbell (1974) wrote *If You Don't Know Where You're Going, You'll Probably End Up Somewhere Else.* Lest the career planner wind up somewhere else, career planning should be directed by a clearly written career objective. The résumé work sheet (Figure 9.4) provides an opportunity to focus career direction by stating an objective.

Education sections typically include the names of educational institutions attended, degrees, (diplomas, and certificates achieved, and relevant accomplishments (awards, honors, course work, special projects). Referencing column 1 on the MUMPs work sheet (Figure 9.2) will aid in the development of the education section. The résumé work sheet provides space for development of an education section.

Experience sections afford career planners the best opportunity to show off skills and abilities. In examining work history, the career planner begins with the skill (using an action verb) and describes the functions being performed at the place of employment. For a résumé to be *truly* successful, résumé writers must do two things: (1) show off skills and abilities, and (2) show success and achievement in using those skills and abilities. In the middle of a difficult job search, it's all too easy to focus on past failures, but it's most important to think about career successes. Column 2 on the MUMPs list will assist in the development of the experience section on the résumé work sheet.

Most résumés have numerous optional sections. Since the résumé is a marketing tool, optional sections should fit the marketing plan (that is, what will sell to an employer in the field of interest). One optional section is a personal section. While personal sections should be used judiciously in adding to a candidate's qualifications (for example, foreign language skills, computer skills, willingness to travel), they are frequently used injudiciously to self-destruct (for example, divorced, smoker, not willing to relocate).

Other optional sections include (but are not limited to) honors and activities, professional memberships, summary of qualifications, and references. The bottom line for deciding whether to include any of these sections is "Will the information in this section help market me?" If it advances a cause, then by all means that information should be included in the résumé. If it doesn't, it should be omitted. Return to the résumé work sheet to add any relevant optional sections.

Omitted from the list of sections in the Figure 9.4 work sheet is the skill section. Many résumés include special skills sections such as computer skills. And the style of résumé called the *skills résumé* (also known as the functional or analytical résumé) focuses on marketable skills, rather than work history (or experience) as in the chronological résumé. Since it is assumed that employers hire based on applicant skills and abilities, what could be more powerful than a résumé that focuses on skills and abilities?

While a skills résumé is a powerful tool, it does have a downside. Because it lacks a work chronology, it has become the preferred style of résumé for "jobhoppers," individuals who move from job to job, unable to maintain stable employment for very long. Employers fear they may be screening a jobhopper's résumé when they see skills combined with no dates of employment and occasionally screen out qualified candidates as a result. For those who like the idea of a skill-based résumé, but fear being labeled a jobhopper, a *combination résumé* might be the marketing tool of choice. A combination résumé combines the veracity and verifiability of a chronological résumé along with the power of skill formatting. Examples of all three styles of résumés can be found in Figure 9.5. The style

Louise King
14 West Parkway
Buffalo, New York 14214
(716) 555-1212
E-mail: King@can.edu

OBJECTIVE: Seeking a position as a career counselor at a college or university

EDUCATION: **Master of Science in Counselor Education,** May 1997. Canisius College, Buffalo, New York. Course work included career development theory, counseling theory, and group counseling.

Bachelor of Arts in Psychology, May 1992. Alfred University, Alfred, New York. Course work included personality theory, learning theory, and abnormal psychology.

EXPERIENCE: **Rotormola Career Development Center,** Lyn, Massachusetts. *Career Resource Assistant.* Provided career resources to employees involved in company career planning program. Taught job search and résumé writing seminars. June 1994–September 1995.

Women's Career Center, Waldrip, Massachusetts. *Employment Counselor.* Assisted clients in developing job search plans. Taught interviewing techniques. Took job orders from area employers. June 1992–May 1994.

PERSONAL: Fluent in Spanish. Working knowledge of Word, Excel, and Word Perfect.

REFERENCES: Available upon request.

FIGURE 9.5   Chronological Résumé

Louise King

14 West Parkway
Buffalo, New York 14214
(716) 555-1212

OBJECTIVE:

Desire a position in which career counseling skills can be utilized along with knowledge of career development theory.

EDUCATION:

M.S. in Counselor Education from Canisius College, May '97. Program included field placement at LightHouse for the Blind Sheltered Workshop. Taught basic work skills to clients. Supervised training of twenty novice workers.

B.A. in Psychology from Alfred University, May '92. As a part of clinical psychology course, learned basic testing techniques, including the administration of the Strong Interest Inventory and Kuder Occupational Interest Survey.

CAREER COUNSELING SKILLS:

Counseled professionals on their career development at the career center of a major electronics manufacturer. Developed career materials for clients and used these materials in training seminars. Ordered resources for career media center. Administered standardized career measures like Strong, Myers-Briggs, and KOIS.

JOB DEVELOPMENT SKILLS:

Networked with area employers to obtain contracts for agency clients. Increased work opportunities by 75 percent over a single year. Set-up computer network to allow clients to search Internet for career leads. Organized area consortium that promoted local job fairs for clients.

COMPUTER SKILLS:

Working knowledge of Word, Excel, Word Perfect, Java, and HTML. Have used IBM compatibles and Apple Macs. Developed home page for counseling center.

REFERENCES:

Available upon request.

FIGURE 9.5 (cont.)   Skills Résumé

Louise King

14 West Parkway
Buffalo, New York 14214
(716) 555-1212

OBJECTIVE: Seeking a position as a career counselor in a college or
university setting.

EVIDENCE OF POTENTIAL: Taught career development seminars to professionals at a Fortune 500
employer. Provided career conseling to individuals wishing to return
to college. Administered career test batteries to facilitate the career
decision making of vocationally undecided clients. Familiar with
the latest computer-assisted career guidance programs, including
SIGIPLUS, DISCOVER, and ChoicesCT.

EDUCATION: Canisius College, Buffalo, New York.
Master of Science degree in Counselor Education, May 1997.
Classes included career development theory, counseling theory,
and group counseling.

Alfred University, Alfred, New York.
Bachelor of Arts degree in Psychology, May 1992.
Classes included personality theory, learning theory, and abnormal
psychology.

EMPLOYMENT HISTORY: **Rotormola Career Development Center,** Lyn, Massachusetts.
Career Resources Assistant. June 1994–September 1995.

Women's Career Center, Waldrip, Massachusetts.
Employment Counselor. June 1992–May 1994.

REFERENCES: Available upon request.

FIGURE 9.5 (cont.)   Combination Résumé

of résumé that best suits an individual will depend on his or her specific situation.

Step 3—Gaining Information on Self and Marketplace

With the awareness of skills comes the question, "Where can I market the skills that I possess?" A number of career software programs can provide interesting analyses of what individuals can do to market the skills they possess. SIGIPLUS, ChoicesCT, and DISCOVER all do analyses and provide career suggestions for using the skills the career planner has. Bolles (1997) developed a skills checklist and references Holland (1992) coding in using it. Individuals checking the skills they have can derive a Holland code and gain career ideas by checking their code in the *Dictionary of Holland Occupational Codes* (Gottfredson, Holland, & Ogawa, 1982). This data can be a helpful resource in creating a résumé.

Step 4—Venturing Beyond Existing Boundaries

It is one thing to have skills, but will there be an opportunity to use those skills? The sapient career planner should be familiar with resources like the *Occupational Outlook Handbook* (1994), *Megatrends 2000* (Naisbitt & Aburdene, 1990), and *Workforce 2000* (Johnston & Packer, 1992), which provide information on employment outlook. Even with moderately favorable forecasts, some career planners hesitate to enter a field of interest. In today's market, no career or profession can guarantee employment. If everyone based their decision to enter a field solely on employment outlook, very few people would be doing anything. The decision to enter a career or profession *involves risks*. Visits to workplaces of interest and information-gathering interviews

remain fine sources for finding relevant career data to help examine career/vocational risks.

CASE STUDIES FROM FOUR DIFFERENT PERSPECTIVES

Career decisions have been made, résumés written, risks taken, and employment gained. What better way to observe career development than through a chronological résumé? For observation purposes, this career microscope will have four lenses applied to it: (1) development, (2) type or trait, (3) individual and work environment, and (4) learning experiences.

Lens 1—Developmental Stages

Super's (1994) model of life-career stages, developmental tasks, and behaviors states that individuals progress through birth, growth, exploration, establishment, maintenance, decline, and death. Some of the developmental tasks faced include stabilization, consolidation, frustration, advancement, stagnating, updating, and innovating. Approaching a résumé from Super's perspective provides much information to counselor and counselee. A senior manager has been recently downsized. Examination of the executive's résumé reveals that little has been done to keep skills current with the demands of today's job market. Data in the résumé suggests that the executive has been in the maintenance stage of career development and stagnating. Career counseling at this stage should suggest the development of new skills and updating for a new era.

Dalton and Thompson (1986) report on four stages of professional development: (1) apprentice, (2) colleague, (3) mentor, and (4) sponsor. One exercise for career planners is to examine the experience section. An examination of positions held should allow the counselor to determine a

Examine J.Q. Executive's résumé. This upper level manager has a strong background in finance and marketing. Junior hasn't actively sought work since graduating from college. What developmental information can be deduced? Can any typological conclusions be derived? Is there a match between person and environment? What career advice would you offer to this executive?

J. Q. Executive Jr.
123 Holland Court
Superville, Texas 76007
(817) 555-1234

OBJECTIVE: Senior administrative position in planning, manufacturing, and quality control.

SUMMARY OF QUALIFICATIONS: Strong leader with excellent communication skills. Am a results-oriented senior administrator with excellent decision-making skills. Have a thorough knowledge of all areas of business operations.

EXPERIENCE: ABC Group, Gottfredson, Texas.   May 1989–Present.
Vice President – Planning. Head administrator for Manufacturing, Quality Control, Purchasing, and Marketing groups. Developed long-term plans. Investigated and resolved production problems. Implemented effective cost control procedures and reduced past-due orders from $1.5 million to $75,000 within a single year.

NMO Manufacturing, Bordin, Oklahoma.   June 1976–May 1989.
Senior Manager – Production / Planning. Prepared forecasts. Investigated and resolved production problems. Prepared study looking into measures for controlling costs. Liaisoned with Marketing and Purchasing departments.

EDUCATION: University of Texas at Arlington, Arlington, Texas.
Bachelor of Business Administration degree, May 1976.
Major concentrations in Finance and Management.

PERSONAL: Dynamic, persuasive, team player geared toward achieving organizational goals. Professional training classes taken include project management, inventory management, and master scheduling.

REFERENCES: Available upon request.

FIGURE 9.6   Case Study

client's development stages. If the positions a client has held have been entry-level in nature, the client is probably in the apprentice stage of his or her career development. A work history showing progressively more responsible positions suggests someone moving from the apprentice stage to a more collegial stage of development. A lengthy work history without any progression into more responsible roles should flash a warning signal to counselor and counselee. Figure 9.6 is a case study to examine from a developmental perspective.

Lens 2—Type/Trait

Type (or trait) is another lens through which to observe an individual while examining a résumé. For example, Holland's (1992) theory can be applied to a résumé. He found six career environments with six concomitant personality types: realistic, investigative, artistic, social, enterprising, and conventional. (For those unfamiliar with the six types, Figure 9.7 summarizes the characteristics.) Many résumés contain personal sections, and it is not at all unusual to see information like the following in a personal section (or summary of qualifications section): "Dynamic, high-energy individual who likes to make things happen" (enterprising type). Careful examination of the personal or experience section of a résumé should lead to clues about the individual's Holland type.

Jung's (1971) theory of personality, in the form of the Myers-Briggs Type Indicator, has become popular with career planners. Four dimensions containing eight characteristics lead to sixteen personality types. Tieger and Barron-Tieger (1995) advise that different types prefer different occupations. For example, an "ISTJ" would prefer accounting or law as these areas demand introspection, attention to detail, logic,

planning, and organization. The skilled career observer should be able to spot type reflected in a counselee's résumé and offer appropriate suggestions and advice based on knowledge of personality characteristics. Check Figure 9.8 to determine the executive's Holland or Myers-Briggs type.

Lens 3—Person-Environment (P-E) Correspondence

Holland's work can be considered as typology, but also certainly can be examined from a person-environment perspective. Résumé content can be examined from a P-E perspective as well. Person-environment theories state that there is a fit or match between individual and career environment. Parsons (1909) began the tradition, and Williamson (1949) took "test 'em and tell 'em" to greater heights. Williamson believed that through analysis and diagnosis the right job could be found for each individual. Dawis (1994) refined and gilded the approach in his theory of work adjustment, suggesting four components: ability, reinforcement value, satisfaction, and person-environment correspondence. Sonnenfield, Peiperl, and Kotter (1988) found that executives sorted themselves into career systems best suited to their needs. Four types of career systems exist, each with distinctly different features, to attract career decision makers: (1) academies, (2) fortresses, (3) clubs, and (4) baseball teams.

According to Sonnenfeld et al. (1988), *academies* are firms that promote from within and reward individual contributions. Hiring from the outside only at the entry levels, academies create barriers to labor exit by developing firm-specific skills and deep-seated (company) loyalty. Employees tend to value self-reliance, honesty, and considerateness. Representative industries

Which of these six types best describes you? By taking the first letter of the three types that best describe you, you arrive at your three-letter Holland code.

Realistic

Prefer dealing with environment in a concrete, objective, and physically manipulative manner.

Like activities involving motor skills, things, and structure.

Enjoy operation of machines, tools, and vehicles.

Avoid supervisory, leadership, and social situations.

Investigative

Prefer scientific vocations.

Tend to be asocial, persistent, and scholarly.

Original, independent, and self-confident.

Skilled at using intelligence to manipulate ideas, words, and symbols.

Have complex outlook and score high in both verbal and mathematical aptitude.

Artistic

Deal with environment by creating art forms and products.

Prefer musical, artistic, literary, and dramatic vocations.

More original than members of any other type.

Higher verbal than mathematical aptitude.

Rely on subjective impressions and fantasies in guiding problem-solving.

Social

Sociable, nurturant, and cheerful.

Tend to have high verbal and low math aptitude.

Concerned about human welfare.

Have positive self-images and consider themselves to be leaders and good speakers.

Enjoy teaching, training, helping others.

Skilled in dealing with others.

Have a need for social interaction.

Enterprising

Prefer sales, supervisory, and leadership vocations.

Aggressive, extroverted, and persuasive.

Dominant, cheerful, and adventurous.

Need for recognition and power.

Enjoy interviewing and public speaking.

Tend to be self-confident and sociable.

Conventional

Deal with environment through goals and activities that carry social approval.

Prefer clerical and computational tasks.

Tend to be neat, sociable, and conservative.

Stable, controlled, shrewd, and frequently rigid.

Reduce stress by social conformity.

Can be more hard-headed and less dominant and nurturant.

Adapted from Holland, (1992)

FIGURE 9.7   Holland Types

include electronics, consumer products, automobiles, and pharmaceuticals. IBM is an example of an academy. *Fortresses* are firms fighting for survival. They promise neither job security nor reward for individual contribu-tions. Fortresses need generalists with turn-around skills. Workers in fortresses had parents who valued curiosity about causes and the importance of mentors. They were less concerned about professional growth, future income, and

Take the Meyers Quick Version* of the Myers-Briggs. Answer the following four questions:

1. **You're planning a dinner party. Would you prefer a lively dinner party with many people or a quiet dinner party with a few people?**
2. **At your dinner party would you rather be seated with an accountant or banker, or with an artist or writer?**
3. **If you were to invite a fantasy guest, because you believe you are more like one than the other, would you find yourself drawn to Mr. Spock (the totally logical chief science officer on *Star Trek*) or Mother Teresa (the caring, Nobel Laureate humanitarian)?**
4. **Would your dinner party be planned and organized in advance of the actual date or would you more likely throw something together at the last moment?**

1. *Extroversion-Introversion*. If you choose a lively party with many peole, give yourself an "E" for Extroversion. A quiet party with a few peole merits an "I" for Introversion. Extroverts favor the outer world of people. As a result, they tend to be more outgoing and plan things on a larger scale. Introverts favor their own inner world of ideas. They tend to be quieter, more introspective, and to plan things on a smaller scale. An introvert would not likely be comfortable in a commissioned sales position where forced to cold call on many customers. An extrovert would not be happy working all day in a cubicle at a computer terminal without any human interaction.

2. *Sensing-Intuition*. If you chose accountant or banker, rate yourself an "S" for Sensing. The artist or writer rates an "N" for iNtuition. Sensing types rely on their sensory faculties and, as a result, tend to be more focused and data- and detail-oriented. They prefer work that is systematic and step by step, which is why they might enter into accounting or banking. Intuitives prefer their subliminal perception faculties and, as a result, tend to be more defocused and wholistic. Thus, intuitives tend to see connections and associations and to be more creative. This attitude lends well to careers in the arts.

3. *Thinking-Feeling*. If you're more like the logical Chief Science Officer Spock, give yourself a "T" for Thinking. If you're more like the caring, humane Mother Teresa, give yourself an "F" for Feeling. Thinkers take a logical and analytical approach to their work. Feelers take a people-oriented, empathic approach to their world. A thinker would be left cold in a work environment where warmth and care were a prerequisite. Feelers would be heartbroken in an environment where they would be unable to relate to others.

4. *Judging-Perceiving*. A planned organized approach gets a "J" for Judging, while the spontaneous planning merits a "P" for Perceiving. Judging types take a planned, controlled, and organized approach to their world. Perceivers are most receptive to the intake of the world and as a result tend to be more spontaneous, curious, and adaptable. Judging types are uncomfortable in a crisis environment; they prefer knowing what to expect. Perceivers would adapt well to crises and would not appreciate having everything planned out and having to meet deadlines.

*Adapted from Myers Briggs Type Indicator (1985).

FIGURE 9.8   Myers-Briggs Types

Academies

Value self-reliance, honesty, and considerateness.

Reward individual contributions.

Representative industries include: electronics, pharmaceuticals, automobiles, and consumer products. IBM—classic example.

Clubs

Value honesty and considerateness, with less regard for self-reliance.

Promotions based on seniority, status, and commitment.

Typical industries include utilities, banks, and museums. UPS—classic example.

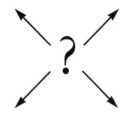

Baseball teams

Employees value future income and personal growth.

Those making the greatest contributions will progress through the ranks.

Representative industries include advertising, law, and software development companies. Apple Computer during its heyday is a classic example.

Fortresses

Employees should value causes and the importance of mentors.

Promise neither job security nor financial reward.

Representative industries include publishing, hotels, and textiles. Continental Airlines during its crisis is a classic example.

FIGURE 9.9   Where Do You Fit In?

societal contributions. Representative industries are publishing, retail, hotels, and textiles. During its financial crisis, Continental Airlines became a fortress. *Clubs* like to hire from within but with a difference from academies. They assign and promote based more on group factors like seniority, status, and commitment rather than innovation or contribution. Typical industries would be utilities, museums, banks, the military, and government agencies. UPS is a classic club example. Club employees value honesty and considerateness. *Baseball teams* use external labor markets for hires. They hire those likely to make the greatest individual contributions. Producers will progress through the ranks. Advertising, law, software development, and broadcast/entertainment are examples of baseball team industries. Employees value future income and personal growth and are less concerned with job security. Apple Computer was a classic example of a baseball team in its formative years, then showed signs of becoming an academy, and most recently a fortress. A creative client with a pioneering personality and independent spirit would be a bad match for a fortress. A better fit would be on a baseball team. Figure 9.9 asks the client whether he or she prefers to "play ball," "join the club," "enter the academy," or "hole up in a fortress." Reference the case study in Figure 9.6 for information that can be gleaned on person-environment correspondence.

Lens 4—Social Learning Theory

Krumboltz (1994) believes that individuals constantly encounter learning experiences, learning that is a function of rewards and punishments received. Parents or significant others provide important career modeling early in life for the career planner. Teachers, television characters, and movie figures may also lead to important career beliefs held by an individual. Career counseling goals (Krumboltz, 1996) focus on the client's learning of new skills, interests, beliefs, values, work habits, and personal qualities, which lead to a satisfying life within a constantly changing work world. In a way, the career counselor becomes a coach or mentor, rather than merely a matchmaker like a counselor operating from a P-E perspective. A skilled career counselor can examine a résumé as a sum total of a life's learning: What kind of skills has this client developed? what kind of work habits? values? Refer to the Figure 9.6 case study: What can be determined about the kinds of social learning influences that may have had an impact on the executive?

CONCLUSION

Much can be gained through the examination of a résumé. A cursory glance can suggest whether an individual has a chance of getting an interview and, consequently, getting hired. But through an in-depth examination of a résumé, a skilled reader can verify whether the owner is on career track. Developmentally, is the applicant where he or she should be in his or her career? Does the individual have the tools (the skills and abilities) to be successful in his or her chosen field? While career success can be a matter of luck (being in the right place at the right time), experienced career counselors know that success will be dependent upon having the client understand self relative to market and consequentially, being ready to take the big risk when the time comes. Knowing self means that the individual must understand his or her development (that's what a chronological résumé is about). Through the course of development, a correspondence between individual and environment begins. Personality characteristics (types/traits) emerge—whether through genetic predisposition, social learning, or a combination of the two—suggesting a path or paths. The skilled career counselor and the wise career manager must take this information and piece it together.

REFERENCES

ABCA Bulletin. (1975). A classic letter of application (December): 19.

Bandura, A. (1977). *Social learning theory.* Englewood Cliffs, N.J.: Prentice Hall.

Bolles, R. N. (1997). *The 1997 what color is your parachute?* Berkeley, Calif.: Ten Speed Press.

Borgen, F. (1986). New approaches to the assessment of interests. W. Walsh & S. Osipow (eds.), *Advances in vocational psychology: Vol. I. The assessment of interests,* 83–126. Hillsdale, N.J.: Erlbaum.

Campbell, D. (1974). *If you don't know where you're going, you'll probably end up somewhere else.* Allen, Texas: Argus.

Dalton, G. W. & Thompson, P. H. (1986). *Novations: Strategies for career management.* Glenview, Ill.: Scott, Foresman, and Co.

Dawis, R. V. (1994). The theory of work adjustment as convergent theory. M. L. Savickas & R. W. Lent (eds.), *Convergence in career development theories,* 33–43. Palo Alto, Calif.: CPP Books.

Dawis, R. V., & Lofquist, L. (1984). *A psychological theory of work adjustment.* Minneapolis: University of Minnesota Press.

Enelow, W. S. (1997). Résumé guidelines for senior executives, *National Business Employment Weekly,* (March 30–April 5): 18–19.

Ginzberg, E. (1971). Toward a theory of occupational choice. H. J. Peters & J. C. Hansen (eds.), *Vocational guidance and career development,* 105–110. New York: The Macmillan Co.

Gottfredson, G. G., Holland, J. L., & Ogawa, D. K. (1982). *Dictionary of Holland occupational codes.* Palo Alto, Calif.: Consulting Psychologists Press.

Gottfredson, L. (1984). Circumscription and compromise: A developmental theory of occupational aspirations. *Journal of Counseling Psychology,* 28, 545–579.

Holland, J. L. (1992). *Making vocational choices: A theory of vocational personalities and work environments.* Odessa, Fla.: Psychological Assessment Resources.

———. (1994). Separate but unequal is better. M. L. Savickas & R. W. Lent (eds.), *Convergence in career development theories* 45–51. Palo Alto, Calif.: CPP Books.

Johnston, W. B., & Packer, A. H. (1992). *Workforce 2000.* Indianapolis, Ind.: Hudson Institute.

Jung, G. (1971). General description of the types. J. Campbell (ed.), *The portable Jung,* 178–269. New York: Penguin Books.

Kennedy, M. M. (1987). The new look in résumés, *Businessweek careers,* 10–13.

Krumboltz, J. D. (1994). Improving career development theory from a social learning perspective. In M. L. Savickas & R. W. Lent (eds.), *Convergence in career development theories,* 7–31. Palo Alto, Calif.: CPP Books.

———. (1996). A learning theory of career counseling. M. L. Savickas & W. B. Walsh (eds.), *Handbook of career counseling theory and practice,* 55–80. Palo Alto, Calif.: Davies-Black Publishing.

Krumboltz, J. D., & Nichols, C. (1990). Integrating the social learning theory of career decision making. W. Walsh and S. Osipow (eds.), *Career counseling: Contemporary topics in vocational psychology,* 159–192. Hillsdale, N.J.: Erlbaum.

Lent, G., & Hackett, R. W. (1994). Sociocognitive mechanisms of personal agency in career development: Pantheoretical prospects. M. L. Savickas and R. W. Lent (eds.), *Convergence in career development theories,* 77–101. Palo Alto, Calif.: CPP Books.

Meyers, H. H. (1984). Writing résumés right, *Journal of Career Planning and Employment,* 44, 19–21.

Myers, I. B., & McCauley, M. (1985). *Manual: A guide for the Myers-Briggs Type Indicator.* Palo Alto, Calif: Consulting Psychologists Press.

Naisbitt, J., & Aburdene, P. (1990). *Megatrends 2000.* New York: Avon Books.

Parsons, F. (1909). *Choosing a vocation.* Boston: Houghton-Mifflin.

Pliner, J. (1990). Staying with or leaving the organization. J. C. Quick, R. E. Hess, J. Hermalin, & J. D. Quick (eds.), *Career stress in changing times,* 159–177. New York: The Haworth Press.

Rounds, J., & Tracey, T. (1990). From trait-and-factor to person-environment fit counseling: Theory and process. W. Walsh & S. Osipow (eds.), *Career Counseling: contemporary topics in vocational psychology,* 1–44. Hillsdale, N.J.: Erlbaum.

Sonnenfeld, J. A., Peiperl, M. A., & Kotter, J. P. (1988). Strategic determinants of managerial labor markets: A career systems view, *Human Resource Management,* 27, 369–388.

Super, D. E. (1994). A life-span, life-space perspective on convergence. M. L. Savickas & R. W. Lent (eds.), *Convergence in career development theories,* 63–74. Palo Alto, Calif.: CPP Books.

Tieger, P. D., & Barron-Tieger, B. (1995). *Do what you are.* Boston: Little, Brown, & Co.

U. S. Department of Labor. (1991). *Dictionary of Occupational Titles,* (4th ed.). Indianapolis, Ind.: JIST Works, Inc.

———. (1998). *Occupational Outlook Handbook.* Indianapolis, Ind.: JIST Works, Inc.

———. (1979). *Guide for Occupational Exploration.* Washington, D.C.: Department of Labor.

Williamson, E. G. (1949). *Counseling adolescents.* New York: McGraw-Hill.

DISCOVER

Its Uses with College Students

JOHNNIE WALKER-STAGGS, M.A., M.ED.

INTRODUCTION[1]

DISCOVER, a computerized guidance program for colleges and adults published by the American College Testing Program (1995), contains nine modules. A review and summary of these follow.

Module 1: Beginning the Career Journey This module teaches the steps of an effective career-planning process, assesses the user's position in the process, and recommends other

DISCOVER modules based on the user's knowledge of the steps of this process.

Module 2: Learning About the World of Work This module teaches the World-of-Work Map for occupations and programs of study and provides the user with an opportunity to browse programs of study and occupations by World-of-Work Map categories, such as regions, families, or clusters.

Module 3: Learning About Yourself (recommended for all undeclared majors) In this part of *DISCOVER* the student learns more about self by completing inventories at the computer of interests, abilities, values, or experiences or by entering scores from having taken these inventories in the *Career Planning Guidebook.* The student may also enter the results of

---

Johnnie Walker-Staggs is the director of the Career Resource Center at Our Lady of the Lake University in San Antonio, Texas.

[1] Editor's Note: There are several excellent computerized career guidance programs in addition to DISCOVER, such as SIGI/PLUS, ChoicesCT, COIN, and more. Because of Ms. Walker-Staggs's demonstrated ability, we asked her to write this chapter about this particular program as a model for using computer-assisted guidance programs with college students. The ACT DISCOVER materials discussed in this chapter are all copyrighted by ACT, Inc.

inventories and tests taken in other print form. Possibilities are:

- Self-Directed Search (SDS)
- Strong Interest Inventory (SII)
- Kuder Occupational Interest Survey (KOIS)
- Career Decision Making system (CDM)
- Career Ability Placement Survey (CAPS)
- Differential Aptitude Tests (DAT)
- Career Planning Program (CPP)
- Armed Services Vocational Aptitude Battery (ASVAB)
- California Occupational Preference Survey (COPS)
- Career Assessment Inventory (CAI)
- Ohio Vocational Interest Surveys (OVIS)

Module 4: Finding Occupations (recommended for all undeclared majors) This module "converts" Module 3 results (data, things, ideas, and people) into World-of-Work Map regions, then into occupational titles.

Module 5: Learning About Occupations (recommended for all undeclared majors) This module provides extensive information about occupations of the user's choice and assists the user in narrowing the identified list to ten or fewer occupations.

Module 6: Making Educational Choices (recommended for all undeclared majors) This module identifies paths of training for the ten or fewer occupations stored in the user's record and programs of study related to each high-priority occupation.

Module 7: Planning Next Steps This module helps users to identify schools with desired characteristics, to gain comprehensive and accurate information about these schools, and to receive information about key job-seeking skills, academic requirements for specific programs and criteria for admission.

Module 8: Planning a Career This module defines career as a combination of all life roles being played at a given point in time and draws the user's current Career Rainbow. It then draws the user's desired future Career Rainbow and helps the user construct an action plan for achieving it.

Module 9: Making the Transition This module teaches users about the nature of transition, assesses the "temperature" of any transition, assists users in identifying factors they may control that are related to the personal transition (thus reducing the temperature), and assists the users in describing specific actions that they can take in order to reduce the temperature of a transition.

DISCOVER will assist students in two ways:

- the **"information only"** approach (option A)
- the **"guidance plus information"** approach (option B)

Option A is used for **accessing information only.** Option B is used for **counseling undeclared majors and career changers.**

Option A of *DISCOVER,* the **"information only"** approach, allows the student to:

- search for occupations by job characteristics or majors
- get information about occupations
- search for two- and four-your colleges, technical and specialized schools, and graduate schools
- learn about financial aid and its availability

- learn about military programs
- learn how to get a job
- get interviewing tips
- get résumé-writing instructions and samples

Option B of *DISCOVER,* the "**guidance plus information**" approach, offers the first step of the career-planning process, the step of learning about self and about the process of setting long-range goals. In the tradition of the best of career-planning theory and practice, this base knowledge provides much of what is needed by a student in order to identify occupations, programs of study, and training options and to prepare for a job placement. From this perspective, **option B** of *DISCOVER* is essential for those who have not yet selected a college major or made definite career choices.

Option B leads to a sequential, relatively long-term use of the *DISCOVER* modules for the purpose of career development. This approach builds a unique user record by name and social security number allowing review by the user at later dates. **Option B** should be used with students who need assistance in exploring career options and choosing a college major and career. With this approach students will be able to:

- follow a complete step-by-step process for choosing a college major and making a career decision
- pinpoint interests (likes and dislikes), abilities, and values
- find occupations that match personal characteristics (likes and dislikes) (Holland, 1985)
- get assistance in pinpointing a college major or course of study
- receive detailed information about specific occupations, such as job descriptions,

salaries, qualifications, and related occupations

A word of caution for first-time *DISCOVER* users, both professional and student—the entire nine modules contained in option B, the Guidance Plus component of *DISCOVER,* should *not* be prescribed for every user of *DISCOVER.* An initial counseling session should be conducted to determine each user's purpose for seeking the guidance and assistance of the *DISCOVER* program. The career counselor should make the purpose of each module clear to the user and make a professional determination regarding the appropriate modules for each user.

Modules 3, 4, and 5 are recommended for undeclared majors only. These modules are designed to help students better understand themselves and are used for helping students find an appropriate career fit. Other modules are recommended based on the user's reason or based on the goal the person visiting the career center wants to achieve.

IMPLEMENTING *DISCOVER* ON YOUR CAMPUS

Getting started with the *DISCOVER* guidance program by ACT is a very interesting and challenging endeavor. The *DISCOVER* system should be presented primarily as an exciting and useful tool for enhancing the university's advisement process. *DISCOVER* should be a routine part of career counseling, academic advising, and course work selection for all undecided freshmen and be part of a general orientation program for all freshmen.

A *DISCOVER* guidance model for advising and counseling students may be promoted on your campus to groups of students, parents, instructional faculty, professional staff, and college advisors through a series of short in-service workshops presented by the career counselor. An in-service format should include:

1. An overview of the purpose of the DIS-COVER program and what to expect from it.

2. The ACT training video.

3. A series of role-playing scenarios.

4. A short processing period, including feedback.

5. Evaluation.

Other methods for promoting DISCOVER on your campus may include:

1. A special information flyer inserted in the freshman information packet describing DISCOVER as an effective and exciting decision-making tool for undeclared majors.

2. A detailed description of DISCOVER and its usage in a Career Services brochure.

3. Letters and/or e-mail to all undeclared majors describing DISCOVER and its use, particularly emphasizing that it helps undeclared majors choose career options and a major that best fit their occupational personality.

Integrating DISCOVER into the ongoing counseling and advising process is the most direct method of getting students to use the system. The first students to use the system have usually been referred by professional staff and advisors. Other students will access the DIS-COVER system because of a friend or classmate who shared their profile results. Yet others will learn about it from group presentations and graduate school psychology class assignments. DISCOVER is introduced to students at Our Lady of the Lake University during freshman orientation, after which a large number of undeclared majors visit the center to schedule an appointment to use DISCOVER. Most students experience positive results with DISCOVER and very often refer other undeclared majors to the center to schedule an appointment to use DISCOVER.

The three most important modules in DIS-COVER for making career decisions are Modules 3, 4 and 5. All students seeking career direction should be required to complete these three modules. Module 3 helps the student determine which career fields are the best fit before choosing a college major. Module 4 generates a list of career fields based on the results of Module 3. Module 5 produces a three- to four-page printout describing each career field in detail: nature of the work, required training and qualifications, earnings, job outlook, and related occupations.

During an initial counseling session, students seeking career guidance will need to be taught how to use the DISCOVER guidance program for career planning, specifically Modules 3, 4, and 5, the career guidance modules.

In the absence of properly trained professionals and proper precounseling, students often confuse questions relating to interests with questions relating to abilities. They seem to answer interest assessment questions from an abilities standpoint, confusing what they would like or dislike with what they can or cannot do. It is crucial that counselors clarify the difference between interest questions and ability questions when preparing students to use DISCOVER.

OUTLINE FOR STAFF TRAINING

Before implementing DISCOVER on your campus, careful and adequate training of staff users is imperative and essential.

Staff training sessions are essential and should include the use of specific parts of the *DISCOVER* program by combining demonstrations of the system with discussions and segments from the ACT training videos.

- Schedule a series of staff training sessions providing demonstrations of and direct hands-on experiences with *DISCOVER*.

- Schedule a series of orientation sessions focusing on the proper procedure for profile interpretation.

- Develop steps for integrating *DISCOVER* with career counseling sessions.

- Provide group feedback sessions for staff trainees.

Use of the *DISCOVER* Guide, other support materials available from ACT, and hands-on practice will prepare and equip the staff for success in using the *DISCOVER* guidance program effectively. Staff members learning to use *DISCOVER* should perform the following steps.

Step 1 Read through the *DISCOVER* materials and become familiar with the contents of the manuals.

Step 2 Complete the entire program on the computer in order to become familiar with the nine modules. This exploration may take several sessions, but it is the most effective way to learn the system and the content contained in the nine modules.

Step 3 View the *ACT DISCOVER* video. The ACT video is an excellent tool for learning and understanding the nine modules and their purpose.

Step 4 Attend at least one yearly *ACT DISCOVER* training workshop.

A clear understanding of *DISCOVER* is important to everyone who will be working with students on the system or referring students to it for career direction or even just for information. The career counselor at the site will need to become very familiar with the program content and be knowledgeable enough to train others in its operation.

After the key leader is familiar with the entire system, it is important to train other professionals and paraprofessionals in order for them to become comfortable with the system and knowledgeable about its applications. Ideally, training should be spread out over several sessions with the staff utilizing and practicing parts of *DISCOVER* between the sessions. The initial training should be designed to help staff understand what *DISCOVER* can do, how the system operates, and the purpose of each module. Each staff member can then begin to explore and get hands-on experience with *DISCOVER* in order to become competent in its application.

An Evaluation Exercise For Staff Training

Exercise handouts are excellent tools for evaluating the staff training session. The ACT Training Manual may be useful as a resource.

Exercise How would you assist the student who brings the following concerns to the counseling center? Answer A and B for each of the ten cases. (ACT Training Manual, 1996).

    A. Identify the *DISCOVER* module to which you would direct the student.

    B. Record your answer to each item.

1. I have just returned to school after being at home with the kids for fifteen years. I have never had any work experience out-

side the home, and I have not learned how to do anything. Can you help me decide about a major and an occupation?

2. I am a business major and I really do not know what kinds of jobs I might be able to get with this background. What can you suggest?

3. I hear that there is a lot of money in computer science. Can you tell me if this is true, what the employment outlook is, and the names of some schools where I can get training?

4. I have decided to major in forestry, and I understand that our college does not have this major. Can you help me find another school on the East Coast? Can you help me identify schools?

5. I think I would like to be a market analyst, but I need to find out exactly what they do.

6. I did well in my first accounting course and may be interested in becoming an accountant, but I need to know more about the occupation.

7. I am a liberal arts major. What can I do with a degree in English?

8. I would like to be an occupational therapist, but I do not know how much training I would need or what the employment outlook is.

9. I decided that I do not want to invest four years in the college's nursing program, but would rather become a physician's assistant. Where can I go for that?

10. I know what I like to do, but I would like to identify some occupations according to my abilities.

More than ten situations may be included in the staff training evaluation exercise.

Each staff training session should include an evaluation exercise for measuring knowledge and skills gained from the session.

A MODEL FOR USING *DISCOVER* AS A COUNSELING AND DECISION-MAKING TOOL

This model is best implemented by scheduling individual appointments or by working in small group settings. This model takes the student through a step-by-step approach to career planning, including inventories to assess interests, abilities, and experiences. (Most students have no relevant experiences.)

Precounseling session (15 to 20 minutes)
Establish purpose, expectations, and goals with students.

■ Stress the importance of honesty in responding to the UNIACT items in Module 3 (ninety-item interest inventory: likes, dislikes, and indifferences).

■ Clearly emphasize during the precounseling session that the UNIACT Interest Inventory is not a measure of abilities, but rather a measure of *occupational personality type* and *occupational interests* (Holland, 85).

Module 3 (15 to 30 minutes)
1. Students get instructions and complete the UNIACT Interest Inventory at the computer (Module 3), or complete a paper and pencil interest inventory and enter the scores into *DISCOVER* Note: The following paper and pencil interest inventories are recommended.

Other inventories are named later in this chapter.

- Self Directed Search (SDS)
- Career Assessment Inventory (CAI)
- Strong Interest Inventory (SII)

2. Students complete the Abilities Inventory (5 to 15 minutes): In this exercise students rate themselves on fifteen abilities essential to career planning. Emphasize to students that it is important to be honest when evaluating personal skills and abilities.

3. Students complete the Values Inventory (15 to 30 minutes): Students respond to a variety of statements about their values as the values relate to career planning.

Module 4 (12 to 20 minutes): Finding Occupations A list of occupations is generated in Module 4 by using the self-assessments from Module 3 (UNIACT Interest Inventory). Counselor and students discuss the list of occupations. After discussion, students narrow the list of occupations. Educational and career goals need to be considered before the student makes a final career decision.

Module 5 (20 to 30 minutes): Learning About Occupations A search of approximately ten or fewer occupations identifying the following information for each is recommended.

- Work task
- Training/schooling needed
- Starting salary
- Related occupations
- Journals/organizations to write for more information
- Advantages and disadvantages
- Growth outlook

Each career field printout consists of approximately three to four pages of information relating to the selected occupations.

A postcounseling and profile interpretation session of test results must be conducted with each user or group of users. This session must be informative, candid, and genuine in nature. Any flat profile score (no clear pattern of interests) must be carefully explained, and completing a paper and pencil instrument and/or retaking the UNIACT should be recommended by the counselor. The SDS (Self-Directed Search) could be administered at this time (paper and pencil or computer version).

A second *DISCOVER* session should be scheduled, reemphasizing to the users the importance of answering questions honestly regarding what they like and dislike. In order for users to arrive at an appropriate career that fits with their personality traits, they must clearly understand the purpose and results of Modules 3, 4, and 5.

UNIACT provides focus to career exploration—not a focus that singles out the "right" occupation, but rather that points to families of occupations in the world of work that individuals may want to explore. In the process of exploration, they will discover things about themselves and where they may best fit into the world of work.

To facilitate career exploration. UNIACT pinpoints six basic types of vocational interests: (R) Realistic, (I) Investigative, (A) Artistic, (S) Social, (E) Enterprising, and (C) Conventional. These correspond to the six occupational interest types in Holland's (1985) theory of careers.

Profile Interpretation

Once the student has completed Modules 3, 4, and 5, a counseling session should be conducted with the student for the purpose of reviewing the *DISCOVER* results. This is to help the student identify personality type (SEA, SAE, and so on) and appropriate careers based on the tasks that the student would enjoy doing. The student should be given a computer printout of results from Modules 3, 4, and 5 and referred to academic advising for career planning and selecting an appropriate major.

Information and Guidelines for Counseling and for Profile Interpretation

- **Technical (Realistic − R): *DISCOVER* Things**

  Working with tools, instruments, and mechanical or electrical equipment. Activities include designing, building, repairing machinery, growing crops, and raising animals.

  Things (machines, tools, living things, materials such as food, wood, or metal). Things tasks are nonpersonal tasks such as producing, transporting, servicing, and repairing. Bricklayers, farmers, and machinists work mainly with things.

- **Science (Investigative − I): *DISCOVER* Ideas and Things**

  Investigating and attempting to understand phenomena in the natural sciences through reading, research, and discussion.

  Ideas (abstractions, theories, knowledge, insights, new ways of expressing something—for example, with words, equations, or music). Ideas tasks are interpersonal tasks, such as creating, discovering, interpreting, and synthesizing abstractions or implementing applications of abstractions. Scientists, musicians, and philosophers work mainly with ideas.

- **Arts (Artistic − A): *DISCOVER* Ideas and People**

  Expressing oneself through activities such as painting, designing, singing, dancing, and writing; artistic appreciation of such activities (listening to music, reading literature).

- **Social Service (Social − S): *DISCOVER* People**

  Helping, enlightening, or serving others through activities such as teaching, counseling, working in service-oriented organizations, engaging in social and political studies.

  People (no alternative terms). People tasks are interpersonal tasks such as caring for, educating, serving, entertaining, persuading, or leading others—in general, producing a change in human behavior. Teachers, salespersons, and speech pathologists work mainly with people.

- **Business Contact (Enterprising − E): *DISCOVER* Data and People**

  Persuading, influencing, directing, or motivating others through activities such as sales, supervision, and aspects of business management.

- **Business Operations (Conventional − C): *DISCOVER* Data and Things**

  Developing and/or maintaining accurate and orderly files, records, accounts, and so forth. Designing and/or following systematic procedures for performing business activities.

  Data (facts, records, files, numbers, systematic procedures). Data tasks are impersonal tasks that expedite goods and services consumption by people (by organizing or conveying facts, instructions, products, and so on).

Purchasing agents, accountants, and air traffic controllers work mainly with data.

A follow-up session needs to be scheduled to ensure that the student has made a decision.

CONCLUSION

DISCOVER is one of the most effective guidance tools available for working with and counseling undeclared college majors and career changers. Each module has a well-defined purpose for its users. Whether the student is only accessing information using Option A or seeking career direction from the guidance-plus approach of Option B, the information gained is precise and useful.

It is necessary to emphasize again the danger of a professional who has had limited training and exposure to *DISCOVER* and its usage. Misinformation and misuse only add to students' frustration and anxiety, and they will often not return to the career center for other services.

Thus, extensive knowledge and training in the use of *DISCOVER* is imperative for the delivery of effective career counseling. If a career resource center does not have a professional counselor that has been trained to use *DISCOVER*, the program should not be used. If the number of trained counselors is limited, appointments may be necessary to ensure that students work with a trained counselor to use *DISCOVER* for choosing or changing majors.

REFERENCES

DISCOVER: ACT Educational Technology Center, Executive Plaza 1, Suite 200, 11350 McCormick Road, Hunt Valley, MD. 21031 (800) 645-1992 or (410) 584-8000.

ACT's *DISCOVER* Action Guide, (1996). Hunt Valley, MD.: ACT Educational Technology Center.

Holland, J. L. (1985). Professional manual for the Self-Directed Search. Palo Alto, Calif.: Consulting Psychologists Press.

Prediger, D., Swaney, K., & Mau, W. (1993). Extending Holland's hexagon: Procedures, counseling applications, and research, *Journal of Counseling and Development,* 71, 422–428.

Swaney, K. (1995). *Technical manual: Revised Unisex Edition of the ACT Interest Inventory (UNIACT).* More information on how ACT Interest Inventory scales relate to World-of-Work Map regions. Iowa City, Iowa: ACT.

11

A Group Approach to Career Decision Making

K. RICHARD PYLE, PH.D.

INTRODUCTION

Groups have long been used to promote career development. Group approaches range from providing information (group guidance) to counseling (group counseling). Career development groups can be organized according to the degree that the approach is directive (information/didactic-oriented) or nondirective (feeling/affective-oriented). Depending on the need, both types are beneficial. For such needs as job trends and occupational specifics, the direct and didactic approach is more useful. For those who are struggling with a career choice or direction, a counseling, affective-oriented group is more appropriate. Career counseling involves both areas. Individuals need to get in touch with feelings and issues of identity while gaining in-

formation that will be of value in choosing a career or occupation. A career counselor needs all the skills of a group counselor along with the ability to personalize and process career information in such a way that the individual can effectively relate to and fully apply the information. Therefore, group career counseling has two major tasks—dealing with feelings and dealing with information.

A review of current literature regarding career counseling groups using computer-assisted guidance systems demonstrates that little research is being generated in this area. This became the impetus for the further development of this model.

This chapter describes both the skills needed and a model that counselors can use to deliver group career counseling. It is intended to act as a guide and is based upon more than twenty years of development and delivery.

K. Richard Pyle is director of School and Career Services, ACT, Inc.

THE PROCESS OF GROUP CAREER COUNSELING STAGES

As has been mentioned, the skills of the counselor involved in group career counseling are the same as those of a counselor in any group counseling. The exception is that additional skills are needed to help with the effective use of information. These skills are highlighted where they are most fully used within the group process. Each of the stages of the group process brings out certain skills that are important to moving on to the next stage.

The first stage is called the *Opening Stage,* when participants meet each other and the counselor and they learn the content of the group program. The second is the *Investigation Stage,* during which the members broaden their thinking about the possibilities that exist for them. The third is the *Working Stage,* in which participants process, synthesize, and make real for their lives the variety and amount of information that has been generated. The fourth is the *Decision/Operational Stage,* since it requires individuals to take actual steps and engage in activities aimed at gathering further information and integrating the information they already have to assist them with their career development. This stage is not an ending, however, because it is the stage that creates in individuals the need and drive to continue learning on their own. If counseling is to be effective, the individual should be involved in some behavioral goals beyond the life of the group.

GOALS

There are two types of goals stressed for each stage. The first is the achievement of *affective* goals. Group counseling, as we have discussed previously, is marked by feelings and the en-hancement of insight through interaction among the members of the group. It is critical that the members feel comfortable and trust both the leader and each other in order for self-disclosure and insight development to take place. Therefore, it is assumed that certain affective goals are necessary for each stage. It is further assumed that if each goal is met, then the next level of goals can be more easily achieved.

The second dimension is *cognitive,* or *information,* goals. As stated earlier, one of the major differences between group career counseling and group counseling is the need to help the client understand and personalize information related to the world of work. It is assumed that the client needs to acquire certain levels of information to help him/her make good decisions and correct misconceptions and myths. The use of appropriate counseling skills makes it possible for these goals to be realized. When well-timed and appropriate, these skills can help achieve the affective and cognitive goals. This is where an art form takes place within counseling. The challenge for the counselor is to weave in the skills that are relevant to interpersonal communication and group process. The cognitive/informational goals provided here are related to the high school, college, and adult career decision-making groups. This is particularly true for Stages 2 and 3. Modifications would be necessary for the elementary/middle school groups, job search support groups and the transitional groups. However, the affective goals remain the same for each of the groups.

Stage 1: Opening

Affective Goals During this stage the individual needs to feel at ease with the group and comfortable with the leadership of the counselor. The counselor needs to develop credibility, trust, anticipation and excitement about the learning opportunities, and a feeling of discovery and the potential for gaining insight into self.

Cognitive/Informational Goals The counselor strives during the first stage to impart certain information and knowledge, including first names of the group members, the rationale for the program, and the times and locations of the sessions.

Counselor Skills The skills the counselor uses during Stage 1 are the most critical to the group process. Being able to establish the tone for the group through the use of effective group counseling skills will make the difference between a successful and unsuccessful group. The skills that are most important to Stage 1 are described below.

A. Attending. The counselor attends in an open and clear manner with each member of the group. This is facilitated by having the group sit in a circle without any tables or other barriers in front of the members. The counselor's goal is to attend to the other, both physically and psychologically—to give himself entirely to being with the other, to work with the other. The counselor listens attentively to each individual, to both the verbal and the nonverbal messages. The counselor keeps asking: What is this person trying to communicate about feelings, about behavior? The attitude of the counselor is one of respect and concern. Attending carefully to another is work that demands a great amount of effort on the part of the counselor (Egan, 1975). How the counselor sits and the nature of his or her eye contact will make a difference in the attending process. If the counselor's body language suggests openness and in-

terest, the participants will more likely model this attending behavior.

B. Concreteness. The counselor clearly specifies the purpose and rationale for the group: how the group has helped others, what is required for success, and that the sessions are designed to increase career maturity and decision-making skills, not to provide magic answers. The times of the meetings and the importance of attendance are emphasized, since the group process is one that builds upon itself and maximizes learning only when everyone attends each session. A crucial part of the group process is assisting peers and providing feedback, and missing just one session can jeopardize both the process and the goals of the group.

C. Genuineness. The offer of assistance cannot be phony. The counselor is spontaneous and open and does not hide behind the counseling role. Above all, the counselor must be real and able to communicate his or her humanness, including humor.

Stage 2: Investigation

Affective Goals During Stage 2 individuals should be achieving a higher level of comfort with the group, including easier self-disclosure and ease with humor. That individuals are listening to one another rather than being preoccupied with what they are going to say next should be apparent to the counselor. Group attention is focused on other members instead of just the counselor.

Cognitive/Informational Goals In this stage the counselor is trying to develop a norm that emphasizes exploration of self and the world of work. Equally important is improving the participants' awareness and knowledge of careers.

An increase in occupational literacy is a very important cognitive goal of the second stage. This includes an overall understanding of the world of work and how it is organized. Accomplishing this is not an easy matter, since individuals often want to get to specific careers as quickly as possible. The cognitive/ informational goals are related to enhancing the participants' alternatives through helping them understand three specific areas of career development. The first area relates to how their general personality makeup (such as values, interests, and abilities) interacts with their career decision making. The second area is to help them see how specific careers relate to their self-assessment information. The third area for them to understand is how psychological barriers such as culturally imposed values and sex role stereotypes can inhibit alternatives and potentially good decisions.

Counselor Skills During the investigation stage the counselor continues to use all the skills of Stage 1. Additional skills are described below.

A. Facilitative Responses. The counselor employs a variety of responses to facilitate self-exploration. These include:

1. Reflection of feeling. As explained earlier, one of the important ways that group counseling differs from group guidance is that attention focuses on members' feelings and reactions as much as on their thoughts. The counselor responds in a way that demonstrates he or she has listened and understands how the individual feels and how it is being said. In some sense, the counselor must see the individual's world from the individual's frame of reference. And it is not enough to understand—the counselor must be able to communicate his or her understanding.

2. Clarifying/Paraphrasing/Summarizing. The counselor repeats information heard from the participants so they can hear it in another way and correct it if necessary.

3. Questioning. The counselor asks questions appropriate to the goals of the stage. These need to be open-ended questions, questions that force deeper thinking, such as "tell me more" or questions starting with "what," "how," or "why." These are the opposite of close-ended questions, which allow the individual to respond with a simple yes or no.

B. Self-Disclosure. The counselor is willing to share his or her own experience with the client *if* sharing will actually help the individual's self-understanding. The counselor is extremely careful, however, not to lay any burdens on the client.

C. Circling. The counselor poses a question or puts an issue before the group and solicits a response from each member in turn. This technique is especially helpful in a group where members are reluctant to respond or when one member tends to dominate the discussions. The counselor must carefully choose who goes first within the group process, since this individual will set the tone for the rest of the group.

D. Pairing/Linking. This is a particularly important skill for drawing the group together and helping members see similarities and commonalities. The counselor notices similar comments or self-disclosures from several participants and feeds this information back through pairing the names of the individuals with one another along with the content.

E. Personalizing. People have a tendency to speak in generalities or to attribute their feelings and thoughts to people in general. Group leaders should encourage members to speak in the first person when sharing reactions and experiences.

Stage 3: Working Stage

Affective Goals In Stage 3, group members should be fully relaxed and at ease with one another, be open and receptive to feedback, and be giving feedback in an appropriate manner. Attentiveness to each other, ability to listen in a nondefensive manner, commitment to exploration, and openness to alternatives should be accompanied by a sense of excitement and anticipation of discovery. Individuals should see more and more clearly the necessity for action. They might be fearful of change and even doubt that they have the resources necessary for change, but should be willing to face up to these challenges and push toward some real action steps beyond the life of the group. In addition, individual members should be seeing more clearly how the group and the other members can help develop a clearer picture of self and the world of work.

Cognitive/Informational Goals During the third stage the counselor helps the group members understand a large number of occupations that have potential for the future. This includes such aspects as the nature of the work, a typical day, what those presently involved in the career area like and don't like, salary information, job security, educational and training opportunities, future outlook, and where to go for more information. The participants should be aware of the pros and cons of each career area they are seriously considering. In addition, they should know something about the process and stages of career decision making, how this process can be used in the future as well as now, and whether they tend to be dependent, objective, or intu-

itive decision makers. Another important cognitive goal is helping the individual learn about career information sources other than those involved in the group career counseling process. This externally generated information can come from a library assignment, a computer-assisted guidance assignment, and testing.

Counselor Skills The counselor continues to use the skills of Stages 1 and 2, but the counseling skills that are most apparent during the third stage tend to be information generating and information processing. These additional skills are described below.

A. Accurate Empathy. The counselor demonstrates an understanding not only of what the group member says but also of what is implied, what is hinted at and what is communicated nonverbally. The counselor begins to make connections between seemingly isolated statements. The counselor must not create anything new, but puts together all of the pieces and signals for purposes of greater clarification and insight development.

B. Confrontation. The counselor challenges the discrepancies, distortions, stereotypes, and preconceived notions of the group members. This skill is particularly necessary to the discussion and clarification of occupational stereotypes.

C. Feedback Development. The counselor facilitates the exchange of feedback among group members to gain information that helps them understand themselves more fully. This skill is particularly important, since so much potential information is available from the group members.

D. Providing Experiential Information. The counselor should guide discussion and thinking with the group members' experiences rather than lectures. Tying and connecting the experiences to the information will help the learning process. For example, by using such stereotypical careers as nurse, doctor, social worker, accountant, pilot, funeral director, and so on, the counselor can help members understand how they each have stereotypes of certain occupations and can lead a discussion on the problems inherent in such limited perspectives. Where does the image come from? To what extent does the stereotype limit them? How powerful is self-concept in determining an occupation? The critical skill here is helping the group members arrive at certain understandings on their own rather than simply telling them what they should know.

E. Information Processing. In this age of information, one of the most important skills a counselor can possess is that of information processing. A number of years ago, IBM, in conjunction with Donald Super and his associates, developed the computer-assisted information system called Educational and Career Exploration (ECES). Field testing provided no significant student benefits. Carkhuff and Friel analyzed the results and concluded that the students did not know how to process the data. Under Friel's guidance later versions of ECES incorporated processing features and produced significant student benefits (Anthony, 1985). Several other studies have provided further support for the importance of the information processing component of computer-assisted guidance and information systems (Cassie, Ragsdale, & Robinson, 1979; Pyle & Stripling, 1976; Risser & Tully, 1977). What are the component skills of information processing? The first is to excite and motivate students to use the information at hand, which in turn helps them at-

tend to it. The second is to help them conceptualize and break down the information by asking them open-ended questions such as "Select five careers from your list of twenty-five that you might seriously consider and select two that you have no interest in whatsoever. Be prepared to discuss the reasons why you chose each one. What is it that makes you want to retain or discard the career area?" These probing questions develop a depth of introspection that is important to information processing. The third component is helping them take action on the information by motivating them to use the information appropriately. Examples of questions to use within the third component are: "What does this mean to you now? What do you need to do in order to act upon the information you now have?"

Stage 4: Decision/Operational Stage

Affective Goals   The final stage should be marked by energy and high morale regarding the possibilities that exist for the future. There should be a feeling of accomplishment and empowerment. A very close feeling should exist among the members of the group, with some sadness that the group process is drawing to a close. The feeling is one of enhanced understanding of self and the world of work and a confidence that one can use both the process learned and the information gained for future decision making. Most important, individuals should feel an interest and motivation to continue their career development activities with the realization that career development never stops, that it is an ongoing activity.

Cognitive/Informational Goals   By this time the group members have a great deal of information about self and careers and have learned to break the information down into manageable and understandable units. They understand what is meant by "learning how to learn" and how this concept can be applied to the future. A specific knowledge of their own strengths and skills should be in place. The next steps that they need to complete should be very explicit, with exact times and dates for implementation.

Counselor Skills The skills the counselor uses during the last stage, in addition to those of the first three stages, are described below.

A. Drawing Conclusions. The counselor helps the group members draw appropriate conclusions from their experience. This necessitates helping them look at what has been learned and how it can be applied to their lives.

B. Elaboration of Action Programs. The counselor helps each person determine concrete and specific tasks that need to be done in order to continue the learning process. These tasks could include (a) talking to someone who is working in a career area under consideration, (b) spending more time in the library researching a specific career, (c) changing a major, or (d) talking to a significant other about what was learned from the group program.

C. Bringing Closure. The counselor helps the members put in perspective what transpired during the life of the group and assists them in building a bridge from the group to their next steps. Assisting the group in processing their time together through a verbal or written evaluation is an approach that can facilitate closure.

D. Follow-up. The counselor needs to plan a session when the group meets to monitor progress and results. Particular problems may be worked through at this time.

A SCRIPT FOR A MODEL GROUP CAREER COUNSELING PROGRAM

To accomplish the goals and apply the skills previously described, counselors need various approaches and methods that they can use within the group process. The methods discussed here have been tested and refined over time and appear to be very helpful in achieving the goals, but they are not the only means. Most counselors have developed techniques to fit their own style. The critical variable is their creativity in using approaches that effectively achieve the goals of each stage.

Several approaches are described in order to reinforce the idea that no one set of techniques has to be used. The model is built around the four major stages of the group career counseling process. The techniques can be modified to fit the ages and developmental level of the participants. The program can be completed in three sessions of approximately 90 minutes each. The process involves out-of-group assignments for generating information. For counselors who are working in settings where one-hour sessions are more appropriate, the model can be modified to four to six sessions. The important aspect of this model is that it is designed to meet the goals of each of the four stages. The program was originally developed as a means of reinforcing the information generated by the System of Interactive Guidance and Information (SIGI) and *DISCOVER,* computer-assisted guidance programs. The model was enhanced through Project Learn, a grant provided by the W. K. Kellogg Foundation.

Session 1: Encounter
and Exploration Stages

Stage 1: Opening

1. Overview

A. Introduce the group program as a potentially useful tool for making educational and occupational plans.

B. Share program goals.

C. Establish group rules for group participation.

   1. Clarify meeting times and locations.
   2. Emphasize importance of attendance.
   3. Explain confidentiality.
   4. Share agenda or objectives for the first session.

2. Introductions

Activity. Have each person introduce self to the group by sharing first name, year in school, major(s), where from, and career fantasy when in the fifth or sixth grade. Ask each person to restate the name of preceding participants before introducing self.

Expectations

A. Task: Ask participants what they hope to gain from participation in the program.

B. Relate participants' expectations to program goals and session objectives to indicate how they might use the group activities to meet their expectation.

Stage 2: Investigation

1. Self-Assessment

A. Values

Activity: "Million Dollar Exercise". Ask participants to write down how they would spend a million dollars if they had just received it with no strings attached. Share information and relate to values (independence, security, leisure time, leadership, high income, and so on). Then ask them to describe the type of work they would pursue if money were not a problem.

Counselor Processing Suggestions. The millionaire story provides a number of opportunities for the counselor to build group cohesiveness and understanding. For example, many times group members of all ages will comment that they would purchase a new car. At this point the counselor might say "Knowing what we know about _____, what type of car do you think he/she would look good in?" This simple question always creates interest and excitement within the group. The focus of the sharing becomes more personal and is directed away from the counselor. The responses have certain elements of feedback contained within them. Such a lead by the counselor is an example of how to personalize the information being shared. A comment by the counselor that has been found to be of value in processing the activity after everyone has finished sharing is, "Why do you think I asked you to enter into such an activity as the millionaire exercise?" Group members often come up with such statements as, "You wanted to see what our priorities are" or sometimes even "what our values are." If the group members can come up with the word "values," it is better than the counselor imposing it on them. This helps keep the group counseling format from regressing into a group guidance session or classroom lecture. Another piece of learning that can be drawn out of this exercise is to ask members to identify the values that the group has in common and those that are different. This helps them conceptualize and visualize the values from an experiential base. The counselor can also ask group members if they can think of any careers that would help them actualize the values that have been mentioned. This is a good time to help them look at the word "entrepreneur," since many of their values will be related to independence. Also, it has been found helpful to point out the importance of giving ourselves permission occasionally to dream without being inhibited or restricted by money. Such a statement also gives the counselor the opportunity to begin emphasizing the value of exploration and creativity as a norm within the group. A final comment by the counselor can be, "Now that we have some idea of how you might lead your life if money were not a problem, let's think of ways you can do these things and make money at the same time."

B. Interests

Activity: "Past Experiences". Have the group members think back to the variety of work-related positions they have had over their lifetimes. These positions can be voluntary as well as paid—for example, candy striper at a hospital, Boy Scout leader, Sunday school teacher, and so forth. Everything should be listed—baby-sitting, mowing yards, working at McDonald's, and regular full-time salaried positions.

After job lists are completed, have participants put a plus sign (+) by each position that was a positive experience, a minus sign (−) by each that was negative, and a zero (0) by those that were neutral.

After participants complete their rankings, have them circle the position that was most positive and draw a line through the one that was most negative. Have the group share their responses.

Counselor Processing Suggestions In order to personalize and provide feedback to this process, have each person simply read their list without saying what was most positive or negative. Then say to the group, "Now that we know _____, let's guess which of the work experiences _____ has been involved in was the most positive and which was the most negative." Such a comment by the counselor and subsequent guessing by the group members helps the group members to fully attend to one another and shifts the focus from the counselor to the group members. The guessing has some form of feedback, since participants often say such things as, "What is there about me that makes you think I liked baby-sitting?"

As individuals respond to most-liked and least-liked activities, it is important for the counselor to ask, "What is there about that activity that caused you to like it?" (or "not like it?") This helps the group members formulate statements related to their interests and abilities. At the end of the session the counselor can use the same technique as was used in the millionaire activity by asking, "Why did we do this exercise? How does it relate to career development?" The group members arrive at conclusions related to interests and abilities without the counselor having to initiate them. After the participants have pinpointed such areas as working with people, data, things, and ideas, the counselor can assist the participants in conceptualizing interests into these four areas. At this point group members might be asked to rank their interests along these four dimensions. The same can be done with their abilities. What skills do they have based upon their experiences? The counselor's task here is to prevent the group members from putting themselves down, since most of us have a tendency to negate our abilities.

2. Decision-Making Stages

Activity. Ask the group members to think about the stages they go through when they make a decision. Use an example of a decision either you or one of the group members recently made. Break the decision down into the steps that led to making the decision. For example, this author often uses the illustration of purchasing a pair of cowboy boots. The first step was to walk into a boot shop and be surrounded by boots. What is the first thing that one does in such a setting? *Explore.* One looks around and begins to check out boots by size, color, shape, and so on. What happens next? One begins to narrow down possibilities. This is called *synthesis* or *crystallization*. At this point one has four or five pairs of boots. What happens next? A *tentative choice* is made and a pair of boots is tried on. At this point what happens? Usually one stands up and checks to see how the boots feel and look. What is this called? *Clarification.*

Counselor Processing Suggestions. This activity is designed to help the participants understand the steps involved in career decision making. After the activity the counselor asks, "What does this activity have to do with career decision making?" Group members begin to draw connections between this process and choosing a career. The next question the counselor asks is, "Which of these stages do you think is most important to making a good career choice and, interestingly, is also the stage people seem to do the poorest job with when choosing a career?" Group members almost always indicate "explo-

ration." The counselor asks, "Why?" A variety of responses come forth, from not knowing how to explore effectively to being in a hurry and rushing to judgment without adequate information. The counselor asks if these four stages are linear or circular, explaining that circular means that one is always going through the process to varying degrees. At this point the counselor asks, "Which stage do we want to be sure to do well in order to help with a good decision?" The members will come up with "exploration" again. By going through this process, the counselor is trying to motivate the group members not to be in a rush to narrow down and come up with the magic answer, but to slow down and attend to generating information before they begin to narrow down. The counselor reinforces the need to leave no stone unturned in the exploration process. By so doing, the chances are increased that a good decision in the proper direction can be achieved.

At this point the reader might ask why so much emphasis is placed on such a simple concept. It has been this author's experience that individuals of all ages, 15 and up, tend to have difficulty doing the research and exploration necessary for career decision making. It is not unusual for people to put more effort and energy into choosing the right shoes, car, or house than they put into the choice of the career.

Closure to Session 1 and Homework Task to Generate Information At the end of the first session the counselor needs to draw appropriate closure by saying such things as, "We are off to a good start, and I have enjoyed working with you." "What was one thing you learned during this first session?" "What did you enjoy about today's session?" At this point negatives are not to be encouraged, since it is important to keep the morale high and the group open to possibilities. The tendency to critique is very much a part of all of us. Once it starts it can dampen the group's enthusiasm. It is important to withhold negative judgment until the group process is completed.

Some type of homework activity should take place between the first and second sessions. This activity should focus on the development and generation of occupations based upon values, interests, and abilities. This can take the form of (a) career library research, using such tools as a keysort, a card deck, or books that discuss occupations by their values, interests, and abilities; (b) computer-assisted guidance and information systems with assignments to specific sections; and (c) tests or self-assessment inventories (paper and pencil activities). Group members should be told very clearly that it is important for them to bring the generated information to their next session.

Session 2: Working Stage

1. Opening
A. Review names.

Activity. Ask participants which of them can name the other members of the group. Have two or three people state everyone's names.

B. Share agenda or objectives for the session.

2. Review Homework Assignment

Activity. Ask participants open-ended questions regarding the information generated from their homework assignment. Solicit reactions and discuss in general terms.

Counselor Processing Suggestions. This is the point at which the counselor begins to assist the group in making sense of the information they have generated. Questions that might be used during this

time are: What were your highest and lowest values? What were your top two interests? abilities? To what extent were your values, interests, and abilities consistent with what we discussed at our last meeting? What surprises came up? Why did that surprise you? (Note: These questions will be most pertinent for individuals going through a self-assessment homework exercise that evaluates their values, interests, and abilities, as with computer-assisted guidance programs.)

3. Review Career Possibilities

Activity. Ask participants to select five career areas that they would seriously consider and two that they don't want to have anything to do with. Have them jot these down for discussion purposes.

Counseling Processing Suggestions. As individuals share their top five careers, involve the other group members in the process by asking, "Which of those surprise you, based on what you know about _____?" or "How do those career areas fit _____'s personality?" Also ask, "What do the top five have in common?" Involve the group in helping to answer this question. Specifically, probe for the reasons they don't want to have anything to do with the two occupations they threw out. Listen carefully for prejudices or stereotypes. This will lead to the next activity.

4. Sex Role Stereotyping and Career Prejudices

Activity. Ask the participants, "Why do you think I drilled you so hard on what it was you didn't like?" Have several of them respond to this question. Bring out the fact that we all have certain perceptions of careers. Ask them to describe what type of person comes to mind when you indicate a specific career area. Ask them to go through a word association process. Mention such careers as nurse, teacher, doctor, pilot, funeral director, and so on. Use any career area that often has stereotypes operating.

Counselor Processing Suggestions. Ask the group if they know anyone that does not fit a stereotype mentioned during the word association. Ask them why they did this exercise. What dangers to each of them are there in stereotypes and occupational prejudices? How do stereotypes limit them and the exploration process? Mention that the next set of homework exercises is to read about and gain information on all the occupations to which they might give some thought. Warn them to be careful not to limit themselves because of stereotypes as they go through the research process.

5. Occupational Enhancement (Cool Seat)

Activity. Ask the group how many occupations there are in the world. After getting some responses, explain that there are over 20,000 occupations in the *Dictionary of Occupational Titles.* Great bedtime reading! (Note: You may want to mention some unusual occupations, such as "Egg Sexer," to add some humor to the discussion.) Mention that the group has just begun to touch the surface of occupations and that most of us are occupational illiterates. We would be hard pressed to name more than forty occupations. Tell them that possibilities should be enhanced before the process of crystallizing thinking begins. Indicate that from the occupational word association activity certain personality characteristics are often related to occupations and that everyone has an "occupational look." Then say, "In order to take full advantage of the fact that we are in a group, we are going to ask each of you to be in the cool seat, which is an empty seat

in the circle. When you are in the cool seat, all you have to do is listen to what others are saying. No response is necessary. After we are finished you can respond. We are going to bombard the person in the cool seat with occupations that come to mind for them based upon what we have learned about them." Have each person take turns sitting in the cool seat and being bombarded with occupations from the group. Take about three to five minutes per person.

Counselor Processing Suggestions. During this exercise it is advised that the counselor act strictly as the facilitator and not enter into the brainstorming of occupations. The reason for this is the power and weight that individuals give to the so-called expert. The counselor asks the group to really stretch themselves and come up with any occupation at all. Use the rules of brainstorming by saying that the goal is to get out as many suggestions as possible in the shortest period of time and that no occupation is too ridiculous or out of order. After the bombardment is over, ask the individual in the cool seat to describe his/her response to the careers mentioned by the group. This is another form of feedback, and the attention, interest, and energy of the group will be quite high during this activity. (Note: It may be of help to provide the group before the bombardment with lists of occupations to stimulate their thinking.) Indicate that how we perceive others' perception of us has a lot to say about identity. Consequently, they may want to look into careers that were mentioned.

6. Summary and Closure

The sequence of exercises mentioned here will take about an hour and a half and could, if necessary, be modified to fit one-hour formats. The counselor draws closure in the same manner as with the first session. The major difference is that the homework assignment changes; it is the task of the group at this time to gather as much specific information as possible on any career area they are considering. Specific reference books and the career library can be used along with computer-assisted guidance and information resources. The counselor may want to include research on educational and training resources as well as career information during this time.

Session 3: Working and Decision/Operational Stages

1. Opening

A. Review participants' names again by using the same procedure as in the beginning of Session 2.

B. Go over the objectives for this session by emphasizing that this is the session in which participants are really going to get into a synthesis and begin to generate some realistic and positive directions.

2. Processing of Information from Homework

Activity. Ask the group how many occupations they were able to fully research. What were some of the questions they asked? What information did they find that was particularly interesting and unusual?

Counselor Processing Suggestions. Use questions and a process very similar to the beginning of Session 2. It is important to help participants place the information in perspective and to review it with the group.

3. Decision-Making Styles

Activity. Mention that as a part of this session some tentative decisions will be made. In order

to do this effectively, it may help participants to know something about their approach to decision making. Mention that there are three styles of decision makers. Ask participants to think of a major decision they have made recently and to jot it down. Share with the group. Now ask them what influenced their decisions. What role did significant others play? What information helped them to make the decision? To what extent did they do what their intuition told them to do? Now share the three styles of decision making: dependent (others make the decision), objective (use of external information such as tests, employment trends, and so on, as major criteria for decision making) and intuitive (gather all the information and make the decision based upon what one feels). Ask them where the decision they jotted down would fall. To what extent did they make the decision and take responsibility for it?

Counselor Processing Suggestions. In this activity the counselor tries to assist group members to understand that their approach to decision making can make a difference in their satisfaction with a particular decision. The open-ended questions suggested above should be embellished to help group members arrive at an understanding of the concept of decision-making style. In order to make effective use of the group, the counselor could ask group members to share their decision-making process, then ask others, "Which style of decision making did you hear coming through?" "What makes you think so?" Again, the counselor is trying to draw the members out and help them get in touch with their approach to decision making. People usually find that they use all three styles at various times. In this instance the counselor is trying to help the group see that when it comes to important decisions it may appear easier either to let others make the decision or to base the decision on some external piece of information rather than to accept ownership for it. Ownership means facing the possibility of failure, and that is difficult for many. It is also helpful during this activity to point out the myth that a career decision happens only once and that a person is stuck with it. Point out that the average person will change careers four to six times in a lifetime.

4. Career Matrix

Activity. This is an approach that helps the participants determine the extent to which an occupation under consideration fits their values and interests. Along the left side of a sheet of paper (going down), have participants list the values and interests that are important to them. For each item listed, a value weight should be assigned (1 is low, 10 is high) to show the relative importance of those items to them. Across the top of the paper at least four occupations under serious consideration should be listed. Then for each occupation they will place a checkmark next to each value/interest item that the occupation would satisfy. By adding up the weights of the items checked for each occupation, they will obtain numbers that indicate the relative satisfaction they might hope to achieve from each occupation. For greater precision, numbers rather than checkmarks can be entered whenever a value/interest item fits an occupation. This "occupation weight" should indicate the extent to which the occupation satisfies the particular item (1 is low, 10 is high). By multiplying the item weight and the occupational weight, then totaling these for each occupation, participants again obtain numbers that reflect the relative satisfaction they might hope to achieve from each occupation. Usually a differ-

ential of ten points or more indicates some significance for one occupation over another.

Counselor Processing Suggestions. Participants should be asked to share their results and reflect upon the significance the results have for them and their decision making. Refer back to how this activity fits into the "decision-making styles" exercise. Group members should see that this is an objective approach that should be taken into consideration but should not be the only factor in their decision making. What is advocated here is an intuitive approach to decision making, but with strong consideration given to what others see and to what objective information is available. As a final step, ask each person to name the occupational area that he or she would go into if forced to make a decision today.

5. Strength Bombardment

Activity. Each group member takes a turn in the cool seat and listens while the others make positive comments on the strengths they have observed about that person.

Counselor Processing Suggestions. This exercise is designed to come at the end of the time together in order to provide participants with a greater sense of the strengths they can use as they move away from the group and initiate their decision making. It is meant to empower each person and to leave a positive feeling regarding the group experience. It is also designed to come immediately before the "next step" exercise in order to enhance the potential for follow-through. It is always a very positive and powerful experience. The counselor introduces it by saying, "In our culture we are very used to critiquing and looking at the negative side of ourselves and others. For a few minutes we are going to focus only on the positives and strengths that we have observed in the individuals in the group. As we leave the group, we will want to be able to think back on these strengths because career decision making can sometimes be a very lonely and frustrating experience. We will want to remember the strengths that people see in us and to keep them in mind when we run into difficulties and frustrations." The counselor stimulates group members to think of positive qualities and facilitates the comments by embellishing them as appropriate. After two to three minutes and after the individual has had a chance to react to the comments, another person should be invited to sit in the cool seat.

6. Next Step

Activity. Ask participants to write down what they consider to be some next steps to take based upon where they are in the career decision-making process. Provide examples of what they might do. For example, they could go to the dean's office and change their major, visit with someone who is working in a career field of interest, conduct further research into a particular career field by using the career library, spend some time with a counselor to further process their thinking, and so forth. After they have written these down, they should select the one they want to implement first. After they have selected it, they are to write down when they will do it, including actual date and time. For example, "I will go to the dean's office this coming Tuesday at 2:00 P.M. to complete the necessary forms for changing my major from computer science to English." Have the group share their responses.

Counselor Processing Suggestions. The most important element of this sequence is that the counselor stress the importance of stating in specific terms what the next step is going to be. By so doing the participants are stating a verbal contract that is more likely to be completed since it is stated publicly. After hearing the next steps, it is not unusual for group members to indicate that they will be checking up on one another. This should be encouraged. The counselor should emphasize the importance of the next steps and that completion of the group process does not mean that the career decision-making process has been accomplished.

7. Closure and Evaluation

Activity. The counselor summarizes briefly what has happened and evaluates the experience. For example, "We have looked at a lot of information about ourselves and the world of work and tried to understand it in terms of a career direction. I appreciate the hard work you have put into the process and hope it pays dividends for you and your future. I've enjoyed working with each one of you. Every time I lead one of these groups I learn something new and thoroughly enjoy the process. I wish each of you the best and I hope you will call on me if I can be of any further assistance." An evaluation should take place at this time. This can be a verbal or written response to these three questions: What did you learn and find helpful? What would you suggest for improvement of the program? What are any general comments you have about the program?

Counselor Processing Suggestions. This final activity is designed to help the participants put their experience into perspective and to serve as a learning opportunity for the future. Counselor comments should be upbeat and encouraging about the future in order to enhance the likelihood that group members will follow through with their next steps.

REFERENCES

Anthony, W. A. (1985). Human and information resource development in the age of information: A dialogue with Robert Carkhuff, *Journal of Counseling and Development,* 63, 372–376.

Cassie, J. R. B., Ragsdale, R. G., & Robinson, M. A. (1979). *Comparative analysis of choices and S.G.I.S.* (ERIC Document Reproduction Service No. ED 180 132). Toronto, Canada: Ontario Department of Education.

Egan, G. (1975). The skilled helper: A model of systematic helping and interpersonal relating. Monterey, Calif.: Brooks/Cole.

Pyle, K. R., & Stripling, R. O. (1976). The counselor, the computer, and career development, *Vocational Guidance Quarterly,* 25, 71–75.

Risser, J., & Tully, J. (1977). SIGI project research summary report. Pasadena, Calif.: Pasadena City College.

12

The Genogram Technique

A Therapeutic Tool for the Career Counselor

NELL PENICK, PH.D.

INTRODUCTION

This chapter provides a brief rationale for using the genogram in career counseling and a description of how to create a genogram. It also covers how to use a genogram in career counseling and offers case examples demonstrating the process. The genogram, a graphic display representing a three-generation family tree, documents the family system visually. A standard tool in the field of marriage and family therapy, the genogram maps family structure, patterns, and events. It facilitates joining, assessment, and intervention (Bowen, 1980; Guerin and Pendagast, 1976; McGoldrick & Gerson, 1985) and improves counselors' familiarity and

recall of clients and their relational issues (Figures 1 through 3). Career counselors will find the genogram technique easy and intriguing to use (Okiishi, 1987). At first it may seem deceptively simple, even simplistic, but it can lead to depth and precision in addressing career development issues.

Research and theory both provide support for examining family influences on career development. Research on the influence of the family on career development has focused primarily on influences as socioeconomic status, birth order, sex, temperament, parental support, parenting style, and modeling (Penick, 1990). In most theories and conceptualizations of career development, family influence was acknowledged as a self-evident truth (Blau & Duncan, 1967; Brill, 1949; Bordin, Nachmann, & Segal, 1963; Crites, 1962; Ginzburg, 1952,

---

Nell Penick is a psychologist in private practice in Raleigh, North Carolina. She has done extensive research in career development and continues career counseling as part of her private practice.

1972; Holland, 1959, 1973; Osipow, 1969; Roe, 1957; Super, Starishevsky, Jordaan, & Matlin, 1963). Super et al. (1963) emphasize that the family plays a major role and provides a context for the development of vocational self-concept. They further describe career exploration as asking questions about self and future and realistically assessing self and situation. Later, Super (1984) describes the family as the most immediate external determinant of adolescent career development.

More recent conceptualizations of career development have incorporated family systems and human development theories (Brachter, 1982; Herr & Lear, 1984; Lopez & Andrews, 1987; Vondracek, Lerner, & Schulenberg, 1986; Zingaro, 1983). Advocates of these career counseling approaches emphasize treating whole persons in their relational contexts (Brown & Crace, 1996; Carlsen, 1988; Cochran, 1987; Manuele-Adkins, 1992; Savickas, 1991, 1995; Super, 1951, 1957; Super, Starishevsky, Matlin, & Jordaan, 1963; Vondracek, Lerner, & Schulenberg, 1986), rather than viewing career counseling as simply giving advice, providing information, or helping a person make one critical decision. Vondracek et al. (1986), in their ecological theory of career development, describe the family's relation to the developing individual as the most important relation of several major relational contexts, including school, workplace, church, and peer group. In their systemic perspective, influence between the individual and the context is reciprocal. This reciprocity of influence is, perhaps, the single most important characteristic of the systemic perspective, because it allows for the consideration of how ongoing interaction of individuals with their context results in change or stability. Thus, the career counselor will find clues to salient interventions in the identification and understanding of clients' family relationships and related reciprocal interactions.

Family Systems Theory

In family systems theory, the family is defined as a unique social system through which has evolved a set of rules, myths, roles, a power structure, and forms of communication, negotiation, and problem solving for effective task performance (Goldenberg & Goldenberg, 1980). Family rules evolve more from interaction than from open negotiation and are often outside the awareness of family members. Rules and myths influence the establishment and maintenance of beliefs, values, and roles for family members, which, in turn, are influential in the development and establishment of family traditions (Brachter, 1982). Many rules and myths are derived from the parents' families of origin. The passing on of these unique family patterns is called the multigenerational transmission process (Bowen, 1976, 1978; Borzomenyi-Nagy & Spark, 1983). Change and stability in the family system are monitored in the family by negative and positive feedback systems. In the case of negative feedback, when a family member changes too much, uncomfortable and threatened family members will respond with negative feedback, signaling the changed member to change back.

Family patterns, rules, and myths may impede career development by interfering with differentiation. Level of differentiation refers to the degree to which individuals are able to separate thinking from emotion. Inability to distinguish between emotion and thinking is associated with higher levels of anxiety (Bowen, 1978). A somewhat similar term, individuation, from psychoanalytic theory, means psychological separation from parents and is believed to precede identity development (Blos, 1979; Dashef, 1984; Erikson, 1959; Polster, 1983). Individuation and identity development usually precede career development (Bordin & Kopplin, 1973; Luckey, 1974; Salomone, 1982; Salomone & McKenna, 1983; Super, 1957). Achievement of an optimal level of differentiation and individuation allows adolescents to master career development tasks. These include: (a) addressing important questions about self in school and work, such as, Who am I? What are my characteristics, values, needs, abilities, and interests and how do they relate to possible career choices? What kind of future do I want for myself? What constraints and opportunities does my situation hold? (b) assuming responsibility for gathering and using predecision information; and (c) arriving at a reasoned independent judgment (Lopez & Andrews, 1987).

One crucial family rule boundary concerns who will interact with whom, how they will do so, and how the interaction will be understood (Simon, Stierlin, & Wynne, 1985). Boundaries determine critical family characteristics (Beavers, 1977; Bowen, 1978; Minuchin, 1974). External boundaries are determined by the difference between the way family members interact with each other and with nonmembers (Simon et al., 1985). External boundaries protect the uniqueness and separateness of the family from the outside world. Internal boundaries differentiate structures within the family, such as parental, sibling, and individual subsystems (Minuchin, 1974). Rigid external boundaries and too permeable internal boundaries lead to enmeshment. Too permeable external boundaries and too rigid internal boundaries lead to disengagement. Enmeshment and disengagement are located at opposite poles of the dependence/independence continuum and have been linked to dysfunction in families (Beavers, 1977;

Bowen, 1978; Minuchin, 1974; Olson, Sprenkle, & Russell, 1979).

Disengaged families are distant emotionally, limit sharing of information, limit interdependence, and view the world outside the family as the main source of satisfaction in life (Beavers, 1977). Enmeshed families are warm and too emotionally close. Their rules require them to think and act alike, and they view the family as the main source of satisfaction in life. Members from disengaged and enmeshed families are likely to be undifferentiated (Bowen, 1978). Persons from enmeshed families may have difficulty mastering career development tasks because they are unable to distinguish their own goals and expectations from those of their parents. They may be unable to acknowledge their own unique qualities because family rules require them to think and act like the family. Persons from disengaged families are already separated from the family by lack of important emotional connections to the family. Unless they develop a significant relationship with someone outside the family, they must define themselves in an interpersonal vacuum. They may have difficulty demarcating their internal worlds, because they have limited interpersonal interaction within their own families. They may have difficulty orienting themselves to the tasks of career development because they lack familial support and a sense of belonging. These limits on self-knowledge and task orientation can interfere with the achievement of career development tasks, such as answering the above-mentioned important questions about self in relation to school and work.

In family systems theory, enmeshment or disengagement results in lack of differentiation and higher levels of anxiety. In linking family systems and individual perspectives, enmeshment or disengagement interferes with individuation and identity development. Thus, career counselors might use the family systems notion of enmeshment and disengagement (as well as rules, roles, power structure, and myths) and associated interventions—among them, the genogram—to enhance their ability to address the whole person.

A MODEL FOR CAREER COUNSELING USING THE GENOGRAM TECHNIQUE

Descriptions of the genogram technique in career counseling appear in several publications (Brown & Brooks, 1991; Dagley, 1984; Gysbers & Moore, 1987; Okiishi, 1987). The authors describe the career genogram as a structured assessment and exploration device. With information gathered from the client, the career counselor draws a genogram on large newsprint for the client to see. The genogram records the client's family members and their occupations across three generations. A complete three-generation genogram is laid out in five rows. The five rows, beginning at the top, represent (1) grandparents, (2) mother, father, aunts and uncles, (3) cousins, (4) parents, and (5) siblings. Extended family members in remarried families can be included—for example, stepgrandparents, stepparents, stepbrothers, and stepsisters—to optimize options for exploration. Figure 12.1 illustrates a selection of frequently used genogram symbols and their meanings.

It is necessary to explain to the client what a genogram is and that one is going to be developed of the client's family. This structured approach follows most descriptions of the genogram technique, which suggest that counselors begin by seeking factual information regarding the dates of births, deaths, marriages, separations, divorces, and illnesses as well as the occu-

pations, education, migrations, and current location of family members. The career counselor can begin by asking whether the client has brothers and sisters and, if so, which sibling position the client holds. The counselor can follow up by asking whether the client's parents are still alive and still married. The next step is to ask what the parents, brothers, and sisters do for a living. The counselor continues to guide the conversation in an effort to identify family factors that may contribute to understanding the client's career dilemma. Brown and Brooks (1991) summarize twelve topics to guide the career counselor's genogram interview:

1. What roles did each family member model?
2. For what behaviors and attitudes were males and females reinforced?
3. For what behaviors were males and females punished?
4. Were other role models besides family members important?
5. What were the important values in the family?
6. Do the client's values fit with family values?
7. Are certain career missions valued (for example, teaching, or business)?
8. Are there generational myths or misperceptions about careers?
9. How does the family address work, family and leisure, and family interrelationships?
10. Have certain boundaries been established that limit career mobility?
11. What are the career patterns that emerge as one looks at the family structure?
12. Do family members try to realize unfulfilled goals, aspirations, and fantasies vicariously through their children? (Brown and Brooks, 1991, 128, 131).

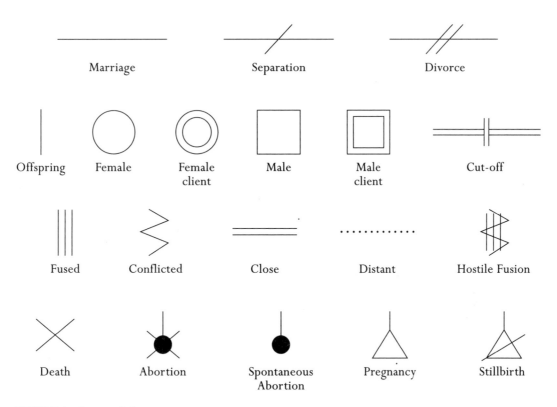

FIGURE 12.1   Genogram Codes

Brown and Brooks (1991) also offer a form designed to gather genogram information that can be used in group settings.

The counselor's knowledge of family influence on development, self-perceptions, attitudes, and views of the world coupled with specific knowledge gained about the child point to potentially relevant areas for exploration and intervention. But gathering this information can result in information overload. How does one do a genogram interview from a systemic perspective, taking into consideration family emotional process and how it may impact career development and indecision? How does the counselor avoid being bogged down in superficial and irrelevant detail? Kuehl (1995) points out that charting three generations is not always

considered necessary. Instead, the focus may be on the present and current family memberships, key events, problematic triangulations, and interactional patterns within one or two generations *as they relate to the career dilemma*. Besides, trying to gather too much factual information during the early stages of brief counseling can interfere with joining, and the client may either feel interrogated (Tomm, 1988) or fail to see the connection with the presenting problem.

If the client is tense, the counselor may begin by simply asking whether the client has brothers and sisters. This question can serve as a joining maneuver early in the first session, as clients often brighten up and relax when talking about their brothers and sisters and their feelings toward the siblings. (It's sometimes easier to talk

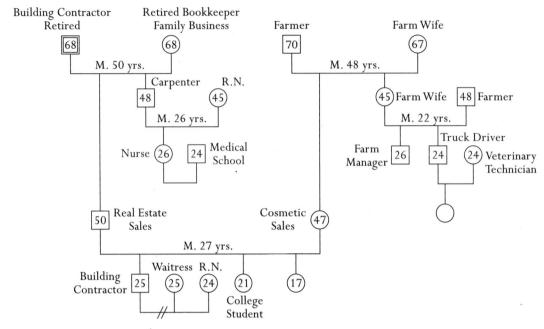

FIGURE 12.2   Five-line Genogram[1]
[1]Genograms made with MacGenogram program (Gerson, 1994)

about someone other then oneself. Most often, however, one can begin by asking what brings the client in. Once the presenting problem is identified, the search begins for an opportune transition to exploring how family members are connected to, affect, or respond to the client's presenting problem. When relevance is established, the counselor can ask about family members' positions, careers, and attitudes toward the client's career issue. This is basically a constructivist approach to counseling.

Savickas (1995) has noted that the constructivist approach fits with recent models of career counseling that address the subjective experience of career development. He points out that constructivism views knowledge as socially produced and legitimized through use. In a constructivist approach, the counselor and client collaborate to blend both their ideas to create

new meaning. At the start of counseling, the counselor leads by following, beginning where the client begins. The counselor seeks to uncover the client's stories and the relevant theme(s) related to the career issue. Clients often describe how they feel oppressed by family-of-origin issues, offering an opportunity for the counselor to begin the genogram (Kuehl, 1995). If this doesn't occur, the counselor may need to find opportunities to connect the presenting problem to family-of-origin issues. The counselor's effort to connect the career problem to family relationships and interaction through client stories and the genogram technique facilitates the ongoing process of joining by conveying respect for client perceptions and acknowledging client autonomy and self-expertise (Kuehl, 1995). Usually, clients feel heard and understood quickly when the counselor connects them to their relational context by learning about the position they hold in their family of origin.

Gathering the genogram information provides the counselor with the opportunity to reframe, detoxify, and normalize clients' perceptions of themselves and their family. It facilitates the development of alternative interpretations and opens up new possibilities for the future (Kuehl, 1995). The counselor may also educate clients about problematic triangles and transactions. Conflict between members of the family of origin, especially parents, often results in dysfunctional triangles that interfere with differentiation, individualization, identity development, and career development. Identifying problematic triangles can lead to interventions that free the client for development.

Eliciting themes related to the career issue contributes to a purposeful and efficient process. Clients stories and plots that relate to the presenting problem may reveal salient themes (Savickas, 1995; Papp & Imber-Black, 1996). Savickas looks for stories about family and heroes and heroines and listens for trouble, imbalance, or deviation in an effort to identify a preoccupation or thematic problem. He says that these identity stories explain how clients plot a future for themselves in order to address the preoccupation. Savickas (1995) provides a list of prompts for the counselor to use to help clients see their career indecision as a purposeful pause:

1. Under what circumstances was your indecision recognized?

2. How does it feel to be undecided?

3. What does this feeling remind you of?

4. Tell me about another situation in which you have had this same feeling.

5. Do you have any idea about what haunts you?

6. What part of your life story is most important to your current indecision? (Savickas, 1995, 368).

Papp and Imber-Black (1996) describe a method of using family themes to facilitate change. They propose constructing a genogram until a major theme becomes evident, then tracing the theme intergenerationally. The theme should be used to identify and suggest a task or ritual that will alter the theme. They offer a set of guidelines for the therapist to follow in this process (Papp & Imber-Black, 1996, 18–19):

1. What are some of the beliefs or attitudes held by family members that have an impact on the presenting problem?

2. What is the daily interactional pattern that takes place in response to these beliefs, and what is the central theme that emerges from this pattern?

3. Using the genogram, ask theme-oriented questions and look for repetitions of the theme intergenerationally.

4. Observe how the theme is carried out in contexts outside the family.

5. Design a set of questions that alter or challenge the theme.

6. Think about possible interventions to address the theme.

Case Example: Susan

The genogram in Figure 12.3 represents work with a client, Susan, age 26, who came in initially complaining about morale in her workplace.

The genogram depicts three households. Susan, an only child, continued to live with her father through college and still lived with him. Her mother had divorced her father when Susan was eighteen and later remarried a divorced man with three children.

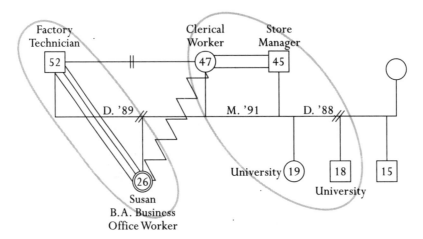

FIGURE 12.3   Sample Genogram, Susan

The initial intake revealed that the client held a low-level clerical position despite her college degree in business administration. Susan said she did not feel in control of her life. She did what clients often do, offering the theme right up front. When asked what other times in her life she had felt a lack of control, she said that she felt that way when her parents separated when she was 18. On further questioning, a potential interpretation emerged of an ongoing triangulation in the parental dyad of this adult child. Susan admitted she had felt compelled to take care of her father when her mother left the home, and she has continued do to so. Susan's caring response to her father's loneliness was noted. Later her mother married a man with other children who, in Susan's eyes, became a major focus of her mother's attention. Susan reported feeling bored with conversations with her mother in which her mother discussed her new stepchildren. Further, Susan reported that she and her father do not talk much. She described herself as more like her dad, preferring to keep things to herself. Susan was feeling stuck and was considering changing careers or moving to a different state where job opportunities might be better. Here was a young woman who at 26 had not yet left home, but was considering a drastic and precipitous change.

Susan took the Strong Interest Inventory (Hansen and Campbell, 1985) and scored a very high interest in social occupations and a high interest in conventional ones. She decided to investigate a graduate degree in psychology. However, after attending a meeting about it, she expressed hesitation about investing two years in graduate school. The observation that Susan's issues with her parents might be clouding her thinking led to interventions to increase her differentiation and individuation. The counselor thought that these interventions might also provide Susan with skills to address her uncomfortable work environment. Using the I-message stem (I feel _____, because _____.), Susan rehearsed what she might express to each parent. Using the empathic-listening stem (You feel _____, because _____.), she practiced how she might respond to the reactions from each. Susan, advised to talk openly with her mother and father, was warned that her parents would

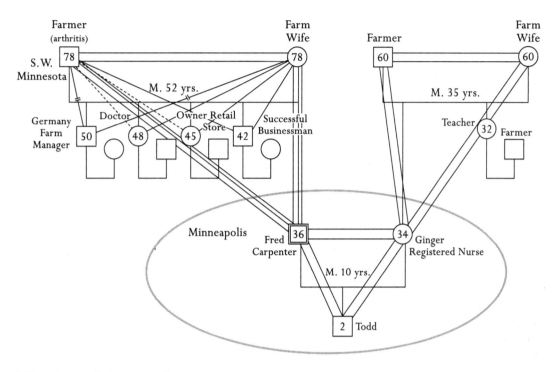

FIGURE 12.4   Sample Genogram, Fred

likely react with negative feedback, being alarmed by the perceived change in the family system.

At the next counseling session, Susan reported having talked with her mother and feeling better about their relationship. She discovered that her mother found the role of stepmother distressing and that she was proud of Susan for completing college and taking care of her father. Their relationship began to have more give-and-take as Susan expressed herself more to her mother. She also began to talk more to her father after she told him of her need to have more conversation with him. Susan joined a health club with the goals of losing weight and getting in shape. Susan also went to her boss and expressed her concerns about interactions of co-workers. And she

began to look to systematically for a better position rather than making a sudden and reactive change.

Case Example: Fred

The genogram in Figure 12.4 represents the family of thirty-six-year-old Fred, who is a carpenter and has a bachelor's degree in biology. Fred's parents offered him the opportunity to take over his father's farm.

The change would automatically improve Fred and Ginger's financial security. The couple, married for ten years, had a two-year-old son, Chad. Fred's mother and father seemed to expect that he would accept the offer of the farm. His brothers and sisters asked him how he could even think of turning down this wonderful opportunity. Being the youngest in the family, the only sibling still living in the state, and the least successful by conventional definitions of success, Fred felt pressured to return home to take over the family farm. Fred was thrown into a quandary and compared himself invidiously to his more established siblings. He assumed that he had no valid reason not to accept his father's generous offer. To add to his confusion, Ginger welcomed the opportunity to return to their hometown and live close to her own parents. Fred became depressed. Until his father offered him the opportunity to take over the farm, Fred and Ginger had been happy with their lifestyle.

Fred considered other career options as he postponed making a decision. He took the Strong Interest Inventory and showed a high interest in the realistic theme and only average interest in the other five. Also, he showed high scores in the basic interests of nature, adventure, art, and teaching. Scores on other questionnaires, the Myers-Briggs Type Indicator (Myers & McCaulley, 1985) and the Values Scale (Nevill & Super, 1986), also suggested that Fred highly valued aesthetics and variety. He aspired to being a quality craftsman and expressed pride in his renovations of his older home. Fred experienced performance anxiety—he worried about letting others down and was slow with projects at work as he sought to perfect them.

When Fred described his visits home and how the interactions with his parents countered his subtle efforts to try to say no, a theme began to emerge of parental control, anxiety, and lack of differentiation. Fred reported that his mother threw out his comic books without asking or even telling him. He said his father was focused only on efficiency and never made farming seem enjoyable. Fred was afraid he would not be able to express himself or have control in decisions over the farm. Fred also seemed to have difficulty expressing himself to his parents and felt he was never heard. He and Ginger reported that Fred's parents had discounted their plans about a home, expressing amazement and disapproval when the couple decided to live in town rather than in an old house on the farm.

Fred was taught I-message and empathic-listening stems and was coached in how to begin to talk to his parents about who he is. Telling his father that he wouldn't be coming to farm with him was also rehearsed. The impact on his aging parents and what their reaction might be was discussed. Alternative interpretations were explored, such as what might be the positive results of Fred's decision to stay put. For example, his parents might find different pursuits and learn to relate differently to their children, and particularly to Fred.

After considerable work, reassurance, and exploration of other career options, Fred told his father. The parents were disappointed but took it well. At the last session, Fred said that he was talking more often and more openly with his father. In addition, he was taking a short course on computers and hoping for a permanent position as a maintenance person at a recreation facility.

CONCLUSION

The genogram technique allows the counselor to begin to see how the client is connected with his or her relational context, especially with that most important context for career development, the family of origin. The counselor and client can facilitate the client's self-understanding as they explore how family patterns, rules, myths, roles, and communication affect the client's career development, career issues, and life themes.

Family systems concepts suggest interpretations and interventions that the career counselor can use to shift beliefs, attitudes, behaviors, and relationships in order to open the client toward greater freedom, flexibility, confidence, and broadened horizons. Not only communication but also thinking become freer as the clients find new perspective and meaning with regard to their place in the family and career-relevant life themes. In the case examples, an understanding of enmeshment, disengagement, and power dynamics suggested the need to balance the relationships of parents and adult offspring. Helping the client rehearse difficult issues with family members, especially parents, opens communications and promotes differentiation.

Career counselors can increase the depth of their work with clients using the genogram technique. Note that the two examples provided in this chapter are very basic. It is recommended that career counselors familiarize themselves with family systems concepts and interventions in order to enhance awareness of primary dynamics to watch for and to provide themselves with optimal options for intervention (Nichols & Schwartz, 1991; Wachtel & Wachtel, 1986). Important influences to be aware of include sibling relationships (Toman, 1969), intergenerational patterns (McGoldrick & Gerson, 1985), the family life cycle (Carter & McGoldrick, 1988), ethnicity (McGoldrick, Pearce, & Giordano, 1982), normative and nonnormative processes (Walsh, 1982), and gender issues (Luepnitz, 1988). The career development specialists cited here who emphasize family influences as a resource for intervention are the career counselor's beginning resources in the use of the genogram in career counseling.

REFERENCES

Beavers, W. R. (1977). *Psychotherapy and growth: A family systems perspective.* New York: Brunner/Mazel.

Blau, P. M., & Duncan, O. D. (1967). *The American occupational structure.* New York: Wiley.

Blos, P. (1979). *The adolescent passage.* New York: International University Press.

Bordin, E. S., & Kopplin, D. A. (1973). Motivational conflict and vocational development, *Journal of Counseling Psychology, 20,* 154–161.

Bordin, E. S., Nachmann, F., & Segal, S. J. (1963). An articulated framework for vocational development, *Journal of Counseling Psychology, 10,* 107–116.

Borzomenyi-Nagy, I., & Spark, G. M. (1983). *Invisible loyalties: Reciprocity in intergenerational family therapy.* New York: Harper & Row.

Bowen, M. (1976). Theory in the practice of psychotherapy. P. J. Guerin (ed.), *Family therapy: Theory and practice,* 42–90. New York: Harper & Row.

————. (1978). *Family therapy in clinical practice.* New York: Jason Aronson.

————. (1980). Key to the use of the genogram. E. A. Carter & M. McGoldrick (eds.), *The Family Life Cycle: A Framework for Family Therapy.* New York: Gardner Press.

Brachter, W. E. (1982). The influence of the family on career selection: A family systems perspective, *The Personnel and Guidance Journal, 61,* 87–91.

Brill, A. A. (1949). *Basic Principles of Psychoanalysis.* Garden City, N.Y.: Doubleday.

Brown, D., & Brooks, L. (1991). *Career Counseling Techniques.* Boston: Allyn and Bacon.

Brown, D., & Crace, R. K. (1996). Values in life role choices and outcomes: A conceptual model, *The Career Development Quarterly, 44* (3), 211–223.

Carlsen, M. B. (1988). *Meaning-making; Therapeutic processes in adult development.* New York: W. W. Norton.

Carter, B., & McGoldrick, M. (1988). *The changing family life cycle.* New York: Gardner Press.

Cochran, L. (1987). Framing career decisions. R. A. Neimeyer & G. J. Neimeyer (eds.), *Personal Construct Theory Casebook,* 261–276. New York: Springer Publishing Company.

Crites, J. O. (1962). Parental identification in relation to vocational interest development, *Journal of Educational Psychology,* 53, 262–270.

Dagley, J. (1984). *A Vocational Genogram* (mimeographed). Athens, Ga.: School of Education, University of Georgia.

Dashef, S. S. (1984). Aspects of identification and growth during late adolescence and young adulthood, *American Journal of Psychotherapy,* 38, 239–247.

Erikson, E. (1959). Identity and the life cycle, *Psychological Issues,* 1, 1–171.

Gerson, R. (1994). *Macgenogram: A graphic utility for producing genograms.* Atlanta: Humanware.

Ginzburg, E. (1952). Toward a theory of occupational choice, *Occupations,* 30, 491–494.

———. (1972). Toward a theory of occupational choice: A restatement, *Vocational Guidance Quarterly,* 20, 169–176.

Goldenberg, I., & Goldenberg, H. (1980). *Family therapy: An overview.* Monterey, Calif.: Brooks/Cole.

Guerin, P. J., & Pendagast, E. G. (1976). Evaluation of family system and genogram. P. J. Guerin (ed.), *Family Therapy.* New York: Gardner Press.

Gysbers, N. C., & Moore, E. C. (1987). *Career counseling: Skills and techniques for Practitioners.* Englewood Cliffs, N.J.: Prentice-Hall.

Hansen, J. C., & Campbell, D. P. (1985). *Manual for the SVIB-SCII* (4th ed.). Stanford, Calif.: Stanford University Press.

Herr, E. L., & Lear, P. B. (1984). The family as an influence on career development, *Family Therapy Collections,* 10, 1–15.

Holland, J. L. (1959). A theory of vocational choice, *Journal of Counseling Psychology,* 6, 35–43.

———. (1973). *Making vocational choices: A theory of careers.* Englewood Cliffs, N.J.: Prentice-Hall.

Kuehl, B. P. (1995). The solution-oriented genogram: A collaborative approach, *Journal of Marital and Family Therapy,* 21, 239–250.

Lopez, F. G., & Andrews, S. (1987). Career indecision: A family systems perspective, *Journal of Counseling and Development,* 65, 304–307.

Luckey, E. B. (1974). The family: Perspective on its role in development and choice. E. L. Herr (ed.), *Vocational Guidance and Human Development,* 203–231. Boston: Houghton Mifflin.

Luepnitz, D. A. (1988). *The family interpreted: Feminist theory in clinical practice.* New York: Basic Books.

Manuele-Adkins, C. (1992). Career counseling is personal counseling, *The Career Development Quarterly,* 40 (4), 313–323.

McGoldrick, M., & Gerson, R. (1985). *Genograms in family assessment.* New York: W. W. Norton & Company.

McGoldrick, M., Pearce, J., & Giordano, J. (1982). *Ethnicity in family therapy.* New York: Guilford Press.

Minuchin, S. (1974). *Families and family therapy.* Cambridge: Harvard University Press.

Myers, I. B., & McCaulley, M. H. (1985). *Manual: A guide to the development and use of the Myers-Briggs Type Indicator.* Palo Alto, Calif.: Consulting Psychologists Press.

Nevill, D. D., & Super, D. E. (1986). *The Values Scale manual: Theory, application, research.* Palo Alto, Calif.: Consulting Psychologists Press.

Nichols, M. P,. & Schwartz, R. C. (1991). *Family therapy: Concepts and methods.* Boston: Allyn and Bacon.

Okiishi, R. W. (1987). The genogram as a tool in career counseling, *Journal of Counseling and Development,* 66, 139–143.

Olson, D. H., Sprenkle, D. H., & Russell, C. S. (1979). Circumplex model of marital and family systems: I. Cohesion and adaptability dimensions, family types, and clinical applications, *Family Process,* 18, 3–28.

Osipow, S. H. (1969). What do we really know about career development? Gysbers, N. & Pritchard, D. (eds.), *Proceedings of the National Conference on*

Guidance Counseling and Placement in Career Development and Education-Occupational Decision Making. Columbia, Mo.

Penick, N. I. (1990). *An exploratory investigation of the relationship between measures of family functioning and adolescent career development.* Ann Arbor, Mich. University Microfilms International Dissertation Abstracts.

Papp, P., & Imber-Black, E. (1996). Family themes: Transmission and transformation, *Family Process,* 35, 5–20.

Polster, S. (1983). Ego boundary as process: A systemic-contextual approach. *Psychiatry,* 46, 247–258.

Roe, A. (1957). Early determinants of vocational choice, *Journal of Counseling Psychology,* 4, 212–217.

Salomone, P. R. (1982). Difficult cases in career counseling: The indecisive client, *Personnel and Guidance Journal,* 60 (8), 496–500.

Salomone, P. R., & McKenna, P. (1983). Difficult career counseling cases: Unrealistic career aspirations. *The Personnel and Guidance Journal,* 60 (5), 283–286.

Savickas, M. L. (1991). The meaning of work and love: Career issues and interventions. *The Career Development Quarterly,* 39 (4), 315–324.

———. (1995). Constructivist counseling for career indecision, *The Career Development Quarterly,* 43 (4), 363–373.

Simon, F. B., Stierlin, H., & Wynne, L. C. (1985). *The language of family therapy: A systemic vocabulary and sourcebook.* New York: Family Process Press.

Super, D. E. (1984). Career and life development. D. Brown & L. Brooks (eds.), *Career and choice development,* 192–234. San Francisco: Jossey-Bass.

———. (1963). Self-concepts in vocational development. D. E. Super, R. Starishevsky, N. Maitlin, & J. P. Jordaan (eds.), *Career development: Self-concept theory* (monograph 4). New York: CEEB Research.

———. (1951). Vocational adjustment: Implementing a self-concept, *Occupations,* 30, 88–92.

———. (1957). *The psychology of careers.* New York: Harper & Row.

Toman, W. (1969). *Family contellation.* New York: Springer Publishing Company.

Tomm, K. (1988). Interventive interviewing: Part III. Intending to ask lineal, circular, strategic, or reflexive questions, *Family Process,* 27, 1–15.

Vondracek, F. W., Lerner, R. M., & Schulenberg, J. E. (1986). *Career development: A life-span development approach.* New Jersey: Erlbaum.

Wachtel, E. F., and Wachtel, P. L. (1986). *Family dynamics in individual psychotherapy.* New York: Guilford.

Walsh, F. (1982). *Normal family processes.* New York: Guilford.

Zingaro, J. C. (1983). A family systems approach for the career counselor, *The Personnel and Guidance Journal,* 62, 24–27.

13

Spirituality and
Career Development

Using the Enneagram

MARGARET M. PINDER, ED.D.

INTRODUCTION

Instinctively as well as culturally, we know that our work is intricately linked with our very being. Yet it is often happenstance at best if we find ourselves working in a field that we love. Why is this so? Could it be that we have lost our way from the path that our Creator intended?[1] In consciously focusing on spirituality as it relates to career development, we explore two possibilities: (1) that each of us finds meaning in work that transcends our individual attainment of things or goals, and (2) that the

world beyond us truly needs what each of us has to offer. Thus, the total design of our world is inclusive of each of us. In fact, its level of wellness is dependent upon the connectedness and contributions of each of us.

Two possibilities are central to well-being. First, any sense of enduring hope is rooted in an identity of purpose or worth. Second, one must feel included by significant others. Career development from a spiritual perspective places clients at the intersection between what is best for the individual and what is best for the whole system. It requires that clients know self and know the world in which they live. For only then can they make decisions that meet the standards of Spirit-in-Action.

Spirit-in-Action is the term that Wilber (1996) has given to spirituality. With this term, Wilber is saying that spirit is not some transcendent creator that keeps itself removed from

Margaret M. Pinder is a professor of counseling at Amber University in Garland, Texas. In addition, Dr. Pinder maintains a private counseling practice in which she often works with adults and career development. The Enneagram is a tool that she frequently uses in her work.

[1]Editor's Note: While this chapter may reflect ideas unique to certain Christian values, the scope of the chapter is meant to be relevant to other religions.

creation. Conversely, the phrase suggests that the Creator is imminently present, always evolving in the process of making Itself known throughout infinity. All levels and breadths of existence, from the least to the most complex of creations, are manifestations of spirit as it chooses to create in time and space. Within this gestalt we find humanity. We human beings, made in the image of spirit, have one ultimate purpose: to completely reflect the absolute truth or reality of our Creator. Spirit-in-Action calls us to live lives of revolutionary vision, compassion, and action. If we believe that our origin is spirit and that our purpose is to perfectly reflect our Maker, then we live out of boldness and freedom.

This is what Victor Frankl (1992) described coming out of his experiences in a Nazi concentration camp. He recounted how the Nazis took all of the belongings from him and his family. Then, when Frankl thought he had nothing else to give, the Nazis took more. They shaved all the hair from the people's bodies. But Frankl and others discovered there was one thing that could not be wrenched from a person—the human spirit (Frankl, 1992). It was out of spirit that the Holocaust survivors found the meaning, hope, and energy to endure the atrocities. And it has been out of spirit that these brave people have drawn from their own pain to teach us the importance of respecting diversity, listening to others' stories, and finding ways to work together for the benefit of us all.

Perhaps now more than ever our world needs this message of Spirit-in-Action. In Africa we see tribal wars in which entire villages are slaughtered and the survivors are running from their homes. In Russia a criminal underground has erupted in the wake of turmoil. In South America drug lords exploit people's hunger for a better life. Here in the United States young people scoff at the idea of earning a college degree in order to work for $28,000 to $30,000 per year when they can earn that much in one month by selling drugs. Record numbers of midmanagers are being downsized with little hope of recovering a similar type of employment. New jobs are being created but many of them are in very low-paying fields. And even among people earning good salaries we hear the cry, "There has to be something more. Sure, I'm making good money, but I have no life. I'm too tired."

We are living in an era when most are suspicious of others. People readily recount stories in which they were betrayed by bosses, therapists, ministers, parents, and friends. In 1993 M. Scott Peck wrote *A World Waiting to Be Born,* in which he described a world devoid of civility. Peck devoted a number of chapters to looking at incivility within the workplace. On page after page he described ways in which co-workers used and abused one another because they were "looking out for No. 1." In contrast to incivility, Peck offered an operational definition of civility as "consciously motivated organizational behavior that is ethical in submission to a Higher Power" (Peck, 1993, 91).

Inherent within Peck's definition is the idea that the Higher Power is calling us to a way of relating or working together. This is the concept of vocation. It implies that a god or a creator who sees and knows everything is calling us to respond to our own inner desires (that which we long to do) and to the heartfelt needs of others (the free-market needs of others as well as societal issues and crises). It is at the intersection of these two types of needs that we find our true vocation. And it is in submission to spirit that we identify this intersection.

The model for thinking about vocation assumes an underlying order to our being. Thus, career development becomes a process of discovering our true nature, then participating with the Creator in a preordered plan of expression. This is in contrast to most models of career development, which are restricted to the arenas of body and soul, omitting the impact of spirit. This doesn't necessarily mean that a person will make an inappropriate career choice when following these traditional models. But it does suggest that it may be incomplete. Only when spirit, soul, and body are all considered and balanced is total fulfillment possible. Soul is defined as the psyche or personality of an individual. Typologies that measure interests, abilities, values, and personality types are thus soul-oriented models. When physical abilities, gender, or physical attractiveness are figured into the career-planning equation then the body is being considered. To consider the spirit of an individual, one has to identify the presence of energy that is sufficient to produce a unique will. The spirit of an individual exists in unity with the Creator. It is a nonphysical essence that requires a soul for expression in the realm of consciousness and a body for expression in the physical realm, but that ultimately transcends both soul and body. The mission of the spirit is to provide both the soul and body with perfect love. strength, and wisdom as they exist in time and space.

A MODEL FOR BRINGING SPIRITUALITY INTO CAREER DEVELOPMENT

When spirituality is brought into career development it is with the understanding that the goal is restoration of the whole person to a position of integrity and of service to a purpose higher than self-advancement.

Not only are priorities among body, soul, and spirit reordered but the individual is ex-

pected to grow and mature through a process of spiritual practice. Schlecht, in a 1997 group discussion, presented three elements of spiritual practice that are found in each of the major world religions. These three are:

1. Touch the sacred
2. Systematic form of self-reflection
3. Commitment to loving service

Touch the Sacred

Various experiential styles and activities exist as methodologies for being touched by the Divine. No one form is practiced by every spiritual disciple, but the common element seems to be finding a practice that opens one's heart to that which is holy. For some people this practice is prayer or meditation. For someone else it could be body prayer or the reading of sacred writings. Practitioners of Tantra describe human sexuality as one of the most profound passageways to the Divine. One's work can also be approached as a path leading both to God and from God through one's self to others.

Systematic Form of Self-Reflection

A daily examination of self is an integral part of the birthing of an authentic self that is at the center of what it means to be a spiritual being. A number of tools exist to help in the process of self-reflection. Regardless of the specific tool used, the process needs to be nonjudgmental, full of extraordinary respect for oneself, and always focused toward the truth.

Psychological inventories can be beneficial in helping a person determine a preferred style of interacting. Often by seeing graphic profiles or descriptive narratives of one's behavior, a person is confronted with personal biases or tendencies that are either self-defeating or limiting. Conversely, this self-confrontation process may bring one face to face with personal strengths that have been ignored, denied, or untapped. Through a process of systematic self-reflection, a person might find oneself returning again and again to the same vision of work to be done. This enduring passion may be the perseverance of the Divine calling a person to his or her true vocation.

Commitment to Loving Service

Bauman (1996) states that we are at our best when we act as channels for that which is greater than ourselves and that we are at our worst when what we do is self-serving. In addition, Bauman suggests that we are meant to serve this higher reality by being its priests. The word priest basically means a person who accepts the role as mediator between the infinite and the finite. A person who knows, loves, and can bring others into contact with the infinite is a priest. Any type of work has the potential for fulfilling this mediative role when it is performed in the spirit of loving service.

This service is not the dutiful doing of righteous things out of compulsion or adherence to dogma but is the expression of self in process. Service is most powerful when the acts are "in sync" with the actor. It is a matter of living so that one's behavior, thoughts, and feelings are aligned in a fashion that opens the channel through which spirit can flow. Work approached from this vantage can be full of joy and satisfaction.

Helminski (1992) uses the metaphor of a mirror to depict the relationship between ego or form and spirit. The ego, which is a combination of genetic predisposition and developed desires and fears, can obscure the mirror so that one is almost completely out of touch with ultimate reality. If one is taught to live life from a perspective of matching (ego) with choices,

one is only partially alert to the whole universe of being. It is easy to become so enmeshed in meeting the demands of ego that one fails to see other perspectives. It is as if the spirit is asleep or disconnected or dead. Individuals need a way of polishing the mirror of awareness so that they can see their own deeper levels of being more clearly. As individuals do the work of acknowledging, respecting, and surrendering ego states, the spirit is freed from control by the ego. These experiences of letting go or of dying to self are an essential part of cleaning the mirror so that one's true nature is reflected clearly. Given that the benefits of living out of spirit include joy, wisdom, and love, it would seem that people would readily do this work of polishing the mirror. And perhaps they would if it were easier. But there is one catch—these experiences are often extremely challenging.

The ego exists to achieve its desires and to defend against its fears. It does not want to surrender. In fact, to do so is quite painful. It seems as if the Creator built within the overall scheme of things a plan that said, "I want all individuals to know that I am trustworthy and that I have created them to be likewise. Now, I know that some individuals will find this very hard to believe, so in order to help them learn just who they are at the deepest level, I will create exactly the types of experiences that cannot be dealt with at a superficial or ego level. Then they will turn inside, recognize who they are at the core, and recognize that I have been here all along to help them."

So we see that the trying experiences are the catalysts for our spiritual development. As we become more and more spiritually mature, according to Helminski (1992), we are "gathered to our own 'I', we are increasing a Divine presence in the world . . . As we polish away conditioning, concepts, and the false, reacting

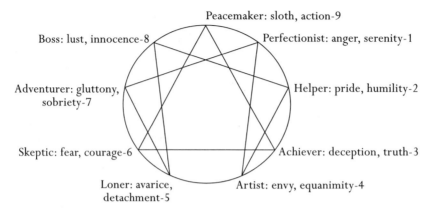

FIGURE 13.1   The Basic Enneagram Names, Passions, and Virtues

self, wherever we turn there is the face of Reality" (Helminski, 1992, 72–73).

With its emphasis upon assessment, traditional career development has laid a firm foundation for helping people grasp the concept of matching who they are with the work they do. Certainly, numerous people have been helped by using tools such as the Self-Directed Search, the Myers-Briggs Type Indicator, or the 16PF to understand how their personality types correspond with various careers. What has not been used as fully is a tool that integrates spiritual development with the matching of personality and career. The Enneagram provides career counselors with a tool that uses a psychospiritual perspective to develop in clients a fuller awareness of who they are as a three-part system (body-soul-spirit) that expresses Spirit-in-Action through careers.

At least 1,500 years before psychology developed as a field and began describing people according to certain personality types, teachers in the spiritual traditions were identifying specific patterns in people's ways of relating. These teachings were brought to the Western world about two hundred years ago by the Russian mystic, Gurdjieff. One hundred years later

Sigmund Freud was laying the groundwork for the study of psychological types. The Enneagram is based upon the mystical teaching of seven capital tendencies or sins that have to be converted to virtues through spiritual practice.

Somewhere around 1970 Ichazo developed a template that integrated two additional tendencies with the original seven and the Enneagram as we know it was born. The graph is drawn as a circle with the nine points distributed evenly around the outer perimeter. (The word enneagram means nine-point graph.) Inner lines show the connections among the nine types. As a person becomes more identified either with Spirit-in-Action or with personality, movement will be seen around the nine-point circle. When functioning at the lowest point of development, the nine points are anger, pride, deception, envy, avarice, fearfulness, gluttony, lust, and sloth. At their polar opposite in development, the traits are serenity, humility, truthfulness, equanimity, detachment, courage, sobriety, innocence, and action. Figure 13.1 shows the Enneagram as it is often depicted with the corresponding number, name, basic tendency, and transformed virtue.

Each of the nine types of the Enneagram has the potential to be transformed to a virtue through a life of increased consciousness and civility. Conversely, each type, in service to itself, will deteriorate into inefficacy and destructiveness. From the perspective of the Enneagram success is not attained via one's passions but by transforming one's passions into virtues through spiritual practice. Said differently, the passion or primary presentation of a person is a vehicle of expression for Spirit-in-Action. This primary tendency is not intended to be used predominantly to meet one's desires or to avoid one's fears. Rather, according to the model, when an individual develops special or unique capacities and presents them in service to the transcendent Creator, the individual is transformed into the likeness of the Creator.

While the Enneagram may at first appear to be solely focused on individual assessment, development, and transformation, its ultimate utility is in its application for entire systems or societies. If we go back to the earlier discussion about effective career development being that of living within the intersection of our passion and society's needs, we see that the Enneagram provides us with a tool for assessing the profile of an entire group or work force. And in assessing the needs of society, individuals make socially responsible choices by developing their competencies to respond to societal needs.

The goal is not to develop one type of society in which one of the nine types dominates but to discover and empower all of the nine types in an integrated and complete Enneagram. Unfortunately, the work culture in the United States today could be considered Type Three on the Enneagram. This achiever type often puts image in front of authenticity in order to get ahead. A danger for the Three is a disconnection from feelings and an insensitivity

to the needs of others. Think of the increasing cry for soul within the workplace. Think of people who have seemingly achieved it all only to say they've never been who they really are. The Enneagram can help us see our hubris in thinking that one way is the best way for everyone. It can help us transcend any one type in order to incorporate the values of each type into an integrated whole that functions as a community to meet each other's needs.

If career counselors understand the underlying philosophy of the Enneagram and apply the tool with critical and creative thinking, they can play a significant role in assisting individuals, groups, and society in fulfilling their purposes.

Don Riso, one of the world's foremost leaders and spokespersons for the Enneagram, states that the Enneagram alone cannot provide spiritual development (Riso & Hudson, 1996). However, he offers extensive theoretical and experiential evidence for the Enneagram as a tool for polishing the mirror of self-awareness. According to Riso, the Enneagram is a complex system for understanding human behavior. As a personality typology, the Enneagram organizes nine personality types into three triads of three personality types. Triad 1 is the Feeling Triad (Riso & Hudson, 1996). It comprises Types Two, Three, and Four. Type Two is characterized by a strong motivation to help or nurture others. Careers often chosen by Twos include counseling, teaching, and sales and service jobs. Type Three is very achievement oriented. Type Threes' careers are often leadership and management positions and influence-oriented fields such as journalism ·or media broadcasting. The profile of Type Four is artistic, turning toward careers such as writing, music, the arts, and entrepreneurship.

The second triad is the Thinking Triad (Riso & Hudson, 1996). It comprises Types Five, Six, and Seven. Type Five people like to work alone and are independent thinkers. They may choose careers in scientific, technical, or other intellectually demanding fields. Type Six is known as the questioning or skeptical profile. Sixes like being part of a team. They wrestle with decision making, wanting an external structure but often rebelling against it as well. Career paths often involved a structured system such as the justice system, the military, or academia. The Thinking Triad is completed by the adventuresome Type Seven. These people love challenges and do not like repetitive work. Many Sevens will choose careers that involve travel, working outdoors, and some form of troubleshooting.

The third and remaining triad is the Instinctive Triad (Riso & Hudson, 1996). It comprises Types Eight, Nine, and One. The Eight is the leader or asserter and often takes the initiative. Eights like responsibility and problem solving. Attractive careers for Eights include self-employment, business, strategic leadership, law, and the sports field. Type Nines are known for their bent toward peace and their avoidance of conflict. Nines tend to be effective diplomats and mediators. They may choose one of the helping professions or may prefer to work in a field that provides security with structure, such as the military, civil service, or other bureaucracies. Type Ones are perfectionists. They believe that the world is a mess, but they accept the challenge to fix it. Type One individuals may enter law enforcement or religious work or may join civic causes or become actively involved in education for social change.

Each of the nine types functions along a hierarchical continuum of nine levels of development that are categorized as healthy, average, or unhealthy. In addition, although the Enneagram organizes personality into nine district categories, it acknowledges fluidity among the types. While individuals have a core type, they also have a wing type, which is one of the two types adjacent to the core type. The core type dominates one's personality. The wing complements and adds important elements to the total personality. In addition, all types move around the nine-point Enneagram in the direction of either integration or disintegration. So a great deal of movement is expected as a person changes, grows, and develops.

The goal for an individual using the Enneagram is to transcend the core type or ego and to integrate all nine of the types. This process is fostered by using the Enneagram to help persons identify their characteristic responses in their daily life experiences. As individuals tell their stories, the Enneagram provides a structure for gaining meaning throughout the life course. Individuals begin to see that they are not a particular personality type but something deeper, wiser, more enduring. According to Riso and Hudson (1996), the Enneagram helps people clarify their goals, desires, fears, typical response patterns, and gifts to offer the world. Furthermore, the system describes how each core type looks when moving in the direction of health or the direction of pathology. Movement in the direction of disintegration is the easiest path for each type. Conversely, movement in the direction of integration always involves conscious choice and effort. But it will not be an effort of striving, straining, condemning, or forcing choices. Instead, it will be the effort of letting go of the old personality patterns and of letting go into Spirit-in-Action. As individuals see that their usual patterns often work against their best interests, they find the encouragement to let go of them, thus making way for a richer, more complete life. This could be defined as love-in-action and frees us to offer our gifts to others.

Given the sophistication and precision of the Enneagram, it is easy to see how it can be useful throughout the lifelong process of career development. Just as other typologies have been used to match personalities with job categories in order to aid a person in selecting a type of work with high potential for success, so too can the Enneagram be used. But the Enneagram can also be used to help individuals discern if they are acting out of ego in a way that is detrimental to spiritual development. Similarly, the Enneagram can be used to shed light upon whether the key motivations for career choices are spiritual or ego-based. Keep in mind that spiritual development occurs through the threefold process of touching the sacred, systematic self-reflection, and ongoing service. The Enneagram provides a viable structure for self-reflection and also provides a typology for outlining areas of service.

It should be kept in mind that the process of spiritual development does not require that one's passions be abandoned, but invites one to bring passions into alignment with a transcendent purpose and a transcendent source of energy. When individuals live and work out of spirit, their lives are characterized by empowerment and community.

Below is a case in which the Enneagram was used to structure a spiritually based approach to career development.

Case Study: Jon Michael

Note: Names and identifying information have been changed, but issues and process are consistent with the actual case.

Jon Michael is a forty-two-year-old divorced father of three daughters. His work history is erratic and fragmented. Currently, Jon Michael works in the petroleum industry. His work takes him abroad frequently, which he enjoys but at the present dreads because of concern for the welfare of his children.

Jon Michael grew up in the rural South in a Christian fundamentalist evangelical extended family. One of Jon's earliest and most significant memories is that of his father being killed by a drunken driver. Jon was three at the time of his father's death and he yearned to die also so that he could be reconnected with his father. Death of family members has been a significant recurring event in Jon Michael's life.

Jon Michael was first asked to create a lifeline to show significant life events from his birth until now. When he presented the lifeline, his first observation was that he found himself wanting to draw lines both above and below the baseline for the same events because they seemed to hold both positive and negative meanings for him.

Then he was asked to complete the Riso-Hudson Enneagram Type Indicator, Version 2.0. He presented as a Type Seven, which Riso and Hudson call the generalist. The generalist is described as enthusiastic and productive. He is extroverted, optimistic, spontaneous, playful, and high-spirited, but can also be overextended, superficial, and undisciplined. Often very bright, a Seven avoids anxiety by staying on the go. Uninhibited, excessive, and self-centered, the Seven can be infantile, demanding, and insensitive to others. When living at the healthiest level, the Seven truly appreciates and celebrates life, is focused upon worthwhile goals, and reflects a true spirituality (Riso & Hudson, 1996).

The Enneagram is divided into three triads, each with a different emotional thrust. The Seven falls within the fear triad. The other two triads are based in anger and greed. The Seven is also known as one of the aggressive types.

Jon Michael approached me with two concerns: (1) he wanted to make more money so he could pursue his lifelong dream of being a writer-philosopher, and (2) he wanted to understand what he kept doing that "pissed off" people and that lessened his possibilities within specific organizations.

As Jon Michael told me his story, several themes emerged:

1. He affixed blame to himself when bad things happened. (God took Daddy because I was bad.)

2. He believed that God was punishing him for being bad by taking first his father, then two of his brothers, and both of his beloved grandparents and by making life overwhelming for his mother and the remaining siblings. (God became an overpowering force that could not be satisfied.)

3. He developed rage as a characteristic way of responding when anxious or threatened.

4. Life consistently seemed threatening to Jon Michael.

5. As a child, he felt bad and helpless. As a teen he sought help because he was extremely depressed. Treatment for Jon Michael compounded the problems because he became addicted to prescription medications. Continuing into adulthood, he seemed helpless even when he attempted to get help.

6. He was very confused about his identity but kept trying to live out his perception of how his Papa (grandfather) had lived in the family.

7. When Jon Michael began to make good money in the oil business, he did not know how to manage it, consequently alternating between extreme abundance and poverty.

8. He felt out of control in all areas of his life. He had rejected both God and country because he blamed them for taking the people he loved and because he felt abandoned by them.

9. Through the readings, relationships, and practices of Buddhism, he began to develop a structure that increased his hope.

10. He reentered therapy, this time with a therapist who helped him work through his grief over his numerous losses and helped him begin to clarify his identity, beginning to believe that he could fulfill his life's dream of being a writer. He recognized that his rage grew in large part out of his frustrations with his own power. He was caught in the paradox of having much energy and ability but knowing that if he developed his talent it would take a great deal of disciplined work and it would also separate him from friends who might not choose to grow or go in the same direction. It appeared easier to rage than to exercise self-discipline.

It was roughly at this point developmentally that Jon Michael came for counseling. He had failed to get a job he really wanted and in his mind he blew the interview because he became enraged at the interviewers.

While listening to Jon Michael's account of the interview, it became apparent that it had been a classic stress-inducing interview designed to see how the job candidate would react under pressure. He tried to calm himself down and to rebound but never felt he recovered. For eight months Jon Michael brooded over losing what he considered to be a perfect job for him.

When reviewing his Enneagram profile, it became clear that he was operating at level 8 of the Type Seven, which is the next-to-lowest level of functioning, and that he was also incorporating behaviors from the unhealthy level of Type One, which meant that he was moving in the direction of disintegration.

Using role playing he reentered the interview situation and explored alternative responses that would have given him more maneuverability. He was also willing to see that he had superficially interpreted the negative experience to reinforce his world view. He realized he had compulsively thrown himself into Buddhism, his work at his technical job, escapism through travel, and his enrollment in a professional writing course. None of these would make his pain go away, however.

The Enneagram was used to slow him down enough for him to see himself in the midst of his experiences.

A plan was devised for Jon Michael to take one of the interviewers, a long-term industry acquaintance, to lunch and ask him to give Jon Michael feedback. Since systematic self-reflection is an important part of spiritual practice, the Enneagram gave Jon Michael a structure for critiquing his own choices and behaviors.

Many characteristics of a Seven on the Enneagram directly relate to Jon Michael. He:

- tends to be depressive, superficial, and addictive

- lays plans for the future, but has difficulty keeping commitments

- avoids things under the surface and copes by repressing anxiety

- is fun to be with, likes to tell stories, and is smart, charming, and fast-moving

- was terrorized in childhood

- wants everybody to feel good

- presents himself as wanting a deep spirituality but resists the depth

- may use spiritual practice to avoid deep spirituality

- is prone to extreme mood swings

- tends not to respect authority

- becomes bored by routine

- grows up emotionally when he disciplines himself

- acts aggressively

- when healthy, is highly responsive, lively, and eager and gifted in accomplishing goals

- when average, has enormous appetites, looks to constantly amuse himself, is a spiritual glutton, and is in constant motion

- when unhealthy, is abusive, impulsive, infantile, in flight from self, and very blunt; at first sign of threat, goes into action by attacking

- tends to burn out

- believes the world is dangerous

- denies anxiety

- finds it hard to become who he is; often feels controlled by his mother and feels guilty for that

As we explored this disparaging picture of a Type Seven disintegrating into the unhealthy patterns of the Five, Jon Michael began to cry. Realizing that he was careening out of control, Jon Michael had thrown all of his energy into trying to work harder and to gain control of his life. He had begun dating a woman who shared his love for literature and travel, and he had believed their relationship would help him make the needed shifts to balance his life. He became obsessed with winning this woman's devotion and would call her from work, almost incapacitated from his fear that she would leave him. Jon Michael realized that he was now becoming enraged and bitter toward this woman because she would not guarantee him that everything would be okay. He admitted that his attempts at growth through control were not working.

As he moved toward health, other aspects of the Enneagram were used to demonstrate how he might grow.

It was clear that Jon Michael had moved up and down the levels of development and that he had more often moved in the direction of disintegration than integration.

The counseling process involved working around the complete nine-point graph, showing Jon Michael how he could become empowered as he made new kinds of choices. It also helped him to slow down in order to live in the present. He worked to reframe his broad continuum of skills, to find ways to be thankful for his technical work, and to learn how to bring his artistry to the technical arena. Ideas from Bolton's *People Skills* (1979) were suggested to help Jon Michael face his aggressiveness toward others and to give him other options when faced with conflicts.

He was aware that he reacted negatively to most employers because he blamed them for his own failure to integrate his life. In fact, Jon Michael saw them in direct conflict with his spirituality.

From a Buddhist perspective, one is truly free when one is connected with one's own true Buddha nature. Using imagery, Jon Michael was asked to connect with his authentic self and then to envision himself relating in a job interview. In a second imagery Jon Michael envisioned himself integrating both his artistic and technical skills in the workplace.

After approximately six hours of working together, Jon Michael had (a) developed a much clearer picture of who he was; (b) had found meaning in past work experiences over which he still obsessed; (c) had identified and practiced new communication skills; (d) had identified steps he could take to complete the learning from the unsuccessful job interview; (e) had considered a more holistic way to view his range of technical to artistic work; (f) had refocused on his responsibilities for living his life; and finally (g) had examined what it could look like to replace his fear of his own power with being empowered.

This case reinforces the contention that we are far more than the sum of our parts. To have reduced career counseling to a technical discussion of his personality and of the demands of the workplace would have severely limited the scope. But by addressing behavioral, soulful (personality), and spiritual aspects of his case, far broader and deeper interventions were possible. The work of integrating spirituality and career development is a daily practice of love.

CONCLUSION

Career development is not about how we develop our talents in order to get all that we want. It is about looking around us to see the needs of our fellow travelers and about knowing ourselves well enough to give freely of our abundance. This can only happen when we first know ourselves relative to our Creator. We know that we are never alone but that our every need will be provided for. It is at this point that we shift from giving out of dependency or need to truly giving out of love.

This is not the end of the process but only the preparation for the next part of the journey. As growing individuals shift to a higher level of spiritual development, they often find themselves in the midst of enormous organizational conflict and perhaps experience disinterest in anything having to do with growth or spiritual development. Because learning is a process, spiritual travelers stumble and fall. Likewise they may experience resistance from coworkers or family members. None of this means that the system is broken or dysfunctional. To the contrary, Spirit-in-Action has constructed exactly the set of circumstances needed to produce spiritual growth and development of all parties involved. On the one hand we are given a passion to produce certain services or products. On the other hand we must learn to receive products and services from others.

It is only as we live and work in community with others who are on their own spiritual journeys that we emerge as fully human. Herein lies the difficulty. As the Enneagram so clearly points out, we individuals differ greatly from each other. Our preferences and our fears create vastly different styles of behaving, which, in turn, create additional biases, prejudices, and blocks to interaction. However, it is exactly this conundrum of competitive, self-serving activity within which lies our hope. Career develop-

ment, approached from a spiritual perspective, is not only about our individual development as persons, but about our evolving as communities of persons who acknowledge and affirm the never-ending cyclical process of growth and development. Our places of work become sacred spaces for creativity as we each recognize our connectedness to the whole. As Fox (1994) stated, we reinvent the workplace by rediscovering who we are and why we are here. It is not an easy process and will require touching the sacred, systematically reexamining self, committing to loving service, and consciously connecting with others. This is the process of love, and its seed has been planted within each of us. The place of our work, whether it be corporate, entrepreneurial, home-based, or volunteer, is sacred space. Let us honor its creator as we enter therein.

REFERENCES

Bauman, L. (1996). *Living the presence*. Telephone, Texas: Praxis.

————. (1995). *Foundations of Christian spirituality*. Telephone, Texas: Praxis.

Bolton, R. (1979). *People skills*. New York: Simon & Schuster, Inc.

Fox, M. (1994). *The reinvention of work*. San Francisco: HarperCollins Publishers.

Frankl, V. (1992). *Man's search for meaning* (4th ed.). Boston: Beacon Press.

Helminski, K. (1992). *Living presence*. New York: G. P. Putnam's Sons.

Palmer, H. (1995). *The Enneagram in love and work*. San Francisco: HarperCollins Publishers.

Peck, M. S. (1993). *A world waiting to be born*. New York: Bantam Books.

Riso, D. & Hudson, R. (1996). *Personality types*. New York: Houghton Mifflin Company.

Schlecht, D. (1997). *Personal Communication* (February). Dallas, Texas.

Wilber, K. (1996). *A brief history of everything*. Boston: Shambhala Publishers.

14

Single-Parent Families

Issues in the World of Work

BONNIE L. FERGUSON, M.S., WITH CARROLL
WILLIAMS AND SR. LUCILLE GARDNER

INTRODUCTION

There are a number of publications on the topic of single-parent families. Many of them focus on the impact of family life as it relates to children brought up by single parents or the outcome of family life as it relates to adjusting to divorce and the impact this has on the children. Although there are many avenues to explore in terms of single-parent families, this chapter focuses on the world of work and issues of career development.

This author has interviewed single parents, completed a literature review, and worked with two other colleagues to (a) develop an understanding of single-parent families, (b) explore issues relating to raising children, (c) identify

available community resources, and (d) address work and career issues. A model of integrating the multidimensions of the single-parent family was then developed. This model is presented visually in Figure 14.1.

According to the U.S. Bureau of Census (1994), 22.3 percent of all families with minor children are single-parent families. Of that percentage, 79.1 percent are single female heads of household and 20.9 percent are single male heads of household. The Commerce Department's Census Bureau also documented that in 1970 there were 5.6 million families maintained by women with no spouse present and that by 1995 this figure had increased 117.9 percent for a total of 12.2 million families now being maintained by women alone. Families with men as single parents grew even more sharply. In 1970 there were 1.2 million such families and by 1995 that figure had grown by 166.7 percent

Bonnie Ferguson received her M.S. in counseling psychology from Our Lady of the Lake University and has lived in a "wider family" setting for several years.

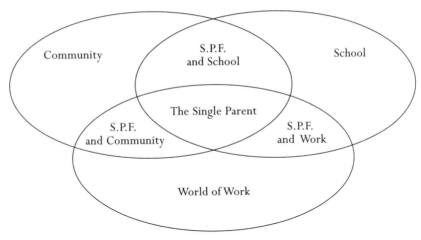

S.P.F. = Single-Parent Family

FIGURE 14.1 Integrating the Single-Parent Family

for a total of 3.2 million families maintained by men with no spouse present.

While the reasons for divorce are varied, it is important to note that there are three common circumstances among divorced families: (1) decreased financial resources (Hanson, 1988), (2) increased daily stresses (Rose, 1989), and (3) reduced social supports (Kissman, 1992). To complicate matters, society traditionally has held a view that divorced families are broken, that they are not whole families, and as such are somehow doomed to fail (Morrison, 1995). In looking at decreased financial resources, it is important to note that 50 percent of single-parent families with an absent father were awarded child support. Of the women due child support, 51 percent reported receiving the full amount awarded, 24 percent received less than the full amount, and 25 percent did not receive any support at all (Lester, 1991).

In a survey of 3,100 single-parent households conducted by Kennickell and Shack-Marquez (1992), 68 percent owned a financial asset in the form of a checking, savings, money

market, or IRA account or a certificate of deposit. The median value of their financial assets was approximately $3,000. By comparison, among married couples under 55 with children, the median value of financial assets was approximately $11,000.

It is also interesting to look at the educational level of single parents. Mulroy (1995) cites that children being raised in a single-parent family are twice as likely to be living with a parent without a high school education as children being raised in a two-parent family. According to the 1990 U.S. Bureau of the Census report, 30.1 percent of all single parents in the United States did not complete high school, 43.1 percent completed high school, 18.3 percent completed one to three years of college, and 8.5 percent completed four or more years of college.

Despite the growth of single-parent families in today's society, there are still stereotypes associated with the single-parent family. Some may believe that because a couple's marriage has failed, the individuals themselves are failures.

Some may believe that the deficits associated with solo parenting preclude developing the closeness that an intact family may develop.

In order to make effective interventions, it is necessary to increase the understanding of what it means to be a family. According to the U.S. Census Bureau a family is "a group of two or more people, one of whom is the householder, living together, who are related by birth, marriage, or adoption." We feel that the context of families is broader than blood relation. In fact, Donati (1995) recognized the same need when he coined the phrase "wider families" to challenge existing social perceptions of what it means to have a family. He further discusses how wider families (1) are outside the traditional and societal definitions of family because they stretch beyond blood relationships, (2) by their existence raise questions about societal norms and legal definitions of family, and (3) reflect the various structures and relationships that are part of current social constructions.

The term wider families more accurately defines today's changing family lifestyle. This rethinking of our concept of the family, rather than ignoring realities, recognizes that families exist as a variety of social constructions, that wider families co-exist with traditionally defined families, overlapping with them in expressing family-like behaviors (Marciano & Sussman, 1991). Thus, wider families come together naturally and serve a useful purpose for all members. They are both similar and different from biological and marital families. They are similar in that the bonds of affiliation and obligation evolve, and they fill needs of time, emotions, and economy. They are different in that they are often choice-based and therefore legally voluntary both in their inception and departure. For example, it is commonplace today to hear of grandparents rearing their grandchildren who live with them either because of divorce, ne-

glect, or financial reasons. Albeit unique, this author's niece lives with her and is considered a primary caregiver. Often friends who have gotten divorced will join households for both emotional support and financial arrangements. These examples of "wider families" are sometimes referred to as "extended" or "surrogate" families.

OVERVIEW OF EMPLOYMENT CONSIDERATIONS

Mulroy (1995) noted that today's restructured workplace has divided workers into two primary groups: unskilled, underpaid, and unemployed workers and well-paid technical workers. The industrial sector experienced a high level of plant closings in the 1980s. The Bureau of Labor Statistics reports that 11.7 million American workers were laid off between January 1981 and January 1990. The report goes on to state that one-third of the laid-off workers remained unemployed or left the work force. The remaining two-thirds had to take service jobs at a drastically reduced wage, but with companies downsizing or restructuring in order to be more profitable, service jobs, among others, are also on the decline.

Yet another factor that single parents need to be aware of is the barriers to employment (Mulroy, 1995). These include (a) affordable housing within close proximity of jobs, (b) access to child and health care, (c) sexual harassment, (d) the cost and time of education and training, (e) self-esteem, and (f) job readiness.

Affordable Housing

According to Mulroy (1995), a common standard in the mortgage lending arena is that "affordable housing means that the family's monthly rent or mortgage and utilities do not exceed 30 percent of their monthly income" (Mulroy, 1995, 89). Affordable housing is generally not readily available in metropolitan areas where good-paying jobs are located. Mulroy states that 70 percent of the public housing programs were cut during the Reagan-Bush administration. If affordable housing is not readily available where the jobs are, then transportation becomes an even bigger factor. Along with commuting expenses, single parents have to consider the additional time required to commute and the reliability of the transportation.

Child and Health Care

Many parents rely on other family members to take care of their young children. Veum and Kahn (1991) have identified that quality, cost, and accessibility of child care are key issues. Equally important is the need to have a benefits package that includes affordable health-care coverage. Single parents who were interviewed stated that appropriate health-care coverage is the primary benefit they look for when seeking employment.

Sexual Harassment

There have been numerous studies on sexual harassment of women in the workplace. Mulroy (1995) reports that "instances of sexual harassment (happen most often to) women who are perceived as 'available,' those women who are either single or divorced; or 'vulnerable,' trainees; those holding jobs previously held by a man; or those with a greater dependence on their jobs, such as single mothers" (Mulroy, 1995, 93).

Cost and Time of Education and Training

Education and training are prerequisites for obtaining good-paying jobs. Most corporations provide educational reimbursement programs for their employees as an incentive to update their technical skills. Most employees, including single parents, want to progress in their technical skills and take advantage of this benefit that employers offer. However, the bind for many single parents revolves around two issues: having the time to take classes and the financial resources to pay for classes. Most of these opportunities are available on an after-hours basis, which means that taking classes would increase the demands and cost of child care. And while some employers reimburse employees for tuition expenses, they are reimbursed only upon successful completion of the course work. Most single-parent families live from paycheck to paycheck and find it difficult to pay in advance for training and additional child care.

Self-Esteem and Job Readiness

Self-confidence and a sense of adequacy are needed to excel in the job search, in interviews, and, once hired, in job performance. Because of the stereotypes about divorced people, they not only have to prove themselves in the job market, but they also have to overcome the image that divorced people are failures. When others' negative perceptions are coupled with the real-world challenge of caring for children alone and holding a job, it is easy to see how self-confidence can become diluted and darken one's hope of succeeding (Mulroy, 1995).

Dinkmeyer (1987) points out that single parents can boost their self-esteem in the work arena by reminding themselves of their skills at home and further recognizing that many of these skills are transferable to the job market. For example, the ability to effectively communicate, to solve problems, to listen, to manage time, and to build good relationships are all important skills required in any job. Single parents

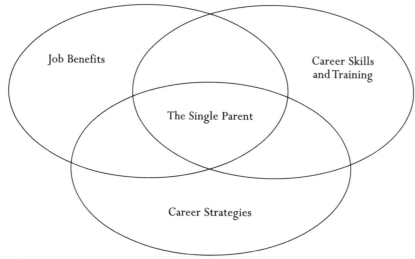

FIGURE 14.2 Single Parents and Work

use these skills to varying degrees each day as they raise their children and maintain a home.

Job readiness, on the other hand, is a barometer of how employable a person may be. Are the person's skills in line with the job being applied for? Are the skills current, especially as they relate to the use of technology? These factors often determine the type of job a single parent can obtain.

A CAREER DEVELOPMENT MODEL FOR SINGLE-PARENT FAMILIES

In developing a model for this population, two broad questions need to be addressed. First, what can the business world do to help balance work and family issues? Are there any specific policies or benefits that can be offered to enhance the quality of employees' work life while remaining profitable? Second, what can single parents do for themselves to enhance their career strategies? Figure 14.2 depicts the three

areas to be explored: (1) job benefits, (2) career skills and training, and (3) career strategies.

1. Job Benefits

Employers have in place a number of human resource policies and programs that are family-friendly in order to comply with federal regulations and to increase profit. For example, in 1993 President Bill Clinton signed into law the Family and Medical Leave Act (FMLA). Companies with fifty or more employees are required to adhere to the FMLA for employees who have been with the company for at least one year and have clocked in at least 1,250 hours. The intention of the FMLA is to provide benefits that enable employees to more effectively balance work and family issues.

The law requires up to twelve weeks of unpaid time off for an employee's serious health condition or that of the employee's spouse, child, or parent. The employee's position or equivalent position must be held open during the specified period of unpaid time off, and during the leave, the employee's group health insurance coverage must be continued at the employer's expense, with the employee continuing his/her contribution (Foster, personal communications, 1997).

Seyler, Monroe, and Garand (1995) believe that family-friendly policies will occur with greater frequency when the benefits from such policies exceed their cost, or in other words, when they have a favorable effect on bottom-line profits. Among the reasons employers provided these policies are to (1) assist employees by minimizing family-based stresses; (2) increase productivity through job satisfaction as a result of having such benefits; and (3) reduce the associated costs of employment advertising, hiring, and training due to employee turnover (Seyler et al., 1995).

Family-friendly benefits are provided in the form of (1) human resource policies, (2) financial aid programs, and (3) information and referral services (Seyler, Monroe, & Garand, 1995). One hundred seventy-eight workers were surveyed, and the findings suggest that the most common human resource policies include flextime, options to work at home, paid sick leave, parenting seminars, family counseling or other EAP (employee assistance program) benefits, job sharing, parental leave, and maternity leave (Seyler et al., 1995). The survey results also indicate that companies offer packages that include such benefits as pretax salary reductions for day care, cafeteria plan benefits, on-site or near-site child-care centers, vouchers to subsidize child-care expenses, and contracts with child-care providers (for sick children only). Furthermore, some employers provide services such as distributing information on local child-care providers, distributing educational material, and contracting with outside resource and referral services (Seyler et al., 1995).

However, not all single parents are fortunate enough to have jobs that provide these types of benefits. Although there are laws that prescribe

the right to equal pay for women, neither the intent nor the letter of these laws are enforced. The 1994 U.S. Census Bureau reported that the average salary of female family heads is $19,872, while the average salary of male family heads is $30,472, a substantial difference. This coincides with research that shows women currently earn 64 percent of what men earn (Cetron, Rocha, & Rebecca, 1988). The gender gap in earnings is closing, but not at a fast enough pace for some people. As stated earlier, single women make up 22 percent of the parents in American families, single men 4 percent. A family with a man as the only breadwinner sees $30,000 per year. A woman doing the same job is making $19,200 per year. The absence of $10,800 per year is a huge difference in the financial resources available to the single-parent family headed by a female. This puts female single-parent families in a lower socioeconomic level than male single-parent or dual-parent families.

However, there are some solutions. The ideal situation for single-parent workers is to find an organization that provides benefits that support family concern issues, such as sick leave, medical benefits, and retirement benefits.

1. Many organizations provide their employees with floating holidays. These days off can positively assist single parents on days their child is ill. Progressive organizations will encourage their human resource professional to ensure consistent administration of floating holidays across the various departments. Frontline supervisors should be encouraged to develop contingency plans so that work can be covered in the event of a last-minute request for a floating holiday.

2. Flextime can also assist single parents in balancing work and family priorities. With adequate planning, flextime enables single

parents to juggle their schedule in order to respond to doctor appointments, school visitations, and days that "don't get off on the right foot." Responsive supervisors make a big difference in these programs. True flextime means that a person's start time can fluctuate between two hours before or after the core business hours. Some organizations do not allow employees to flex their hours each day but rather require that they choose one starting time that is the same every day.

3. Progressive organizations also offer on-site child-care programs or subsidized child care. Private industry can be brought on campus to provide this service to employees. This not only reduces the commute time for single parents, but also provides more continuity in the day by allowing parents to visit their children during lunch or break times. For example, *Working Mother* magazine's top-rated companies generally provide on-site day care. This is a tremendous benefit for the single-parent worker.

4. Alternative work environments, such as telecommuting, job sharing, and part-time jobs with full benefits are new ways in which employers are responding to the changing needs of workers. Unpaid but job-protected leave of absence policies also provide families with emergency support in critical times of need when it is necessary for single parents to have extra time for their children.

Many organizations are also trying to respond to personal care issues and career development needs of their employees by offering a number of noontime or after-work company-sponsored activities. Most of these activities are free to employees and include seminars covering a wide range of subjects, including parenting and child care, retirement, health and diet, social activities, opportunities for hobby development, exercise programs, industry-specific training, stress and time management workshops, communications-building seminars, and subsidized meal programs. A forward-looking and responsive organization will also provide employee assistance programs for addictions, family crises, and other counseling needs. Responsiveness to the needs of employees has not always been an explicit factor in the development of company policies. But with the number of women in the work force continuing to increase, many of them single parents, progressive organizations are developing new programs to ensure that women can pursue management positions and develop their potential for increasing financial gain.

Among the services some organizations provide are connections to the community. Organizations advise employees about community services that help with family issues, such as United Way agencies, local YMCA programs, and after-school day-care programs.

2. Career Skills and Training

Assessment Tools Whether the single parent holds an entry-level position or is working in a specific career track, there are assessment tools available, such as the Career Assessment Inventory, Career Development Inventory, Career Directions Inventory, Self-Directed Search, and Campbell Interest and Skill Survey. These can assist individuals in making choices about additional training and skills in order to help improve their situation. A particularly helpful instrument is called Working. It measures nine competencies and helps the individual build on strengths and minimize weaknesses. Assessment tools as well as computerized guidance systems for occupational information are available for a nominal fee at local colleges and universities, and counselors who specialize in career counseling are available for consultation.

Seminars and Employment Agencies There are a number of professional organizations that offer seminars for a nominal fee or as a courtesy to the working professional. Presentation topics include information about job-seeking skills, self-concept building, interviewing skills, résumé writing, and portfolio development. Local and state employment centers, women's resource centers, community colleges, and universities also offer seminars.

A major career strategy in the 1990s is to sign up with temporary agencies. This permits a flexible work schedule, gives the employee a realistic preview of a job prior to accepting fulltime employment, and often entitles the worker to free technical training sessions, such as in word processing and spreadsheet programs.

Educational Assistance Most major organizations today offer educational assistance to facilitate career growth through job certification, training, or obtaining a degree. Local community colleges, universities, and school districts offer reasonably priced evening and weekend courses. The larger the school, the more likely the class schedule is to accommodate various work schedules.

3. Career Strategies

Résumé and Personal Portfolio Chapter 9 in this book will be helpful.

Mentorship Programs Finding a mentor is highly recommended. A mentor is someone who spends time with an individual, providing meaningful feedback on situations that the individual wants to discuss and insight into specific industries and organizations. Most important, mentors provide recommendations about work and offer assistance in preparing for future opportunities. This is especially important for women who are entering a career field.

Being Visible and Productive All employees, no matter where they land on the organizational ladder, are in a position at any time to be visible within their organization. As such, it is imperative to be productive. People who produce results and are ready for new challenges are in the best position to maintain good performance and take on new opportunities. This is especially important as American businesses continue to downsize, leaving fewer people to do more work.

Having Inside Knowledge of Organization Company newsletters, statements of priorities/goals, meetings with managers and peers, and so forth, are ways to be aware of what is happening within an organization. Having this awareness enables employees to see the big picture and focus on how they can contribute to this process. It also helps employees to network better and to anticipate ways in which they can become even more useful to the organization.

Cross-Functional Moves Up is not the only way to enhance a career. Today, people who are generalists are in a good position to move within the organization. In fact, many larger organizations will encourage cross-functional moves by paying a bonus to employees who make these kinds of moves. Employers recognize the value of bringing in fresh ideas, building on skills and interests that can enhance work processes, and providing opportunities for creating new team leaders and managers. To be prepared when these opportunities arise, an employee must always be learning new skills.

Professional Organizations Keeping in step with what is happening within an industry is essential in order for employees to show their employer that they are continually learning and growing. Additionally, professional organizations create a powerful means of networking with other professionals, which enhances business knowledge, helps to develop a sense of team spirit with people with similar interests, and provides information about other potential jobs and career moves.

Social Attending social functions within an organization or industry provides a grass-roots way to discuss common interests and problems and to gain new insights and knowledge in order to develop new solutions to current work problems. Social functions also allow for balancing work demands with the need for social interaction and recreation. This does take time away from family, which needs to be considered when developing the wider families concept. It is important to have other adults who can share the child-rearing responsibilities, including cooperative exchanges when a single parent needs to attend a professional social function.

There are a number of ways in which this model can be incorporated in a therapeutic setting. Keep in mind that the aim is to look at avenues in which the community, school system, family, and world of work can be incorporated into meaningful solutions to the challenges of single parenting. Possible solutions from the perspective of the practitioner as well as school counselors follow.

Implications for the Practitioner

The world of work includes an array of issues for any single parent, whose concerns may include broad goals such as career exploration, career development, or retooling for a new job skill set. Issues may also include very practical and real situations such as balancing the demands of work, home, and child rearing. Specific considerations may include:

- reviewing the career assessment instruments listed earlier.

- discussing how your client can best juggle work and home demands. What new strategies may prove helpful in this process?

- inviting clients to imagine a miracle and describe how things would work in their home if there were fewer pressures associated with their varied roles.

- referring clients to someone who can assist in financial goal planning and help them maximize the benefits their company provides.

- providing therapy that would enable clients to further explore self-narratives and discover new meanings to the way they view their situation as a single parent, single person, and professional.

- applying parenting skills to the work environment—learning problem-solving skills, negotiating skills, communication skills in a group environment, time management skills, and so on, are useful both on and off the job.

Implications for the School Counselor

- School counselors can look for strategic interventions. One important issue to recognize is that single parents are using their resources to do what traditional families do with two parents. When there is a problem at school it may be productive to request that the parent *assist* the school in solving the child's particular problem. Believing that the parent knows their child best enables the school counselor to keep the parent in charge and builds on the parent's expertise rather than insinuating that the child's problem is a result of poor parenting (Lewis, 1986).

- Help develop a family hierarchy. One of the challenges in a single-parent family is the need for appropriate boundaries. Single parents may focus all of their attention on the children and not engage in rebuilding adult relationships, or the reverse may be true. Children in single-parent families may be too involved with their parent and not involved enough with their peers, resulting in an inability to learn appropriate boundaries and the loosening of generational hierarchies.

- Encourage parents and children to have time together that is not focused on problems or behavioral issues. This will help the family have quality time together that doesn't involve conflict.

- Support both children and parents. The family structure needs extra encouragement since the family often experiences limited resources, needs emotional support, and is adjusting to the loss of a partner and parent. Furthermore, the noncustodial parent may visit. This can be a source of problems for the children and the parents, since each parent adopts a different role with the children. It is much easier to spend money on a weekend and let the child have extra freedoms (often the visiting parent's role) than to provide the necessary structure during the week that includes a schedule, discipline, chores, and school-related tasks.

CASE STUDY

A 36-year-old female client began therapy when her marriage of ten years was coming to an end. She has one daughter, age seven. Unfortunately, the client was not able to financially make ends meet on her own. She explored several options such as moving to a different apartment, getting a roommate, and looking at her personal budget to see how her monthly expenditures could be reduced. Eventually, she sought refuge and solace by moving back in with her parents. While it had been quite some time since she had lived at home, her parents were supportive of her situation and enjoyed having their granddaughter around.

This single parent remained in therapy for a little over a year. She had to deal with many issues—anger about the situation in general, regret and doubts—wondering if she could have done things differently in order to make their marriage work, frustrations in parenting a child, juggling demands from both sides of the family, and so on.

Of particular concern to the client was the fact that she was finding it difficult to get her daughter to school each morning and arrive herself at work on time each day. She felt extra pressure to do even a better job than she routinely did because her job meant even more to her now that she was totally dependent on her own salary to make ends meet. She also felt that her co-workers were looking at her differently; as if they were judging her for becoming a divorced woman and the manner in which she was raising her daughter. She also noticed that her manager, while sensitive to her personal situation, became distant and assigned her "special projects" on a less frequent basis.

Her therapist initially laid out all of these challenges and helped the client prioritize the issues. She determined that her daughter's welfare was her number one priority; her job situation was second; the changes as a result of the divorce were third; and finally readjusting to living at home was fourth. The client and counselor spent a great deal of time pursuing the meaning of each role in her life and how she viewed herself as a single parent. Initially the client was quite overwhelmed with the changes in her life and did not feel she was adequately performing any of her roles. In time, she developed consistent routines with her daughter which included an effective discipline program. She made changes in her routine that enabled her to get her daughter to school each day and make it to work on time. She even noticed herself volunteering for new assignments at work and becoming more appropriately assertive.

As she began making these changes in her life some very interesting things began to occur. She started looking at the various resources available to her. She enrolled her daughter in a local softball team and swimming lessons at the YMCA. She went back to church and made friends with people who were supportive of her situation. Her church also told her about some financial assistance available through the local United Way agency. Through networking, she met some people in a singles group that informed her of a new job opportunity. Over a period of six months she was able to get a new job at a higher salary and one that provided benefits. She was grateful for the new friends she had met through the church and even began volunteering some of her own time one Sunday each month helping with children's programs.

Her relationship with her daughter improved and they became even closer as they began the process of rebuilding new family ties and traditions. While the process seems very natural to most, the client looked at resources available within herself, her family, the community, and the world of work and by using

these resources was able to achieve appropriate goals for both herself and her daughter.

The counseling experience was invaluable to the client, as she was able to express her feelings about going through her divorce. She found the counseling experience to be a supportive environment for her to explore the meanings she attached to being a divorced woman, a single parent mother, and an employee who needed to make improvements in her career, work environment, and salary. Her counselor helped her change her world view of what it meant to have a family, by creating a "*wider family*" that include blood relation, community, school, and the world of work. She learned new techniques in parenting and was able to improve her own self-esteem, which enabled her to go for a new job that provided the challenges she was looking for and at an increased salary. In time, she doubted herself less, and developed new relationships and a consistent routine that helped balance the many roles in her life.

SUMMARY

Single-parent families continue to grow as a recognized family constellation. In 1994, single parents headed 22.3 percent of all families, and these figures are expected to continue to grow. The combination of being a caretaker, worker, and homemaker and caring for self is a big responsibility. Working single parents, who are mostly women, are often in a lower socioeconomic level than married counterparts for a number of reasons. Many women are paid less than men in the same positions, women are often in lower-paying jobs due to skills and education level, and the child support that many women are awarded is often not paid at all or only partially paid.

Single parents have unique needs due to their complex roles and responsibilities. Schools, businesses, and the community at large can assist the single parent in many different ways. The primary way in which practitioners can assist the single-parent family is by being aware of the multiple demands placed on this population. Single parents need understanding, encouragement, and a willingness on the part of those who help them to assist with practical activities such as day care, household chores, and social activities.

Practitioners have a wide range of options for assisting single-parent families. Individual counseling with single parents can build self-esteem and sound decision-making skills and help the families on both sides of the single parent understand what is occurring within the single-parent family. Group counseling can provide the needed support and encouragement that single parents need in order to maintain their multiple roles and responsibilities.

REFERENCES

Cetron, M. J., Rocha, W., & Rebecca, L. (1988). Long-term trends affecting the United States, *The Futurist,* 1, 29–40.

Donati, T. (1995). Single parents and wider families in the new context of legitimacy, *Marriage and Family Review,* 20(1/2), 27–42.

Ferguson, B., Williams, C., & Gardner, L. (1994). *Single-parent families: The integration of school, work and the community.* Paper presented at Texas Counseling Association Conference, November 11, 1994. Houston, Texas.

Foster, M. (1997). Personal Communication. October 13, 1997. Dallas, Texas: Wausau Insurance Company.

Hanson, J. (1987). *Clinical issues in single-parent households.* Rockville, Md.: Aspen Publishers.

Kissman, K. (1992). Single parenting: Interventions in the transitional stage, *Contemporary Family Therapy: An International Journal,* 14, 323–333.

Lester, G. (1991). *Child support and alimony: 1989.* U.S. Bureau of the Census. Washington, D.C.: U.S. Government Printing Office.

Lewis, W. (1986). Strategic interventions with children of single-parent families, *The School Counselor,* 375–378.

Lino, M. (1989). Financial status of single-parent households headed by a never-married, divorced/separated, or widowed parent. R. Walker (ed.), *Families in transition: Structural changes and effects on family life,* 151–160. Proceedings of the 1989 pre-conference workshop of the Family Economics Home Management Section of the American Home Economics Association.

Marciano, F. D., & Sussman, M. B. (1991). Wider families: An overview. F. D. Marciano & M. B. Sussman (eds.), *Wider families: New traditional family forms.* New York: The Haworth Press, Inc.

Mednick, M. (1987). Single mothers: Review and critique of current research, *Applied Social Psychology Annual,* 7, 184–201.

Morrison, N. (1995). Successful single-parent families, *Journal of Divorce and Remarriage,* 22, 205–219.

Moskowitz, M., & Townsend, C. (1998). The 100 best companies for working mothers," *Working Mother.*

Mulroy, E. (1995). Successful single-parent families, *Journal of Divorce and Remarriage,* 22, 204–219.

Rose, S. R. (1989). Teaching single parents to cope with stress through small group intervention, *Small Group Behavior,* 20, 259–269.

Seyler, D., Monroe, P., & Garand, J. (1995). Balancing work and family: The role of employer-supported child-care benefits, *Journal of Family Issues,* 16, 171–193.

U.S. Department of Commerce, Bureau of the Census (1994). *Comparison of income summary measures by selected characteristics,* 1–2. Washington, D.C.: U.S. Government Printing Office.

U.S. Department of Commerce, Bureau of the Census (1996). *Household and family characteristics: March 1995,* 20–188. Washington, D.C.: U.S. Government Printing Office.

15

Prisons

A Vocational Counseling Model

DOM GARRISON, GREG DEWALD,

DONNA METCALF

INTRODUCTION

The Oklahoma Department of Vocational and Technical Education (ODVTE), an Oklahoma state agency, has operated vocational training programs for prisoners since February 1971.[1] For years, the inmate population in the state was relatively static and the benefit of the few vocational programs offered was unquestioned. It was assumed that if inmates participated in a training program they would be more likely to succeed once released from prison.

Since the inception of the first programs, the inmate population in Oklahoma has skyrocketed to more than 15,000 offenders. This has resulted in the state allocating an increasing percentage of state revenues to the incarceration of felons. The ODVTE, through its Skills Center School System (SCSS), experienced an increase in the number of training programs and campuses during this time. Today, the SCSS has campuses on the grounds of fifteen state correctional facilities. The SCSS trains offenders in many occupations, such as welding, automotive service, commercial food service, carpentry, commercial building maintenance, computer technology, plumbing, and additional construction-related trades. Training in each of these occupational areas is designed to meet the specific needs of business and industry. Business and industry representatives serve on advisory committees that provide

Dom Garrison is the superintendent of the Skills Center School System with the Oklahoma Department of Vocation and Technical Education; Greg Dewald is the state coordinator for the Skills Center Special Projects; and Donna Metcalf is the state coordinator of Student Services for the Skills Center.

[1]Editors' Note: Oklahoma has developed a significantly integrated vocational/career program within its prison system. It is possible to adapt this program to other states for this growing population.

guidance in the development of the training programs' curricula, including implementation of practical experience for students.

In 1995, the Oklahoma legislature passed the Juvenile Justice Act. This act established the state's Office of Juvenile Affairs, which is responsible for the incarceration of juvenile offenders. Currently, the state owns and operates three secure juvenile detention facilities and contracts for several group homes. These facilities house the state's most dangerous juveniles. During 1997, the SCSS began operating training programs in two Level E group homes in Oklahoma and will soon begin program operations in two more juvenile facilities. Level E group homes are designed to house juvenile offenders who are at risk of flight and in need of intensive supervision. Typically, these offenders have no history of aggravated, violent criminal activity.

This heightened emphasis on securing and detaining individuals (of all ages) convicted of crimes is eroding the state's budget. Thus, the state has mandated that all programs aimed at reducing growth rates of prison populations be more accountable for results. This mandate has led the SCSS to allocate greater human and financial resources to determine offenders' ability to benefit from the services the SCSS provides. Public and legislative support for educating and training offenders is extremely limited. There is, however, some public support for locking offenders away and punishing them by removing privileges.

The fact is, most offenders will be released and will return to society. This creates a need for meaningful education and training programs targeted at preparing the individual offender for success in the workplace and in society. No offender returns to prison solely due to a lack of welding skills or a low score on an academic achievement test. The lack of life skills causes most exoffenders' failures. These skills include knowing how to: (a) resolve conflict in an acceptable manner, (b) effectively manage anger, (c) access and manage resources, (d) remain free from chemical dependence, (e) work as a team member, (f) secure meaningful, satisfying employment, and (g) make acceptable decisions.

This complex set of issues has caused the SCSS to develop and implement processes for identifying individuals who can benefit from specific services. Prior to October 1994, staff members at the Oklahoma Department of Corrections' (DOC) Assessment and Reception Center (A&R) provided all assessment and counseling for adult offenders entering the correctional system. In October 1994 the SCSS and the DOC entered into a partnership in the area of inmate assessment. Through a reallocation of human resources, the SCSS assigned two assessment specialists the task of assessing and providing career guidance to individual offenders entering the corrections system. Today these assessment specialists are able to serve twenty-five of the approximately 160 offenders who enter the system weekly.

The cost to incarcerate offenders is high. Training and education programs add to this cost. It is important that these programs meet the unique needs of individual offenders and keep them from becoming repeat offenders. Thus, a comprehensive approach to assessing individual needs, aptitude, interest, ability, and academic attainment is imperative.

Dramatic increases in the numbers of hard-to-serve offenders of all ages have caused us to assess the services offered and strategies for delivery. Proper, upfront offender and periodic reassessment are necessary for identifying services needed by the offender and for providing guidance on how to tailor these services to meet the unique needs of the "whole person."

DEVELOPMENT OF THE MODEL FOR A PRISON POPULATION

The Skills Center School System provides vocational skills training to individuals who are under the supervision of the Oklahoma Department of Corrections or the Office of Juvenile Affairs (OJA) and provides funding for five dropout recovery programs for at-risk youth. The SCSS has adopted School-to-Work as its primary operational philosophy and is the lead organization in implementing this transition system in a corrections environment. School-to-Work provides a framework for the delivery of services that helps ensure the offender's successful transition from inmate to employee.

School-to-Work is not a program, it is an educational system with many interconnected components that helps prepare students for work in a systematic manner. The School-to-Work system begins with career development, which includes assessment of aptitude, interest, ability, and career awareness followed by career exploration and career guidance. Plans of study are built for each student at the appropriate juncture of education. This plan of study is flexible and is based on student interests and needs. The plan of study defines the steps necessary for students to become successful in a chosen career and helps students become aware of the competencies that must be achieved in order to succeed in the workplace. The Oklahoma School-to-Work system encourages students to enroll in the appropriate academic classes and helps them understand the need for appropriate technical or other schooling beyond the twelfth grade. Through this system, students as well as teachers are discovering the relevance of education to the real world.

For incarcerated individuals School-to-Work is a framework for success as well. A successful transition from school to work can mean a crime-free and prosperous life for graduates upon their release from prison. In conjunction with School-to-Work, Oklahoma has adopted the ten Key Practices of the Southern Regional Education Board's (SREB) High Schools That Work as the secondary education model for School-to-Work. These nationally recognized, SREB-developed practices are indicators of integrated, high-quality, challenging education for high-school-aged youth. The Key Practices can be translated to learning environments outside high schools—they have educational significance applicable to programs for students of all ages.

The Key Practices are:

1. Set higher expectations and get all students to meet them.

2. Provide rigorous and challenging vocational and technical studies that incorporate mathematics, science, language arts, and problem-solving skills in the context of modern workplace practices and in preparation for continuous learning.

3. Provide rigorous academics that teach essential concepts through functional and applied strategies.

4. Have all students complete a challenging program of study that includes both a rigorous academic core and a career pathway.

5. Provide a structured system of school-based and work-based learning.

6. Have an organized structure and schedule that allows academic and vocational teachers to do joint planning.

7. Have all students actively engaged in the learning process.

8. Have all students in an individualized career guidance system.

9. Provide a structured system of extra help.

10. Use student and system performance data to continuously improve curriculum, instruction, school climate, organization, and management in order to advance student learning.

The ten Key Practices are the guiding principles for developing individualized instructional plans, closely supervising and directing project participants, developing a structured system for delivery of services based on the needs of participants, scheduling cooperative planning for teachers and other program and service providers, setting high expectations of all learners, integrating all services, and continuously improving the system. Following the Key Practices while developing the SCSS system for delivery of services has led to participants becoming lifelong learners and opens doors to their successful employment in high-wage jobs.

A major component in the Oklahoma School-to-Work transition plan is reentry skills training. Reentry skills, or life skills, including the abilities to resolve conflict, solve problems, manage resources, and remain free from substance abuse, are primary factors in increasing student success. Reentry skills also have an impact on cognitive learning abilities. By integrating all services into students' individual strategies and basing the focus of these services on their chosen career path, the time frame necessary for competency attainment is compressed.

Successful implementation of this process provides offenders with the skills to successfully enter and reenter society, including job and life skills that satisfy their unique personal, social, and workplace needs. The processes described in this chapter can also have an impact on the quality of services for other populations in a workforce development model, for example, transitional welfare clients seeking to enter and reenter the work force and out-of-school youth.

USING THE MODEL FOR OKLAHOMA OFFENDERS

Screening Process

The Skills Center School System strives to make educational opportunities accessible to those offenders with an identified need. As new offenders are processed, they receive an orientation to academic and vocational education opportunities, a medical and psychological assessment, and a substance abuse screening. Treatment recommendations are made available to case management staff and educators for use in program planning. Because resources are limited, a screening process is used to determine which new offenders are most likely to benefit from academic or vocational education. All new offenders are screened, using a questionnaire that requests information about past education and work history, earnings upon entry into the correctional system, and employment potential and financial obligations upon release.

All self-reported information is verified by a correctional intake officer. Through this process it is determined if a youthful offender has an active Individualized Education Plan (IEP). It is also determined if an adult or juvenile offender has pending charges or parole violations.

Although the state of Oklahoma has 15,130 adult offenders housed at minimum, medium, and maximum security facilities, the SCSS only has resources for 564 training slots. To ensure that all offenders who have an identified "vo-tech and/or academic need" are afforded access prior to release, the SCSS uses screening results and projected discharge date (or parole date) to target those offenders returning to the community first.

Using this process, the following types of offenders are identified for further evaluation and assessment:

1. offenders who will not be self-sufficient upon release with existing education, work experience, and technical skills.

2. offenders with adequate basic skills to participate and graduate from a vocational education program within the next twelve months (some basic skills remediation may be necessary).

3. offenders who will have the opportunity for employment within ninety days after vo-tech graduation.

Offenders returning to the community in the shortest time are provided the earliest access to career assessment, career guidance, and development of an ISS. The remaining offenders are placed on a waiting list for guidance services so that no offender is denied access to services.

Assessment

The Test of Adult Basic Education (TABE) Battery has been chosen as the instrument used to assess academic achievement. The results of the TABE Battery are retained as part of the client's objective assessment. The TABE Survey and Locator are used appropriately to determine which form of the TABE Battery will yield the most valid results. Offenders must have at least a 5.1 grade equivalency on the TABE to enroll in vo-tech. Offenders who have a "vo-tech and/or academic need" are referred to the correctional

system for participation in appropriate academic preparation programs. The delivery system is flexible. Offenders may complete basic skills remediation prior to entry into a vocational education program or while they are enrolled. Offenders may also participate in treatment programs while they are enrolled in academic and vocational education programs. At some sites, the academic and vocational education delivery system is totally integrated within one classroom.

The Career Occupational Preference System (COPS), the Career Ability Placement Survey (CAPS), and the Career Orientation Placement and Evaluation Survey (COPES) have been selected as the instruments for assessing vocational aptitude, ability, and work values. Using all results available from medical, psychological, and educational assessments, offenders are given the opportunity to participate in a career guidance session.

Planning and Referral

The desired outcome of the career guidance session includes development of an Individual Service Strategy (ISS) or referral to DOC for programs that will better meet the offender's needs. Using all information available, offenders are provided with the opportunity to make guided career decisions about academic and vocational education opportunities that enable them to be self-sufficient upon release. The Oklahoma Career Search program is the guidance tool used to provide current work-force data. An ISS is developed for each offender. The purpose of the ISS is to outline the appropriate mix and sequence of services and programs and justify the decisions for each, to indicate any need for supportive services, and to develop an individualized continuum of services that will lead to the desired employment goal.

When the graduate enters placement services, the ISS is used by the employment coordinator, the School-to-Work coordinator, the site guidance specialist, and the instructor as a means of sharing information and making sure the graduate is successful in securing employment upon release from the correctional institution. Movement efforts and job search efforts are documented on the ISS as they occur so all involved staff are aware of the graduate's status. When the ISS is reviewed, it is easy to determine the specific actions that were taken to assist the graduate with job search and movement.

Decisions reached during the development of the ISS are made in partnership with the student and are determined in conformance with applicable Office of Civil Rights provisions. During their career guidance session, offenders are asked to sign a participant concurrence statement, which affirms their commitment to completing the service strategy. Gaining this personal commitment to the ISS is a critical element in the offenders' accepting personal responsibility for their behavior and achievements. At the conclusion of the career guidance session, a memorandum is prepared for the unit classification meeting. This memorandum includes a facility recommendation, program needs, and tentative enrollment dates in specific academic and vocational education, life skills, and treatment programs.

While the offender is receiving services, the vocational education staff documents ongoing assessment at least once a month. The ISS is periodically updated to ensure relevancy to the offender's current status. The vocational education staff works cooperatively with each student to ensure that technical competencies are obtained, employment portfolios are completed, and employability readiness skills and life skills are developed to an acceptable level.

Training and Job Placement

During the training phase, vocational education students complete pretests and posttests in their chosen occupational area. These tests are a critical element in the development and updating of the ISS and are useful documentation for students. The results of these tests serve as a good motivational tool in an unpleasant environment where at-risk students are prone to developing negative attitudes.

At graduation, each student receives a competency-based certificate. If state-certified occupational competency tests are available, and the student has achieved the desired level of proficiency, the student will also receive appropriate state occupational competency certificates.

An important part of job placement services occurs during training. Each student is instructed on how to search for a job and actually completes a job application and a résumé and prepares an employment portfolio. Many students have no work experience, so they complete work-based learning prior to graduating from vo-tech. The vo-tech instructor and/or employment coordinator helps the graduate by providing job search assistance and assistance in securing clothing and supportive services from other state and community agencies. Each graduate is expected to obtain training-related employment within ninety days after graduation and is tracked for one year after release. Training-related placement rates are a major performance measure for the SCSS, and all personnel involved in serving the offender are held accountable for them.

CASE EXAMPLE

In 1994, a forty-eight-year-old offender named Ron was housed at a minimum security prison in Oklahoma. He was a third-time offender who was the victim of chemical dependency. Each time Ron had been in trouble with the law it was the result of drinking. His first incarceration occurred at the age of nineteen immediately after he graduated from high school. He had received an excessive number of traffic violations for driving while under the influence of alcohol. He served eight months on a two-year sentence at a nonsecure, community-based DOC facility where he was allowed to go on work release after one month at the facility. He spent his nights at the DOC facility and worked for a private employer each day. His wages were returned to the correctional facility each week and a portion was deducted for food and lodging. He did not participate in any type of substance abuse program prior to being placed on probation. He discharged his sentence at the end of two years. Ron started drinking as soon as he went on probation, but it was undetected. He married, became the proud father of two children, and worked his way up to being manager of an auto dealership in a metropolitan area. Ron never quit drinking, he just became more experienced at hiding the problem. His family suffered the consequences of living with an alcoholic, but his problem did not seem to interfere with his career. Ultimately, however, Ron went on a drinking binge that resulted in a conviction for vehicular manslaughter. Ron was sentenced to a medium security facility. Although his case manager had recommended that he participate in a substance abuse program, Ron never did. Ron saw no reason for it—he felt he had so many other survival problems facing him upon release that it was not worth the effort.

In 1994, Ron was transferred to a minimum security facility where vocational education opportunities were available. He was within twelve months of being eligible for work release when he decided to go see the vo-tech guidance specialist. Ron admitted that he had no idea how he was going to support himself when he went home, and he was afraid to return to the community where technology had changed everything that he had previously known. He agreed to participate in career assessment and to take the TABE. The vo-tech student coordinator and Ron reviewed the results and, to everyone's surprise except Ron's, he had a fourth-grade reading level. He admitted that he'd made it through school on good behavior and athletic ability. He had low self-esteem and great doubt that upon release that he would be able to be self-sufficient and sober. During the guidance session, Ron made a commitment to increase his reading skills by participating in ABE and the tutoring program that was available at the facility. Ron also made the guided career decision to enroll in Auto Service Technology, to participate in substance abuse training, and to attend AA at least three nights a week for the remainder of his sentence. During the twelve months that Ron participated in the academic and vocational education programs, his self-esteem and self-worth increased, his reading level increased to 12.9, and his math scores went from 3.4 to 12.9. Much of this growth can be attributed to ongoing guidance efforts and good instructional practices.

When the student coordinator and Ron originally developed the ISS, they decided that the first vocational objective Ron should achieve was "acquisition of the competencies for the Auto Service Excellence (ASE) competency areas of front end alignment and brake repair," realizing that most students only had time to complete two ASE areas. The academic and vocational instructors consciously made a commitment to coordinate with each other and with the substance abuse educator. Ron's successes in the academic, vocational, and substance abuse classrooms were openly acknowledged and recorded on the ISS. At each review, new objectives were established. This positive reinforcement motivated Ron to excel. As Ron's reading skills increased, his achievement rate in the vocational program increased. Upon graduation, Ron successfully passed the competency tests for all four ASE competency areas. Ron was the first student in that program to complete all four competency areas.

Prior to Ron's being transferred to a community-based facility, the student coordinator provided the case manager at the facility with information about Ron's problems, successes, and continued needs. They agreed that by working together they could better serve Ron. The instructor arranged several job interviews for Ron before he graduated and the employment coordinator made arrangements for appropriate clothing. Immediately upon graduation, Ron was transferred to a community-based correctional facility. Upon securing employment, the employment coordinator and the employer made an agreement with Ron that a certain amount of his wages each week would be deducted for the cost of tools.

The employment coordinator, the case manager, and Ron updated the ISS and created a new plan that would result in sobriety twelve months after discharge. The instructor, the employment coordinator, and the case manager checked on Ron once a month. The instructor and employment coordinator communicated with the employer and Ron on a regular basis to determine if additional training or services were needed to make Ron a successful employee. Ron discharged his sentence on time. Today, Ron is employed by the same firm. He is earning $14.50 an hour. He routinely contacts his instructor and his student coordinator. Ron has not touched alcohol, but he readily admits that it is a daily battle. To maintain sobriety, Ron continues to participate in AA three nights a week and acts as a mentor for new AA members. Ron has been instrumental in helping three vo-tech graduates secure employment. Ron attributes his success to caring educators who took the time to help him set goals and create a structure that allowed him to acquire self-discipline, self-esteem, and self-worth. The student coordinator eagerly awaits Ron's routine calls and Christmas cards. Ron knows that the Skills Center System is a support base that will always be available to him.

CONCLUSION

In July 1991 the Skills Center School System implemented a structured process for providing career development that includes assessment, career awareness, career guidance, and development of an Individualized Service Strategy prior to enrollment.

Prior to implementation of the career development model, offenders were placed in SCSS vocational programs based on their expressed interest in a particular program and availability of a training slot in the program. Prior to implementation of the career development model, the annual dropout rate was 38 percent. Within the corrections environment, approximately 10 percent of the dropout rate can be attributed to security issues, such as protective custody issues, disposition of pending chargers, misconducts, and custody assessment. Since implementation of the career development model, the average annual dropout rate has decreased to 25 percent. Much of this gain in student retention can be attributed to student commitment to program completion. Today, offenders make an up-front, conscious decision about program choices after reviewing the assessment results, participating in career exploration activities, and making guided decisions about future employment preferences and earning potential. Upon completion of the career guidance session, each offender signs a participant concurrence statement to affirm commitment to completing the identified education and treatment programs (as outlined on the ISS) in the prescribed sequence. At the same time, the offender is assured that the SCSS will coordinate with the DOC on movement and placement issues to increase accessibility to programs and services at the appropriate time. This has provided a more streamlined, outcome-based approach for delivery of services and provides the offender a reason for setting short- and long-term career-planning goals.

Having an individualized, needs-based plan for each offender has made it easier for the DOC and the SCSS to manage inmate movement issues in an overcrowded prison environment where security is paramount and movement on a central transport unit (CTU) between facilities is costly. In 1996, the CTU drove 47,168 miles transporting offenders between DOC facilities within the state of Oklahoma. As a result of the career development program, it is now possible to target offenders to specific sites for specific programs at a specific time, which has allowed the DOC to reduce the number of unnecessary, costly moves. This has also allowed the SCSS to maintain full enrollment by ensuring that each training slot in each program is filled on an as-needed basis, which was not previously the case. Prior to implementation of the career development model, for example, there was a week during which thirty-eight of the 540 training slots were va-

cant. Now, with enrollment based on documented assessment outcomes, the SCSS has improved its ability to partner with the DOC by forecasting which offenders need to be moved to what site within a set time frame. This has resulted in the development of a pipeline of potential students, and the average slot utilization during 1996 and 1997 was 99 percent.

In 1991, the job placement rate for Skills Center's graduates was 52 percent, but only 38 percent of the graduates secured training-related jobs. In 1997, the training-related job placement rate for SCSS graduates was 65 percent. This can be attributed to offenders being trained in an appropriate program, which empowers them to assume personal responsibility for acquiring employability skills and to believe they can market those skills for legitimate personal gain upon release. The increase in job placement can also be attributed to documented needs (identified during the enrollment process) being addressed as the offender reintegrates into the community.

Plans can now be developed to address many of the common barriers to offender employment, and these barriers can be addressed prior to release. One of the more common is housing, since many offenders will be homeless upon release. Transitional living arrangements are negotiated prior to the offender leaving the DOC facility. Efforts to acquire a social security card, which is essential for a job search, can be initiated while the offender is in training, thus reducing the amount of preemployment time the offender would face upon release (which can result in new offenses or the resumption of substance abuse due to anxiety about basic survival needs). Interviews can be arranged by the instructor prior to completion of training so the offender can conduct a purposeful job search that has been enhanced through personal contact that the instructor has had with potential employers. This value-added approach has resulted in an increased number of offenders who are now successful, tax-paying members of communities.

REFERENCES

Introducing a Premier Educational System That Transitions Students from School to Work (1995). *Oklahoma School-to-Work Model* [Brochure]. Stillwater, Okla.: ODVTE.

Moskowitz, M., & Townsend, C. (1998). The 100 best companies for working mothers, *Working Mother.*

Office of Juvenile Affairs (1997). *OJA Web page: Statistical information* [Online]. *www.state.ok.us/~oja/ oja.html.*

Oklahoma Department of Corrections (1996). *1996 Annual Report.* Oklahoma City, Okla.: Department of Corrections.

Oklahoma Department of Vocational and Technical Education (1995). *Implementing Oklahoma's System of Career Portfolios and Career Passports.* Stillwater, Okla.: ODVTE.

Oklahoma Department of Vocational and Technical Education (1996). *1991–1996 Completion/Follow-up Report.* Stillwater, Okla.: Information Management Division, ODVTE.

Oklahoma Department of Vocational and Technical Education (1997). *Slot Utilization Report.* Stillwater, Okla.: Skills Centers Division, ODVTE.

Skills Center School System School-to-Work Transition Plan (1995). *Skills Centers School System School-to-Work Transition* [Brochure]. Stillwater, Okla.: ODVTE.

Southern Regional Educational Board (1993). *Redesigning and refocusing high school vocational studies.* Atlanta, Ga.: Gene Bottoms.

Southern Regional Educational Board (1992). *Making High Schools Work.* Atlanta, Ga.: Gene Bottoms, Alice Presson, & Mary Johnson.

16

Impaired Workers

A Multidisciplinary
Approach to Work Hardening

FELIPE G. MARTINEZ, M.A.

INTRODUCTION

Work Hardening is a physical therapy program. It is designed to measure what an injured person can do physically and to provide treatment to improve that level of functioning. Specifically, work hardening refers to preparing the client to return to work through simulation of work tasks at different levels of weight that provide physical conditioning. If a client is not capable of doing the same level of work as before the injury, specific levels of functioning can be identified. This program was developed by Matheson (1982; Neimeyer and Jacobs, 1989) in California. It was designed specifically for industrially injured workers receiving worker's compensation.

When a person is injured on the job and receives worker's compensation, unusual dynamics come into play. The Work Hardening program addresses the subsequent situation with specific techniques to meet the special needs of this population. The goals of Work Hardening are: (a) increasing work tolerance through conditioning; (b) learning pain-control techniques through simulated work samples; (c) decreasing fear of reinjury through simulated work; and (d) learning worker characteristics that employers like. To accomplish this, a varied team of experts are engaged in the treatment.

This type of program is multidisciplinary as defined by the Commission on Accreditation of Rehabilitation Facilities (CARF) and the National Advisory Committee on Work Hardening. Besides dealing with the physical improvement of the injured individual, Work Hardening

Felipe G. Martinez has worked as a rehabilitation counselor for twenty years and is currently working as a vocational consultant for OPTUM in San Antonio, Texas.

is intended to address psychosocial issues and worker behaviors (Neimeyer and Jacobs, 1989), since many clients act as if they are being paid to stay sick. The team typically includes a physical therapist, an occupational therapist, assistants for both, aerobics instructors, physical trainers, a vocational counselor, and a psychologist. Some programs include a person to do biofeedback therapy and a social worker to make referrals to appropriate agencies.

The vocational counselor assumes several roles in order to meet the dynamics of this very special group of people. Typical responsibilities include: (a) administering assessments to help the client make appropriate vocational decisions; (b) assessing the client for gaining skills for job placement and the world of work; (c) preparing a functional job analysis of the preinjury job; and (d) counseling the client to deal with depression or the lack of or distorted motivation and other quasitherapeutic functions. Some of these tasks include relaxation training and facilitation of a group process. Most processing of problems is done at a very low level of intensity and does not deal with deep-seated emotional components. The process focuses on the irrational thinking that can be detrimental to being able to return to work. A rational emotive therapy approach has been used in many cases and has been helpful.

The Relationship Between Malingering and Clients in the Work Hardening Program

The primary psychosocial issues for worker's compensation clients center around issues of deception and malingering. The Diagnostic and Statistical Manual of Mental Disorders IV (1994) sets a standard for identifying malingering that indicates several factors:

1. Malingering is more prevalent among people with a personality disorder and occurs in a medicolegal context.

2. A discrepancy exists between what is reported and what is factual.

3. There is a lack of cooperation with evaluation and a lack of compliance with treatment.

4. A diagnosis of malingering includes a diagnosis of antisocial personality disorder.

Counselors' experiences in Work Hardening programs corroborate many of these factors. However, although a certain number of participants come from the fringes of acceptable social behavior, many clients who seem to practice what appears to be deception are not typically disordered personalities. Therefore, a broader context is needed to understand and to deal with the issue of malingering or deception.

Forensic Deception Analysis

Hall and Pritchard (1996) propose a broader context within which to explain and detect distortion of symptoms that is the hallmark of malingering. The authors propose a model for detecting deception called Forensic Deception Analysis (FDA). The model assumes that distortion is typical of all types of personalities, not just antisocial, and postulates three issues that help define deception for gain:

1. What is the level of usefulness of the symptoms in achieving the goal? For example, victims of a car accident may exaggerate functional limitations. They may say their pain is all over or more intense or long-lasting than it really is in order to gain a larger settlement.

2. What is the response style to the efforts to detect deceptive behavior? Hall and Pritchard (1996) suggest that the way a person deceives is a marker that helps the FDA detect deception. The authors also believe that not all "fakers" fake intentionally. In their model, they argue that some distortion is not intentional but accidental. Other behavior types include those who exaggerate (faking bad) or minimize (faking good) real symptoms. Some people try to invalidate testing through disruptive behaviors while some mix several of the above styles at the same time (mixed response styles). Finally, some fake and then stop due to fatigue during long testing or due to the belief that they have been found out. These behaviors are important in providing the evaluator with information on what to look for to detect faking (Hall & Pritchard, 1996).

3. What are the strategies for detection of deception that the evaluator will use? The following three strategies are listed in order of efficacy:
   a. Multimethods are best because clients become confused and lose control of their faking. When faced with several tests, the person being evaluated does not know when faking is being tested, especially when the test does not obviously address the target symptom. For example, a person is suspected of faking a back injury but is required to take a Minnesota Multiphasic Personality Inventory that tests for veracity.
   b. The evaluator needs to explicitly use alternative testing, which refers to using tests that measure similar stimuli with different instruments. For example, objective personality testing can often identify individuals who would typically distort. The validity of this strategy is decreased by the assumption that normal people do not fake.
   c. Clinical interviews can be valuable but are more subject to examiner error and lack of objectivity.

FDA is specially designed to provide a model for detection of faking for the forensic expert so that information can be gathered for a legal proceeding. That, however, is not the goal of Work Hardening. Faking or malingering is an important concept but its detection is only important in the context of clinical treatment.

Symptom Magnification

Faking is one of many issues that is ubiquitous to industrially injured clients. Matheson (1985, 1988) and Neimeyer and Jacobs (1989) proposed a change in the basic assumptions that define faking, or malingering as it is more commonly known. According to Stedman's *Medical Dictionary* (1972), malingering is defined as feigning an illness usually so as not to work. Matheson interprets this concept in a more innocuous form that removes the negatives from what some describe as faking behavior. His is a more benign idea that leads to more effective treatment of the industrially injured client. He observes that some injured persons easily become victims of injury circumstances. The behaviors they exhibit are verbalization of symptoms or the acting out of symptoms, whether consciously or unconsciously. These behaviors are destructive but, by definition, reinforced socially. Dealing with symptoms becomes the most important aspect of the injured person's life. If there is no intervention, suggests Matheson, depression follows, leading to learned helplessness.

However, there is another way to interpret this progression of events. As the client realizes that life is miserable being an injured worker, as the financial pressures mount, and as the people surrounding the client become disillusioned over the morass the client is in, depression occurs, setting the stage for rehabilitation to occur.

If symptom magnification is socially reinforced, then the primary role of the vocational counselor is to provide interventions that will extinguish the maladaptive behaviors. Whenever a client utilizes maladaptive symptom behavior, the injury should be treated as real. In the beginning of treatment, much clinical attention is given to show good faith. However, if there is no response the client should quickly be sent to a physician, who, recognizing there is no compelling reason to stop the treatment, usually sends the client back to Work Hardening. A "go slow" approach is used for the first day or two so the client can be helped to recognize what brought on symptoms. When this awareness is explored, the client is expected to resolve the problem by not increasing the pain through taking control of its basic cause. As the client's functional capacity increases and as control of what exacerbates the pain is mastered, the counselor and all other staff provide social reinforcement in a variety of ways. Sometimes clients need to be recognized publicly for taking the correct steps to prevent pain. Clients are told they will be watched carefully by the clinical staff to ensure that they are applying proper body mechanics and are doing only as much as they can physically handle.

An understanding of behavior modification techniques is necessary for a Work Hardening program. The counselor should also train the staff on the importance of extinguishing and reinforcing behaviors and should provide the language necessary to accomplish this.

Studies done at one of the Work Hardening programs where this counselor worked indicated that workers of different ages performed differently when Functional Capacity Evaluation results were compared. Clients who were eighteen to twenty-nine years did the best. It appears their age was the major factor. Those thirty to thirty-nine years achieved the worst results. They were not willing to work through painful exercises and exhibited a "live for today" mentality. Those forty to forty-nine years did better but still did not seem to reach their true capacity as judged by the staff. The fifty and older, however, matched the youngest subset of clients! It is possible that they were so worried that if they lost their job, they would never get a good job again, or they would have trouble getting a job and have to start at the bottom. They were also more mature and more dedicated to their occupation.

THE MODEL

A program called Special Olympics was implemented to remove client resistance to activity. Safe activities were designed for a competitive format. Clients were competed in teams, rather than competing as individuals. Some of the games involved lifting safe levels of weights. The competitive yet fun atmosphere, coupled with the peer pressure to win, encouraged clients to do their best. The staff recognized that the best a client could do occurred during these games. Faking behaviors were often dropped at this point as the clients took pride in their achievements. It should be noted that the programs set up by the physical and occupational therapists for the individual needs of each client were more important than what happened during these Special Olympics. In other words, clinical treatment was the real basis for a client's success during these games.

The recognition given each client for achievement throughout the program provided probably the best social reinforcement of all. Clients received certificates for perfect attendance during a weekly graduation party. Daily grades for safe lifting, cooperative behavior, timely participation and other valued worker characteristics were rewarded with a T-shirt. This particular reward was very important to the clients, as demonstrated by the extra effort they made to get a T-shirt before leaving the program through graduation. The proud wearing of the T-shirt when the clients returned just to visit indicated how important this recognition of effort was.

The role of the counselor is to enhance these reinforcements of appropriate behaviors in individual counseling sessions. The gradual emotional and physical progress of clients is easily observable by a counselor during the sessions and that progress should be recognized and enhanced by the counselor through counseling techniques. A technique based on cognitive behavioral theory is recommended.

THE ROLE OF THE VOCATIONAL/REHABILITATION COUNSELOR IN WORK HARDENING PROGRAMS

Therapist

Clients that are industrially injured are compensated during the period of injury and treatment as well as during the posttreatment period up to a certain point. This remuneration is often the basis for some injured workers to stay sick as long as the compensation is forthcoming. Compounding this problem is the thinking that makes many workers resist getting well. Cognitive behavior theory (Rachman, 1997; Gelder, 1997) explains not only the reinforcement of illness behaviors but also the thinking behind the behaviors.

Beck (1964) proposed that schemata are used by patients to screen, code and evaluate. These schemata act like mental filters. From my experience, it appears that bias enters into the evaluative process when using schemata. Some people tend to see things negatively, as in the case of depressed patients. When a person is injured on the job, several assumptions are inherent: (a) "I have been injured" (this is true in the majority of cases); (b) "This is my chance to make some money through a legal suit"; and (c) "The greater the degree of my injury or the longer it lasts, it is for more money—." These assumptions can drive injured workers to stay ill far beyond what is considered typical.

None of these models addresses the role of embarrassment at being seen as a faker. Whether the injured worker is faking or not, the perception almost always is that the individual is faking, so the client comes under attack by the employer, fellow workers, family, and treatment professionals. At this point, the client starts to find justification for illness behaviors, often leading to the development of a filter or schema. It is probable that as the "story" and the symptoms are rehearsed, distorted logic makes the story all the more real. Like an implanted early childhood script, the original injury story takes on a life of its own. Since the client is perceived as a faker even if the injury was real, there is a loss of face. The embarrassment leads to an increasingly stronger story and the development of illness behaviors to make it more believable.

The original story, especially if false, sits like a computer virus, reshaping all subsequent data. The client, therefore, becomes very sensitive to criticism, and the role of the counselor must be influenced by a strong ethical sense of what is hurtful to the client. It is very important not to confront the client regarding the truth of the injury-related behavior. One physical therapist states that if a client complains of pain, the therapist assumes that it is true and provides appropriate and genuine treatment. This engenders strong rapport with the client that can often lead to a breakthrough with chronic pain behaviors. For example, a person that fakes a limp starts to modify the behavior after genuine and respectful treatment, having found an open door that allows for saving face upon resuming more normal behavior.

As a cognitive therapist, the counselor's first task is to counter the false premises or cognitions that clients have. In fact, these false premises can lead to such negative and destructive consequences that it is incumbent on the counselor to make clients evaluate their schemata. One such schema is that "a worker's compensation suit will lead to lots of money." The reality is that worker's compensation laws are designed to limit liability. In Texas, few cases go to trial, and when one does, the benefits are limited to what the client would have gotten without a lawsuit. Once the inaccurate cognition is countered, it should be replaced by a reasonable one. A reasonable one for the above example is to point out that clients without lawyers receive as much compensation as those with lawyers.

Depression takes on many faces in the Work Hardening program. Clients' first encounter with the Work Hardening program is during the orientation. At this time clients sign forms and the program is explained. The description of one group follows.

While some clients were feisty during the orientation, other were disheveled and exhibited poor hygiene. Even the feisty clients were seen as needing a morale boost and their anger was addressed politely, avoiding confrontation. The anger was placed in perspective and not seen as reflecting on the staff. Any hostile accusations or insinuations were treated appropriately and the clients were shown respect.

Within two weeks almost all of the clients experienced a total turnaround. The reasons for this are not known. Perhaps the best explanation is that the clients did physical exercises, mostly aerobic and stretching activities, and the endorphins caused a concomitant mood change. Perhaps the clients found a welcoming and social environment where they were respected and treated with unconditional regard. Whatever the reasons, the changes were dramatic.

The problem of depression, however, is ever-present to a counselor. While it is usually situational, in some cases it is of clinical intensity. Out of approximately 3,000 to 3,500 clients personally seen by one counselor, there were two suicides. Both were fairly young men, one in his forties, the other in his thirties. Neither gave any outward sign that they were suicidal. Recognizing that depression is typical of injured clients, some programs routinely measure it by use of psychological services. However, many insurance carriers resist paying for psychological assessment and interventions, insisting that their focus stay on physical rehabilitation.

Nevertheless, the role of the vocational counselor has to include dealing with depression when it occurs. Classes providing coping skills are very useful in providing clients with an understanding of what depression is, how it is generated, and how to deal with it. Clients willing to share their experiences and feelings provide a perfect lab for learning "how-to" techniques in classes and groups. In many cases, clients find that their feelings of being overwhelmed are not isolated experiences. Solutions that have worked for others are presented and discussed. Most important, the benefits of returning to work can be discussed as a way out of a depressing situation.

In this type of setting, the vocational counselor will also need to know how to intervene with a subgroup of chronic pain patients that are not amenable to improvement—they have become totally debilitated. They report severe pain and act as if they have severe pain. At the same time, there is no evidence of injury sufficient to support this pain. These individuals are recognized by staff, including the medical doctor, as being emotionally handicapped. Typically, there are very serious family or mental problems that coexist with the pain problem. These clients are truly entrenched in their pain, which appears to be a powerful and necessary crutch in their lives. The role of the counselor is to assess the emotional situation and to request a referral to a treatment professional capable of providing long-term treatment. Dealing with these clients' emotional problems is more important than providing them with physical treatment.

Motivator

The most difficult aspect of doing vocational rehabilitation in an industrial rehabilitation facility is to motivate injured workers to move forward. The workers' agenda is often in direct opposition to that of the treatment personnel. The workers must perform physical activity that is fairly demanding, and creative strategies need to be developed and implemented to provide the kind of rationale that allows them to set aside their own plans for those of the Work Hardening program.

When individuals are referred to a Work Hardening program, they are in a downward spiral. Typical individuals will have been in the system for more than six months and are considered chronic pain patients. Some still expect great wealth from the system and are waiting out creditors until the settlement is granted. Consequently, there is major financial stress.

Other individuals at this stage of the game are pegged as exaggerators and may manifest distrust, insulted feelings, anger, and hurt pride. Many clients feel they are sent to a rehabilitation program to be investigated. These clients arrive at the program guarded and worried that they are going to flunk this latest attempt to prove they are not really injured. They feel a smoldering anger that is directed at the staff. This behavior must be confronted as a first step in redirecting motivation.

Finally, regardless of which category a worker falls into, an increase in body weight for the idled injured worker is almost guaranteed and this weight gain has a devastating impact on morale.

Kanfer (1996) defines motivation as movement toward fulfillment of drives. He describes change as possible partly due to the client's capacity to develop incentives and goals and to move toward these goals. This is accomplished by means of anticipatory self-regulation, that is, knowing that something good will occur through application of effort. The counselor's task is to help the client set new goals based on more accurate assumptions. To make work more compelling, the counselor may have to increase anxiety by pointing out all of the bad things that can happen. While expectations of a large settlement increase anticipatory self-regulation to maintain pain behaviors, fear of failure can be used to change the expectations. The counselor should clearly explain the pros and cons of failing and of succeeding in the Work Hardening program. In this manner, the client has a clear picture of how choices affect the direction of one's life. The counselor helps in the evaluation of choices.

This task requires that the counselor explain to the client (individually and in classes or group) the consequences of delay in resolving treatment or of not returning to work. A lot of time needs to be spent on stories of other peoples' decisions and the consequences, whether good or bad. Individual analysis of the client's particular situation helps in identifying distress and in generating solutions to resolve the distress. Once the stress is recognized and possibly increased through accurate analysis, solutions and goals, even if long-term, can be set. The client can be motivated to move toward changing ineffective behavior and getting back to work.

Teacher

Applying techniques without the client knowing what is being done is a traditional approach to interventions. The counselor, however, can increase the confidence of the client in treatment by making sure they know what the professional goals are. A client who learns to deal with stress by understanding the therapeutic steps applied can resolve problems in the future. Consequently, teaching clients how to avoid reinjury by teaching them how accidents occur and why the body breaks down makes for a better result. The same applies to counseling goals: The client who knows how to solve problems will learn to deal with life more productively.

Teaching what the worker's compensation rules are and how they work is important. Clear information leads to good decisions. Classes on the rules and how they are misused by clients have been well received by clients. In fact, explaining that the worker's compensation rules were developed because of abuses helps clients see that abuses by some changed benefits for all. At the same time that clients are learning how compensation is regulated, subtle messages are conveyed about how a person fails in the system. The whole process is a change of cognitions and of the false premises typically made by clients. Many clients accept the new situation and, while not happy about it, change their behaviors. Understanding the rules correctly leaves them no other choice. By the end of the Work Hardening program, they start seriously to work toward returning to work rather than toward staying sick for as long as possible.

Return-to-Work Coordinator

One fear experienced by work-injured clients is concern that they may not have a job to return to. The worker's compensation system can offer a lot of security and leaving can seem like a jump into the unknown. Also, a lot of employer hostility exists toward the injured worker and many do not want the worker to return. In one case, a client who admitted he had abused the system was allowed to return but was fired that same day. Fortunately, one of the vocational classes that emphasized recognizing one's value to employers in terms of experience allowed this client to go to a former employer and get a promise of a job within a matter of days. Relying on the preinjury employer for a job is difficult for the worker. There can be anger and a strong fear of rejection. The counselor has to counter the reluctance to return to the old job by recognizing that the fear is legitimate and by providing options to fall back on should their fears prove correct. One strategy is to tell the client fearful of being fired that applying for employment from the unemployed position allows prospective employers to call former employers. A better position to be in is to return to the old job and wait to be fired, as that would make the employer liable for unemployment benefits, a situation the employer does not want. In addition, that is the best time to apply for other jobs. If a prospective employer wants to talk to the current employer and the applicant is still on that job, the applicant can request that the prospective employer not call the current employer without raising suspicions as to why not.

The main reason for getting injured workers back to the old job is to give them an opportunity to show their stuff, especially their newly learned safework practices. This is emphasized to the employer.

Job Analysis

Figure 16.1 provides information for concrete and quantifiable physical demands. If necessary and with the permission of the employer, the job analyst goes to the job site to collect data. Knowledge of the physical demands is more accurate with on-site information. Also, the employer gets an opportunity to provide input. Many employers complain that once a worker is injured, they never hear from the person again. The on-site visit provides an opportunity for the employer to make a report on the worker. Some employers also provide material or work items, such as pallets, tires, mattresses, sand bags, and even tools for the Work Hardening task. In one instance, a car was even donated.

CASE VIGNETTES

Case 1

Polly was a nurse in a country jail. She was in her late fifties and seventy or eighty pounds overweight. She had been out of work with an injury for well over a year. Her job was ex-tremely sedentary, which is why she liked working in the jail. Most of her patients had minor injuries, such as cuts, bruises, or sprains, or were medication cases. In the Functional Capacity Evaluation, she was unable to squat to do some lifting and, in fact, had to be lifted herself. She was guaranteed her job back, but she was convinced that she was too ill to return. Her employer was convinced of the same thing.

Vocational Counselor Task At staffing, it was decided to find out if the client could return to her job, as her physical therapy goal was to lift up to ten pounds on an infrequent basis, or for less than 10 percent of her workday. She could sit, stand, and walk at her discretion. She was supposed to be capable of doing a takedown (forcibly and physically restrain a prisoner), but this had never happened during her decade-long employment with the jail. She had guards who were readily available to do that.

Both employer and client had assumed that she would never recover sufficiently to return to her job. In fact, both were correct. She had a herniation of the L4-5 disc that was not repaired, as the operation would probably have resulted in little relief. She needed continual home exercise so that she could regain her strength, stamina, and flexibility. While she would always have her herniation, the job would not make it worse. She could do the work without putting stress on her injury, and the home treatment would keep her from hurting and would make her strong enough to avoid reinjury.

The vocational counselor needed to make both parties understand that returning to the job was not a danger. Both could benefit, the client by returning to meaningful employment and the employer by retaining a valued and ex-

Job Title: Vocational Counselor

Place of Employment: State Rehabilitation Commission

Informant(s): Client and Employee Supervisor, Joe Martinez

> Client: Frank Smith
> Date of Injury: 1/1/1998
> SSN: 555-55-5555

Job Description: The vocational counselor provides personal interviews, collects assessments of disability data, and performs educational assessments to develop vocational rehabilitation plans.

The counselor sits most of the workday, dealing with clients, doing paperwork, and working with computers.

Driving is required to do field work and to attend meetings with other agencies.

Lifting is limited to sedentary levels with an occasional medium demand to carry equipment such as a toolbox or crates of other equipment.

Physical Demands:

Standing	Occasional	10% of day
Walking	Occasional	15% of day
Lifting/Carrying I	Occasional	10% of day
Lifting/Carrying II	Very Rarely	2% of day
Pushing/Pulling	Not applicable	0% of day
Reaching	Continuous	66% to 90% of day
Manipulating	Continuous; types at computer, writes notes	33% to 66% of day

The demand is frequent (33 to 66% of day) for working with a computer monitor, and client experiences cramping and pain in the neck from this activitiy.

FIGURE 16.1 Job Analysis

perienced employee. The course of her treatment in the Work Hardening program would convince the client that she could handle the work. A work trial with the option of not keeping the client should she not be able to perform her job duties gave the employer a sense that they would not be taking back an "accident waiting to happen." The client responded by losing her concerns of being unemployable and an invalid and by regaining the energy to return to work, causing her to overcome some of her depression.

Case 2

Client Steward was a thirty-seven-year-old male who had sustained a back strain. He had been out for almost two years, well beyond the normal recuperative period for a simple soft-tissue injury. He was, however, very touchy about allusions that he was faking. He was a musician. He was well over 200 pounds in a 5′8″ frame. In testing, he was hardly able to twist, complaining of severe pain. In fact, he was unable to twist more than just a few inches to either side. While in the break room, however, he was able to completely twist around to throw an empty can of soda into a trash can behind him. He did not seem to be in any pain when he did this, not evidencing any of the facial expressions he did when reporting unbearable pain. His appearance could be judged as being angry. During his contact with the program, he would tell other clients to not let themselves be taken advantage of and that the counseling staff are their employees as they are paying the counselors' salary.

Vocational Counselor Task This client did not stay for treatment, but the vocational counselor would have taken on the task of providing very accurate information on the benefits of the system to make sure that the client and those around him understood that: (a) all participants are there for their own benefit; (b) they are all in control of what they do, so no one would be pushed beyond their endurance; and (c) all are there to get better, so some pain was necessary to lead to some gain and, hopefully, reemployment. The staff would need to be firm in providing good, professional treatment and to be honest with clients. This type of client will cause others to become distrustful but caring care will result in a good counter to misinformation and instigation by a very negative client.

If Steward had stayed in the program, he would not have been able to sustain the feigned pain behaviors. He would eventually have fallen victim to too many inconsistencies to keep up the façade. Eventually, he would have had to respond to exercise and professional treatment and demonstrate sufficient improvement to show some progress.

Case 3

Client Homero was a fifty-four-year-old male from Mexico. He did not speak English. Whether he was a legal immigrant was not an issue for the Work Hardening program, as all the services he was getting were through a benefits program paid for by his employer. Homero was a road-paving crew member. His job was difficult in that he had to do stoop labor, but the weight demands were not over fifty pounds, within his capacity. The multimember team set goals of getting him to be as physically strong as he could get to insure that he did not reinjure himself. His doctor had already indicated that the preinjury job was feasible if he attained the required demands.

Vocational Counselor Task The vocational counselor contacted the employer, who was willing to take the client back if the man was capable. The difficulty that would be encountered if the man were required to change jobs was emphasized to both the client and the employer. With limited language skills, with no vocational skills except as a laborer, and with a compensation claim in his employment history, finding new employment would be difficult. A very specific job analysis was generated from interviews with the client and the employer and from data collected on-site.

Counseling with the client focused on the realities of finding work for an older immigrant worker. Ensuring that he understood his rights in the worker's compensation system was emphasized. Worker's compensation clients always worry about being short-changed, and the counselor needs to assist the client in understanding the system and maneuvering around it effectively. Clients who are not guarding their backs make for better rehabilitation clients. The counselor also helped the client understand everything that was happening, including everything that was in writing. When this client completed the program, he was able to return to his employer without any problems. At the time of follow-up, he had been with his employer for nearly a year and was doing well.

Case 4

Client Terrica was a thirty-two-year-old female. When she started the program, she missed days and made lots of excuses as to why she was not there. She had a minimal physical problem, and her doctor wanted her to be in the best shape possible before he released her. The Work Hardening program was implemented to provide the required conditioning and strength training. The problem was that she participated too little to ensure effective results.

Vocational Counselor Task Counseling, with an eye to making the client comfortable discussing her problems, was provided. The reason the client was missing frequently was that she had little money. Her benefits were minimal, and she had no money for baby-sitting and had

no transportation. She was referred to several agencies that provided her with what she needed. Some effort was made to have her sign up with a program to train her at something better, but she was not really interested. Since her lack of education was problematic, she was not pushed any further. The social services that she received and the encouragement to not be absent allowed her to complete the program successfully. She returned to her preinjury job.

CONCLUSION

Even though this treatment model may be used for any person injured on the job, the focus in this chapter has been on those whose injuries have kept them from returning to work. One of the issues addressed in this model is the detecting of deception by administering the Forensic Deception Analysis (FDA). The chapter also focuses on deception or distortion of symptoms, which is the hallmark of faking or malingering. This is a factor in a disinclination to return to work. It is important for the vocational counselor to be able to detect malingering and intervene to extinguish such maladaptive behavior.

The program designed by Matheson and others has been used successfully across the country. The role of the rehabilitation counselor was developed by the author, based on his experience with the presenting problems and needs of the clients.

REFERENCES

American Psychiatric Association (1994). *Diagnostic and statistical manual of the mental disorders* (4th ed., rev.). Washington, D.C.: Author.

Gelder, M. (1997). The scientific foundations of cognitive behavior therapy. D. M. Clark & C. G. Fairburn (eds.), *Science and practice of cognitive behavior therapy*. New York: Oxford University Press.

Hall, V. H., & Pritchard, D. A. (1996). *Detecting malingering and deception: Forensic distortion analysis (FDA).* Delray Beach, Fla.: St. Lucie Press.

Kanfer, F. H. (1996). Motivation and emotion in behavior therapy. K. S. Dobson & K. D. Craig (eds.), *Advances in Cognitive-Behavioral Therapy.* Thousand Oaks, Calif.: Sage Publications, Inc.

Matheson, L. N. (1982). *Work capacity evaluation: A training manual for occupational therapist.* Trabuco Canyon, Calif.: RISC.

————. (1984). *Work capacity evaluation: Interdisciplinary approach to industrial rehabilitation.* Anaheim, Calif.: ERIC.

————. (1988). Symptom magnification syndrome. S. J. Isernhagen (ed.), *Work injury: Management and prevention.* New York: Apen Publishers.

Matheson, L. N., Ogden, L. D., Violette, K., & Schultz, K. (1985). Work hardening: Occupational therapy in industrial rehabilitation, *American Journal of Occupational Therapy* (5), 314–323.

Matheson, L. N., & Ogden-Niemeyer, L. (1987). *Work capacity evaluation: Systematic approach to industrial rehabilitation.* Anaheim, Calif.: ERIC.

Niemeyer, L. O., & Jacobs, J. (1989). *Work hardening: State of the art.* Thorofare, N.J.: Slack.

Rachman, S. (1997). The evolution of cognitive behavior therapy. D. M. Clark & C. G. Fairburn (eds.), *Science and practice of cognitive behavior therapy.* New York: Oxford University Press.

The Williams and Wilkins Company (1972). *Stedman's medical dictionary* (22nd ed., rev.). Baltimore, Md.: Authors.

Turk, D. C. (1996). Cognitive factors in chronic pain and disability. K. S. Dobson & K. D. Craig (eds.), *Advances in cognitive-behavioral therapy.* Thousand Oaks, Calif.: Sage Publications, Inc.

17

Chronic Mental Illness
and Work

An Integrated Vocational Life-Planning Model

MARJORIE T. KYLE, M.ED., M.S.

SCOTT PERSINGER, L.M.S.W.-ACP

INTRODUCTION

Personality and work environments have been linked in many career development theories, including Parson's trait-factor theory of career choice and Holland's theory of types (Kjos, 1995). However, a particularly difficult problem in career counseling is created when an individual demonstrates a personality disorder that interferes with occupational functioning. Kjos (1995) writes that "little attention has been paid . . . to the relationships among abnormal personality, career development, and interven-

tions in career counseling" (Kjos, 1995, 73). Education programs that provide rehabilitation services on a college or university campus for psychiatric disabilities have been described as promising for vocational and educational support of young adults (Anthony & Unger, 1991; Unger, Anthony, Sciarappa, & Rogers, 1991).

In a study of the quality of life for adults with severe mental illness, Fabian (1992) suggested that work contributes to and improves the quality of life for those individuals. However, in the past, economic and social forces combined to effectively exclude individuals with mental illness from the work force (Cohen, 1990). Palmer-Erbs and Anthony (1995) state that "the philosophy of psychiatric rehabilitation has emphasized that persons with psychiatric disabilities have the same goals and dreams as any other person, disabled or not. People with psychiatric disabilities want a decent place

Marjorie T. Kyle is a student in the doctorate of psychology program at Our Lady of the Lake University, San Antonio, Texas, and is employed as a consultant for the San Antonio Head Start Program. Scott Persinger is director of the Crisis Center for the Alamo Mental Health Group in San Antonio, Texas. He worked for six years with the chronically mentally ill at the San Antonio State Hospital.

Editor's Note: This chapter differs from others in that the case example is integrated into the comprehensive model.

to live, a suitable work environment, social activities, and friends to turn to in time of crisis" (Palmer-Erbs & Anthony, 1995, 38). Psychiatric rehabilitation programs vary on their focus, approach, and implementation, but, as Palmer-Erbs and Anthony (1995) point out, the primary focus of psychiatric rehabilitation is "in treating all participants as people with skills and abilities first, then evaluating the extent of the disability" with the "promotion of choices, self-determination, and individual responsibilities" (Palmer-Erbs & Anthony, 1995, 40).

An evaluation of a supported employment program for people with psychiatric disabilities found that by maintaining a client-centered approach to vocational rehabilitation, clients were able to exercise control over their career choices, which engendered feelings of empowerment and hope (Block, 1992). Recent studies of the relationship between psychiatric symptomatology, work skills and future vocational performance (Anthony, Rogers, Cohen, & Davies, 1995; Rogers, Anthony, Cohen, & Davies, 1997) suggest that "knowledge of someone's psychopathology provides only moderate evidence of that person's functional capacity for work" (Anthony et al., 1995, 357). The relationship between demographic indicators and work skills is weakened by clients who have a developed vocational goal and were in a community-based vocational program designed to help them meet that goal.

The following case example illustrates a community-based program that focuses on the individual, not the illness, to allow the individual to exercise control over career choice. Through a multidisciplinary approach, this program assessed the client's intellectual abilities, his personality, and his educational achievement to identify areas of difficulties that needed to be addressed in order to be successful. A thorough vocational assessment was made to determine the client's potential to benefit from a specially designed program for work readiness. An individualized plan to address the client's needs and to develop his interests, skills, and abilities was constructed and implemented.

CASE EXAMPLE

Perry Q. was eighteen years old when his mother died after a protracted battle with cancer. He was especially close to her as she was his emotional support and social connection to the world. Perry's father, while a good man, had extreme difficulty expressing his feelings to anyone around him. Mr. Q's comments to his son generally consisted of statements meant to correct behavior that sounded critical and demeaning. Perry felt disconnected from and even fearful of his father.

Perry finished high school with much special attention and encouragement from his mother. Intellectual assessment results obtained during his middle school years indicated Perry was of average intelligence with no learning or developmental disabilities. Given his continued marginal school performance and inadequate social functioning, extensive psychological testing was performed by the school district in Perry's junior year of high school. The Minnesota Multiphasic Personality Inventory-2 indicated a pattern of schizoid traits that was borne out in clinical interview and supported by collateral data gathered from teachers and family members. Resulting from this battery of testing, Perry was referred to a local psychologist for individual and group psychotherapy. At the time, Perry's parents felt such treatment was not necessary and, therefore, did not follow through with the recommendations.

Perry continued to function marginally in all areas until his mother's cancer progressed. As her condition worsened, Perry became increasingly sullen and withdrawn. Mrs. Q. died shortly following her son's high school graduation. At this time, Perry's condition began to worsen significantly. He became severely depressed and agitated. Within two months of his mother's death, Perry was sleeping irregularly, eating poorly, losing weight, behaving erratically, and consuming increasing amounts of alcohol. Perry became extremely paranoid, displaying delusional thoughts. He believed the local police department had placed bugging equipment in the family home to monitor his father's supposed illegal activity. He was also convinced that this equipment produced ultraviolet rays, which had caused his mother to contract and die of cancer.

One night after becoming intoxicated and severely agitated, Perry went home and retrieved a semiautomatic rifle from his father's gun cabinet. He then proceeded to seek out a local police officer to avenge the death of his mother. Perry entered a local restaurant in his small town verbalizing threats against the police. After leaving the establishment Perry was approached by several police cars. He slipped into an abandoned building where he held officers at bay for several hours firing poorly aimed shots at them. Fortunately, Perry was apprehended without further escalation of the incident.

Perry was committed to the state mental health facility where he spent the next twelve years of his life. Treatment consisted of various anti-psychotic medications and sporadic group and individual counseling. He was finally released at the age of thirty-one, having been judged to no longer be a threat to self or others. By this time, Perry's father had relocated to Texas where he lived alone in a small town. Reluctantly, Perry's father allowed him to move in. Perry spent the next three years in virtual isolation, co-existing with his father in a tension-filled house. As he became increasingly depressed and paranoid, he sought mental health care from a psychiatrist in a nearby large city.

Given his current psychiatric condition and past history, Perry was referred and admitted to a psychiatric day hospital program. In previous months, Perry had unsuccessfully attempted to utilize state rehabilitative services, but none were offered, given his chronicity and poor prognosis for rehabilitation. The day hospital program offered a perfect opportunity for Perry to receive comprehensive treatment and to participate in a rehabilitation program.

Perry endured several days of assessment by various disciplines (psychiatry, psychology, and social work). The tests included the Wechsler Adult Intelligence Scale-Revised (WAIS-R), the Minnesota Multiphasic Personality Inventory (MMPI), the Thematic Apperception Test (TAT), the Rorschach, and the Wide Range Achievement Test (WRAT). These instruments were used by the various disciplines to assess Perry's intellectual abilities, his personality, and his educational achievement and to identify any areas of difficulties that needed to be addressed in order for Perry to be successful.

In addition to this basic battery of psychometric assessment instruments, the treatment team requested that the psychologist perform an extensive vocational assessment as an addendum to the team assessment. Perry was given the Strong Interest Inventory (SII), the Career Assessment Instrument (CAI), the Campbell Interest Skill Survey (CISS), the Myers-Briggs Type Indicator (MBTI), and the Values Scale (VS). This test battery assessed four areas associated with career and vocational development:

interests, skills, personality, and values. The vocational assessment determined Perry had the potential to benefit from a specially designed program for work readiness. Vocational testing indicated Perry's career interests were in the human services field. He expressed enthusiasm for the medical field—in particular, he wanted to become an emergency medical technician (EMT). The following is a description of the career counseling model used and its application to Perry's circumstances.

COMPREHENSIVE MODEL OF REHABILITATION FOR THE CHRONICALLY MENTALLY ILL

The day hospital program that Perry entered consisted of group, family, and individual psychotherapy along with psychiatric and nursing care. The majority of clients in the program had been admitted following acute psychiatric hospitalization. In the early days of the program, it became evident that the chronically mentally ill were underserved in the community. A special treatment track was devised to serve a limited number of these individuals. All treatment was provided by appropriately licensed professionals in the various disciplines.

The chronically mentally ill track consisted of two group therapy sessions each day. The morning group was process-oriented, giving clients an opportunity to discuss issues of immediate concern, such as family problems, interpersonal interaction, and intrapsychic issues. The afternoon group consisted of various topics designed to enhance personal skills, including assertiveness, social interaction and relationships, stress management, time management, and cognitive-behavioral training focusing on the

relationship between thoughts, emotions and action, and rational versus irrational thinking.

At the beginning of each day, a community meeting was held. During this meeting, participants addressed the daily schedule and daily chores, assigned a buddy to new members, and discussed issues or concerns of the members. Once a week at this meeting, a president, vice president, and secretary were elected for the week.

The nursing staff conducted a medication and health group twice weekly. The group topics varied, but focused on the importance of compliance, nutrition, drug interactions, and side effects.

Recreation therapy provided three sessions per week with emphasis on leisure skills and structuring and planning of free time. The recreational therapists conducted arts and crafts sessions, facilitated locating community-based leisure activities, and encouraged social interaction and relationship building. As the day program matured, a Reality Oriented Physical Experience Services (ROPES) component, which is an obstacle course intervention that focuses on building self-esteem, teamwork, problem solving, and goal attainment, was added. This improved and enhanced learning dramatically through all aspects of the client's experience in the program.

Career Counseling and Assessment Model Used

Because of the comprehensive philosophy of this program, it was deemed that Krumboltz's social learning theory of counseling (1996) provided the most appropriate career intervention. According to Krumboltz, there are four factors that influence career paths—genetic endowment and special abilities, environmental conditions and events, learning experiences, and task approach skills.

According to Krumboltz, genetic endowment and special abilities are "inherited qualities that may affect people's abilities to acquire certain educational and occupational preferences and skills" (Mitchell & Krumboltz, 1996, 237). Perry's genetic endowments and special abilities included a normal intellectual functioning with no sensory or motor impairments. He was of average height and demonstrated normal motor coordination patterns.

Task-approach skills, according to Mitchell and Krumboltz (1996, 237), include one's study skills, work habits, ways of learning, and ways of responding emotionally. Perry's way of responding emotionally was characterized as aloof and detached with little emotional warmth or rapport. And he expressed a desire to become an EMT, for which, in some instances, the ability to remain detached from a situation (a gruesome automobile accident, for example) could be considered an asset. Perry also considered working as an EMT because there were well-defined tasks and explicit instructions combined with limited decision-making responsibilities.

Perry had experienced significant environmental conditions and events that influenced his career path. Mitchell and Krumboltz (1996, 237) define these events as usually beyond the control of the individual. The events include some or all of the following:

1. Number and nature of job opportunities
2. Number and nature of training opportunities
3. Social policies and procedures for selecting trainees and workers
4. Monetary and social rewards of various occupations
5. Labor laws and union rules
6. Natural disasters
7. Availability of and demand for natural resources
8. Technological developments
9. Changes in social organizations (for example, welfare)
10. Family training experiences
11. Social and financial resources
12. The educational system
13. Neighborhood and community influences

Perry's opportunities for employment and occupational training had been severely limited by his institutionalization. Due to his strained relationship with his father and the death of his mother, Perry's family experiences were not optimal for developing career options. The fact that Perry was interested in the medical field is not surprising, given his relationship with his mother and her protracted battle with cancer. Since Perry's father had extreme difficulty expressing his feelings, it was probably his mother who was most influential in Perry's learning experiences. Since those experiences most likely revolved around Mrs. Q's battle with cancer, Perry's positive regard of the medical profession as his vocation of choice is understandable. The fortuitous relocation of his father near a large city afforded Perry the opportunity to participate in a day hospital program that offered comprehensive treatment and rehabilitation and afforded job training opportunities, thus greatly enhancing Perry's occupational opportunities. Another environmental event that influenced Perry's career path was that he was befriended by his father's neighbor, who was an emergency medical technician.

Perry's learning experiences had also been limited by his institutionalization. He had received some therapy-based training in social skills and had worked in various janitorial jobs at the hospital as part of his behaviorally based therapy. He had developed a reasonable comfort level in groups through the group therapy he had received during his institutionalization and continued to function well during the group sessions in the day program. His task-approach skills had been formed based primarily on the behavioral program at the institution, which had given him privileges and a small salary for his janitorial work.

Perry was given individual attention in the areas of interview skills and résumé writing. He demonstrated increased self-confidence and an improved ability to interact with others. Perry took the initiative to gather information on training and educational requirements, and he spent a great deal of his free time at the local fire station in his small town conversing with and observing the EMTs.

Given his mental health history, the drawbacks of such a career were discussed at length by the treatment team and with Perry. Since Perry was seeking employment in the years prior to the implementation of the Americans with Disabilities Act, the implications of revealing his history were also thoroughly explored. Specific recommendations for consistent aftercare were provided. It was determined that psychiatric medications would be continued, as they offered no impediment to functioning. In fact, his response to antidepressants had been excellent. Individual psychotherapy was also recommended to assist Perry in dealing with day-to-day stressors presented by intensive educational training and interpersonal interaction, especially with authority figures.

At last report, Perry had completed the six-month training course for emergency medical technicians and had been offered a part-time position at the local fire station. He has performed well with only minor difficulties in interpersonal relationships. Work performance has been good. The long-term prognosis for Perry is cautiously optimistic.

CONCLUSION

Perry's career decisions are easily understood when viewed through Krumboltz's social learning theory. The genetic endowments and abilities that influenced Perry's career decision were his average intelligence with no learning or developmental disabilities. However, his schizoid personality disorder and dysthymia were qualities that needed to be addressed through vocational rehabilitation to increase his chance of success in his chosen career.

The influence of environmental conditions and events occurred not only through the events discussed above, but also through the specially designed program for work readiness and the availability of the six-month training course required for becoming an emergency medical technician. The fact that Perry was able to spend a great deal of his free time at the local fire station in his small town conversing with and observing the EMTs also contributed to his success. Mitchell and Krumboltz (1996) state that "career counselors who do not conceptualize personality characteristics as permanent traits but rather as primarily learned are in a position to devise learning experiences to help their clients develop personality characteristics that the client themselves want" (Mitchell & Krumboltz, 1996, 257). The willingness of Perry's therapy team to consider and support his decision was instrumental in creating a successful career decision.

A vocational rehabilitation model that promotes meaningful work in a community enhances the quality of life for the individual and is critical to the rehabilitation and recovery of individuals with mental disabilities. As new laws are enacted that integrate individuals with disabilities into the mainstream of American life, this dream may become a reality for many.

In recent years, with the passage of the Americans with Disabilities Act (ADA), the vocational support of persons with mental disabilities has become a political and legal issue. The ADA's definition of a disability is limited to individuals who have substantial limitations in major life activities, which obviously includes people with physical disabilities. However, the ADA also explicitly includes people with mental disabilities. Recent rulings by the courts have helped clarify and define the issues addressed in the ADA. Guidelines have been released by the Equal Employment Opportunity Commission (EEOC) that discuss "how to determine whether a condition is covered under ADA, disclosure of a disability, requesting reasonable accommodations, examples of reasonable accommodations, when an employer can discipline a worker for misconduct resulting from a disability, direct threat, and professional licensing" (Bazelon, Center for Mental Health Law, 1997).

To meet the ADA's criteria for substantial limitations in major life activities, individuals with mental disabilities may have limitations in caring for themselves, thinking, concentrating, and interacting with others (Bazelon, Center for Mental Health Law, 1997, 1). The EEOC Title I of the act prohibits employers from "discriminating against qualified individuals with disabilities in job application procedures, hiring, firing, advancement, compensation, job training, and other terms, conditions, and privileges of employment" (Bazelon, Center for Mental Health Law, 1997, 1). An employer is required to make reasonable job accommodations for individuals with disabilities, including individuals with a mental impairment that substantially limits one or more major life activities. Reasonable accommodations may include "modification to work schedules or policies, physical changes to the workplace, adjusting supervisory methods, providing a job coach, and reassignment to a different position" (Bazelon, Center for Mental Health Law, 1997, 2). Changes such as these in the laws influence political and environmental factors, which in turn influence the occupational career choices available to individuals with chronic mental illness.

REFERENCES

Anthony, W. A., Rogers, E. S., Cohen, M., & Davies, R. (1995). Relationship between psychiatric symptomatology, work skills, and future vocational performance, *Psychiatric Services,* 46 (4), 353–358.

Anthony, W. A., & Unger, K. V. (1991). Supported education: An additional program resource for young adults with long-term mental illness, *Community Mental Health Journal,* 47 (2), 145–156.

Bazelon Center for Mental Health Law (1997). *Facts About the Americans with Disabilities Act* [Online]. Web site: *http://www.bazelon.org/bazelon/eeocguid.hml.*

Block, L. 1992). The employment connection: The application of an individual supported employment program for persons with chronic mental health problems, *Canadian Journal of Community Mental Health,* 11(2), 79–89.

Cohen, L. J. (1990). Work and mental health: Personal, social, and economic contexts, *Social Psychiatry and Psychiatric Epidemiology,* 25, 108–109.

Fabian, S. E. (1992). Supported employment and the quality of life: Does a job make a difference? *Rehabilitation Counseling Bulletin,* 36 (2), 85–96.

Kjos, D. (1995). Linking career counseling to personality disorder, *Journal of Counseling and Development, 73,* 592–597.

Mitchell, L. K., & Krumboltz, J. D. (1996). Career choice and counseling. D. Brown, L. Brooks, & Associates (eds.), *Career Choice and Development* (3d ed.), 233–280. San Francisco: Jossey-Bass, Inc., Publishers.

Palmer-Erbs, V. K., & Anthony, W. A. (1995). Incorporating psychiatric rehabilitation principles into mental health nursing, *Journal of Psychosocial Nursing, 33* (3), 36–44.

Rogers, E. S., Anthony, W. A., Cohen, M., & Davies, R. R. (1997). Prediction of vocational outcome based on clinical and demographic indicators among vocationally ready clients. *Community Mental Health Journal, 33* (2), 99–112.

Unger, K. V., Anthony, W. A., Sciarrappa, K., & Rogers, E. S. (1991). A supported education program for young adults with long-term mental illness. *Hospital and Community Psychiatry, 42* (8), 838–842.

18

Battered Women

A Group Vocational Counseling Model

NADENE PETERSON, ED.D.

GEORGIA PRIOUR, M.S.

INTRODUCTION AND RATIONALE

This chapter provides a brief review of the literature and rationale for developing a comprehensive occupational and life-planning model for abused women who seek counseling at a battered women's shelter. An occupational group model is described with specific activities for each of eight sessions.

There were several studies from 1975 through 1982 (Gaylord, 1975; Gelles, 1976; Parker & Schumacher, 1977; Hilberman & Munson, 1978; Strauss; Gelles, & Steinmetz, 1980; and Bowen, 1982) dealing with abused/battered women and their common characteristics that emerged, such as low self-esteem, ac-

cepting responsibility for the abuser's actions, passive behavior, inability to make clear decisions, severe reactions to stress, economic depression, and fear of relationship failure (divorce). Even though these characteristics are still common in abused women, there has been little current research on the topic.

Ward, Wilson, Polaschek, and Hudson (1995) described factors that contribute to the experiences of battered women from a social contextual perspective. These factors include the "frequency, variety, and seriousness of their partner's violent acts, the sociological attitudes to violence of both the perpetrator and the victim, the range and quality of formal and informal social and financial support and assistance available to the victim, and the effectiveness of the criminal justice system in protecting victims" (Ward et al., 1995, 27). They conclude it is essential for mental health practitioners to understand the social and cultural factors and not

Georgia Priour earned a master's degree from Our Lady of the Lake University and has worked in a battered women's shelter for several years.

to "pathologise" women (Ward et al., 1995, 27). The authors further assert that "[c]ognitive deconstruction is thought to occur in battered women whose expectations about themselves and their intimate relationships are violated by violence" (Ward et al., 1995, 31). Often these women exhibit concrete thinking only while focusing on the moment; furthermore, they are aware of their inability to develop long-term goals or plans. They understand why they experience difficulty making decisions and solving interpersonal problems, but, finding their beliefs and behavior incongruent, often feel as if they have no control. This leads to a "passive approach to problems and a sense of personal ineffectiveness and emptiness" (Ward et al., 1995, 32), which develops a belief in their own powerlessness and helplessness. If cognitive deconstruction is being used as the coping strategy, then therapeutic intervention involves challenging the woman's attributions, such as her stating, "It's all my fault," thus taking responsibility for provoking the abuse, or "Leaving the relationship would mean I was a failure." If these cognitions are modified, they can increase the woman's self-esteem and lead to a more positive self-evaluation.

Bowen (1982) suggests that counselors working with abused women need to understand that economic survival is the women's most immediate need, which makes the counselors' being trained in vocational counseling as essential as their ability to understand the developmental and psychological needs of these women. The basic interventions that these women need are: (a) guidance and information regarding occupational opportunities; (b) personal counseling to overcome fears; and (c) coaching on interviewing and job-seeking skills. Many programs suggest group counseling sessions as a method of providing support and affirmation.

Vocational Group Models
for Battered Women

A survey of the literature identified two models, which are described briefly. Ibrahim and Herr (1987) described a developmental life career group model that has eight phases:

1. Inner preparation
2. Acknowledgment of feelings of loss and fear and the introduction of exercises to build self-esteem and identify skills
3. Intensive family involvement
4. Vocational experimentation
5. Vocational implementation
6. Vocational analysis
7. Vocational resynthesis
8. Provision of vocational development resources

This model seems particularly appropriate for women who have been out of the work force for a while or have never developed specific vocational skills.

Cox and Stoltenberg (1991) developed a group treatment program for battered women that includes five modules: (a) cognitive therapy, (b) self-assertiveness and communication skills development, (c) problem-solving skills development, (d) vocational counseling, and (e) body awareness. The emphases in these groups are to assist women in (a) identifying the cyclical patterns of abuse, (b) improving their self-concept and interactional skills, and (c) preparing them for the world of work. Mawson and Kahn (1993) found that group participants valued the affective component of occupational/career groups and that it was this component that assisted in the increase of self-confidence, self-worth, and a sense of hope.

DEVELOPMENT OF THE MODEL FOR BATTERED WOMEN

While battered women and their plight have received attention from the media, there are few vocational programs available at battered women's shelters, and little data has been collected regarding their effectiveness. Several shelters across the country were contacted, and none offered any consistent type of vocational counseling service that included both self- and vocational exploration, providing systematic assessment of traits, interests, values, skills and aptitudes. A few offered job placement services with minimal vocational and technical training, but offered little or no assistance in helping women make occupational choices based on a match of interests, traits, and personality factors.

With this in mind, we decided to develop a program for a battered women's shelter in the area, drawing from the models described combined with our own experience. Basic to the model is Holland's typology, which has very specific categories that describe both personality characteristics and job environments. Accordingly, most jobs and people can be identified by any combination of these characteristics. Holland has divided personalities into six types: investigative, artistic, social, enterprising, conventional, and realistic. Environments can also be identified according to these same classifications. The relationships between different personality types and environments are described by a hexagon format in which the similarity between groups is inversely proportional to the distance between them. Holland proposes that persons seek out and are more satisfied with environments that are congruent with their personalities, and behavior is determined by an interaction between personality and the characteristics of the environment. This model has

been used on adult populations. For a more complete discussion of these relationships see Holland (1995) as well as Chapter 4 in *The Role of Work in People's Lives: Applied Career Development and Vocational Psychology* (Peterson & González, 2000).

The group consisted of six women who had been out of an abusive relationship for at least one year. They had all been attending a weekly support group for battered women for at least six months. Their ages ranged from twenty-four to forty. Of the six women who completed the study, all were divorced. At the time of the first meeting, three were employed full time and the others were unemployed. Three of the six women had completed high school, and the other three had not.

Since one of the most common presenting problems for women in abusive relationships is low self-esteem, the emphasis in the first three sessions was to assist in strengthening these women's sense of self-worth and self-confidence. The next five sessions moved to vocational exploration. Since half of the women had not finished high school, the assessment exercises were geared to the general educational level of the women in the group.

By the end of the group sessions, each of the six women in the group had identified a vocational area of interest and was pursuing it. The facilitator of the group lives in the small city where the program was administered and sees some of the women on occasion. The responses to the program have been positive. The women are continuing to work and report they are satisfied with their jobs. In an informal evaluation, the women observed they had developed an enhanced sense of control and feelings of empowerment. One woman, for example, combined interests in singing and baking and started a business in which she bakes and delivers birthday cakes to children's parties and sings for them; she also bakes and sells cakes for special occasions. She has also maintained a steady job working in a school cafeteria.

A GROUP VOCATIONAL MODEL FOR BATTERED WOMEN

Since women in this population often do not have adequate financial resources, all of the materials, assessments, and activities were selected with this in mind.

Session 1. Pretest and First Steps to Self-Discovery[1]

(Administer the Goals Checklist: Self- and Vocational Development. [Appendix A].

Self-Discovery: Who Am I?

1. On a piece of paper write three words that describe your strengths.
2. Write several words that end in "–ing" or "–able" that describe your personal traits.
3. Share the results with other group members.
4. Reflect on what you learned about yourself.
5. Complete the Adjective Self-Description (Appendix B) and have a friend fill out the same form about yourself.
6. Complete the Observation Sheet (Appendix C). (Have each woman keep all materials in a folder for use in developing her own personal file.)

Assignment Complete the following.

1. Score the Adjective Self-Description.

2. Complete Ten Things I Love to Do (Appendix D).
3. Complete the Values Survey (Appendix E).

Session 2. Further Along the Road to Self-Discovery and Values Definition

1. Discuss results of the Adjective Self-Description, particularly the answers that were marked 5 [really like me], then answers of 1 [not at all like me]. (This helps to develop a vocabulary of words that can be used to describe the person.)
2. Discuss responses of the Values Survey, looking at self, others, and the world at large. (Self includes items 1, 3, 5, 6, 7, 10, 11, 12, 13, and 16. Others are items 4, 8, 14, and 15. World-at-large items are 2, 9, 17, and 18.) Discuss how this reflects your values.
3. Discuss Ten Things I Love to Do, with emphasis on the questions at the bottom of the sheet and how these things relate to your values.
4. Complete the Observation Sheet.

Assignment

1. List eight to ten achievements/accomplishments.
2. Complete the Motivated Skills Chart (Appendix G) using these achievements/accomplishments.

Session 3. Identifying Skills and Achievements

1. Discuss the Motivated Skills Chart. (Use small groups. Have each individual discuss one accomplishment she is proud of with the others in the group.)

[1]The instructions to group members stand as written. The instructions for the facilitator are in parentheses.

2. (Encourage group members to identify the skills each one has that will help her accomplish her goals. Have them total the number of times a skill was used for each of the achievements. This gives each individual an indication of the skills she has as a result of these achievements.)

3. Complete the Observation Sheet.

Assignment

1. Complete the Work Factors Inventory (Appendix F).

2. Begin a work autobiography with a brief history and paragraph about each job held.

Session 4. Exploring
My Relationship to Work

1. Discuss the Work Values Inventory. Discuss what was clearly important to you.

2. Using the work autobiography, take one job and identify skills acquired for that specific work situation using the Motivated Skills Chart as a resource for skill areas. Identify things you enjoyed or did not enjoy about each job.

3. Complete the Observation Sheet.

Assignment Complete Holland's (1994) Self-Directed Search [SDS] assessment test.

Session 5. Exploring My Interests

1. (Check scoring of SDS.) Use the Occupations Finder to identify compatible job categories and clusters by the Holland codes. (Occupations Finder is ordered at the same time as SDS.)

2. Out of all the possibilities, list three jobs that you would like to explore further.

3. Complete the Observation Sheet.

Assignment Go to the local library or a career resource center at a high school or college in the area. Using the *Dictionary of Occupational Titles* (DOT), the *Occupational Outlook Handbook* (OOH), a computer-assisted guidance program such as DISCOVER, SIGI, or COIN, and the Internet, gather information about the three job areas you chose.

Session 6. Exploring
Job/Career Possibilities

1. (Bring in a speaker from a local employment commission who can give the women an overview of jobs available in the area, types of training needed, where the training is available, and other pertinent information. Emphasize the nontraditional occupations, since there are more jobs available in these areas and the pay is usually better. Some possibilities include refrigeration, computer repair, building maintenance, plumbing, and airplane mechanics.)

2. Complete the Observation Sheet.

Assignment Bring all the materials from the past six sessions and make a list of interests, personal traits, values, and skills that best describe you.

Session 7. Putting It All Together

1. (Have each person explain her list of interests, traits, values, and skills, and put them on a chalkboard or flip chart. Have all members brainstorm about job possibilities for each person based on the information. This can be a creative time to help them integrate all the information.)

2. Complete the Observation Sheet.

Assignment Complete the Goals Inventory (Appendix H).

Session 8. Wrap-Up and Closure

1. (Using the Goals Inventory, have each woman identify a goal and possible obstacles. Suggest resources as needed, whether an informational interview, training programs, or educational requirements. Then have them each make a plan of action for the next month and set a meeting time for follow-up.)

2. Complete a final Observation Sheet.

3. Complete a posttest Goals Checklist: Self- and Vocational Development.

SUMMARY

Battered women's shelters and domestic violence programs appear to be important venues through which to offer vocational group counseling. Our observations confirmed that this is a population that can benefit from a vocational/career counseling group that provides elements of both personal and vocational exploration and that is sensitive to the importance of matching skills, interests, and personal traits to the available job opportunities. Simply offering job placement services and work training programs without the component of self- and vocational awareness is not adequate. If these women gain a positive sense of self and develop economic independence, there is less chance that they will return to an abusive relationship. This is not just finding someone a job, but assisting the person in finding empowerment, self-discovery, hope, and a realization of an inner locus of control. For many, it means shattering generational patterns and creating a new paradigm for themselves and their children.

Even though most battered women's shelters have limited staff, there are grants available in most states from school-to-work programs, work-force development initiatives, and other resources. A vocational/career counselor can be contracted to develop and facilitate these groups on a continuing basis. This is our recommendation.

REFERENCES

Bowen, N. (1982). Guidelines for career counseling with abused women, *Vocational Guidance Quarterly,* 31, 123–127.

Cox, J. W., & Stoltenberg, C. W. (1991). Evaluation of a treatment program for battered wives, *Journal of Family Violence,* 6, (4), 395–411.

Gaylord, J. (1975). Battered wives, *Medical Science Law,* 15, 237–245.

Gelles, R. (1976). Abused wives: Why do they stay? *Journal of Marriage and Family,* 3, 659–668.

Haldane, B. (1988). *Career satisfaction and success: How to know and manage your strengths.* Seattle, Wash.: Wellness Behavior.

Hilberman, E. & Munson, K. (1978). Sixty battered women, *Victimology International Journal,* 2, 460–470.

Holland, J. L. (1992). *Making vocational choices: A theory of vocational personalities and work environment* (3d ed.). Englewood Cliffs, N.J. Prentice Hall.

Holland, J. L. (1994). The Self Directed Search: Professional Manual. Odessa, Fla.: Psychological Assessment Resources.

Ibrahim, F. A. & Herr, E. L. (1987). Battered women: A developmental life-career counseling perspective, *Journal of Counseling and Development,* 65, 244–248.

Mawson, D. L., & Kahn, S. E. (1993). Group process in a women's career intervention. *The Career Development Quarterly,* 41, 238–245.

Parker, B., & Schumacher, D. (1997). The battered wife syndrome and violence in the nuclear family of origin: A controlled pilot study, *American Journal of Public Health,* 67, 760–761.

Penney's Forum (1972). *Twenty things I love to do.* (Spring/Summer): Author.

Peterson, N. (1978). Effects of two distinct life-planning group models upon several personal and vocational outcome measures in adult women. Dissertation: Unpublished.

Rokeach, M. (1973). *The nature of human values.* New York: Free Press.

Psychological Assessment Resources (1996). Self-Directed Search, *Assessment Booklet and Occupations Finder.* Odessa, Fla.: Psychological Assessment Resources.

Strauss, M. (1978). Wife beating: How common and why? *Victimology International Journal,* 2, 443–458.

Strauss, M., Gelles, R., & Steinmetz, S. (1980). *Behind closed doors: Violence in the American family.* Garden City, N.Y.: Doubleday/Anchor.

Veldman, C., & Parker, U. (1971). *Adjective Self-Description* (monograph 11). Austin, Texas: University of Texas Research Methodology.

Ward, T., Wilson, L., Polaschek, D., & Hudson, S. M. (1995). Explaining some characteristics of battered women: A cognitive deconstructionist approach, *New Zealand Journal of Psychology,* 24, (1), 26–38.

APPENDIX A

GOALS CHECKLIST: SELF- AND VOCATIONAL DEVELOPMENT

Please rank the following goals with a, b, c, or d:
  a. Committed to this goal and have accomplished (achieved) it.
  b. Committed to this goal and will work on it in the next month.
  c. Committed to this goal but will not work on it in the next month.
  d. Not committed to this goal.

1. Determine an academic major or degree.
2. Determine a vocational program.
3. Determine job areas for which I am best suited.
4. Find information on training, employment opportunities, and job application procedures for particular jobs.
5. Decide whether to stay in school.
6. Decide to start back to school.
7. Decide to work part time.
8. Decide to work full time.
9. Decide to volunteer in a specific area.
10. Have the ability to cope with uncertainty.
11. Be aware of my own emotional responses.
12. Be positive and optimistic.
13. Overcome feelings of guilt.
14. Have confidence in my own abilities, decisions, and skills.
15. Determine not to procrastinate.
16. Develop perseverance.
17. Have realistic self-expectations.
18. Accept personal limitations.
19. Have a sense of direction.
20. Have a sense of identity and personal worth.
21. Clarify personal goals and values.
22. Determine to take responsibility for my own life and decisions.

APPENDIX B1

ADJECTIVE SELF-DESCRIPTION

D. J. Veldman and G. V. C. Parker

NAME: _____
(Please Print)   Last   First   Middle or Maiden

SOC. SEC. NO.: ☐☐☐☐☐☐☐☐☐   **DATE:** _____

SEX: ☐ M ☐ F   **LEVEL:** ☐ E ☐ S

Circle **one** of the five numbers after each of the following descriptive words to represent how well it describes you. Try to describe yourself as you really are, rather than as you would like to be.

	NO				YES		NO				YES		NO				YES
1. Anxious	1	2	3	4	5	20. Kind	1	2	3	4	5	39. Sharp-witted	1	2	3	4	5
2. Charming	1	2	3	4	5	21. Lazy	1	2	3	4	5	40. Shy	1	2	3	4	5
3. Cheerful	1	2	3	4	5	22. Loud	1	2	3	4	5	41. Silent	1	2	3	4	5
4. Clever	1	2	3	4	5	23. Moody	1	2	3	4	5	42. Soft-hearted	1	2	3	4	5
5. Complicated	1	2	3	4	5	24. Nervous	1	2	3	4	5	43. Sophisticated	1	2	3	4	5
6. Efficient	1	2	3	4	5	25. Obnoxious	1	2	3	4	5	44. Spontaneous	1	2	3	4	5
7. Emotional	1	2	3	4	5	26. Organized	1	2	3	4	5	45. Stable	1	2	3	4	5
8. Foolish	1	2	3	4	5	27. Outgoing	1	2	3	4	5	46. Steady	1	2	3	4	5
9. Gentle	1	2	3	4	5	28. Pleasant	1	2	3	4	5	47. Sympathetic	1	2	3	4	5
10. Good-looking	1	2	3	4	5	29. Polished	1	2	3	4	5	48. Talkative	1	2	3	4	5
11. Good-natured	1	2	3	4	5	30. Practical	1	2	3	4	5	49. Temperamental	1	2	3	4	5
12. Handsome	1	2	3	4	5	31. Precise	1	2	3	4	5	50. Tense	1	2	3	4	5
13. Idealistic	1	2	3	4	5	32. Quiet	1	2	3	4	5	51. Thorough	1	2	3	4	5
14. Impulsive	1	2	3	4	5	33. Reckless	1	2	3	4	5	52. Timid	1	2	3	4	5
15. Indifferent	1	2	3	4	5	34. Reflective	1	2	3	4	5	53. Touchy	1	2	3	4	5
16. Individualistic	1	2	3	4	5	35. Reserved	1	2	3	4	5	54. Unconventional	1	2	3	4	5
17. Industrious	1	2	3	4	5	36. Rude	1	2	3	4	5	55. Warm	1	2	3	4	5
18. Insightful	1	2	3	4	5	37. Sexy	1	2	3	4	5	56. Worrying	1	2	3	4	5
19. Irresponsible	1	2	3	4	5	38. Shallow	1	2	3	4	5		1	2	3	4	5

APPENDIX B2

Items Selected for the Adjective Self-Description Instrument

Factor I. Attitude

3. Cheerful

9. Gentle

11. Good-natured

20. Kind

28. Pleasant

42. Soft-hearted

47. Sympathetic

55. Warm

Factor 2. Behavior

8. Foolish

15. Indifferent

19. Irresponsible

21. Lazy

25. Obnoxious

33. Reckless

36. Rude

38. Shallow

Factor 3. Efficiency

6. Efficient

17. Industrious

26. Organized

30. Practical

31. Precise

45. Stable

46. Steady

51. Thorough

Factor 4. Orientation

22. Loud (rev.)

27. Outgoing (rev.)

32. Quiet

35. Reserved

40. Shy

41. Silent

48. Talkative (rev.)

52. Timid

Factor 5. Anxiety

1. Anxious

7. Emotional

23. Moody

24. Nervous

49. Temperamental

50. Tense

53. Touchy

56. Worrying

Factor 6. Ideology

5. Complicated

13. Idealistic

14. Impulsive

16. Individualistic

18. Insightful

34. Reflective

44. Spontaneous

54. Unconventional

Factor 7. Attractiveness

2. Charming

4. Clever

10. Good-looking

12. Handsome

29. Polished

37. Sexy

39. Sharp-witted

43. Sophisticated

APPENDIX B3

EXAMPLE OUTPUT OF SELF-DESCRIPTION REPORT GENERATOR

Summary Report of Adjective Self-Description for Code 00011

Raw Scores = 26 12 39 29 23 25 26

On each of the scales below, the X marks your score.
The zeros show the middle half of a large student group.

Social Attitude
```
                              X
Cold    1 ..............2 ..............3 ..............4 ..............5    Warm
                                             000000
```

Social Behavior
```
                X
Courteous   1 ..............2 ..............3 ..............4 ..............5    Annoying
              000000
```

Performance Habits
```
                                                    X
Careless    1 ..............2 ..............3 ..............4 ..............5    Efficient
                                           000000
```

Social Orientation
```
                                  X
Outgoing    1 ..............2 ..............3 ..............4 ..............5    Reserved
                   0000000000
```

Emotional Stability
```
                              X
Serene    1 ..............2 ..............3 ..............4 ..............5    Anxious
                     000000000
```

Ideological Orientation
```
                              X
Practical   1 ..............2 ..............3 ..............4 ..............5    Idealistic
                         000000
```

Appearance and Charm
```
                              X
Plain    1 ..............2 ..............3 ..............4 ..............5    Attractive
                     0000000
```

APPENDIX C

OBSERVATION SHEET

On a scale of one to five please rate your reactions to the focus/activities in this session. Include a sentence about each area.

1. Little or no significance
2. Somewhat significant
3. Moderately significant
4. Very significant
5. Extremely significant

_____ Exploration of my own feelings in the group

_____ Clarification of my own feelings about my personal attributes

_____ Clarification of my own feelings about my job/occupational goals

_____ Exploration of job possibilities

_____ Input from the group leader

_____ Input from the other group members

What specifically was most helpful in this session?

What specifically was least helpful in this session?

Other comments:

APPENDIX D

TEN THINGS I LOVE TO DO[1]

1.						
2.						
3.						
4.						
5.						
6.						
7.						
8.						
9.						
10.						

List ten things in life that you really love to do. Then, using the code below, code the ten items you listed.

1. Place the $ sign by any item that costs more than $10 each time you do it.
2. Place an *R* by items that involve some RISK. The risk might be intellectual, emotional, or physical.
3. Place a *P* by items that you prefer to do with PEOPLE and an *A* by items you prefer to do ALONE.
4. Place a *2* by items that would not have been on your list two years ago.
5. Place a *3* by items that you think will not be on your list three years from now.
6. Indicate the date when you last did each activity.

Reflect on this list:

Can you identify any patterns in the things you love to do?

Did you learn something new about yourself?

Is there anything that you would like to change or add? How might you go about it?

Are there some things you love to do that you have not done lately? What could you do about this?

[1]Adapted from Penney's Forum: Spring/Summer 1972.

APPENDIX E

VALUES SURVEY[2]

Rank these eighteen values with "1" being the highest and "18" being the lowest.

_____ A comfortable life (prosperous)

_____ Equality (brotherhood, equal opportunity for all)

_____ An exciting life (stimulating, active)

_____ Family security (taking care of loved ones)

_____ Freedom (independence, free choice)

_____ Happiness (contentedness)

_____ Inner harmony (freedom from inner conflict)

_____ Mature love (sexual and spiritual intimacy)

_____ National security (protection from attack)

_____ Pleasure (enjoyable, leisurely life)

_____ Connection to a higher being

_____ Self-respect (self-esteem)

_____ A sense of accomplishment (making a lasting contribution)

_____ Social recognition (respect, admiration)

_____ True friendship (close companionship)

_____ Wisdom (a mature understanding of life)

_____ A world at peace (freedom from war and conflict)

_____ A world of beauty (beauty of nature and the arts)

---

[2]Adapted from Rokeach (1973). *The Nature of Human Values.*

APPENDIX F

WORK FACTORS INVENTORY

Following are fifteen different factors or values that can be applied to work. Please study this list carefully. Then select the four that are most important to your job satisfaction. Write *MS* (most significant) in front of these four. Now select the four you consider least important to your job satisfaction. Write *LS* (least significant) in front of these four. If it is possible for you to identify the one factor or value that is most necessary to your work satisfaction, circle that item.

_____ Security (steady work, sure job)

_____ Prestige (job that is highly respected)

_____ Salary (high-paying job)

_____ Interesting work (a job that I can enjoy)

_____ Advancement (a job with a chance to get ahead)

_____ Working conditions (a job with good hours and pleasant surroundings)

_____ Relations with others (a job where I can work with people I like)

_____ Independence (be my own boss or work on my own)

_____ Benefits (vacation, social security, health insurance, retirement plans)

_____ Service to others (help other people)

_____ Leadership (set example for others)

_____ Power (be a boss)

_____ Self-expression (express feelings, ideas, talent, or skill)

_____ Fame (make a name for myself or become famous)

_____ Other (name it) _____

_____

APPENDIX G

MOTIVATED SKILLS CHART

Instructions: Start with No. 1 of your seven greatest achievements. In Column 1, check off those items strongly applicable to your No. 1 achievement. Do the same with your No. 2 achievement in Column 2, and so on with the others.

	1	2	3	4	5	6	7	8	9	10	Total
Analysis											
Artistic											
Budgets											
Controls											
Coordination											
Creative											
Design/art											
Details											
Energy/drive											
Economical											
Figures											
Follow-through											
Foresight											
Human relations											
Ideas											
Imagination											
Individualist											
Initiative											
Inventive											
Leader											
Liaison											
Manager											
Mechanical											
Memory											
Negotiations											
Observation											
Organizer											

	1	2	3	4	5	6	7	8	9	10	Total
Outdoors/travel											
Ownership											
People											
Perceptive											
Persevering											
Personnel											
Persuasive											
Planner											
Policy making											
Practical											
Problem solving											
Production											
Programs											
Promotion											
Research											
Sales											
Service											
Showmanship											
Speaking											
Systems/ procedures											
Things											
Training											
Trouble-shooting											
Words											
Writing											

APPENDIX H

GOALS INVENTORY

Given my current values and priorities:

1. What are some goals I have for my vocational growth? List at least three.

   _____

   _____

   _____

2. Choose one of the goals you listed above and answer these questions:

   a. What skills do I have to accomplish this goal?

      _____

      _____

      _____

   b. What skills do I need to acquire in order to reach this goal?

      _____

      _____

      _____

   c. What obstacles could keep me from reaching this goal?

      _____

      _____

      _____

3. If there are obstacles, what can I do to overcome each obstacle?

   _____

   _____

   _____

4. What do I plan to be doing in three months regarding this goal?

   _____

   _____

   _____

   in six months?

   _____

   _____

   _____

   in one year?

   _____

   _____

19

Military Personnel

A Career Transition Counseling Model

for Those Leaving Active Duty

SUSAN KNOBLOCH PRENGEL, M.S.

INTRODUCTION

The population addressed in this chapter is primarily active duty military personnel within one year of retirement after serving an average of twenty years of service. Most of these members joined one of the military branches (Army, Navy, Air Force, Marines, or Coast Guard) right out of or soon after graduation from high school. Most of this population do not have work experience in the civilian work force and are only familiar with military careers. The transition is difficult because the civilian job market is relatively unknown and service members are making the transition during middle age. The average retiring person is from thirty-eight through forty-four years old.

There are two distinct groups of military members within this population. The enlisted members form one group and the officer members the other group. The groups are distinguished not only by rank structure but also by function: Officers comprise the middle to upper levels of management and enlisted personnel comprise middle management level to skilled workers. There is a great difference in educational level between these two groups. Officers have college degrees and enlisted members have high school diplomas. Among the officers, there are two groups: the commissioned officers with at least a four-year degree, usually with a master's by the time they retire, and warrant officers who usually have a two-year degree by the time they retire. This difference in functional skill level and educational level translates into a big difference in how prepared members are for retirement and how much help they need from

Susan Prengel is a guidance counselor with the Army Continuing Education Services since 1981.

the counselor. Most officers have already chosen a civilian career (probably in management or technology) and only need résumé services and a computer job bank to find the desired civilian position. Many officers, both commissioned and warrant, have already secured a job by the time they are ready to retire.

The majority of clients that will be using the transition model are the enlisted members with some college who have not chosen a civilian career and are relatively unprepared for the transition. They need a lot of guidance in (a) career exploration, (b) review of transferable skills, (c) assessment of available resources, (d) writing a résumé, (e) interviewing, and (f) securing an appropriate position in the marketplace. The counseling focuses on how to reengineer learned skills to prepare for entry into a new job market and on assessing the need for further training. Some of these skills are not transferable directly to a new career because they are military in nature (for example, the skills of a tank crewman, an infantryman, and an artillery crew member), but many of the component skills, such as organizational leadership, training skills, and technical skills, can be transferred. Although most personnel do not have a job waiting for them as they leave the service, they do have many veterans' benefits, among which are educational funds, loans, medical care, and a retirement check to help cushion the shock of transition. A large group of enlisted members also need career exploration guidance because they are planning to use their education benefits to finish a degree. Most of these need help selecting an appropriate career and an appropriate educational institution and may need additional financial aid while attending school.

While the counseling model is designed as an ideal package—from assessment of present work values, acquired skills, an available support group, and financial means to an exploration of career interests, personal style, résumé and interview preparation, and job search—not all service members use the complete model. Some members have plans in place to attend a specific college, others already have family or other connections to a job, and still others will have waited too long and will not have enough time to go through the process before separating from the military.

The career transition model presented in this chapter is actually carried out by several different agencies and different types of counselors. The education counselor is mainly responsible for assessing education level and helping the service member prepare for college. Included in this counseling are helping the service member: (1) choose an appropriate career, (2) choose an appropriate college program, (3) secure refresher courses if needed, and (4) assess credit already acquired so that the member can continue on a degree plan without repeating courses unnecessarily. It should be kept in mind that military members change duty station every two or so years, so a twenty-year member may have served at eight or twelve different locations throughout the world in a given career span and may have attended as many as six or seven different schools or colleges.

The transition counselor in the transition office is prepared to help the service member with the following services: (1) career exploration, (2) assistance in preparing the résumé and styling it for different positions, (3) improving and perfecting job interview skills, and (4) conducting a job search through the use of an automated computer job bank.

The family services center counselors are prepared to help the service member with these concerns: (1) family support, (2) financial planning assistance and emergency aid, and (3) special family needs such as unusual or difficult health or educational needs for family members.

Department of Veterans Affairs (VA) counselors are prepared to: (1) brief service members on their health, education, financial, and other benefits, (2) provide vocational rehabilitation assessment and program placement, (3) provide help with employment, and (4) provide career exploration for veterans who have not yet chosen careers. The VA provides services to retired members and the other agencies provide services to members still on active duty.

Although the career transition model that is presented could easily be done entirely by an education counselor, generally résumé preparation, interview skills development, and assistance with the job hunt are done in the transition office and the assessment of the family support system is done in the family counseling center.

THEORETICAL APPROACH

The theoretical approach to counseling for this model is basically client-centered. This approach is used to explore personal values, assess skills and accomplishments, and clarify transition concerns. The client-centered approach involves several core conditions for a good relationship:

- Understand the client.
- Have respect for the client.
- Be genuine.
- Be concrete and specific.

The function of the counselor in this approach is to provide these core conditions, and the function of the client is to engage in self-exploration. Self-exploration is essential in career counseling, and this process should proceed

in a spontaneous way with clients moving at their own rate and in their own way without being limited by the counselor. The counselor's role is one of getting clients to obtain more information about values, interests, and the world of work by involving them in the information-gathering process. Although person-centered counseling is nondirective and involves listening and clarifying client responses, the process is to present choices that are as logical, cognitive, and rational as possible. Choices and decisions that come from the client rather than being directed from without are their own and involve a commitment that would otherwise be lacking.

Instruments used for career assessment and development of a career plan are based on the Holland model for career assessment and exploration. The assessment instruments used are the Strong Interest Inventory (SII) and the Myers-Briggs Type Indicator (MBTI). This helps the client select career fields that are appropriate for specific interests and style. Most clients will choose a career based on past training and on skills they already have. Some choose a career based only on what they think will bring the highest financial reward. It is an eye-opener for clients when they learn that interest and personal style not only can be measured, but can be effectively matched up to a career choice. This information usually brings renewed energy and openness to the career exploration experience.

MODEL FOR

VOCATIONAL COUNSELING

The model for vocational counseling for the transitioning service member consists of two phases, the Life Review and Focusing on the Future. The steps are as follows:

Life Review

1. Exploring transition concerns
2. Exploring the family support group
3. Exploring veterans' benefits and other financial support
4. Exploring present values, goals, and interests
5. Reviewing career background
6. Identifying past accomplishments and present job skills

Focusing on the Future

1. Exploring future career goals and interests—SII
2. Exploring personal style—MBTI
3. Putting it all together—matching career interests with personal style
4. Researching matching careers
5. Developing realistic career goals and job preferences
6. Preparing the résumé
7. Developing good interview skills
8. Transferring work skills to a new career

The object of the first phase is to address transition concerns and assess past work and training experience. The object of the second phase is to assess interests and personal style, to develop career goals, and to either find a job or secure acceptance at an appropriate training institution. The second phase is based on measuring work factors and personal styles, matching them to an appropriate career, and developing a plan to enter the career field. Most people in this population begin to prepare for their transition somewhere between one year and six months before separating from the military. Time spent on the model varies greatly depending upon the client, with most clients needing a moderate amount of career explo-

ration. All clients have been trained in at least one military specialty, probably in two by the time they have finished a twenty-year career. Service members know what they like and dislike about their military jobs, but they need updated information on the civilian job market and the entry skills required to secure a desired position. Clients also need guidance on selecting an appropriate career and appropriate training institutions should further training be necessary. Many have spent years in a job that they either have outgrown or do not want to pursue as a second career. Many clients are elated with this chance to explore interests and do something they always wanted to do, but generally they are confused about how to go about doing it.

The model proceeds session by session through the fourteen transition steps. In each of the sessions there is an agenda of tasks to accomplish, but besides these the counselor needs to keep in mind that there is an emotional process occurring. The client is progressing from initial shock, happiness, or denial through gradual acceptance and planning phases to the final, successful completed transition. The client's feelings need to be addressed in each of the steps, and the counselor must strive to get all concerns out in the open so that progress will not be blocked. The counselor also needs to be aware that the steps do not progress evenly or neatly from one to the other. A typical counseling session is between thirty and forty-five minutes, but this may vary from agency to agency. A minimum of thirty minutes is usually required to adequately address a few issues and make progress.

Sessions 1 and 2: Life Review— Exploring Transition Concerns

These are crucial sessions, as they set the tone for the remainder of the process. The following information needs to be determined: (1) Where is the client in the transition process? (2) Has a career been chosen? (3) Are there support systems in place to help? While the counselor is attending to client issues, good rapport with the client needs to be established and the counselor needs to be aware of the ongoing process. What is the client's reaction to the counselor? What is the client's mood? Is the client happy about the transition? Is the client making light of the transition while actually in denial of feelings of fear and anger? These concerns will begin to flow after the client is more comfortable with the counselor. Clarification is important in order to make sure that the counselor is hearing what the client is really saying. It may be helpful to have the client draw a simple self-portrait surrounded by representations of the feelings currently being felt (clouds with words, faces showing emotions, and so on). Pictures are very powerful for expressing and clarifying feelings, especially when the client is having trouble verbalizing them. There is also a cathartic effect in using pictures—the client can express feelings and is relieved of a load in the process. This leads into the third session, exploration of the family support group. The spouse, indeed all the major players, should be present for this session.

Session 3: Life Review— Exploring the Family Support Group

This session covers the family network that will be available to the client during the transition. Having the spouse present contributes to bringing concerns out in the open that may not have been voiced yet. For most service members, retirement involves a move of household goods, car, and family (including pets) to a hometown or to a favorite area where the member had been stationed. This transition involves much more than finding a new job or securing further education. Connections with new support systems, concerns about new schools for the children, transportation of household goods, purchase of a home, possible change of country, changes (sometimes drastic) in geographical area and climate, and possible time unemployed are all concerns that the family has to face.

The strength of the immediate and extended family group (brothers, sisters, mother, father) will be very important for needed support. Support is a great fear reducer and often the client needs to see that everything does not have to be done alone, but that tasks can be delegated to and help solicited from family members.

A technique that is very useful at this stage for planning the transition is "mind mapping." Mind mapping allows the client to plan details in a nonlinear fashion and to make connections between all the things to be accomplished. Mind mapping is a holistic approach to problem solving and allows the client to think in a circular fashion. A mind map of the support group can be done as homework. It shows who is in the support group and what tasks each will do in the transition process. The mind map, besides allowing the client to plan the transition, helps the client use available sources of help.

Session 4: Life Review— Exploring Veterans' Benefits and Other Financial Support

In this session the counselor shares information on veterans' benefits with the client. Since counselors for both the VA and Transition Point cover all the benefits, the education counselor can concentrate on the education benefits. In a few cases, the retiring service member may not have contracted for educational benefits. In these cases the counselor should discuss scholarships, grants, loans, and other sources of financial aid for students. Peterson's series (1997) on sources of financial aid is one resource for locating money for education. Financial aid applications do require personal assets to be listed, and these funds are taken into account when the award is made (in other words, personal assets are used first). The counselor can assist the client in obtaining financial aid information, student-study arrangements, and information on part-time employment possibilities.

If the client does not plan on going to school for further training, the counselor should stress that veterans' benefits can be used to enhance career skills, cross-train for other careers, or obtain an additional credential. Often, the client does not realize that additional job skills may be necessary at a future date either to keep a current job or to be promoted to a more desirable position. Also, the counselor should make sure the client knows that education benefits do have a time limit.

Session 5: Life Review—Exploring Present Values, Goals, and Interests

This session is devoted to the exploration of present work values, goals, and interests. Leisure as well as work activities should be included in the exploration. Completing a values scale or rating activities on a scale can draw out preferred patterns. A values scale of some kind should be used to rate work values and activities. The books by Bolles listed in the references at the end of this chapter contain good materials for categorizing values and activities and seeing patterns.

The client is now in a position to choose a second career with information on likes and dislikes. The client already has plenty of work experience and can benefit from seeing patterns in preferred values and activities.

The results of this session should be documented or recorded in some manner so they

can be used during the research portion of the process in Phase 2, Sessions 3 and 4. Work values will also be included as part of the career assessment portion of the model, but it will be helpful to have a record of this informal measure for later comparison with test results and subsequent discussion of patterns.

Session 6: Life Review—Reviewing Career Background and Identifying Past Accomplishments and Present Job Skills

This session is devoted to reviewing career background and identifying past accomplishments and present skills. Now that transition concerns have been addressed, available resources have been identified, and a strategy for transition has been made, the client is ready to move into the career exploration process. This process begins with identifying what the client has already accomplished and what skills have already been acquired in the world of work.

In this season the counselor should encourage the client to remember past accomplishments that were milestones. The client can begin to remember some of these by making a list. Also in this session, the counselor should begin to explore job skills already acquired. The counselor can encourage the client to talk about these skills and the client can begin a list of them as well. This work will be valuable for later comparison to results from the SII and MBTI.

Session 7: Follow-Up to Life Review— Exploring Career Background, Accomplishments, and Skills

This session should be used to wrap up any loose ends from the past six sessions. Skills and accomplishments should be sorted into two categories: (1) those that can be directly transferred to a civilian career, and (2) those that are indirectly transferable to civilian careers that were learned from and achieved in combat teams and other military jobs. This information will give the client confidence that he or she has a list of available skills and accomplishments that have brought past success on the job and that can be used to secure a future position.

Session 8: Focus on the Future—
Exploring Future Career
Goals and Interests

This session will be devoted to taking the Strong Interest Inventory (SSI). It is important that the client know that this test is not a mental measure, but an interest inventory. In cases where the client has difficulty choosing an answer, the client should be told to just go ahead and select one. The test itself is usually scheduled and given in a controlled testing environment, although the test materials do not need to be strictly controlled.

Test results for military members and their dependents are scored by a contractor in Princeton, New Jersey, and the results may take up to two weeks to reach counseling centers in the United States and four or more weeks to reach overseas centers. Clients already out of the military may take their test in one of the many education centers in the United States that have their own computerized testing equipment, in which case results are scored and printed out immediately. It is best to wait until the results are available before scheduling the next session.

Session 9: Focus on the Future—
Interpreting the SII

This session is devoted to exploring the results of the SII, its personal indicators, preference for activities, and the resulting similarities to select careers fields based on Holland's RIASEC model. The computer printout version of the SII provides a lot of material for the counselor to use in interpreting and helping the client understand the SII results. The SII workbook listed in this chapter's references can help the client to understand the information presented and to organize it in a clear and usable fashion.

The object of the interpretation is to isolate a few (no more than ten) careers that can be further explored by the client using library or education center resources. Excellent sources of information are the *Occupational Outlook Handbook* (OOH), and the *Dictionary of Occupational Titles* published by the Department of Labor. After reading this, the client can judge which career should be further researched. These resources are listed in this chapter's references and both are available on the Internet.

Session 10: Focus on the Future—
Exploring Personal Style

This session is used to take the MBTI and to interpret the results. There are a variety of materials available from the publishers of the MBTI that can be used to help clients understand their personal style. The counselor can relate some of the previous skills identification to the results of the MBTI. The books by Myers and Myers (1995) and by Quenk (1995) can be used for outside work if clients wish to do further investigation of their personal type.

Session 11: Focus on the Future—
Putting It All Together

This session explores the connection between the MBTI and the SII and their resulting implications for the world of work. An excellent resource to use for this session is the *Strong-Myers Briggs Career Development Guide,* which indicates careers related to both tests. This resource will help the client narrow the number of suitable careers down to two or three.

Usually the client has already thought, maybe seriously, about most of the careers that came out of the searches. The match-up of these two instruments verify those thoughts and feelings and reveal careers that the client either did not know about or did not previously consider. This may require further research on the client's part if they have not come up with specific career choices.

Sessions 12 and 13: Focus on the Future—Developing Realistic Career Goals

These two sessions focus on the development of a realistic plan for achieving the desired career goal. If the list of careers has not been narrowed down to two, at most, now is the time to do this.

Once the career field has been identified, the next step is to determine if additional skills and training are needed to enter the career field. At this point the counselor should explore the client's past educational background (if this has not already been done). If further education or training is needed, or if a certificate or exam is required, the counselor can assist the client in researching appropriate institutions and costs. Any of the resources listed in this chapter's list of references (Peterson's, College Board, College Blue Book) can be used. Once the educational institution has been located, the counselor can assist the client in requesting an application. The client should estimate the cost of attending by estimating the cost of tuition, books, and living expenses minus available financial aid.

Sometimes the client has the necessary skills, experience, and certification required to enter the chosen career without further education. If this is the case, the client can move on to the résumé and job search sessions.

Session 14: Focus on the Future—Refining the Career Plan

This session is spent on refining the career plan and assessing prior training, college credit earned, and certification exams taken. This session is for clients who have some college/technical training and need to estimate how many credit hours they still need in order to reach their educational goal. This session is not necessary for the client who does not need further training. Resources for the unofficial evaluation of credit are "The 1996 Guide to the Evaluation of Educational Experiences in the Armed Forces" and "The National Guide to Educational Credit for Training Programs." In any event, this review is only an approximation, as the educational institution the client attends will do an official evaluation upon enrollment. The unofficial evaluation is useful for planning purposes to give the client a feel for how much more time and money will be needed to reach the career goal.

Sessions 15 and 16: Focus on the Future—Preparing the Résumé

These two sessions focus on writing the résumé. (See Chapter 9.) Some helpful references for connecting matching military occupations to civilian job titles are *Military Careers: A Guide to Military Occupations and Selected Military Career Paths,* published by the U.S. Department of Defense, and *Dictionary of Occupational Titles* published by the U.S. Department of Labor, Employment, and Training Administration. In writing the résumé, it helps the service member to use the proper job titles. Through careful reading of position requirements, the client can cite experience, skills, and training that fit the desired position. Résumés can be sent to the prospective employer as they are completed.

Sessions 17 and 18: Focus on the Future— Developing Good Interviewing Skills

The counselor can use the medium of videotape very effectively in these two sessions. The client and counselor can take turns playing prospective employer and prospective employee. This gives the client a chance to play and see different interviewing styles and questioning techniques that might be used. This is an effective way to understand the difference between a good and a bad interview. There is no substitute for seeing yourself on videotape. The effect is clearly visible, body language and all! Subsequent practice sessions with and without videotape can help boost confidence and prepare the prospective employee for unexpected questions and approaches.

Session 19: Focus on the Future— Transferring Work Skills to a New Career

This is the final session and should be used to clear up any unfinished business. The résumé needs to be continually updated, job offers need to be answered, and up-and-coming interviews need to be researched and practiced. By this time the client is probably near the point of departure from the military post. The final out-processing session can be used to review any relevant concerns before the service member departs the service for civilian life. VA offices around the country and state and city agencies will continue to assist the service member until employment is located.

DETAILED CASE STUDY

The case study involves a thirty-eight-year-old Hispanic male, Raul, who began his transition process about eleven months before retiring from a twenty-year military career. Raul enlisted directly upon graduation from high school. Now, twenty years later, he wanted very much to finish a four-year degree but was not sure what major he wanted to follow. Raul started the transition process early because he wanted to be set up to attend college upon retirement. The first few sessions established that he wanted to go back to his extended family in South Texas. He had come from a large family and had brothers, sisters, and parents living in the hometown area. He and his wife, Diana, had bought a home in that area fifteen years ago, and the mortgage was now completely paid. Raul and Diana had two children—Roger, who had just completed his first year of high school, and Marta, who had completed her third year of high school. Both children were looking forward to going back to their cousins and friends and enrolling in the hometown high school.

Diana was concerned about finding employment to help support Raul while he attended college. She expressed her wish to help support the family now, as he had been the main provider for the past twenty years—it was her turn. During Sessions 3, 4, and 5 it was established that she had office experience and had worked on and off when she could find employment as she and Raul went from place to place. She did work full time after the children entered high school. She had developed good computer skills and had computer and office training. Diana had a high school diploma and had worked full time for the government for the past two years. She would be able to retain her hiring preference status if she could secure a federal position back home.

Raul and Diana had worked out their expected income from his military retirement check plus the expected monthly educational benefit from full-time enrollment in college. They had calculated the tuition at the local university plus living expenses and figured they would need another $800 to $900 per month in additional income. Diana was confident that she could provide this amount. The counselor urged Diana to enroll in some college computer and English courses to brush up her skills during the time they had left on post until Raul retired. The counselor helped Diana apply for federal student aid. She received a small grant and enrolled in a few courses for the next several months.

Meanwhile, Raul completed several values scales. Important to him were (in order of values weight): (1) independence, (2) family security, (3) a comfortable life, (4) a sense of accomplishment, (5) high income, and (6) harmony.

In Sessions 6 and 7, a review of Raul's military career background showed he had trained in two major occupational specialties: communications electronics and unit supply. The communications electronics specialty involved in-depth training in electronic theory and hands-on skills in communications systems, communications devices, and inspection procedures for checking the installation and operation of equipment. The unit supply specialty involved skills in working with an automated supply system, managing and accounting for inventory, computing usage factors, and applying data processing techniques to filing and processing. This specialty also involved skills in applying security procedures to sensitive, controlled items.

Raul had been a senior noncommissioned officer, which meant that he trained, supervised, and managed teams of soldiers (five to ten in a team, depending on unit and rank). He had attended leadership schools and had been trained in supervision. His skills and accomplishments centered around electronic equipment; computer skills; solving logistical problems for getting supplies where they were needed; leading, training, and supervising; and rating the performance of his assigned team of soldiers. Most of his skills and accomplishments seemed evenly divided among people, data, and things. Raul preferred working with data and things. He enjoyed working with people a small percent of the total work time. So far, Raul was leaning toward a program in communications electronics. This is what he knew, was most familiar with, and liked doing very much.

Sessions 8 and 9 were spent on taking and interpreting the SII. Raul's results showed a preference for occupational themes (in order of similarity): CRS—conventional, realistic, and social. His personal style scales showed a slight preference for working alone with data and things. Raul showed a strong preference for a learning environment that is practical and short-term. His leadership preference revealed he was more comfortable doing the job rather than directing others to do it. Results also showed Raul preferred activities with a low level of risk taking. He had a fairly good grasp of various occupations, but showed low preference for academic subjects. Knowledge of work activities was fairly broad, but leisure activities were not well explored. The counselor suggested Raul spend some time trying out new leisuretime activities to expand his interests. His range of preference for different types of people was small, indicating he did not like a large range of different types. This preference fit his desire to work mostly with data and things; however, the counselor pointed out that Raul needed to be aware of this, since he was bound to be working with people in some way (at least a boss) in future employment.

Careers that showed a strong similarity to Raul's interests were (in order of strength of similarity): (1) computer activities, (2) data management, (3) mechanical activities, (4) athletics, (5) religious activities, and (6) military activities. Specific occupations that showed strong similarity were: (1) banker, (2) credit manager, (3) medical records technician, (4) bookkeeper, (5) plumber, (6) radiological technologist, (7) small business owner, and (8) parks and recreation coordinator.

Session 10 was spent on taking and discussing the results of the MBTI. Raul's result was ISFJ, which indicates characteristic qualities of being dependable, practical, traditional, realistic, patient with detail, consistent, conservative, tactful, sympathetic, and preserving. He preferred an established routine, which matched well with his preferred conventional occupational theme from the SII. Raul was basically a shy person and indicated that he preferred not to be the leader all the time and liked to do a job himself. These preferences matched his preferred working and leadership styles from the SII. He had strong family ties and his immediate family was a strong and supportive unit. This configuration matched his MBTI, which showed a preference for being a devoted family person.

Raul began to explore careers and researched various career fields under data management, radiological technologist, and small business owner. He was drawn to the computer technology careers. Not only had he worked with electronics and electronic devices most of his military career, but he liked this work and found it rewarding. He decided he wanted to be an electronic tech-

nician. He wanted to complete a degree in computer electronics. Raul was also interested in eventually taking courses in business, with the thought in mind that he would eventually own his own computer electronics business. The counselor assisted Raul in his research for a two-year technical institute near his hometown that also offered degrees in business. A search of his education records showed that he had completed nine semester hours of general college courses, had taken a Spanish language exam worth about twelve semester hours, and had a possible fifteen to twenty hours in military credit. He wrote for an admissions packet, and the counselor assisted him in completing the application and having college, testing, and military transcripts sent in for evaluation.

Meanwhile, Raul visited the transition office to get help in preparing a résumé. Diana went also so she could have her résumé ready when she returned home. Raul's résumé was a stop-gap measure in case he needed part-time employment to support the family while he was studying. He was fairly sure that he could always find work repairing electronic equipment if he needed extra cash. The counselor at the transition office advised Raul that Texas awarded educational benefits to veterans and that if he needed more training after his veterans' benefits expired, he could get state funds. Raul did not use the computerized job bank at the transition office since he planned on enrolling in full-time studies upon his return. He did, however, practice his interviewing skills with the transition counselor.

Raul was admitted to the desired technical institute for the fall semester and was awarded twenty semester hours from his credit sources. Since the program was sixty semester hours, this meant that he had saved about a semester's worth of expenses.

Raul and Diana left the post to retire in Texas, fully prepared to make the transition to their new life. He began the computer electronics program. She had a lead on several full-time positions through help from relatives back home. They had sent transcripts to the local high school to enroll their children, Roger and Marta, for the upcoming school year. The family was moving into their house, which had been rented but was now empty. Raul and Diana had worked out their budget and found that Raul's tuition and books were more than covered by veterans' benefits. His retirement check from the military would cover about three-fourths of the family's monthly expenses, and Diana was confident that she could provide the remainder. Their transition was successful because it was well planned. Raul and Diana had taken advantage of the model. They had taken advantage of the services offered them and therefore had a smooth and successful transition.

REFERENCES

U.S. Armed Services Publications

Army occupational handbook, RPI 975 OCT. 74, GPO (1974). 651–451. Washington, D.C.: U.S. Government Printing Office.

College career workbook (1993). (Rev. ed.). Published by DANTES (Defense Activity for Non-Traditional Education Support, an agency of the Department of Defense), Code 31, 6490 Saufley Field Road, Pensacola, Fla.

Military careers: A guide to military occupations and selected military career paths (1992–1994). Washington, D.C.: U.S. Department of Defense.

VA Pamphlet 22-90-2 (1996). (Rev. ed.). Washington, D.C.: Veterans Benefits Administration.

U.S. Government Publications

Counselor's handbook for postsecondary schools (1994–1995). Washington, D.C.: U.S. Department of Education Student Financial Assistance Programs, Federal Student Aid Information Center.

Dictionary of occupational titles (1991). (4th ed.). Vols. I & II. Washington, D.C.: U.S. Department of Labor, Employment and Training Administration.

Occupational outlook handbook, Bulletin 2450 (1998). Washington, D.C.: U.S. Department of Labor, Bureau of Labor Statistics.

Assessment Instruments and Related Resources

ACT-American College Testing (1996). Iowa City, Iowa: The American College Testing Program.

SAT-Scholastic Aptitude Test (1996). New York: The College Entrance Examination Board; Princeton, N.J.: Educational Testing Service.

Dobbin, J. L. (n.d.). *How to take a test: Doing your best.* Princeton, N.J.: Educational Testing Service.

DISCOVER, Hunt Valley, Md.: ACT Educational Technology Center.

Myers-Briggs Type Indicator (1985). Palo Alto, Calif.: Consulting Psychologists Press.

Strong Interest Inventory (1994). (Rev. ed.). Palo Alto, Calif.: Consulting Psychologists Press.

A workbook for understanding your Strong results (n.d.). Distributed by Consulting Psychologists Press.

Hammer, A. L., & Kummerow, J. M. (1997). (Rev. ed.). *Strong and MBTI career development guide.* Palo Alto, Calif.: Consulting Psychologists Press.

Test of adult basic education: Examiner's manual for Level D (1976). Monterey, Calif.: CTB/McGraw-Hill.

Tests of adult basic education: Form 5, Level A: Reading, math, and language with Book for Norms (1987). Monterey, Calif.: CTB/McGraw-Hill.

Other Resources

Accredited institutions of postsecondary education (1996–1997). Phoenix, Ariz.: Oryx Press.

Armed services veterans education guide: A guide to education and career opportunities for today's military veterans (1997). (8th ed.). New Rochelle, N.Y.: School Guide Publications.

Bolles, R. N. (1991). *How to create a picture of your ideal job or next career, advanced version (revised) of the quick job-hunting (and career-changing) map.* Berkeley, Calif.: Ten Speed Press.

———. (1999). *The 1999 what color is your parachute? A practical manual for job-hunters and career-changers* (Rev. ed.). Berkeley, Calif.: Ten Speed Press.

———. (1981). *The three boxes of life and how to get out of them.* Berkeley, Calif.: Ten Speed Press.

Buzan, T., & Buzan, B. (1994). *The mind map book.* New York: Penguin Books-Dutton Books.

The college bluebook: degrees offered by subject, narrative descriptions, occupational education, tabular data, and scholarships, vols. 1–5 (1989). (22nd ed.). New York: Macmillan Publishing Company.

The College Board guide to college costs and financial aid handbook (1996). New York: The College Entrance Examination Board.

The College Board index of majors and graduate degrees (1996). New York: The College Entrance Examination Board.

The College Board handbook for transfer students (1993). New York: The College Entrance Examination Board.

Fitzpatrick, W. G., & Good, C. E. (1990). *Does your résumé wear combat boots?* Charlottesville, Va.: Blue Jeans Press.

The guide to the evaluation of educational experiences in the armed forces, vol. 1: Army; vol. 2: Navy; vol. 3: Air Force, Coast Guard, Department of Defense, and Marine Corps (1996). Washington, D.C.: The American Council on Education.

Krannich, R. L., & Krannich, C. R. (1994). *Almanac of international jobs and careers: A guide to over 1,001 employers* (2d. ed.). Manassas Park, Va.: Impact Publications.

Manual on certification and preparation of educational personnel in the United States (1991). Dubuque, Iowa: Kendall/Hunt Publishing Company.

Mitchell, J. S. (1990). *The College Board guide to jobs and career planning.* New York: The College Examination Board Publications.

Myers, I. B., & Myers, P. B. (1995). *Gifts differing: Understanding personality type.* Palo Alto, Calif.: Davies-Black Publishing.

The national guide to educational credit for training programs (1995). Chicago: The American Council on Education, published by the Program on Non-Collegiate Sponsored Instruction (PONSI) of the Council for Adult and Experiential Learning.

The official GRE/CGS directory of graduate programs; vol. A: natural sciences; vol. B: engineering and business; vol. C: social sciences and education; vol. D: arts, humanities and other fields (1995). Princeton, N.J.: Educational Testing Service.

Paré, M. A. (ed.). (1996). *Certification and accreditation programs directory: A descriptive guide to national voluntary certification and accreditation programs for professionals and institutions* (1st ed.). Detroit, Mich.: Gale Research, Inc.

Peterson's annual guide to two-year colleges (1997). Princeton, N.J.: Peterson's.

Peterson's annual guide to four-year colleges (1997). Princeton, N.J.: Peterson's.

Peterson's guide to vocational and technical schools and programs: East (1996). Princeton, N.J.: Peterson's.

Peterson's guide to vocational and technical schools and programs: West (1996). Princeton, N.J.: Peterson's.

Peterson's guide to job opportunities series: The environment (1995). Princeton, N.J.: Peterson's.

Peterson's guide to job opportunities series: Engineering and technology (1995). Princeton, N.J.: Peterson's.

Peterson's guide to job opportunities series: Health care (1995). Princeton, N.J.: Peterson's.

Peterson's guide to job opportunities series: Business (1995). Princeton, N.J.: Peterson's.

Peterson's national college databank: The book of questions and answers (1993). Princeton, N.J.: Peterson's.

Peterson's college money handbook (1997). Princeton, N.J.: Peterson's.

Peterson's guide to paying less for college (1997). Princeton, N.J.: Peterson's.

Quenk, N. L. (1993). *Beside ourselves: Our hidden personality in everyday life.* Palo Alto, Calif.: Davies-Black Publishing.

Sacharov, A. (1988). *Offbeat careers: The directory of unusual work.* Berkeley, Calif.: Ten Speed Press.

Schlachter, G. A., & Weber, R. D. (1994–1995). *Financial aid for veterans, military personnel, and their dependents.* San Carlos, Calif.: Reference Service Press.

20

Career Development in Business and Industry

WYN BUMGARDNER, M.A.

INTRODUCTION

The purposes of this chapter are: (1) to present an overview that integrates career development theory with actual career counseling and career development practices in the 1990s in U.S. (primarily) business and industry; (2) to describe three career development programs representing different industries and organizations; (3) to introduce a hypothetical career development model within a single organization that is flexible enough to address the changing life and employment needs of employees, contractors, interns, and individuals representing other forms of employment; (4) to illustrate how said model can address many of the ongoing employment needs of workers, whether or not the workers remain with the organization; (5) to demonstrate the use of this model with a hypothetical client, one who has been a long-term employee of the organization; and (6) to briefly discuss evolving changes in career development and how they link to organizations' objectives.

Historically, published research has focused on an individual's career within a single organization, while the competitive and rapidly changing global business environment in the 1990s has resulted in multiple organizational structural changes and fewer full-time, benefits-eligible employees in traditional jobs. The career development model described in this chapter is unique in that it takes into account this changing status of employment. Also, career counseling has traditionally been viewed as appropriate for individuals in educational settings who are selecting a school-to-work program or

Wyn Bumgartner is a career consultant in Houston, Texas. She has worked with Mobil, Chevron, and Levi Strauss & Co. in career development initiatives in many states. She has worked with individuals, groups, and organizations to maximize career satisfaction.

a college major and who do not return for career counseling once a trade or profession has been chosen. Therefore, career counseling has been confined primarily to educational institutions while the world of work, represented in large part by business and industry, has focused on training, developing, and promoting employees to meet the business and succession needs of the organization, and, more recently, on ensuring the organization's ability to remain competitive, which includes careful management of its human resources. But this model, again unique, focuses on the career development needs of those who are already in the world of work, and it does so from within an organization. And, finally, a third unique aspect of this model is that it integrates traditional career counseling assessment tools and results with tools and inventories used in business and industry, such as multirater feedback instruments, planning and implementation of skills and competencies development, and the matching of individual interests with broad categories of business interests.

Many individuals in today's labor market experience a variety of working arrangements with multiple employers, including full-time, benefits-eligible positions, part-time jobs, internships, consulting, short-term and long-term contract work, business ownership, and more. Companies, no longer able to offer lifetime employment, promote the message that employees are in charge of managing their own career. There is a need for flexible career development models and practices that take into account a person's total career—a series of learning and employment experiences with multiple employers throughout the individual's work life.

As increasing numbers of individuals have been laid off and have accepted alternative forms of employment, it has become less the norm to think of all workers as having full-time, benefits-eligible, and permanent jobs. Less than half of the work force in the industrialized world will hold what has been thought of as a standard full-time job by the beginning of the twenty-first century (Handy, 1990).

During the economic boom that preceded the late 1970s, many organizations grew fat, with ranks of employees swelling as prosperity abounded. Employees believed they were entitled to a job, and the prevailing attitude centered on what the organization owed its workers (Buhler, 1995). Many employees went to work for an employer immediately after completing school and remained with that employer until retirement. Organizations took care of their employees in what is now described as a paternalistic manner. The employer-employee contract, whether explicit or implicit, was that the employee would have a job for life barring any huge infractions of company rules (Buhler, 1995).

Following the tumultuous period of initial downsizings and restructurings in an effort to reduce costs and remain competitive, many companies discovered that the employees who remained were demoralized. Productivity declined as employees who had survived one or more downsizings, mergers, or restructurings worried about whether or not they would keep their jobs or be laid off in the next reorganization. Not surprisingly, fear was a lingering effect of downsizing for many employees in many companies. Job satisfaction declined. Morale was low among employees in delayering organizations (Holbeche, 1995). Companies that cut many management layers and jobs had few promotional opportunities to offer their employees. Career plateaus, while not new, reached an unprecedented magnitude and presented a major challenge to many organizations (Weiner, Remer, & Remer, 1992). Minimizing the negative impact of plateauing—maintaining or enhancing individual productivity and job satisfaction when an employee reached a career plateau—became an increasingly important focus (Tan & Salomone, 1994).

Tremblay and Michael (1993) identified the difference in objective career plateaus (job stability) and subjective career plateaus (subjective evaluation of having reached a dead end). The difference between structural career plateauism (lack of upward advancement and mobility) and content career plateauism (lack of opportunities to learn and use new skills) became an increasingly important distinction for managers and supervisors who had to advise employees on the impact of structural career plateauism while resolving or preventing the existence of content plateauism (Joseph, 1996).

Organizations needed to consider a new role in employee career development in the absence of corporate paternalism and hierarchies that had made it fairly easy for both company management and employees to discern a path along which the employees would move. Colby (1995) noted that employees needed support, information, and tools to master their expanded career ownership role. For employees to be successful, employers needed to provide open, timely communication on current business performance and future business plans, and they would need to offer honest feedback on performance. Human resources needed to work with line management to identify skills needed for key positions and succession planning. Basic career-planning seminars needed to be offered to employees along with career development tools (skill and interest assessments, for example) to direct employees in developing a career action plan (Colby, 1995).

Organizations and employees realized that the old employer-employee contract had van-

ished due to the unprecedented changes represented by the increasingly competitive global economy and the necessity to survive in a rapidly changing world. Companies reengineered their work processes, placed increasing attention on market share and customer retention, outsourced noncore functions, did more work with fewer people, and placed more emphasis on team rather than individual contributions. Organizations began to focus on a new employer-employment contract: An individual's career became a joint responsibility between the company and the employee. This new approach means that the company is responsible for providing information about its strategic business direction, information about employee skills and competencies required now and in the future, access to position descriptions and job postings, training and development opportunities to upgrade existing skills and develop new skills, and tools for employees to use to manage their own careers. And it means that employees are responsible for individual assessment, career planning, internal career options exploration, and, together with their manager, setting career goals that best maximize the joint intersection between the individual's skills, interests, and motivators and the organization's strategic business direction and desired outcomes.

The Boundaryless Career (Arthur & Rousseau, 1996) represents "leading edge" thoughts and research concerning careers in business and industry. The authors describe the boundaryless career in a number of ways: (1) as the opposite of an organizational career; (2) as a career that moves across the boundaries of separate employers; (3) as a career, like that of an academic or a carpenter, that draws validation and marketability from outside the present employer; (4) as a career that is sustained by external networks and information; (5) as a career that is the result of traditional organizational career boundaries being broken; (6) as a career that happens when an individual rejects existing opportunities for personal or family reasons; and (7) as a career that is seen from the perspective of a boundaryless future, regardless of structural constraints. Running through all these descriptions is the common theme that boundaryless careers are independent from, rather than dependent on, traditional organizational career arrangements.

One factor to consider when working with individuals in today's rapidly changing business environment is what Mary Catherine Bateson calls deviant résumés (Bateson, 1994). Her comments include the following: "Résumés full of change show resiliency and creativity, the strength to welcome new learning; yet personnel directors often discriminate against anyone whose résumé does not show a clear progression. Quite a common question in job interviews is, 'What do you want to be doing in five years?' 'Something I cannot now imagine' is not yet a winning answer. Accepting that logic, young people worry about getting 'on track,' yet their years of experimentation and short-term jobs are becoming longer. If only to offer an alternative, we need to tell other stories, the stories of shifting identities and interrupted paths, and to celebrate the triumph of adaptation" (Bateson, 1994, 83).

Another factor to consider is networking from the perspective of social capital, defined as "the structure of individuals' contact networks" (Arthur & Rousseau, 1996). In Raider and Burt's (1996) chapter from *The Boundaryless Career*, the authors use Burt's 1992 assertion that the concept of social capital is formalized by using the structural hole theory, which describes how certain network structures offer a competitive advantage by providing access to more opportunities. Network structures that offer a competitive advantage are large networks composed of disconnected contacts. Disconnections among contacts are the structural holes, and it is the structural holes that enable access to diverse sets of information, that control flow of information between disjointed parties, and that determine the form of projects that bring together the disconnected contacts. This type of network structure offers a competitive advantage because individuals who connect those who are disconnected are more autonomous and have more opportunities than individuals with smaller networks composed of interconnected others. Individuals who have broader, disconnected networks have advantages in access to dissimilar information, timing in receiving information, and referrals to distant third parties. This social capital is important in boundaryless careers when it comes to job seeking as well as career attainment (Raider & Burt, 1996). Managers in entrepreneurial firms, especially at the boundary of the firm, are a good example—they rely upon their networks to position their firms competitively. Aldrich and Baker (1996) report that job seekers with networks containing many structural holes find better jobs, and find them faster, than those with networks whose members are almost all interconnected. This information is certainly important for career counselors and others who work with people on career-related issues.

CURRENT CAREER DEVELOPMENT PROGRAMS IN BUSINESS AND INDUSTRY

Many corporations, companies, and organizations are currently offering career development programs that are aligned with the individual company's missions, values, and strategic business plans and that emphasize hiring and retaining new workers. Re-recruiting current employees during the continuing acquisitions, restructurings, downsizings, and other ongoing changes is also a key factor for many organizations (Robinson & Galpin, 1996). Five career development program managers in companies with more than 500 employees have stressed the importance of top-down management in the design of career programs (Morris, 1994). Upper management should supply directives and information to human resources and additional management members to conduct career development programs. The following six program steps make up a representative model:

1. Program orientation from executive management

2. Program support from upper management

3. Establishment of a program focus

4. Instructional design

5. Selection of presenters

6. Design of evaluation

Variations of this method have been used with career development programs, particularly those in which consultants have been hired to make recommendations on program scope and content. Brief descriptions of three such programs follow.

Career Development at Amoco

Amoco Corp., a Chicago-based international oil and gas company with 40,000 employees, uses a career management system to assist managers and employees in balancing rapidly changing business needs with individual development (Baumann, Duncan, Forrer, & Leibowitz, 1996). The company uses a four-step system for goal setting and goal achievement. Amoco decided on a long-term system to balance business needs with employees' needs for personal growth and career satisfaction. Additional design considerations included strengthening the shift toward employees taking more responsibility for their own careers, implementing a flexible system that could be customized to meet the needs of eighteen business groups, and making a commitment to advance the philosophy of strategic renewal. Amoco Career Management (ACM), the name of the resulting career development system, includes four parts: (1) education, (2) assessment, (3) development planning, and (4) outcomes. Employees may participate voluntarily in a half-day educational program called "Exploring ACM"; supervisors or team leaders attend a mandatory two-day workshop, "Supporting Employee Development." In subsequent training, employees conduct a self-assessment that addresses both individual skills and company goals. An additional workshop, "Maximizing Career Choices," focuses on future career planning, positions, and job enrichment. Corporate information and computer job postings make it possible for employees to see and apply for jobs electronically from their own computer. Employees meet with their team leader to discuss their completed individual development plan (complete with specific career goals and action plans) and get information from the team leader on the team's development strategy, the team's projected direction and challenges, and competencies needed by the team. After the development plan has been finalized, outcomes are determined and actions to achieve them are implemented.

Twenty-five percent of employees completed an individual development plan, and 60 percent of employees believed that Amoco had an effective process for developing employees, as opposed to 34 percent prior to ACM rollout.

Career Development at Sears Credit

Sears Credit launched a major career development initiative to better align employees' skills and workloads following a major reorganization and reengineering effort that closed many small units and offered a large voluntary retirement program. Significant career implications of the reorganization included redefining existing jobs, creating new jobs, eliminating career paths, hiring from the outside at all levels to obtain new talent, and developing new skills in the current work force (O'Herron & Simonsen, 1995). Senior management at Sears Credit wanted the company to be more open in its communication about career opportunities, individual development needs, and new staffing procedures. There was a need to help managers and employees reframe their mindset from "the company will take care of me" to a more proactive approach in which success is redefined as what is important to the individual, other than fast upward movement on a career ladder. Managers needed to coach and support employee development, and employees needed to take on more responsibility for managing their own career. In a partnership to ensure that individuals at all levels could continually add value to Sears Credit, the organization needed to provide information and resources to employees so that they could take the initiative in their individual career development.

Sears Credit chose a comprehensive, organizationwide career development process that included senior management sponsorship and defined the skills and competencies needed in restructured jobs. Exempt employees attended a mandatory two-day workshop, "Managing Your Career Within Sears Credit," that in-

cluded: (a) a new model of career development, (b) self-assessment activities, (c) organizational information (including the new detailed skills and competencies), and (d) a development planning process. Managers attended an additional mandatory workshop called "Managing Career Development" to learn career coaching skills needed for employee discussions.

Manager/peer assessment and self-assessment inventories were developed and distributed to allow employees to self-identify growth areas. A strong commitment to meaningful performance reviews was supplemented with a separate and optional employee/manager career discussion initiated by the employee. New employee position descriptions were written and position summaries were made available to all employees via e-mail. A databank of employees' desired career goals was created for use in organizational planning and staffing decisions. It included such items as "next job aspired to," "preferred location," and "education needed." Human resources implemented a broad new compensation program that rewarded developmental lateral moves not previously entitled to promotional increases. A new quarterly newsletter entitled "Career Developments" highlights various aspects of Sears Credit and includes a section that describes employee career directions and another that reviews career-related books.

The Sears Credit comprehensive career development program has been a critical factor in organizational success following major restructuring.

Career Development at United Parcel Service

United Parcel Service (UPS) is a leader in the rapid package-distribution service business, with 285,000 employees in 185 nations and territories worldwide. During the 1980s when the company was facing powerful competitors and economic pressures, a strategic decision was made to move to electronic package-tracking technology. A second business strategy decision directed UPS to ensure that all employees would have the skills, knowledge, and experience needed to perform well in increasingly complex jobs and to handle any upcoming changes. A critical issue involved development of management ranks, 49,000 people worldwide, to ensure that manager and supervisor capabilities were state of the art and to link this system to management and selection training (Leibowitz, Schultz, Lea, and Forrer, 1994). UPS therefore decided on a top-down introduction of its career development process. The company believed that all managers needed to be familiar with the career development plans and needs of those below them, emphasizing different developmental issues at different organizational levels. UPS decided to link the management appraisal process with a new development process in which employees thought about their careers in the context of upcoming business needs. The management development program was called the UPS Career Development Process (CDP).

As the program works, managers throughout a district become aware of employees who are ready for specific opportunities. The managers also become knowledgeable in the short- and long-term training and development experiences that the company needs to offer. The ultimate result is a "master operating plan" for each district, complete with training plans and development activities. UPS has trained at least 85 percent, or 8,000, of its district and regional managers, who are now introducing the process to their employees. Initial results from manager workshops showed that 90 percent of managers understood CDP and their roles in it, with more than 85 percent indicating a positive commitment to their participation in CDP (Leibowitz et al., 1994).

A MODEL FOR CAREER COUNSELING IN BUSINESS AND INDUSTRY

Many approaches are utilized to incorporate career and personal counseling as well as continuous learning into career development programs in business and industry. The following figure depicts one such approach, using traditional career counseling methods and specific organizational approaches to career development inside one organizational setting. Although this figure represents a hypothetical program, it demonstrates comprehensive human resources development/career development and learning program resources utilization. All of the traditional career counseling interventions, as well as the organizational career development interventions listed, operate within this model.

This setting represents a hypothetical comprehensive career development and learning center inside a large organization. It offers a full range of services to employees, contractors, interns, and others in a large organization. There are a variety of reasons the center is used:

1. to introduce the concept of a career and learning center

2. to confirm or validate a new career direction

3. to find out what is "out there" in the way of jobs and careers

4. to explore job satisfaction concerns

5. to consider a change to another business unit within the organization

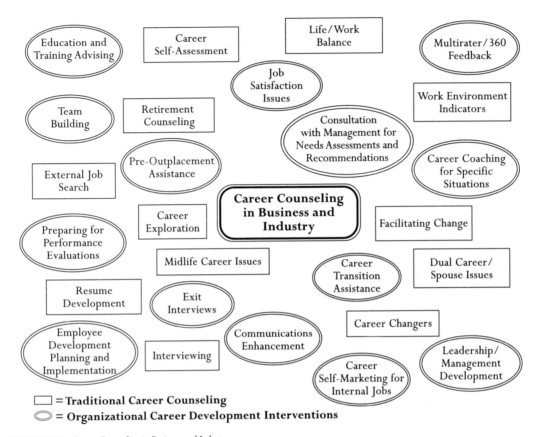

FIGURE 20.1   Career Counseling in Business and Industry

6. to explore relocation options to other cities within the organization and for dual-career couple concerns

7. to create a personal development plan, including training and skills upgrade

8. to use media services available, both in the center and to check out

The center is equipped with media materials, books, Internet access, and computer programs. Individual and group career counseling and related subjects are offered to in-house and offsite workers.

The center also is involved in many organizational human resources development initiatives, including:

1. preparation for annual performance reviews

2. multirater feedback and individual development planning

3. the application/interview process for internal jobs

In addition, career counselors:

1. work with individuals who are leaving the company, assisting these employees with retirement planning and career transition issues

2. work with employee families, including spouses, college and high school children, as well as summer interns

3. conduct exit interviews at the request of human resources and/or management

4. offer consulting services to management

Furthermore, career counselors assist individuals with planning and implementing development needs for the future, such as when the company announces a major downsizing, or develops a new competency model containing specific employee and management competencies needed to help the company retain its competitive advantage. They also develop computer-based training programs using self-directed learning, "just in time" training needs, and employees at multiple sites. As new organizational initiatives emerge, the career development center establishes a solid record of partnering with human resources, management, and employees to ensure that organizational objectives are met.

CASE STUDY:
A LONG-TERM EMPLOYEE
SEEKS A FRESH START

Roy is a white male over fifty who was employed by a major chemical company for seven years and a major engineering company for eighteen years. Roy has a bachelor's degree in chemical engineering with some postgraduate work in chemistry. Roy's formal education took place at the traditional college age, after which he went to work. Roy is curious and considers himself to be independent and a continuous learner with a well-developed sense of humor. He is an intelligent, hard-working, innovative person who conceived, developed, and implemented several major programs that earned his employers millions of dollars. Roy has a record of continuing accomplishments throughout his employment with both companies, focusing on new approaches to existing work processes that increased efficiency as well as on business development opportunities that brought in new customers and substantial revenues.

Roy was puzzled by difficulties in professional relationships with a few of his former supervisors and managers during his twenty-five years of employment. For example, his last manager at the chemical company had been so difficult for Roy to work with that, at the end of an annual performance review in which Roy was not evaluated well despite a year of excellent professional accomplishments, Roy notified his supervisor that he would look for another job outside the company and would leave within three months. Roy located a new job at the engineering firm and left the chemical company.

Although Roy thoroughly enjoyed his work at the engineering firm, he came for his initial visit to the internal career development and learning center baffled as to why he had received another mediocre performance review. He wanted to continue to work for another ten years and knew that in spite of his continuing value-added accomplishments produced for the engineering company, work was not nearly as satisfying to him as it had been at other times during his career. Roy also had the option of looking for another job within the engineering firm, although jobs at his higher level of expertise and salary were scarce. His self-esteem was low and he lacked confidence in his abilities.

Roy and his career counselor spent a lengthy first session exploring his career history and what work he found satisfying and dissatisfying, then began to consider employment options that were compatible with Roy's skills and competencies, interests and values, family situation, and ultimate financial goals. At the completion of the initial session, Roy and his counselor partnered for a career development process that included extensive assessment and career testing, career options generation, career exploration and decision making, planning for an internal job search, résumé development, all aspects of the actual job search, and salary negotiations for his new job.

Roy identified and prioritized his three types of skills—transferable, work content or technical, and self-management or personal. He also identified his areas of competency, prioritizing those that brought him the greatest satisfaction. He reviewed his work history, avocations, and other interests to identify additional possibilities for industries and companies. Roy completed a comprehensive series of career inventories, including the Strong Interest Inventory, the Campbell Interest and Skill Survey, and the Myers-Briggs Type Indicator. He also identified and prioritized his top ten values and completed a questionnaire to further confirm his interest in upward career mobility, adding responsibilities to his current job, making a lateral move, returning to a position of lesser responsibility but possibly greater satisfaction, and looking for work in another organization.

Roy spent five to six sessions reviewing his career history, additional assessment exercises, and the results and integration of his three career inventories with his career counselor. Over this extended period of time Roy began to realize how much satisfaction he derived from being innovative, creative, and developing new business development ideas, from which his companies had benefited greatly. He commented that he had been in an uninnovative area of the engineering company during the past several years, and his attempts to implement cost-savings procedures and suggest new business development opportunities had met with consistent resistance by his manager. Roy's enthusiasm for his work had declined greatly during this period.

Roy shared several performance appraisals as well as the results of a recent multirater feedback instrument in the next session with his career counselor. He made the significant realization that his lower performance appraisals and the lower-rated sections of his multirater feedback pertained to two areas: situations in which he was primarily charged with keeping existing systems, procedures, and client relations at their current level, or "business as usual," and communications with his manager on the status of his work. Roy determined that he had not communicated with his manager frequently on the status of his current projects because he believed that all he was to do was maintain the status quo. He had not reported what he thought of as minor problems to his manager, correcting them on his own. Roy then speculated that his manager may have believed that Roy was exceeding his authority by acting alone, depriving his manager of necessary information and possibly causing the manager's status to erode with the manager's peers.

Roy and his counselor developed a plan for discussing these thoughts with his manager in a nondefensive manner. Roy then visited his manager. At his next visit to his counselor, Roy was visibly enthused. His manager had validated Roy's thoughts and opened up an additional discussion about Roy's many strengths. Roy stated that this was the most candid discussion the two of them had ever had and that each had left the meeting with the friction between them having dissipated.

After extensively researching possibilities, Roy determined to seek work in another division of the engineering company, in a related industry that prized innovation and his technical expertise. Roy believed that his wife was concerned about this choice because this job would represent a significant risk in terms of continued employment and their reaching their financial goals for retirement. Although Jane, his wife, was employed, Roy's income was much greater. Roy and his wife held an extended session with his career counselor so the three of them could realistically take a look at how he would approach this job search, address his wife's concerns, and put a job search plan on paper. At the end of the session Roy had a structured plan of job search activity for the next four to six months, and his wife believed that his choice was sound. Her insights into Roy's work history and job satisfaction underscored the need for his career redirection.

Roy continued to see his career counselor for résumé development, interview preparation, including a video interview with counselor feedback, and implementation of his actual job search. Throughout his search for companies and job responsibilities that were a good fit, Roy's enthusiasm remained high. Roy chose from two attractive internal job offers that met his criteria and negotiated a salary comparable to what he was currently making with the potential to be much more lucrative through increased stock options and other benefits. At last report, Roy was doing very well with both his professional accomplishments and his relationship with his new manager, and he continued to be enthusiastic about his work. (See Appendix for additional interventions, inventories, and tools.)

CONCLUSION

A proliferation of career development programs in business and industry has followed major structural changes in organizations and in the world of work that began in the 1970s. As companies downsized, restructured, merged with other companies, and reengineered work processes many employees were laid off from full-time, benefits-eligible jobs and needed to find work with another employer, consulting work, contract work, part-time work, or entrepreneurial work. The rethinking of work as consisting of these and additional alternative forms of employment became necessary.

Traditional career development theory and practice, confined for many to an educational setting for selection of school-to-work programs and selection of college majors, is increasingly becoming an ongoing part of the work life of many adults. Outplacement, human resources development activities for employees, the concept of individual career resiliency, career development programs in organizations, and an increasing emphasis upon achieving and maintaining a competitive advantage through human resources have all positioned career counseling and career development as factors contributing to sustaining individual and organizational success. A review of recent career counseling literature underscores the necessity for integrating career counseling with personal counseling and other aspects of an individual's life. A description of three career development programs in companies provided an overview of some current career development practices in organizations. The future of career development in business and industry appears to be evolving toward an integration with organizational business objectives and work-force development. An emphasis upon continuous learning, skills enhancement, and proactively managing one's own career are elements for consideration in the work life of each individual. Many new tools and inventories have been developed with specific applications for adults working in a business environment. Career counselors can use these tools in addition to traditional career counseling tests and inventories in working with adults in groups and individually to highlight additional factors contributing to the quality of each person's career and life choices.

As career development increasingly becomes part of the employment life of individuals, attention needs to be focused on the positive and negative aspects of computerized and online career development assessments and materials, as well as on the quality of the counseling relationship with the individual client, in order that the client and the career counselor consider an integrative approach to career development.

REFERENCES

Aldrich, H. E., & Baker, T. (1996). Prometheus stretches: Building identity and cumulative knowledge and multiemployer careers. M. B. Arthur & D. M. Rousseau (eds.), *The boundaryless career* (pp. 132–159). New York: Harper Collins.

Arthur, M. B., & Rousseau, D. M. (1996). *The boundaryless career.* New York: Oxford University Press.

Bateson, M. C. (1994). *Peripheral visions: Learning along the way.* New York: Harper Collins.

Baumann, B., Duncan, J., Forrer, S., & Leibowitz, Z. (1996). Amoco Primes the Pump. *Personnel Journal,* 75, (2), 79–84.

Buhler, P. (1995). The changing workplace of the 90s, *Supervision* (July): 24–26.

Burt, R. S. (1992). *Structural holes.* Cambridge: Harvard University Press.

Carr, J. V. (1996). Comprehensiveness of career planning: The third C—comprehensiveness. *Journal of Career Development,* 23, (1), 33–42.

Colby, A. G. (1995). Making the new career development model work, *HRMagazine* (June): 150–152.

Handy, C. (1990). *The age of unreason.* Boston: Harvard Business School Press.

Holbeche, L. (1995). Why delayering also flattens staff morale and ambition, *People Management* (November 30, 1995): 45.

Joseph, J. (1996). An exploratory look at the plateauism construct, *Journal of Psychology,* 130, (3), 237–244.

Leibowitz, Z., Schultz, C., Lea, H. D., & Forrer, S. E. (1994). Shape up and ship out, *Training & Development,* 48, (8), 38–42.

Morris, L. (1994). How do we really design programs? *Training & Development,* 48, (1), 66.

O'Herron, P., & Simonsen, P. (1995). Career development gets a charge at Sears Credit, *Personnel Journal,* 74, (5), 103–106.

Raider, H. J., & Burt, R. S. (1996). Boundaryless careers and social capital. M. B. Arthur & D. M. Rousseau (eds.), *The boundaryless career* (pp. 187–200). New York: Harper Collins.

Robinson, D. E., & Galpin, T. (1996). In for a change. *HRMagazine* (July): 90–93.

Tan, C. S., & Salomone, P. R. (1994). Understanding career plateauing: Implications for counseling, *Career Development Quarterly,* 42, (4), 291–301.

Tremblay, M., & Roger, A. (1993). Individual, familial, and organizational determinants of career plateau: An empirical study of objective and subjective career plateau in a population of Canadian managers, *Group and Organizational Management,* 18, (4), 411–435.

Weiner, A., Remer, R., & Remer, P. (1992). Career plateauing: Implications for career development specialists, *Journal of Career Development,* 19, (1), 37–48.

APPENDIX

SELECTED CAREER ASSESSMENT EXERCISES FOR INDIVIDUALS WORKING IN BUSINESS AND INDUSTRY

I. Skills Identification and Competencies Assessment
   A. Career counselors can use career instruments, checklists, and card sorts with clients to identify:
   - technical skills
   - personal or self-management skills
   - transferable skills
   B. Career counselors can use organizational instruments and guidelines with clients to:
   - assess individual organizational competencies
   - identify competency gaps
   - develop personal development plans to increase skill levels in current competencies
   - create personal development plans to add additional competencies required for future jobs

One such instrument is CareerAgent, an Internet-based career development tool that engineers, programmers, and developers can use to make career decisions, assess their skills, and locate local training they may need.

II. Identification of Interests
   A. Career counselors can use a variety of career testing instruments and inventories with clients, such as the Self-Directed Search, Strong Interest Inventory, Campbell Skills and Interest Inventory, and others, and clients can ask themselves the following questions:
   - What have I always wanted to do? What do I want to do now?
   - Who are three people with whom I would like to change jobs? What is it about their jobs that I like?
   - What am I doing when I lose track of time?
   - What are the industries, companies, products, and services about which I am curious?
   B. Career counselors can use business and industry instruments with clients, such as CareerFocus, an Internet-based business career self-assessment program consisting of three inventories whose profiles indicate how your interests and desired work rewards may or may not be satisfied in twenty-four business careers. Skills necessary for success in each of these fields are included.

III. Identification of Values
   A. Career counselors can use a variety of instruments, checklists, and card sorts with clients to identify:
   - intrinsic values
   - work-related values
   B. Career counselors can use the Values-Driven Work card sort with clients to identify and prioritize their work-related values, to determine the alignment of their most important values with the organization, and to develop an action plan to satisfy important values not yet fulfilled.

IV. Personality. Career counselors have a variety of personality indicators, such as the Myers-Briggs Type Indicator, from which to choose to assist employees in identifying personality matches with a variety of different jobs.

V. Person/Environment Fit
   A. Career counselors can assess, with their clients:
      - job satisfiers and dissatisfiers
      - career motivators
      - "best fit" working environment

   B. Career counselors can use Career Anchors.

   C. Career counselors can use the Career Leverage Inventory, a questionnaire that sorts clients' answers, based on their current job, into six categories for employment: five within the current organization and a sixth that involves looking for employment elsewhere. Clients prioritize their six choices after considering additional factors.

21

Unemployment Issues and Outplacement Interventions

CARLA CAMPBELL, M.ED.

INTRODUCTION

Within the field of career counseling there is perhaps no greater ambiguity and confusion than exists in the field of outplacement. The term outplacement also refers to the job club concept. Outplacement is a behavioral approach to job seeking, combining specific job search behaviors with counseling and/or group support. The process of finding employment involves complex social, personal, and economic factors. There is universal agreement that a number of psychological, economic, behavioral, and social problems emanate from the condition of unemployment. The outplacement, or job club, concept seeks to improve the

hiring process while providing varied support services to the job seeker with the goal of reducing the time of unemployment. This serves to mitigate the severity of the psychosocial stressors for society as a whole and, most especially, for the individual who is seeking productive work.

UNDERSTANDING THE UNEMPLOYED

If a career counselor plans to work in the area of outplacement, it is essential that he or she understands the specific concerns of unemployed people. The following philosophy describes the equilibrium people strive to achieve in life and aids in the understanding of the impact of unemployment: Personal happiness derives from a balance in life of having meaningful work, or

Carla Campbell is director of Corporate Relations for Rush Enterprises, Inc., of San Antonio, Texas. She is also adjunct faculty at the University of Incarnate Word. She was the founder of the San Antonio Job Club and is its director.

something to do that you love, meaningful relationships, or someone to love, and a spiritual base, or something to believe in. This speaks to the interconnectedness of vocational, relational, and spiritual needs.

It is important that the career counselor is cognizant of the emotional and psychological implications for out-of-work workers. Selling oneself in a job search is inherently stressful. As stress rises, physical ailments are not uncommon, and self-esteem plummets. A prolonged job search can lead to clinical depression. The "something to do that is loved" is missing.

Most unemployed people experience intense feelings of loss of control over what is happening and will happen. The world can feel like a chaotic place. The person attempts to cope with depression and the growing unease of the situation by withdrawing or becoming angry and may exhibit increasing paranoia about the theys and thems whom the unemployed worker feels are causing this condition. Projection, rationalization, euphoria, apathy, and many other conflicting feelings are experienced. These feelings tend to become more intense as the job search is prolonged, if there have not been successes during the search, if a job offer had to be turned down, or if financial or personal resources diminish.

The "someone to love" is affected as friendships formed in the workplace, held together by the commonality of the workplace, suffer, cutting off an important social and emotional support system. This occurs for many reasons. Those still employed face time pressures no longer experienced by the unemployed and are less available to the former co-worker. Also, they often feel secret relief that it is the other who is unemployed, and they feel guilty about that. Finally, they simply may not know what to say or do to be supportive. This makes them uncomfortable. To cope with these feelings, the employed person may avoid the former co-worker with every intention of picking up the relationship once the unemployed friend has found another job. Then they can celebrate, rather than commiserate, with the person.

Cognitive dissonance plagues the unemployed. They feel like damaged goods, and avoid those whom they once regarded as less successful than they were. Many suffer from low self-esteem and do not want others to know how bad they are feeling. Attempts to hide the "shameful" unemployed status can result in extreme behaviors, such as spending all savings in an attempt to maintain a former lifestyle and getting ready for work daily, departing, and entering the house at the former work times to avoid having the family know. These behaviors can exist for months. Meanwhile, the unemployed worker is in a downward spiral. These individuals are more likely to be at risk of suicide because of the quiet depression and guilt they feel in keeping up the charade. Risk increases as unemployment continues.

Any problem behaviors exhibited prior to unemployment are intensified during unemployment. Spousal abuse, drug and alcohol abuse, dissent in the home, problems with children—all are magnified by the unemployment condition. Personal relationships suffer as money becomes an issue or when well-meaning spouses who have not experienced unemployment can't understand why it is taking so long to find a job. The spoken and unspoken censure is that the unemployed person is lazy and not trying hard enough.

Even the most well meaning ask, "Have you found a job YET?"—a phrase so dreaded by the unemployed that they often want to scream, "If I had, don't you think you'd be the first to know?" Children, who often are not able to understand or appreciate the stress of a tightened financial situation, can be the unwitting source of deep remorse and guilt on the part of the dislocated worker. The "someone to love" suffers as the worker pushes away family members because of a sense of failure or lack of self-worth.

As the person is caught up in this strange and stressful state of unemployment, the "something to believe in" may become another source of conflict. Many find little solace in the spiritual. For instance, they may harbor feelings of anger if their church does not provide the immediate support of a job offer through those in the congregation who know the unemployed worker. They may feel their higher power is punishing them or has turned a deaf ear to their suffering. The lack of faith in themselves and their plummeting self-esteem can cause a crisis of belief and faith.

Some individuals base their spiritual renewal outside organized religion. For these persons, their object of spiritual renewal becomes tied to financial aspects or is caught up in the syllogistic logic of the can'ts, shouldn'ts, or won'ts. For example, those who golf do not play because they can't afford to or don't want to let others know of their unemployed condition. Movie buffs shouldn't take time out to relax at a movie because they should be out searching for a job, and so on. What was once a pleasurable, renewing experience becomes one more pressure. The stability of "something to believe in" is missing.

It has been observed that the unemployed experience the same stages of grief as one experiences with the death of a loved one. Job loss is comparable to a form of death for many. Most experience feelings of shock, denial, anger, grief, and finally acceptance and resolution. These feelings are not necessarily experienced in that

order. It is not uncommon for the unemployed to experience several variations throughout the job search. For example, the person may not attain the resolution phase for years after the unemployment trauma. The competent vocational specialist must be prepared to recognize and assist the person through these stages and help the person maintain their confidence and sense of purpose through this process. Outplacement support combined with behavioral techniques provides the structure to lessen these stages and hasten the progress to resolution.

A vocational practitioner must be prepared to assist the person with issues that surface as a result of job loss that had been successfully suppressed prior to job loss. More than in many other fields of counseling, the vocational practitioner must be prepared to serve the client in a dynamic relationship that may include personal issues counseling, marital counseling, family counseling, career assessment, mental health assessment, dealing with situation depression and prolonged depression (which can be mitigated with antidepressant medication), career coaching, financial and credit counseling, and, finally, suicide or substance abuse counseling and interventions. The models that follow provide the career specialist with a full-service framework to help combat the many negatives experienced by the unemployed.

OUTPLACEMENT
INTERVENTIONS

Numerous programs are classified as outplacement options. Varieties include: (a) government programs, such as state-run employment commissions, (b) private employment agencies, (c) volunteer or community-based job club formats, (d) private outplacement firms, and

(e) federally funded programs under the Job Training Partnership Act within various government agencies.

State employment commission (also known as work-force commission) programs typically offer job search skills and job placement/matching services. The plus for job seekers is that employers can place job listings within this database free of charge. This gives the job seeker access to positions statewide. On the minus side, service tends to be impersonal due to the mass-population approach, resulting in a lack of ongoing individualized support, and any training offered is noncomprehensive. Also, the commission generally has fewer executive and professional job listings because private sector employers are less willing to list those positions in the mass forum of a public agency.

Three specific types of outplacement services are described below.

THE JOB CLUB

A job club format that is described later in this chapter is now being offered by some state employment commissions. These services are referred to as one-stop centers and are funded by a combination of Job Training Partnership Act money, federal funds under the Wagner Pisner Act, and work-force development programs. Participants who meet the stated eligibility criteria are able to access the services offered at no charge. Readers interested in this concept should contact their state employment commission or local private industry council for additional information regarding services that may have been implemented.

Typically, private employment firms or agencies offer only job placement services, and usually within a narrow framework of occupational specialization. Fees, which are due upon successful placement, are paid by the employer, job seeker, or both in a 50 percent split-fee arrangement. Emphasis is placed on quickly matching the job seeker with an available opening. This works well if a match exists. However, without an immediate match the job seeker is maintained as a name in a database until a potential match occurs, if it does. There is no support to the job seeker in the interim. These services can be costly, and some employers erroneously believe they are paying for the person instead of for the service provided by the firm, and they reduce the starting salary to make up the fee. Job seekers should research the market value of their services prior to committing to a position referral.

The job club concept as a formal outplacement program and an informal support group structure has stood the test of time as a positive model to assist the unemployed. As early as 1980, the *Job Club Counselor's Manual: A Behavioral Approach to Vocational Counseling* was developed in southern Illinois. This model was the first definitive approach to combining behavioral psychology with interactive career counseling.

In the job club format individuals are assisted in a planned program that combines practical training and job search skills with group peer support and professional counseling. Job clubs can offer comprehensive services and support in a professional career center dedicated to this purpose or be limited to informal peer group gatherings of unemployed individuals who meet regularly to offer mutual support and networking through a club, church, or civic organization.

Both approaches usually define the group to be served to ensure commonality among members. For example, 40 Plus clubs have been active in numerous cities for over twenty years. Typical members are forty years old or older, although the groups do not discriminate or prohibit younger members from participating. In the 1980s, groups formed around a specific layoff or corporate downsizing, with all members in the group having been affected by the action. Characteristically, job club members are professional or paraprofessional workers faced with unemployment or a career change. Workers at a lower wage and with lower job skills are more likely to find work without the support of a job club group because positions that pay higher salaries and require a higher level of skills are less plentiful in today's economy. A month of job search for each $10,000 of salary is the normal time frame of an active job search. Someone who earns minimum wage is likely to secure another minimum wage job within a month, while someone earning $40,000 per year may face a search of four months or longer. Many other factors have an impact on the time required as well, such as the area's unemployment rate or the ability of job seekers to sell themselves as a qualified candidate. Therefore, the time frame outlined above should be viewed only as an estimate.

Workers with less education and fewer marketable skills are less likely to seek out the networking support of a job club and more likely to be disenfranchised. In order to gain the trust and participation of such workers, special recruitment efforts may be necessary, including educating these workers on the services offered by a job club and on the benefits of belonging to such a group.

Civic self-help groups usually have a nominal membership fee. The fee may be assessed on a per-meeting or monthly basis, depending on the group. Groups sponsored by a church usually offer free membership.

FOR-PROFIT OUTPLACEMENT SERVICE PROVIDERS

Private outplacement firms differ little in terms of services offered from the job club concept. The main difference lies in fees charged for services. Retail outplacement organizations are groups that provide services directly to the unemployed. Fees are the responsibility of the individual who uses the services. Retail outplacement services are available from for-profit companies that advertise individualized services tailored to the person. Typical services offered are coaching, résumé preparation, network lists, interview preparation, use of office space, message taking, and computer support. The emphasis on peer group supportive counseling is minimized and is often not a service option. If offered, the client has the freedom to join the group or not. Rates vary from a low of $1,200 to the more common $3,000 to $5,000.

Individuals should carefully review the cost versus the services offered before signing a contract. Some questions to ask are:

1. How long has the service been in business?

2. Do they have references from people who have used the service recently?

3. What success have they had with others in your field?

4. What services are offered, and at what price? Are there any add-on costs?

5. How long can the client use the services for the price quoted?

6. What does job placement include? Will your résumé be sent to numerous employers on a mailing list or matched carefully to openings in specific firms looking for a person with your skills?

7. Will there be formal job search skills assistance, such as training in, preparation of, and ongoing assistance with résumés and cover letters? Are there networking opportunities? Is there training and practice in interviewing skills, or will the service be limited to a videotaped mock interview?

As with all contracts, the buyer must separate the sell from the service and evaluate cost versus gain.

In contrast, there are outplacement firms that do not offer retail services to the individual. Instead, marketing efforts are directed to companies. The fees, paid by the company, are for a menu of services that vary depending on how much support the company is willing to offer to individuals being separated. The outplacement firm and the company enter into a contract. The person receiving the service is then limited to the contract terms. Assistance is provided until the person is reemployed or until the contract termination date.

Most often, outplacement firms of this type cater to executive-level participants because companies are willing to offer outplacement to such workers as part of a separation package. Fees are similar to those charged by retail agencies to individuals. The service menu can include:

- career and personality assessments
- individualized coaching and support
- office support, ranging from providing a work space to computer, fax, and copier services

- resources such as books, videos, and Internet access
- training in interview and other job search skills

Job referral and job placement services vary widely. Typically, individuals are given initial training and support and are then free to use the office as their work center in a self-directed search mode.

FEDERALLY FUNDED
PROGRAMS

Federally funded outplacement services are from public or nonprofit agencies. Most receive funding through a competitive bidding process in response to a published proposal calling for specific service provision. Under the Job Training Partnership Act (JTPA), delivery of services is set up in accordance with the strict funding guidelines of the titles listed as eligible in the actual statute. Because programs are federally funded through tax dollars, there is never a charge to the eligible participant. The various titles and the workers eligible for the services include: (a) Title II-A, which serves disadvantaged adult workers who meet specific eligibility requirements and whose income is classified at poverty level; (b) Title II-B, which supports disadvantaged youth; and (c) Title III, which supports dislocated workers who have been laid off or separated due to economic conditions or who have been unemployed for a prolonged and specified time period. Other titles offer specific funding for senior workers, veterans, and other specified groups. Service delivery is from nonprofit public assistance agencies or as a subset of state work-force or employment commissions.

Agency services can include: (a) intake and certification (to ensure eligibility criteria are met); (b) participation in a job club, job search assistance, and paid retraining in demand occupations; (c) job placement assistance; (d) on-the-job training contracts in which part of the employee's salary is paid through federal JTPA funds; (e) training in work-force readiness skills; (f) career and vocational assessments; and (g) business readiness classes on such topics as appropriate dress and business etiquette.

Listings of agencies participating in JTPA-funded programs can be obtained by contacting local private industry councils, which are designated as the substate grantee to administer funds through the county council of governments, the state or federal Department of Commerce, or the U.S. Department of Labor.

MODELS FOR OUTPLACEMENT CENTER SERVICE DELIVERY

The Trauma Model

The trauma model's primary goal is to give and receive support. Individuals attend weekly meetings held in community centers, churches, offices, or restaurants. The leadership revolves among members, and members remain until employed. The focus is on emotional stability until reemployment is achieved.

The Skills and Educational Model

The primary goal of the skills and education model is to learn to achieve career goals. The group composition may change from week to week, and the leaders are graduates of the program.

Increased job search skills, employment strategies, networking and uncovering job leads, and self-help are the key outcomes.

The Private Practice Model

The private practice model's primary focus is minimizing isolation, shame, and stigma. The group is open to any unemployed person and is facilitated by professional vocational specialists. The focus is to work through the stages of job loss and remove isolation. Networking and self-help are emphasized.

The Outplacement Firm Model

For-profit outplacement firms provide services for clients. The clients are usually senior executives who earn more than $150,000 annually, advanced management personnel who earn $90,000 or more annually, and basic management personnel who earn about $70,000 annually. The corporation who releases the employee pays for the services.

Leadership is provided by career transition specialists whose backgrounds are characterized by personal success in upper level corporate management and who have earned advanced degrees. The specialist is likely to be very visible within the corporate community and is active in many professional associations. Staff is rounded out through skilled professional trainers and counselors.

The services offered typically follow a plan of career assessment planning, one-on-one counseling, design of a marketing strategy, communication and presentation skills (including résumé preparation), and use of administrative help and facilities. Clients are free to use resources for the duration of the contracted period as agreed by the employer and outplacement firm.

For further information about outplacement firms, refer to Reedie & Company, Inc., and Drake, Beam, and Morin, Inc.

A CAREER TRANSITION CENTER MODEL

The following career transition center model combines the most effective features of the four most common models of outplacement service delivery. This is described to provide steps for developing a center.

Supplies

- work area sufficient to accommodate a minimum of ten participants and staff
- secretarial assistance
- telephones with a minimum of four outside lines plus extension telephones for each workstation
- computers for staff and participant use and a quality laser printer for résumés
- facsimile machine
- copier
- typewriter (or printer with capability to address envelopes)
- workstations and chairs
- file cabinets
- television, VCR, and video camera for mock interviews
- reference library that includes: books, audio tapes, CDs, and videos on the topics of job search techniques, business management, self-help, and so on; newspapers; criss-cross directories; telephone books; ZIP code directories; professional journals focusing on business trends; listings of the largest employers in the area; job-line telephone numbers; and chamber of commerce and tourist information
- office supplies: folders, staplers, pens, stationery, envelopes, stamps or postage meter, overnight delivery envelopes, message pads, paper clips, scissors, and so on

Services to Participants

Intake This should include a personal interview history. The person's experience, education, salary history, and past, current, and future goals should be thoroughly discussed.

Assessments Outplacement differs from other assistance programs in that it emphasizes placement rather than vocational counseling testing. But testing has valid uses in terms of assisting the client in exploring career options and aptitudes. A variety of assessment tools are available to the vocational specialist.

The vocational specialist should ensure that the client understands assessments are useful tools, but may not contain the answer to "What do I want to do in my work?" Lifestyle choices and options must be reviewed with assessment results. For example, a vocational test may reflect that a person has the attributes of an attorney, but a divorced person with two young children may not have the time, money, interest, energy, or motivation to pursue this career.

Counseling Services Vocational, self-esteem, marriage and family, group dynamics, stress management, and crisis intervention expertise are all supportive services that can and may need to be offered. It is helpful to have diagnostic specialization available either as an internal resource or as an external referral. For example, a person who by self-report or family disclosure has indication of personality change and mood swings may suffer from situational depression accompanying job loss. This is normal under the circumstances. The practitioner must assess the individual to determine if the behavior is temporary from situational stressors, is severe or chronic life-limiting depression, or is from a physical cause such as a brain tumor. Referral for medical evaluation may be appropriate.

Many individuals who seek career counseling will disclose personal concerns. Generally, many clients, especially men, would never pursue therapy in any other setting but feel less stigma in seeking career counseling. For those individuals, disclosing feelings within most therapeutic settings carries a stigma of mental illness, or they may fear others would see them as being emotionally weak or unable to handle their problems. With the safety of seeking career assistance, there is comfort, and topics can arise naturally.

Vocational specialists also need to be prepared to handle suicide interventions and make appropriate referrals. There are few circumstances in life more devastating than job loss. At risk are those who experience: (a) a prolonged search, (b) rejection due to age or ethnicity, (c) rejection due to not having a current skill base, (d) being offered positions at substantially less than previous earnings, and (e) multiple personal and relationship issues coupled with the stress of job search.

Access to financial counseling is often needed. Consumer Credit Counseling Services is a nonprofit credit counseling assistance center available nationwide. They have a reputation of offering solid and reliable expertise in this area. Beware of volunteer assistance from financial counselors who are employed in for-profit insurance or brokerage firms. They may be attempting to secure new clients.

Peer group, or job club, meetings are held to explore plans, problems, and progress, to provide networking opportunities, and to serve as a social outlet to replace the workplace relationships.

These group meetings have a powerful dynamic and are proven effective in reducing the stressors of unemployment. Separate spousal support groups are beneficial to assist spouses in understanding and coping with the stress and changes unemployment brings. This helps ensure their commitment to the process so that sabotage that undermines the job seeker, whether willful or inadvertent, is minimized. A children's group allows children to safely express fears they may have while helping them to understand and support the parent's job search efforts.

Having group alumni who are reemployed serve as guest facilitators is a powerful confidence builder for the group. Networking opportunities occur, social and personal relationships are expanded, and hope is generated. Current job seekers can model their search on the proven success methods of others. Individualization occurs when the person realizes that even while they are the same in some ways, they are also unique, and there are numerous paths to success.

JOB COACHING AND JOB SEARCH SKILLS TRAINING AND SUPPORT

Training and assistance may include the following, or a combination of these services:

Job Search Skills Training

- preparing a job search
- analyzing the market

- researching positions, companies and salaries
- evaluating the benefits of a "do-for" job (a job that is not the targeted goal but will do for now—an example is a part-time job to allow continuance of the primary job search)
- dressing for the interview
- résumé preparation
- cover letter preparation training
- follow-up and thank you letter training
- business etiquette (world-of-work skills targeted to less experienced clients)
- stress management techniques
- networking
- interviewer personality types
- interview questions
- salary and benefit negotiation
- weighing offers and alternatives

Job Coaching This is a service that is customized for the individual and is intended to maximize readiness for the interview. Coaching extends support while reinforcing behaviors learned in the job search skills. An example of coaching is conducting and videotaping a rehearsal interview, then playing it back and discussing it.

Job Club Job clubs hold group meetings to cover a job search skills topic in depth, to achieve networking and peer support, to get guidance from alumni who have successfully concluded their search, to have employer panels or speakers who can provide the business perspective, and so on. Job club meetings are held to provide a forum for plans, problems,

and progress of members as well as information and training.

Support Services Depending on funding availability and a center's budget, a variety of support services are available. These include rent or mortgage payment assistance, utility payments, grocery stipends or payments, credit counseling, mileage reimbursement to interviews, day care, transit fares such as subway or bus tokens, book and tuition stipends, and so on.

Job Referral/Job Placement Assistance This service attempts to match individuals with available position openings. Most often this is accomplished by posting leads within the center. Job opening information is obtained from individuals who use the center, employers, job-line telephone numbers, the Internet, and classified advertisements. Some outsource firms encourage clients to review the postings daily. Others contact clients with the referral information.

Office Support Services vary from providing a fully equipped office workstation for the individual to use to simply offering computer access, facsimile access, and copier access. Some centers provide a message service to sustain the image of a professional with a secretary for employers to contact, letter and résumé typesetting, and computer software instruction.

SUMMARY

It is essential that vocational practitioners/specialists understand the psychological aspects of job loss and unemployment in order to be supportive in their interactions. A career trauma center model was described as a multifaceted service that can provide both personal and career counseling for people who are unemployed, changing careers, or facing career transition.

This type of center needs to be available in all cities to those who need the service. The need for trained vocational specialists to administer services is crucial, as is the need for funding.

REFERENCE

Riordon, R., & Kahnweiler, W. (1996). Job support groups: Three configurations, *Journal of Counseling and Development,* 74, 517–520.

22

There Is Life After Work

Re-creating Oneself in the Later Years

BONNIE GENEVAY, M.S.W.

INTRODUCTION

This chapter addresses four groups: (1) people who are prematurely forced out of the workplace because of ageist firing and employment practices—in other words, because of their chronological age, not their lack of skill or productivity; (2) people searching for less demanding or part-time employment commensurate with diminishing life energy; (3) people who want more time to find meaning in life beyond work; and (4) retired people who still need to utilize their workplace gifts and talents in some way in order to feel valuable and that they are contributing to society.

The impact of ageism in employment is subtle and insidious. Joan was a sixty-

one-year-old bookkeeper who had worked in an agency for fifteen years. She was well liked and was an excellent bookkeeper. A new executive, hired to cut costs, decided to terminate Joan because her salary and benefits were more costly to the agency than a new and less experienced employee's would be.

Joan had arthritis and occasionally complained about her fingers. The executive never used written or verbal language that could contribute to an age discrimination suit, but he frequently commiserated with Joan about how hard it must be to "keep up with her work" with arthritic fingers.

He kept his voice empathetic and his words benign, but Joan was fearful and he was able to force her out through subtle intimidation. Joan lost Social Se-

Bonnie Genevay is a nationally known trainer and consultant in gerontology. She is the co-author of *Countertransference and older clients*. She received the 1995 American Society on Aging Award for contributions to the field of gerontology.

curity benefits and other retirement benefits. She eventually found another job with lower salary and fewer benefits, but she had to work many more years in order to be able to afford retirement.

People in the United States are more ageist than anywhere else in the world. Ageism is the abhorrence of growing old and the worship of looking young. Because old age signifies unemployment, illness, and decline to many people, it elicits pathological fear in our culture. A deeply ingrained Puritan work ethic, which tells us we must continue to work to be valuable, combined with ageism results in very few creative vocational road maps to and beyond retirement.

Preretirement planning in most firms and corporations focuses narrowly on financial and legal information and ignores the extension of one's skills and experience beyond the work years and the psychological stressors involved in ending this phase of work life.

Retirement is a misnomer to many older people, since the question of retiring from what to what is seldom addressed. It's assumed older people want to buy a recreational vehicle, travel for a year, then play golf for the rest of their lives. Older people don't often consider seeing a vocational counselor to plan their postretirement years, yet it is vocational counseling that can help provide what they need in order to plan for the rest of a fruitful life.

Re-creating one's work life in older age is the continuation of career. The assumption that when work ends, career ends, is a very narrow definition of what human beings are about. The meaningful skills developed in the workplace over a lifetime can be transferred to retirement years in order to provide satisfaction and high self-esteem for people beyond formal, or paid, employment. But few think of transferrable skills, and many dread disabilities that will curtail work life.

Bert, an expert technician in ship rebuilding and repair, is sixty-eight. He maintains that his expertise is valuable and says he will continue his work as long as he can physically crawl around in the bottom of ships on his hands and knees. He has never thought about how his knowledge and work experience can be utilized when he is no longer physically able. I asked Bert what he would do if he had a stroke and couldn't work, and he said angrily, "I won't get a stroke!"

One popular school of thought on aging is the "use it or lose it" school, which often translates to continuing to work—never retire or you'll become senile and sexless. A variant on this productivity ethic injunction is if you must retire, for heaven's sake, volunteer! This is part of the old rule that many of us have grown up with about idle hands leading to sin and sloth. While continuing to work and volunteering until you die are both reasonable options for some people in later life, the great diversity of older people must be taken into account. In old age we are more diverse in our needs, desires, and goals than at any other developmental stage of life (Erikson, 1963).

For instance, some older people need to work parttime; some need to do nothing but reflect and finish unfinished business; some need to do something entirely new; some need to satisfy a passion in life that has always been there but was never attempted. It can be exciting and challenging in the second half of life to try something new that one had always wanted to do. It can help in the last stage of life, a stage that is truly one of integration, the stage of integrity versus despair (Erikson, 1963).

Many older people would like to translate lifelong work skills that have great meaning for them to a much less demanding time frame. It is not only deceptive but dangerous to attach meaning to chronological age in older people—a very vital eighty-year-old may still be an effective full-time employee, while a depressed or stressed forty-year-old may be unproductive. Older workers are generally found to be more loyal and more productive, and they use less sick leave (Hall, 1996).

"Other strengths of older workers are their positive attitudes and good work habits . . . [C]hronological age will work in favor of some older workers in tomorrow's economy. The . . . marketplace will . . . present new opportunities for older workers to be involved in the design, manufacture, and sale of products aimed at the elderly" (Hall, 1996, 289–290).

Work often stabilizes the health of older people. They appear to respond positively to the satisfaction and well-being they experience when their skills are utilized. Some very old people want to, and do, continue to work because it is extremely meaningful to them.

> Dan had been a printer all his life and was deeply depressed when his firm laid him off at age 76. He had developed few other life interests and felt valuable as a printer. His wife died one year after he was terminated from his job, and the only way he continued to function was to go to the printer's union hall each day. He survived by hanging around the hall and the coffee shop he'd frequented for years and by watching television at night. Dan was filled with unexpressed grief and was fearful of changing any patterns, even though they no longer sustained him. When asked what he did he always responded, "I was a printer." He had no other identity. Dan developed high blood pressure, glaucoma, bursitis, and an ulcer following his forced retirement.

Although many psychologists have formulated theories about the last stage of life, Erik Erikson's (1963) description of the stage called integrity versus despair comes closest to this author's personal life experience and that of many older clients. Cumming and Henry (1961) posit that older people uniformly manifest withdrawal from work and activities in late life, a natural and mutual process in which society disengages from old people and they withdraw willingly from life. And an opposite point of view, the activity theory, implies that old people are the same as middle-aged people. Old people who age optimally must stay active and maintain the activities of middle age as long as possible, and they must find substitutes for work when forced to retire and substitutes for friends and loved ones lost to death (Havighurst, Neugarten, & Tobin, 1963).

Since we are more different as we grow old, not more alike, neither of these theories—withdrawal or activity—fits for the broad spectrum of older people.

Peck's (1964) elaboration on Erikson's last stage—integrity versus despair—is helpful because Peck subdivides Erikson's last-stage tasks. He places an emphasis on *being* rather than on *doing;* on knowing one's self; on inner accomplishments (mental, emotional, and spiritual) rather than outer manifestations of success; and on letting go of expectations in favor of understanding and integrating the meaning of life.

Erikson's midlife stage (generativity versus stagnation) overlaps with the integrity versus despair stage in many older people. This could be due to our living so much longer and staying healthy longer, which results in our still trying to generate—to create something valuable—at the very time we become redundant in the work force. We stagnate when we still have the capacity to generate but cannot find meaningful outlets for this creativity.

Super's (1984) description of the minicycle is also appropriate to older people in the last transition of life. He indicates that the five stages of a career that he defined in 1957 (growth, exploration, establishment, maintenance, and decline) involve a recycling through all the stages at each transition. For example, people in the decline stage of their careers often do life review involving their entire work history—remembering the excitement and anxiety of hirings, the security of some jobs, the feelings of competence and rejection, and the loss of work role and identity. The minicyle is a way of integrating, letting go, and accepting—integrating and letting go of what happened and what one might have done differently and finally accepting both the positive and negative in each stage as that which had to be. Retired people who find meaningful involvement at the end of life may experience emotional and spiritual growth, even though they may not have time or energy to pursue certain activities in any depth. They may maintain this emotional/spiritual growth for only a short while before physical or mental decline set in, yet it may be extremely meaningful to them.

According to Greddie and Strickland (1984), renewal is a transitional stage in which people ascribe meaning to past decisions, make new decisions, and plot a course of action to implement their decisions. This is possible at any age

or life stage, barring severe illness or dementia. Many older people have the maturity and the skills, acquired over a lifetime, to review their past decisions and make excellent decisions based on their experience.

Ellen, in her eighties, has been an actress and community activist all her life. She made a conscious decision not to give up these activities—paid or unpaid—when she retired. When she fills out forms she lists her occupation as whatever she is doing at the moment—actor, writer, community organizer. She never writes "retired." Ellen continues to perform, write plays for causes that are meaningful to her, and help sponsor community events. "I don't do these things 'just to keep busy,'" she says. "I do them because it's my life work to bring people together, to enrich my community, and to change the future."

Ellen ascribes great meaning to her lifelong vocational decisions. She made an end-of-life decision to continue her career into retirement and old age, and she implements this course of action each day as her energy permits.

Williams and Savickas (1990) cite tasks to be performed during career renewal: (1) reappraisal of career commitment and choice; (2) integration of the polarities of one's personality; and (3) modification of one's life structure (Williams & Savickas, 1990, 166–175). These can easily be translated to the older or the retiring worker. Reappraisal of career choice becomes a part of the life review process, either proactively or posthumously. Integration of the polarities of one's personality is occurring naturally at this life stage, regardless of where the older worker is in her or his work cycle. Modification of life structure is probably already happening with the older or retired worker due to such circumstances as housing changes, adjustment to loss of a partner, and income adjustment.

One of the challenging books on creative aging (a relatively new concept) is a perspective on meaning making (Carlsen, 1991). An ageist society does not easily attribute the adjective creative to aging, but it is a very useful concept in terms of vocational counseling with older people. Also helpful to counselors is an understanding of what many older people experience—the ageless self (Kaufman, 1986). It is a common experience for old people to see themselves in a store window and not recognize themselves for a moment, thinking "Who is that old person? Surely it's not me! I feel as young as I ever did." In a society that tends to define people by their appearance only—there is little emphasis given to the timeless, ageless feelings of self we all carry until we die.

AGE DISCRIMINATION
AND OLDER WORKERS

The scene is changing slowly in terms of age discrimination. In some U.S. businesses and organizations employees are viewed as "over the hill" at extremely young ages, their forties and fifties. However, the aging population is growing rapidly. What are we to do with our time and our talents from age fifty to 100 in a work ethic society if those who wish to be employed are unemployable? Many will continue to be mentally, psychologically, and physically fit to work into their seventies and eighties.

The author was asked to speak on "Aging and Changing" at a lavish monthly luncheon for retired bank managers. Seventy impeccably dressed men and a handful of women listened as I talked about the great potential and the creative possibilities of aging. Then I asked them, "How does this bank utilize all the skills and wisdom you accumulated in the years you worked here?" There was dead silence, and finally one man stood up angrily and shouted, "They don't! There's so much we know that *isn't* outdated. We could mentor younger employees, we could consult. I'd be glad to volunteer!" There was murmuring and others stood up to echo the first man. I learned that they hadn't even had a part in planning the luncheon meeting. Speakers like myself were scheduled without any input from the retirees. A vice president explained it this way: "We put on this program for them because they're tired. They just want to come here once a month and be entertained." That was *not* my perception.

People over forty may now appeal termination on the basis of age discrimination. In the past few years those who are discriminated against on the basis of age have received higher monetary awards than for either race or gender discrimination. Some organizations now coach older people who are trying to reenter the work force, helping them face discriminatory hiring practices that focus on chronological age rather than qualifications or experience. Because many baby boomers have chosen to start their families later in life, there will be a whole generation of older people in 2000 and beyond who need to work past traditional retirement years in order to support their families and educate their children.

Some older people have let their job skills become obsolete, especially those stagnating in a job when career renewal is highly indicated. But some employers discriminate in distributing training and development funds, assuming that young, newer employees need the training most, when renewal of a competent older worker through retraining enhances both the employees and the organization.

There appears to be a myth that older workers can't learn new technology. Many managers still subscribe to the "old dogs can't learn new tricks" belief, even managers who are older themselves. They apply ageist stereotypes to others and are oblivious to their own age and life stage. For example, one manager called an older employee "an old bag" out of her hearing and implied that she couldn't keep up with computer skills. In truth she was taking all the required classes and adapting quite well. The manager, however, was threatened by new technology and didn't attempt to learn, not trusting himself to master the skills.

This author has observed that many older people are attracted to computer classes for the sheer joy and challenge of it. Technology classes geared toward older people are springing up in several areas of the country. Interestingly, the classes are often taught by older people who have become computer buffs and are eager to enlist their peers!

A MODEL FOR RE-CREATING ONESELF IN THE LATER YEARS

Douglas Hall and Associates (1996) tell us that careers will never die if we redefine them as a series of lifelong work experiences and personal learnings. This is the perception that makes most sense in terms of older people re-creating themselves in later years: being a lifelong learner. A positive outlook and personal satisfaction are even more critical to older people who may be ending their last job, downsizing to part-time work, volunteering, or choosing to do nothing! (People who find happiness by thinking, reflecting, and making sense out of their lives are never "doing nothing.")

Re-creating oneself in old age builds on all the work and life experience that has gone before and requires the nurturing throughout life of identity, self-esteem, and constructive life-coping skills. The care and maintenance of personal and work identity involves an *evaluation* process and an *action* process and rests on the core identity of the person. Ongoing renewal occurs throughout life through utilization of all parts of the person—mind, body, emotions, and spirit—regardless of age. This model is illustrated graphically in the Shamrock Model developed for this chapter, as seen in Figure 22.1.

Evaluation includes: (1) utilizing the past through a process of life review in order to capitalize on past and current goals, skills, and abilities; (2) being selective about the use of time and activities by continually reprioritizing them and refusing to get stuck in work or life tasks that no longer have meaning; and (3) engaging in self and professional evaluation through scheduling reflection time, keeping a log or journal, and committing to individual and/or group vocational counseling testing at key life transitions.

The action process includes: (1) grieving the changes and losses connected to the work role; (2) creating personal and professional feedback and support systems through colleagues and small peer support groups; (3) creating an action plan with specific steps to follow in the transition and in the new life phase; and (4) consciously anticipating and planning for aging, being proactive

Utilizing All of the Older Person's Resources

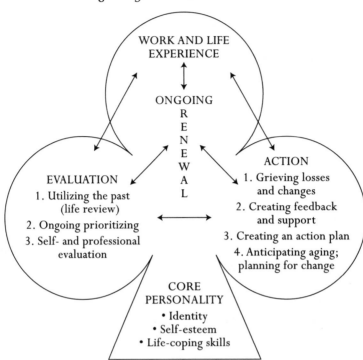

FIGURE 22.1 The Shamrock Model

rather than reactive to change. Change is the one constant we can count on, and we can adapt much better when we get our heads out of the sand of age and death denial.

There are several highly appropriate action steps for older people. These include setting individual and long-range goals, becoming a mentor, seeking out others who do similar work, nourishing a sense of humor, planning a sabbatical, rewriting a job description, creating a vision of what a job or profession could be, and taking short breaks throughout the day to renew energy. Most of these strategies are very empowering—and empowerment is something older people need as they age. An action plan for a sixty-nine-year-old woman retired from full-time work for seven years who is now considering downshifting from half-time work to quarter-time work might look like this:

1. List your reasons for work-time reduction.

2. Identify what you are still passionate about in your job.

3. Assess your life energy and health.

4. Be sure you are facing the inherent losses in reducing your time.

5. Rewrite your job description and analyze the meaning of reduced time.

6. Follow your heart—allow yourself to know the meaning of the change you propose.

Four of the evaluation and action steps of the Shamrock Model require additional comment as they apply to older workers and retirees. They are life review, prioritizing, griefwork, and creating support.

Life review is a process first identified by the geriatric psychiatrist, Robert Butler (1963). It is an inner experience of integrating and reviewing the meaning of one's life and occurs universally in older people. Life review includes experience, relationships, events, and work life. It is characterized by the conscious awareness of past experiences such as conflicts, joys, and sorrows.

> The life review, as a looking-back process that has been set in motion by looking forward to death, potentially proceeds toward personality reorganization . . . (it) is not synonymous with, but includes, reminiscence . . . the process is active, not static, (and) the content of one's life usually unfolds slowly (Butler, 1963, 488).

The occasional, spontaneous insights about the meaning of past behaviors, thoughts, and feelings (successes, failures, critical life changes) often do not imprint on our minds in a way that has an impact on our planning for the future. We are aware of these thoughts and feelings, but let them go without attributing meaning to them. It is necessary to be nonjudgmental and factual about what worked and what didn't work and to record these insights in some way (a diary, journal, audiotape, or videotape) in order to take advantage of this knowledge about the self and to plan for the future.

Vocational counselors and career planners can be extremely helpful in terms of guiding and facilitating life review so that the older individual can create a plan for the use of his or her diminishing life energy and time that focuses on the highest priorities and choices. There is never enough time or energy to do it all, and lifelong perfectionists have a very difficult time letting go of items on their list. The counselor or coach may need to give a lot of permission for letting go of tasks and activities that no longer have meaning, that are wedded to duty or habit.

Steps in Life Review

1. Tell your story unabridged, reflecting on its meaning for you and the important themes that emerge.

2. Identify key life and work transitions and describe the meaning of each.

3. Forgive yourself for past mistakes and focus on what you've learned from these mistakes.

4. Share how you're going to choreograph your life to take advantage of all you've learned.

5. Share dreams, fantasies, and visions of how you'd like things to be.

6. Ask for feedback and reinforcement from others.

Prioritizing is a critical function in later life because it is a life stage that requires selectivity as energy diminishes. Many older people remain locked in meaningless rituals, such as ironing things that don't need ironing, doing repetitive tasks out of habit rather than because they're necessary, and refusing to eliminate unnecessary burdens and activities. Letting go of many of the things we were able to do when younger, but no longer have the interest or energy to do in later years, is critical to personal or job satisfaction.

For those still employed, prioritizing may mean renegotiating the job agreement so that instead of feeling guilty and being overwhelmed by too many job expectations, the employee can be selective and command a reasonable and manageable work load. Or it may mean the older employee needs to cut back on the hours or days of the work week in order to perform at the level of excellence both employer and employee desire. An older employee may choose fewer hours per week and less job stress—even though it might mean working a few years longer in order to achieve adequate retirement income.

One of the major phenomena of aging in America today is caregiving as middle-aged and older children assume increasing responsibility for caring for older parents and relatives. Much of this is long-distance caregiving, which can be just as stressful as hands-on caregiving. The prioritizing of time by working caregivers is absolutely critical to their health. This is distinctly a workplace-combined-with-gender issue because a majority of caregivers are working women. Many of them are older and trying to work full time and care for parents, in-laws, and other relatives.

In no arena is prioritization more important. Some women remain stressed and unhealthy for years while juggling work, home, spouse's and adult children's needs, grandchildren's needs, and eldercare. The fact that women continue to try to do it all points to a great need for workplace caregiver support groups and employee assistance programs that counsel caregivers and provide long-distance case management. As people live longer, we are increasingly seeing sixty- and seventy-year-old caregivers for parents in their eighties, nineties, and 100s. Prioritizing means realigning one's whole life so that there is adequate rest, pleasure, and diversity to support the heavy demands of work and caregiving components of life.

Griefwork takes on new and unexpected meaning when applied to the changes and losses currently occurring in the workplace. The massive changes taking place in business, in health and human services, and in many other organizations in the 1990s create an atmosphere of fear and anxiety for some employees. For others the chaos spells opportunity and challenge. Whether viewed positively or negatively, there are many losses that must be grieved in the workplace and few managers who understand that grieving needs to be acknowledged and applied to organizational change and loss.

Work is so meaningful to many older people that some are bereft without it. Grieving the losses associated with job reduction and termination is a crucial element of mental and emotional health at any life stage, but particularly so in the last developmental stage of life. The last job of a lifetime is worth grieving over in a work ethic society!

Losses accumulate throughout life and many people have never learned to grieve. Older people particularly were socialized to suppress their grief, and they often swallow the sorrow, anger, anxiety, fear, guilt, and other emotions that grief comprises. By the time they retire from, or are terminated from, their last job there may be an accumulation of unresolved grief. The ending of a job is often "the straw that breaks the camel's back," when all of the losses of a lifetime rise to the surface.

This is a gender issue as well. Many older men have no other identity except that attached to work. If they do not express the loss they experience at the ending of their work life, their grief may spiral down into clinical depression. Ultimately, some become suicidal. It's easy to say in hindsight that a man should have planned for old age and created a separate identity by developing hobbies and activities other than work. But our own ageism, our denial of aging and death, prevents us from planning well for the postwork years, and we do not receive a lot of reinforcement for developing peripheral interests in the period when employment demands excessive time and attention.

In addition women caregivers who are employed seldom keep up with their grieving. They say they don't have time to grieve. Some defer grief until the caregiving period has ended and consequently remain depressed and stressed, which deeply affects their work life. Caring for and watching a loved one deteriorate inch by inch while trying to muster the energy to carve out a life at work and home for oneself requires the therapeutic expression of grief on an ongoing basis. When the grief is expressed and resolved to some degree, both men and women experience a new surge of interest and life energy and are more open to new options.

Creating support from friends, co-workers, and family members allows older people to weather the temporary and even long-term pain of separating from the work force. Women share their feelings and their lives more easily in support groups than men do; older men often depend on one-on-one relationships or rely on one friend and are bereft if that person moves or dies.

> Bea knew she would feel isolated and miss collegial support when she retired. So she created a support group of women in her field just before retirement. The six women who formed this group have been meeting for seven years now and rarely does anyone miss a meeting. All are employed full-time except Bea. The monthly breakfasts sustain them personally and professionally. In addition, Bea belongs to a life review group that began long before she retired. She says that being able to count on the regular support and caring of these groups enables her to feel

included, valued, and in touch with the world as she ages.

Some ground rules are important for support groups. Each member needs to:

1. Commit to confidentiality
2. Commit to regular attendance as well as starting and ending on time
3. Be responsible for each member receiving fairly equal time for his or her story
4. Commit to sharing difficulties as well as joys
5. Refrain from giving advice (feedback may be structured, that is, "What I need from you now is. . . .")
6. Express appreciation to the others for the privilege of being together

These are examples of guidelines that enable members to support each other. It's best if each group develops its own ground rules. Slowing down and the loss of life energy are inevitable occurrences if life is long enough, and they have some advantages. It gives more time to focus, to reflect on what is really important, and to choose how to use time, eliminating those activities and behaviors that no longer have meaning. Assessing life energy leads to questions like "What is it that I really need to do today?" and "What is it I absolutely must do before my life ends?" Reviewing one's life may have brought to consciousness regrets, failings, and omissions as well as accomplishments and brilliant successes. Now, in the later years of life, it is hoped that we have honed our skills to measure what's been done and what there is left to do. This can serve as a motivator to finish some unfinished business and to end careers well, both very useful gifts as life energy diminishes and one draws nearer to death.

Some professional counselors are afraid to work with old people in helping them sort out their lives before they die. There is no higher calling than to enable people in the last stage of life to (a) discover a new perspective on all the hours of life spent working, (b) grieve over the ending of work life, or (c) pursue their careers and vocations to the end in some real or symbolic way. This is an opportunity to weave a tapestry of meaning, to enable a painting of hope, desires, and reality.

One powerful way to elicit this kind of meaning is the Life Identity Exercise. This may be written, discussed with a friend or vocational counselor, or shared in a support group, or it may be part of an ongoing journal or diary. The critical component is the reflection required—mental, emotional, and spiritual. Meditation techniques are useful in accomplishing this exercise.

Life Identity Exercise

1. Reflect on *who I was* in the past. Include all of remembered life until now (family, school, love, friendship, and work life). Write down what you have done and roles you have played.

2. Reflect on *who am I now,* at this moment in time. Include all aspects of yourself: mental, emotional, physical, spiritual, and social.

3. Reflect on *who I may still be* in this lifetime. Remember dreams and fantasies from the past, including what you wanted to do and be when you were young and things you have not yet attempted but always wanted to do. List desires and hopes, regardless of how impossible they seem now. Grieve the losses of your dreams.

4. Imagine all the possibilities before you die—tasks you'd like to finish, things you could still do if you were willing to risk more, what you'd like to change, and all the things you are willing to grieve and let go of. Then mentally and emotionally let go of all of it. Now imagine a blank canvas in front of you, and paint your life from now until you die.

5. Discuss this at length with someone you trust—a partner in a group or a close friend—then write a life plan.

Hopes and dreams lie somewhere deep within older people, and pieces of them are still attainable and translatable to life at any age if we choose to access them. Imagining them provides life energy and resolution, even if we do nothing about them. It is therapeutic to remember them, grieve over the loss of the dreams, then lay them to rest. There *is* life after work! Re-creating oneself in old age is one of the greatest challenges of life.

CONCLUSION

In an ageist society older people are often devalued. Yet they are more diverse than at any other life stage. Not only is retirement a misnomer, but traditional options for postwork life are limiting to many. Age discrimination in the workplace is subtle and insidious, and much needs to be done regarding employment practices involving older people. Much more research and writing is needed to address the potential and creativity possible for old people today.

A model for creatively planning the end of work and life after work utilizes life review, prioritizing, self- and professional evaluation, griefwork, support, an action plan, and planning for aging and change.

REFERENCES

Butler, R. (1963). The life review: an interpretation of reminiscence in the aged. B. Neugarten (ed.), *Middle age and aging,* 486–496. Chicago: The University of Chicago Press.

Carlson, M. (1991). *Creative aging: A meaning making perspective.* New York: W. W. Norton.

Cumming, E., & Henry, W. (1961). *Growing old: The process of disengagement.* New York: Basic Books, Inc.

Erikson, E. (1963). *Childhood and society* (2d ed.). New York: W. W. Norton.

Erikson, E., Erikson, J., & Kivnick, H. (1986). *Vital involvement in old age.* New York: W. W. Norton.

Frankl, V. (1959). *Man's search for meaning.* Boston: Beacon Press.

Greddie, C., & Strickland, B. (1984). From plateaus to progress: A model for career development, *Training* 21 (6), 56–61.

Hall, D. & Associates (1996). *The career is dead—long live the career.* San Francisco: Jossey-Bass.

Havighurst, R., Neugarten, B., & Tobin, S. (1963). Disengagement and patterns of aging. Unpublished paper presented at the International Association of Gerontology (abridged). (August): Copenhagen.

Huyck, M., & Hoyer, W. (1982). *Adult development and aging.* Belmont, Calif.: Wadsworth.

Kaufman, S. (1986). *The ageless self: Sources of meaning in late life.* New York: New American Library.

Peck, R. (1956). Psychological developments in the second half of life. B. Neugarten (ed.), *Middle age and aging,* 85–92: Chicago: University of Chicago Press.

Super, D. (1957). *The psychology of careers.* New York: Harper & Brothers.

———. (1984). Career and life development. D. Brown, L. Brooks, & Associates. *Career choice and development,* 192–234: San Francisco: Jossey-Bass.

Williams, C., & Savickas, M. (1990). Developmental tasks of career maintenance, *Journal of Vocational Behavior,* 36, 166–175.

TO THE OWNER OF THIS BOOK:

I hope that you have found *Career Counseling Models for Diverse Populations*, 1st edition useful. So that this book can be improved in a future edition, would you take the time to complete this sheet and return it? Thank you.

School and address: _____

_____

Department: _____

Instructor's name: _____

1. What I like most about this book is:_____

_____

_____

2. What I like least about this book is: _____

_____

_____

3. My general reaction to this book is: _____

_____

_____

4. The name of the course in which I used this book is: _____

_____

5. Were all of the chapters of the book assigned for you to read? _____

    If not, which ones weren't? _____

6. In the space below, or on a separate sheet of paper, please write specific suggestions for improving this book and anything else you'd care to share about your experience in using this book.

_____

_____

OPTIONAL:

Your name: _____ Date: _____

May we quote you, either in promotion for *Career Counseling Models for Diverse Populations,* or in future publishing ventures?

Yes: _____ No: _____

Sincerely yours,

Nadene Peterson

Roberto Cortéz González